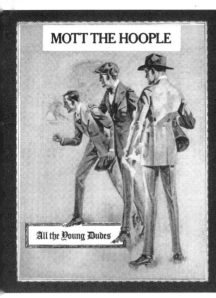

rock 'n' roll sweepstakes

rock 'n' roll sweepstakes

ian hunter

the authorised biography
campbell devine

volume one:
mott's the story

OMNIBUS PRESS

London / New York / Paris / Sydney / Copenhagen / Berlin / Madrid / Tokyo

For Guy Stevens (1943–1981) and Steve Hyams (1950–2013)

Shades Off

Where do you go, when you've somewhere to run
But the time isn't right, and there's things to be done
And you're trapped half-way up, you don't wanna go back
So you keep going on compromising the lack

And you see the green fields, as you travel on by
And you look at the things, you've forgotten to try
And you wish you were young, and you wish you were old
For the song's always sung and the story's been told

And you thought you were different, but what did that mean
For you tricked yourself trying, life's still unseen
As it is, as it was, as it always will be
Will you find out at all what it is to be free

See it never was easy to live with a head
So, I kept to the back room and I live there instead
What comes from the front room's only for friends
I have a bay window, but that's where it ends

And it's here I see pictures and my madness is clear
And there's no longer logic, so therefore no fear
And I'm almost dead with uncontrollable light
Sometimes when I've written a song, it's alright.

Ian Hunter (1973)

Contents

Preface

Rock 'n' Roll Sweepstakes is Ian Hunter's story – the life, the art and the heart – the purpose, the passion and the perception – in his own words and the tales of colleagues and collaborators.

"Long, long time ago", in November 1992, I was invited to compile a new fanzine feature on the late-lamented Mott the Hoople. Eventually, I surrendered and interviewed Verden Allen, and a wonderful trip to Hereford became the launch pad for a book.

Over a six-year period my original biography project was underpinned with input and support from Ian Hunter, the original members of Mott the Hoople and many associates of the band. Of note, the most active participant in that book was Mott drummer, Dale Griffin. After six years of work, *All the Young Dudes: The Official Biography of Mott the Hoople and Ian Hunter* was released by Cherry Red Books as a companion to *All the Young Dudes: The Anthology*, a box set that I instigated with Sony Music and their superb team of Phil Savill, Chris Black and the late Hugh Attwooll.

The "journey" preparing the *Dudes* biography was interesting to say the least, confirming that the outside world largely sees one aspect of the music business – the positive side. Fans and the record-buying public alike are mostly sheltered from the darker, niggling and negative elements and so, whilst I tried to document stories told and untold in that 1992-1998 period, I also embraced loyalty and humour. Crucially, I respected "the code of the road". There were differing recollections and morsels of bitterness, particularly in the complex twisted "tail" of Mott the Hoople, but the original official biography was affectionately written as an accurate and genuine celebration of the players and their music. I have continued to adopt the same tone and intent.

This biography, fully authorised by Ian Hunter, is based on acres of new work and fresh collaborations. After *All the Young Dudes*, a wider field opened up and over 200 people have assisted directly on this project through interview, discussion and e-mail. The biography tackles the rough with the smooth and many of the inevitable Mott contradictions are still included as it was vital to acknowledge how the participants recalled certain events.

Ian Hunter's special life story spans fifty years of accomplishment and musical magic, so Omnibus Press decided that Ian's unique and impressive journey should be travelled via two volumes.

Rock 'n' Roll Sweepstakes, Volume One covers Ian's youth and formative rock 'n' roll days alongside the likes of Freddie 'Fingers' Lee and Miller Anderson. It traces Mott the Hoople's formation, David Bowie's intervention as a fan of the band, Mott's rise to international stardom and their acrimonious break-up.

Volume Two reflects on Hunter's partnership with guitarist Mick Ronson, his collaborations with the likes of Jaco Pastorius, The E Street Band and Ringo Starr, and his colossal solo achievements across an astonishing artistic landscape.

Collectively, *Rock 'n' Roll Sweepstakes* looks in depth at Mott the Hoople's classic albums – *Brain Capers*, *All the Young Dudes* and *Mott* – as well as Hunter's eclectic solo recordings – from the commercially successful *Ian Hunter* and *You're Never Alone with a Schizophrenic*, through the left-field *All-American Alien Boy* and *Short Back n' Sides*, to the astonishing *Shrunken Heads* and *Fingers Crossed*.

Devoid of borrowed information and re-cycled press clippings, *Rock 'n' Roll Sweepstakes* contains inside stories, controversial quotes and previously unpublished views. The author has collaborated with Ian Hunter who provides revealing anecdotes and there are personal contributions from all of Mott the Hoople, The Rant Band, Queen's Brian May, Def Leppard's Joe Elliott, Roxy Music's Andy Mackay and many other important sources.

With personal input from key players, *Rock 'n' Roll Sweepstakes* traces musical strife and stardom with honesty and humour. Peppered with untold tales, this is a story of determination, adversity and triumph. It is a unique and exciting musical journey that will be welcomed by committed and casual rock readers – and by all Dudes – young, post-young and now quite old.

Twenty years after publication of *All the Young Dudes* the time had arrived to update Ian Hunter's remarkable story – not just because his decade as the driving force behind *Brain Capers*, *Mott*, *The Hoople*, *Ian Hunter*, *All-American Alien Boy* and *You're Never Alone with a Schizophrenic* assured him legendary status – but because he remains one of the most interesting figures in popular music via a stunning quintet of albums, starting with *Rant* in 2001 and extending to the recent, fantastic *Fingers Crossed* – because these remarkable, riveting and resonant recordings have been widely acclaimed – and because Ian consistently delivers emotional performances that put many younger artists to shame.

Hunter's influence on fellow musicians has been significant. In 2005, *Classic Rock* presented Ian with their first-ever 'Classic Songwriter Award' and, in 2016, his career was celebrated with the thirty-disc box set *Stranded in Reality*. The book from that project included a section titled, "Go Tell the Superstar" and I received dozens of quotations from luminaries and legends who were all eager to pay homage to Ian. Longer passages were written by some of the collaborators and so, adopting a Hunter-styled, "Do what you want to do" mantra, four wonderful essays are presented around both volumes of *Rock 'n' Roll Sweepstakes*.

It has been a privilege to share such close and unprecedented observations of Ian's work and life. He has defied the recognised arc of commercialism by being his own man – delivering some of his best music over the last twenty years.

It was once expounded that anything is classic if it endures.

Ian Hunter has.

Campbell Devine
January 2019

Foreword

PIRATES OF THE CARIBBEAN

Hey! Mott the Hoople were the first Rock 'n' Roll band we ever knew. I don't mean ever heard, or heard OF – because we'd heard loads, by the time we precocious young boys of 'Queen' started out into the world. I mean this was the first Real Band we ever were close enough to touch, smell and share our lives with. I vividly remember the first day we turned up to the rehearsal theatre for the tour we were about to embark on, as support group to Mott (the only time Queen EVER supported anyone). We were pretty full of ourselves and probably already felt we knew it all – we knew the theory, we had made our first album and we were fast discovering our own style in music, ethos, clothes and staging. But as we surveyed the excitingly huge amount of gear on the Mott stage, up strolled the Band. They looked 'The Business' – they were obviously 'IT', seemingly without trying. They appeared as an agglomeration of bright colours, bizarre shapes, scarves, leather, sunglasses, velvet, huge boots, strange felt hats, blending seamlessly into the masses of hair, beer bottles, fags, battered guitar cases covered with stickers and SWAGGER. They looked lived-in; they exuded Attitude and easy humour and the utter confidence born of 'Knowing you are Good'. They were.

They were friendly to us and courteously treated their warm-up group as equals from the start, but in the following months, as we toured Britain and the USA with them, I was always conscious that we were in the presence of something great, something highly evolved, close to the centre of the Spirit of Rock and Roll, something to breathe in and learn from.

Travelling a lot together, we soon learned the Mott language as we shared countless buses ("It was OPEN, Stan I'm starving!!!"), planes ("Esheven Lags this tour, Rog..."), hotel bars ("Raging Pits"), shopping expeditions ("to the Shawn Pops!"), and philosophical discussions. I vividly remember Ian's advice to me, late one night, realising I was missing my home comforts ("If you need your things around you, Brian, you're in the wrong business" – he was right...). I remember Ariel Bender and Morgan Fisher crashing through my hotel door as one body, with a bevy of beauties in tow, with the cry, "Looking for a bit of head, Bri?!" (I was too shy). I remember the whole world of rock and roll girls Mott attracted and felt so at home with – they became a big part of our world too. I remember standing around back of stage in an arena in Memphis, seeing the place erupt to the first chords of 'All the Way from Memphis', truly a great moment of re-connection to the original capital city of White Rock. I remember the night-long party afterwards in a Holiday Inn on the banks of the steamy Mississippi, a scene comparable with the 'Pirates of the Caribbean' ride in Disneyland with a seemingly endless traffic of revellers in and out of everybody's rooms... and a lady who said, "I'm going to make you a Rock Star" – and so much more...

Oh, and there was the Music! We worked our butts off on the tour, with great success; luckily for us most of the Mott fans took to our style. But there was never any doubt who was the Headline Act. Mott would swing relentlessly and unstoppably into their show every night, like a marauding band of outlaws and every night there was something close to a riot – the kids couldn't get close enough to the stage – they simply couldn't get enough. Every night the legendary Silver-Cross-Painted-on-Chest Overend

Watts would be winched on stage in his impossibly high boots, to thunder deafeningly, and menace the audience from on high. Ian Hunter (the unwritten Boss) would plant himself centre stage behind his shades and DARE anyone to remain seated, pianos would be pushed off stage, amps would be thrashed, dedicated roadies would scuttle tensely across the stage, always aware of the possibility that the strong and silent Buffin would suddenly lose his rag and trash the drum kit over their heads. Ariel Bender played – screamed – on guitar, with his whole body and spirit, rushing around the entire stage, on his feet, on his back, guitar behind head, or held aloft or however the mood took him – an inspiration. And it ROCKED. It was raw, fun, angry, glorious and jagged. It was everything except normal or predictable.

All things must pass. Mott the Hoople passed away much too soon. But it all lives on in our heads. And in the surviving recordings there are hints – echoes of those days of Danger and Wonder. God bless 'em!

Brian May
Queen

Acknowledgements

I would like to thank the following for their support and contributions:

Ian Hunter, Trudi Hunter, Helen Akitt, Verden Allen, Miller Anderson, Richie Anderson, Dick Asher, Hugh Attwooll, Alan Baguste, Russ Ballard, Ariel Bender, Jet Black, Leee Black Childers, Trevor Bolder, Angela Bowie, Tony Brainsby, Patrick Brooke, Mel Bush, John Cambridge, Simon Cantwell, Chris Carter, Philip Castle, Michael Chapman, Keith Cheeseman, Tim Clark, Zal Cleminson, Martin Colley, Jeff Dexter, Richard Digby-Smith, Joe Elliott, Bryan Ferry, John Fiddler, Morgan Fisher, Pete Frame, Andy Fraser, David Fricke, Craig Fuller, Mike Garson, Debra Geddes, Dana Gillespie, John Glover, Imogen Gordon Clark, Nicky Graham, Kirby Gregory, Dale Griffin, Derek Griffiths, Luther Grosvenor, Ross Halfin, Steve Harley, Bob Harris, Laurie Heath, Fred Heller, Keith Herd, Robert Hirschman, Gerry Hogan, The Horse, Steve Hyams, Paul Hyde, Barry Imhoff, Alex Jaworzyn, Paul Jeffery, David Johansen, Phil John, Mick Jones, Chris Kimsey, Simon Kirke, Marty Kristian, Ray Laidlaw, John Leckie, Freddie 'Fingers' Lee, Alec Leslie, Dan Loggins, Andy Mackay, Ray Major, Gered Mankowitz, Willard Manus, Phil Manzanera, Benny Marshall, James Mastro, Brian May, Chris Mayfield, Robin Mayhew, Ted McKenna, Laurence Myers,

15

Gabi Nasemann, Les Norman, Brian Parrish, Annette Peacock, Richard Polak, Steve Popovich, Mick Ralphs, Adrian Rifkin, Bob Rock, Mick Rock, Mick Ronson, Suzi Ronson, Peter Sanders, Ken Scott, Terry Slesser, Gene Simmons, Johnny Smack, Gordon Smith, Ray Smith, Diane Stevens, David Stock, Roslaw Szaybo, Roger Taylor, Dave Tedstone, Billy Thunder, Stan Tippins, Martin Turner, George Underwood, Tony Visconti, Joe Walsh, Overend Watts, Pete Watts, Blue Weaver, Richard Weaver, Barrie Winship, Jackie Winship, Muff Winwood, Roy Wood, Woody Woodmansey, Trevor Wyatt, Robin Zander and Tony Zanetta.

I also acknowledge *Classic Rock*, Ian Crockett, Sven Gusevik, Island Records, JJM Music, Anthony Keates, Michael O'Connell, Justin Purington, Scott Rowley, Phil Savill, Sony Music, Universal Records and Warner Bros Records.

My special appreciation is extended to:

Iain McNay and Cherry Red Books who supported and published my first biography, *All the Young Dudes*, in 1998, when there were few "True Believers" left standing, who remained actively interested in Mott the Hoople and Ian Hunter. Iain came to the party then and has blessed this new project; I will always be grateful to him…

David Barraclough of Omnibus Press who has been a tremendous supporter and ally. David has given this biography project huge commitment – without him, and his great team, you might not be reading this…

Debra and Hunter for enduring the music mania…

Billy Henry for empathy and encouragement…

Brian May and David Fricke for their wonderful reflections…

Ian Hunter Patterson for his involvement and the *Rock 'n' Roll Sweepstakes* title, his preferred branding for *Diary of a Rock 'n' Roll Star* published in 1974, until commerciality came calling. As Ian says, "If you wait long enough…"

I send special appreciation to the incredible Trudi Hunter…

And thank you once again to four gems: the gentle Steve Hyams, the charming Hugh Attwooll, the wonderful Richie Anderson and the incredible Mick Ronson. They were all "Hoopled" but remained four of the finest, fun people I ever met. Boy do we miss them!

Now it's recreational skull-diving time, so… plunge in, think and enjoy!

Campbell Devine
January 2019

CHAPTER ONE

The Loner

I was terribly insecure.

This is Ian Hunter's musical journey – a story of success and survival, that shines a light on the highs and lows of stardom and the music business lifestyle.

Hunter has been described as a rock phenomenon – an icon who has created era-defining music – a writer that still has an influence on many groups and artists. For five decades, he has remained true to the creation of inspirational music; penning words that extend beyond routine "boy-girl" love songs; presenting lyrical vignettes that reflect on history, express social and political frustration or paint truthful pictures of the people in his life and the events around him.

Ian Hunter has written over 200 songs, recorded over twenty original studio albums and released several hit singles. His compositions have been covered by dozens of artists including Barry Manilow, Status Quo and The Monkees. He was acclaimed by Britain's leading music magazine, *Classic Rock*, as their inaugural 'Classic Songwriter'. However, like his musical hero Bob Dylan, he has not sold-out or endeared himself to expectation. Ian Hunter has done it his way – creating a rock 'n' roll legacy laced with intelligence and humour – with no commercial compromise – all crafted in the singular hope that listeners might "zero-in" on his thinking.

Hunter's public image has often appeared mysterious and sometimes fearsome, his forthright opinions the stuff of "PR" dreams but, behind the forbidding façade of corkscrew hair and ever-present shades, lies a self-critical, sensitive and magnanimous core – a frank and truthful man who retains heart, skill and determination.

Ian Hunter first found fame as the leader and focal point of Seventies rock stars Mott the Hoople. In a small London studio, in June 1969, Ian auditioned for Island Records A&R man Guy Stevens and joined a little-known Herefordshire band named Silence. Guy was central to Mott's development and without him they would never have existed; he was on a mission and his vision was a group that placed the primal rock 'n' roll power of The Rolling Stones alongside the poetic balladry of Bob Dylan, with an added dash of Procol Harum keyboards. Stevens re-christened Silence, Mott the Hoople; he thought the name would look good written down, but it confused some people – "Mott the Who?"... "What the Hoople?"... "Mouser Hoop..." – "Oh, Mott the Hoople..." – a classic band that would sculpt a history as sensational as its moniker. Oozing style, attitude and wild unpredictability, they believed they could – they almost didn't – but eventually they did!

Moulded to Guy's blueprint, Mott the Hoople built a formidable reputation as a colossal live act. Fuelled by Ian as their creative core, the band released seven diverse studio albums in just five years and, adopting a non-elitist élan, Hunter possessed a desire to reach out communicatively to fans and audiences – which he did with style. Crucially for the group, the man at the Hoople helm was Ian Hunter – a journalist's delight – the tousle-haired, be-shaded, raspy-voiced, sometimes controversial rocker – a key figure who would arm Mott with a stockpile of stunning songs – an astute writer and a fascinating persona that generated interest and attention.

Through the mists of time, Mott the Hoople are now regarded as one of the most important British rock groups of the Seventies. If not "the greatest" in commercial terms, then they were certainly one of our most valuable and influential bands. Mott and Ian resonated with many fans because they seemed to channel universal feelings of frustration and angst; they were watched by Slade, young pretenders and the future Pretenders; they were appreciated by Status Quo, Robert Fripp and Ozzy Osbourne; they left an indelible mark on the likes of Queen, Mötley Crüe and Def Leppard. Mick Jones of The Clash would admit, "If it hadn't been for Mott, there would be no us"... and, more recently, Hunter has been acclaimed by Gene Simmons of Kiss, Cheap Trick's Robin Zander and actor-cum-rocker, Johnny Depp. The legendary David Bowie was also a secret fan who "raved" over *Brain Capers*, and he benevolently gifted 'All the Young Dudes' to Mott the Hoople – a song that Ian made his own, fashioning it into one of popular music's most amazing anthems.

Having snared success and following five years of increasing intensity, Hunter found a friction with fame and left Mott the Hoople in December 1974, charting a new course. Forty-five years on, Ian's "solo" repertoire features some of rock music's more refreshing songs and albums. Unleashed from the mad shadows and constrictions of Mott, fun, intelligence and critical success has shone throughout Hunter's solo work, revealing a remarkable writer who possesses the entertainment industry's scarcest commodity – honesty – as a person, in his attitude to life and within his artistic endeavours.

Ian was born in Oswestry, Shropshire, on 3rd June 1939, making him a Gemini – a star sign representing two personalities in one. Character traits suggest that Gemini people are expressive, quick-witted, serious and restless. They are also said to have awful memory retention, are more interested in the accumulation of knowledge than money and are excellent communicators; apt qualities for this unique lyricist and a summation reflecting the nucleus of his story.

20

Hunter would become an accomplished writer and Shropshire, with its castles and hill forts was known as a centre of tales, legends and myths, inspiring many authors. Ian's birthplace is only forty-five miles from Hereford, the cathedral city of Herefordshire and a county forever associated with Mott the Hoople, but he would not encounter his future band mates until thirty years later.

Ian Hunter Patterson was the son of police constable, Walter Walker Paterson and Freda Mary Potts. Walter had been born in Hamilton, Scotland, in 1910, his popular Scottish surname deriving from the ancient term "patrician" or "son of a noble father". Walter's last name was originally Paterson with a single 't', but he changed the spelling following a family feud. Ian later traced his Scottish roots back to the MacLarens, a clan known for battling at Bannockburn and Flodden – loyal men who stood by James III, James IV and Mary Queen of Scots. Ian's mother, Freda Potts, was born in Wellington, Shropshire, in 1916 and she married Walter in Wellington, in 1938. The couple and had two sons: Ian and eight years later, Robert, born in Market Drayton in 1947. It was first intended that Ian would be christened Ian Jarvie Paterson, the middle name Hunter being a late substitute, courtesy of his father's heritage.

Ian Hunter: "My Scottish 'lot' go back to two MacLaren brothers who had a row round about the 12th Century. My dad never wore trousers, socks or shoes until he was seven years old and he had to move away from Scotland, like many before him, to make a living. I think the Scots are unique; they just about invented everything. My father could quote Robert Burns and did on many an occasion. He was an active communist in his youth and had worked for the Forestry Commission in Scotland and led some kind of rebellion in the forestry industry when he was nineteen. Then, with the chaos before the war, he travelled south, down through Britain, working on fairground dodgems. He met my mother in Shropshire, a beautiful English garden county. She was from a heavy Methodist family and, somehow, they wound up married. My dad was a tearaway, but the Second World War made him a different person. The commissioned guys were falling like flies in the war and my dad was non-commissioned, so he turned himself round and became a self-made man. He didn't have a good life with one thing after another. In fact, I think he had a miserable time and when I was a lad, my dad and I didn't get on at all, so I beat a swift retreat. Looking back now, I understand him and what he went through. It wasn't easy for him, but my parents survived as a couple for over forty years."

Infant Ian spent his first few months in Oswestry, at Eaton Villas, a "two-up two-down" late-1800s terraced house at 6 York Street but, by the end of 1939, Mrs Patterson fled with her son to Scotland. On 1st September that year, two days before the declaration of World War II, the British Government implemented the Anderson Committee Evacuation Scheme, relocating over three million citizens away from urban locations to escape the risk of German air bombardment. Freda Patterson headed to Hamilton, eleven miles south-east of Glasgow, working in the city while Walter's younger sister, Janet Ferguson – "Aunt Nettie" – looked after Freda's child. Ian loved Scotland as a youngster and whilst he grew up under a very strict father, he felt there were mitigating circumstances.

IH: "My parents had a tough time, especially my dad, who had a real cheerful life. He was born in 1910. Then the First World War started in 1914 and went on for a bit, which wasn't much fun. Then there was the Great Depression, which was a barrel of laughs and went on for a bit. After that there was the Second World War, when my dad was posted overseas. Then he came home and was moved around all over the place with his jobs in the police force. Then there was Elvis – then me!

22

"I was born in Oswestry but only stayed there for a few weeks. At that time Britain was at war – England was in chaos but the Germans didn't seem quite so interested in Scotland. Danger was looming, and all my mother wanted to do was to get me out of harm's way. She was standing with me on the station platform, leaving her home. She was twenty-one, had never been out of England and had never even been on a train before. We went to Scotland because my father had a sister there called Nettie. My dad's whole family in Scotland were amazing. They were nuts, the lot of them. As it turned out, my kids are the same!

"Mum and I lived with Nettie at Peacock Cross in Hamilton until I was six years of age. Nettie was married to my uncle, Willie Ferguson, who worked at the Clyde Alloy Steel Company in Motherwell. My dad's brother Jack and his wife Elsie also lived next door at Peacock Cross. Mum had passed some exams, so she could work at Boots the Chemist in Glasgow, which was a nice job and far better than going into the Munitions Factory. Aunt Nettie looked after me while my mother worked in nearby Glasgow. She stayed there all week and came back to Hamilton at weekends. I remember being taken to the cinema in Glasgow when I was about four years old and they had a tree growing up from the floor in the middle of the foyer.

"Nettie's family lived in a tenement building above a pub on Wellhall Road and it had a communal backyard where they did the washing, with a little 'green' for the kids to play on. It's still there and one of my early best mates, Jim Feeney, lived for years in the apartment opposite ours. The place was so full of life and I loved it. Uncle Willie was a great guy – a gentle man who would sing songs to send me to sleep each night before he carried me through to bed. Willie was a drinker and would often sneak out to the pub. Sometimes I'd hear him and would call out, 'Nettie, he's going out the door.' She would ask him where he was going 'at night' and he would say, 'Oot.' Nettie would say, 'Where oot?' to which Willie would reply, 'Just oot!'

"I loved Scotland and still support Hamilton Academical Football Club because I lived not far from the ground and went as a small child. They were the first football team I ever saw, at the original Douglas Park. I still go to the town of Hamilton when I play gigs in Glasgow or Edinburgh and usually visit Equi's restaurant which is still there and still great. The tenements are a bit more knackered now. In those days it was clean, and the steps were white. People seemed to take more pride in their houses in the old days.

"I remember my Scottish grandmother, my dad's mum, so well. She was Margaret Jarvie but was known as Peggy. My first-ever memory is being taken for a walk by her and she caught a bird – she just plucked this creature from mid-air and put it in her pocket. I was desperate to see the bird, but as soon as she took her hand out of her pocket it flew away. I suppose you'd call Peggy a character. She was incredible. She was married two or three times, was into anything theatrical, was a poet and was married to a miner. They lived in a tenement at the top of a pit and everywhere was black – the house was black, and the rooms were black – but she'd write poetry about the one little daisy that was growing through all the coal. They were great poems, and some got published."

One powerful piece that Peggy wrote, 'Two Minutes Silence', commemorating Armistice Day 1934, was published in *The Hamilton Advertiser* in the late Thirties. Peggy wrote other poems about her family including 'Jack' and 'Nettie', describing Jack Patterson as "noisy", Janet (Aunt Nettie) as "the gaffer" and Ian's dad, Walter, as "an honest serious plodder".

IH: "Peggy was in the Rotary Club, which was men only at the time, but she blasted that one apart and she was head of the Drama Society too. She'd bet on the horses every day and the day Peggy died she had a winner and left eleven shillings. That was her will and she left it to me, to be used in case of emergency. The eleven shillings lasted five minutes. I remember my gran's house was always full of people and there were instruments everywhere. Neither of my parents were the least bit musical and my father wouldn't even allow a guitar in his house, but my grandma had a guitar, piano and accordian. I guess I must have got those genes from her. Peggy was a magical lady so if there's any DNA involved it probably comes from her."

At the end of the war, when Ian was six years old, the Patterson family returned to Wellington in Shropshire.

IH: "When we moved back to England, I missed Hamilton so much. I do feel Scottish as I think the first five years in anybody's life are pivotal – plus, if your dad's Scottish, you are! We went back to England because I think my mother wanted to be near her father, who owned a boot and shoe store on Walker Street in Wellington. We had the flat above – No.8. I recall D-Day in Wellington and being scared of the fireworks. After the war it was still chaos with ration books and 'one egg a week'. My favourite Christmas memory would have been in Wellington, in 1945, over Grandad's shop. My dad wasn't back from the war yet, but I'd always wanted a football – and there it was – under the tree."

Originally a police constable when Ian was born, his father had attended the Officer Cadet Training Unit at the Royal Military Academy, Sandhurst. Walter Patterson was admitted in 1941 and became a non-commissioned officer and a captain in intelligence in Sicily during the war. Following the hostilities, Walter rejoined his family in Wellington and was re-employed in the police force. A few months later, the Pattersons moved from Ellesmere to the small town of Market Drayton in north Shropshire, but only for a further year.

> **IH:** "We stayed in Wellington for a little while, but I don't think my dad got on well with my mum's father, Percy Potts, so we moved to Ellesmere where I went to school for the first time. The only job my father could get was as a policeman and that meant he got a free house, but they couldn't figure out where to put him, so they kept moving him every few months. My mum stayed at home and looked after me as it was a mark of shame to let your wife work in those days. Dad wouldn't allow it, so she stayed 'stuck' at home and got bored. My earliest musical memory was 1947. I remember the police force in Market Drayton had a Family Christmas Party and they hired a guy who played piano accordion and banjo. I sat at his feet totally transfixed and was enraptured all evening. It looked and sounded very cool. I know I was eight at the time.
>
> "I also remember the song 'A Nightingale Sang in Berkeley Square' playing on the radio when I was growing up. I was firmly convinced that the people were in 'the wireless' and got smacked for trying to turn the dial once. I can remember lying on the floor in the police house at Market Drayton, sun streaming through the windows and 'A Nightingale Sang in Berkeley Square' was on the wireless. Somehow London was magical and everybody from the sticks wanted to go there. It's all very emotional – Abbey Road and Elgar flash through your mind. Somehow that square is quintessentially London, so I guess that's why it stuck with me. I eventually incorporated the song in my live set, not that I'm that kind of singer, but I dedicated it to my mum, and it completed a circle."

Young Ian Patterson attended various educational establishments in a relatively short space of time, so his early life was already chaotic and unsettled. The family relocated to Whitchurch where Ian attended Claypit Street School.

> **IH:** "I fell in love there for the first time, with my teacher, Miss Ashley. I was about ten years old. I went to twenty-one schools before I was eleven and I couldn't read or write until I was ten, but then I adored this teacher, so I learned to read and write really quickly. I passed my Eleven-Plus examination as I fell madly in love with Miss Ashley and because my old man said he'd buy me a bike if I passed. I imagined it would be a Raleigh three-speed; it was, in fact, a Hercules safety model – no gears – no lights – not quite so glamorous!"

Ian moved up to Whitchurch Grammar, a school with large grounds which he enjoyed, but his father was given a further police transfer to Shrewsbury and the family lived at 23a Swan Hill, a house that would later be immortalised in song. Ian really became "a loner" in Shrewsbury, a quiet town where he formed no real friendships.

> **IH:** "I moved to Shrewsbury when I was eleven. Swan Hill is a street behind the Music Hall and 23a is still there. The Priory Grammar School that I attended, wedged between St Chads and the river, was ten minutes' walk from the old house. My dad was a police sergeant by then and the wages were only eleven quid a week, but the house was free. They never paid coppers much but gave them free housing, electricity and coal. The idea was you didn't have enough money to live and you couldn't save, but you lived well – kind of like MainMan and Motown! My brother Bob and I slept on the second floor facing the street. I remember the Police Club which could be entered over the bike sheds illegally and there was a garden at the back where Dad permanently parked his Morris 8 car, taken out only for annual holidays

and trips to Scotland. I remember it broke down one year on our way to north Wales. The back axle went, and he had to spend any money he had getting it fixed. We spent a night in a bed and breakfast and then when we got to our caravan, he was really angry – it's a small world when somebody's angry in a caravan."

The Priory Boys School that Ian attended was located on Priory Road in Shrewsbury, near the meandering River Severn, Barker Street and The Quarry recreational park, and was modelled on the more illustrious public school across the river, whose pupils were called "Nellies" by the Priory lads. The sporting side of The Priory embraced rugby, not football. Teachers were called "Masters" and boys stood up when one of them entered a room, while pupils sat in rows in alphabetical order and were addressed by surnames. The Priory was not a happy place for Ian. It was an establishment that placed Latin and Greek ahead of modern languages, with a motto on the school crest that translated as, "They can because they think they can" – probably the most relevant thing that Ian learned there.

> **IH:** "I hated every minute at The Priory – and they didn't like me either. I think I tended to be very stubborn as a child and I got comments like 'Hostile' written on my school reports. My brother Bob joined just after I left, and they called him into the headmaster's office on the first day and said, 'Look, if you think you're going to be anything like him you can forget it. We'll stop it right here.' That was very unfair on him, because Bob is totally different from me. I didn't think that I'd been that bad at school but, apparently, I was a bit of a lad. I spent most of my formative years in snooker halls. Shrewsbury is a much nicer town now. When I was young there was the Music Hall, the Sabrina Dancing Academy – good for girls, and the Morris Ballroom – good for getting your head kicked in."

Whilst Ian had "a terrible time" at The Priory, it was there that signs of a writing gift appeared. Aged eleven, he wrote a poem called 'The Floods Roll On' but was cruelly accused of plagiarism by his English teacher, Mr Nicholas J Dunne. Described in school records as a lively master who gave "quick tests", Dunne used question and answer techniques to ensure pupils grasped precise meaning throughout. 'The Floods Roll On' was a big moment for Ian and he later referenced the poem in the opening verse of a song, as the "put-down" became an early reverse psychology situation in his life.

IH: "'Duck' Dunne was my English master and one of the many biased idiots called 'teachers' at that time. I know they were all crap because I had a great teacher for one term. His name was Mr Scott and he was magic. I wrote this poem titled 'The Floods Roll On'. It was great and the first decent thing that I'd written. I'd never done anything like that before, so I showed it to Mr Dunne, who went red in the face and accused me of stealing it from a book of poetry. He said I couldn't have written it because I was too young. He was rather angry, but I thought his reaction was great as it was the first real compliment, albeit back-handed, that I'd ever had. Education widens your options, or at least it's supposed to, but my education consisted of reverse psychology. 'You stink!' 'No, I don't!' Not for the faint of heart – but I was good at English literature and grammar at school, plus art, so they didn't kick me out. The problem is that teachers have to be great and that's rare.

"Aside from my poem, I had a painting on the BBC once in a kid's art competition, but I lost 'The Floods Roll On' somewhere along the road. I forget what the poem was about, but it was strong, and I regret having lost it. I sent some poetry to publishers when I first joined Mott the Hoople but whatever I'd done was rejected or I was told to forget it – I just thought, sod 'em. The next hint I had about writing ability was when I was fifteen. I was sitting on the back of a truck in Germany, in the school cadets on an exchange, and I heard a song with an orchestra playing in the wind. I asked my mates if they could hear it and none of them could, but it was loud and clear to me. Nobody thought I could sing as a youngster. The first time I tried was in the school gymnasium. I thought I sang well but everybody ran away. I cleared the place."

Ian often stood on the terraces at Shrewsbury Town's Gay Meadow football ground and, with his school chum, Tony Powell, he attended Chipperfield's Circus in the town one day to see Randolph Turpin, the Warwickshire boxer who became World Middleweight Champion in 1951, when he defeated American Sugar Ray Robinson.

IH: "Randolph Turpin had boxed for the circus whilst learning his trade and had always said if he ever became world champ he would return to Chipperfield's and do an exhibition tour – and Randolph was true to his word. At Chipperfield's we waited all day at the fairground exit. Finally, he emerged, and we ran up and asked, 'Please Mr Turpin, can we have your autograph?' 'Piss off' came the reply – and who were we to argue!"

Frustrated educationally and domestically, music would provide inspiration and escapism for Ian. He sung in the church choir with his brother and liked music by the famous British harmonica soloist Ronald Chesney, who introduced teaching of the instrument in the UK via BBC school broadcasts.

IH: "My parents were disciplinarians and wanted Bob and I to go to church. It was so convoluted, and no one really got it, but there was a good feeling. I was a choirboy and I got 3/6d for funerals and 2/9d for a birth, so it was quite nice. The first song I ever loved was a toss-up between 'Blue Tango' and 'Little Jimmy Brown'. The first record I had was 'Blue Tango' by Ronald Chesney, the harmonica player; it was a song that stuck in my head and I couldn't get rid of it. The first concert I attended was The Chessmen, at the Music Hall in Shrewsbury, when I was sixteen. The Chessmen had a No.1 hit with 'What Do You Wanna Make Those Eyes at Me For'."

Ian hated the stifling, hypocritical nature of the educational system, so truancy became an occasional pastime. He once claimed that his only achievement at school was learning how to cheat in exams, but he showed prowess at English and art. He also had some sporting success at The Priory and, in 1954, fifteen-year-old I.H. Patterson won an Athletics Award for the Class 'B' High Jump. He was also a cadet in the Priory School Army Cadet Force attached to the Queen's Bays B.A.O.R. 30.

IH: "I had terrible trouble getting past the snooker hall in Shrewsbury, and more often than not I failed. There were cool guys in there with skintight drainpipe trousers and I would stand, trying to pull my baggy trousers tight to look like everybody else – a slave to fashion. I wanted these trendy black trousers with green stitching that were all the rage, but my dad said, 'No'. Then I acquired a pair and I had to hide them in our damp garden shed and change into them when I went out. I think I was a city kid and I was brought up in the country, so I was at odds. I got into trouble from time to time. I was in the wrong place.

"My father was sporty and forced me to do athletics at school. I hated every minute of school athletics but, in my forties, I was running about thirteen miles every other day and now I walk six miles a day. I remember being captain of the middle school for athletics and I was in the records for the high jump which, of course, I did my way. I was still doing the 'Splits' while they wanted you to do the 'Fosbury Flop'

31

or the 'Western Roll'. My father was a betting man and he took me to Haydock Park racecourse when I was a kid. We often returned home in silence after a 'bad day'. Dad had also been a good boxer – so, at school I did boxing. One of the teachers who didn't take to me fixed up this bout with a kid who was a great fighter. The boy could have killed me, so I soon became mates with him in the hope that he'd go easy on me in the ring – and he did."

Frustrated by school and realising that he couldn't find a soulmate, Ian soon became a lone figure, occasionally lapsing into fits of depression.

IH: "I was a loner because I had to be and because I couldn't find anyone else who was on my wavelength. I did think I was crazy or ill at one point and my parents were talking about having me committed, and that was only because I couldn't mix with 'normal' people. I thought the normal people were idiots at the time and it took me years to find out that they *were* idiots. My parents *did* think there was something seriously wrong with me at one point, but Britain was really in upheaval at that time. The youth had rebelled, and it was a bit of a shock to the older generation. I was just this tearaway and as my dad was a cop, it made things even worse because when I got into trouble it reflected on him. My parents did the best they could, but I was the opposite of them. My dad was aghast at me slobbing out and Mum was a typical Victorian grandfather's daughter who read *The Daily Express*. My parents were very normal people and wanted me to have employment where I didn't get dirty, so that the neighbours wouldn't look at their son and think he had failed. I ended up in a factory anyway."

Ian left school and had various jobs in the Shrewsbury area. He was employed as a trainee journalist at a local newspaper office, worked as a labourer and then started an apprenticeship at Sentinel (Shrewsbury) Limited, originally a Glasgow-based engineering company that made trucks and railway locomotives.

> **IH:** "For a short while I was a cub reporter for *The Wellington Journal* in Shropshire. I had to learn typing, which I was quite good at and shorthand which I couldn't stand. It was like learning Chinese. As a cub reporter I got all the mundane tasks – Shrewsbury Town Reserves mid-week football fixtures and births, deaths and marriages. Every week I had to see the Reverend A.T. Agnew and get the church news and I hated doing that because he was a bachelor and had thirty-two cats and his place stank. I spent three months as a cub reporter, and I was fired. My dad had got me the job and was mortified when I was sacked. He was very upset, so I went into the factories and worked for Rolls-Royce at Sentinel in Shrewsbury as an apprentice for a couple of years. I earned thirty bob a week – £1.50 – and had to give my mum half of it."

Ian also took up employment with McGowan & Co Fruit Company, transporting greengrocers' produce to retailers but he "got into trouble" in Shrewsbury and the small-town mentality alienated him even more.

> **IH:** "I worked at McGowan's Wholesalers when I was sixteen. We used to go up to Liverpool docks from Shrewsbury at 4am, load up a five-ton truck with fruit and veg early in the morning and take it back to the local shops. Shrewsbury is about fifty miles west of Birmingham but not much goes on there. It's the kind of place you try to get away from. It's a lot nicer now than when I lived there, a quiet and lazy kind of agricultural place. Although Shrewsbury never has been a haven for rock 'n' roll, I started to get into music. Even when Mott the Hoople got big we never played around

Shropshire; I think the nearest we got was Birmingham. I never felt that I had anything in Shrewsbury and the whole Patterson clan never seemed to make friends easily. I don't really have friends in the music business today, because I don't seem to be in tune with most people.

"My father was big on reverse psychology, but I happen to function well on that. The more people told me I was crap, the harder I tried. My dad wasn't flush with flattery and to be honest there wasn't much to be flattering about. My father was a copper and I was daft, so there were multiple arguments before I managed to get out of the Patterson home. Now that I'm older, I can see things more from his point of view. My dad had been thrown out of Sandhurst and became a non-commissioned captain who fought in Italy during the war. So, he must have come back, looked at this slob – me – and asked himself, 'Did I go through all of that for this?' He'd hauled himself out of the gutter, so it was pretty hard for him to see me prancing about, playing snooker instead of learning and not doing well at school. I couldn't seem to learn anything and with him being a self-starter, it was a problem.

"We had very little and I was a typical working-class kid in post-war Britain. It's hard to believe but we could only buy one cigarette at a time. When Elvis Presley happened, I suddenly thought it's either music or sport because that was the only way out or you wouldn't get anywhere. I really wanted to be a footballer at one point, and I tried so hard, but I was crap, so it was music. It was more an overriding feeling that I'm not good at anything else and I was not quite as lousy at music as football. I hadn't been able to learn in school, but I think I had to create. I realised that I wanted to be a musician, so Ian Patterson started out on an Ian Hunter career.

"My first instrument was a bass harmonica, but things really started when my father's brother, Uncle Jack, handed

34

me a guitar when I was fourteen. The instrument was a bit of a mess; it was like a bow and arrow as it had no truss rod, and your hands would certainly bleed. You learned C, F and G chords in those days; now it's E, D and A. I never had any music lessons, so I first learned some chords from a car park attendant. In Shrewsbury there was this guy who sat in a small booth in a car park and he played guitar – he was also gay, so the game was to go into the booth and get three chords off him before he made a move. I got all the basics and am eternally grateful to him for the chords because Shrewsbury was a hard place to learn to play. My father hated that guitar in the house, so it had to be 'kept' in the shed outside, which had an earth floor and was damp. The fretboard ended up about six inches away from the strings. It was not an auspicious start. My dad thought it was the devil's music. I remember my guitar broke once and it was £17 to get it fixed, but my dad wouldn't give me the money as he didn't think there was any point. Nobody thought I had a cat in hell's chance of doing anything in music."

Ian started to play in Shrewsbury bands including The Rhythm Boys Skiffle Group, The Pattersons and Wardle's Harmoniacs. Inspired by the seven-piece Morton Fraser's Harmonica Gang, an ensemble who appeared on Fifties and early Sixties stage and television variety bills, Ian regarded Wardle's group as his first proper band.

IH: "I saw Morton Fraser play in Shrewsbury. The very first 'real group' I was ever in was The Tony Wardle Harmonica Band. I had a bass harmonica as I was the worst player, but it was a proper set-up. My first gig with Tony was in Shrewsbury, in 1955 and we never got paid. I got them to try an old Olympics number, 'Western Movies' and they did it, very reluctantly, halfway through the set. People looked at us like we were idiots – and they were right."

Ian was also a member of The Rhythmatics with Tony Wardle and the group played a Boxing Day concert at Shrewsbury Prison. In a 3rd February 1956 *Shrewsbury Chronicle* article, 'Young Rhythm Experts', the paper reported that The Rhythmatics had just failed to make the finals of 'The Carol Lewis Show' at Wolverhampton Hippodrome, despite their 'Cock of the Hoop' introduction. The *Chronicle* added that band-leader Tony Wardle (22), Ronald Pugh, Johnny Green and Ian Patterson (16), "have enough enthusiasm to go far". Music was taking a hold of Ian and whilst there was friction between father and son, Walter tried to keep Ian on the straight and narrow. Hunter realised that his dad helped him in later life by subconsciously imparting a degree of discipline in Ian's adult years.

> **IH:** "I'm afraid I had an intense dislike of my father and he had an intense dislike for me, but I think my dad's discipline did help me later. Fortunately, I've never been one for drugs – I've dabbled – and I certainly drank plenty of beer in the Sixties and Seventies, but I never had that addictive personality. For all the problems me and my dad had, it was probably his attitude to life that saved me. If ever I was going off the rails, I'd hear his voice in my ear saying, 'Everything in moderation son.' It kept me on the straight and narrow – sort of!"

By 1957 Walter Patterson and his eldest son were falling out frequently. Home was an unhappy place for Ian and two of his later songs – 'The Loner' and '23a Swan Hill' – tell the tale of domestic frustrations and psychological barriers during his early years. Ian had "major confrontations" with Walter who was "old school", although Hunter recalled his dad had been a wild kid too, before his world-view changed with the Second World War.

> **IH:** "For my dad, life was about doing as you were told, looking smart and getting a decent job. When I was fifteen

and suddenly discovered rock 'n' roll, I wanted to grease back my hair and listen to Jerry Lee Lewis, but dad was having none of it. At that time, it was austerity Britain where children were seen and not heard. It was a pretty miserable existence. My dad and I did have some fun though – I ran – and he ran after me! The fighting gene avoided me fortunately, but he had bronze medals for boxing, and like an idiot, I messed with him. He had been an army boxing champion, who'd think nothing of taking you in the back room and hitting you in the guts. He'd come back from the war having saved us, but all I wanted to know was Little Richard. It didn't make any sense to him. Music was diametrically opposed to anything my dad ever stood for and then he had this ponce that was into wild music; I get how he felt. Looking back, my parents were great, but I didn't know how great until I was forty. The only thing I could do was move so, at sixteen, I left 23a Swan Hill."

Having helped in intelligence during the war, Walter Patterson worked in the C.I.D. (Criminal Investigation Department) and, for a short period in later life, joined Britain's Security Service, MI5. Walter became secretive, partly because he worked for Sir Roger Hollis a journalist, intelligence officer and Director General of MI5 from 1956 to 1965. Hollis would later feature heavily in *Spycatcher*, the notorious book about the Cambridge Spy Ring.

IH: "My dad was a piece of work and wasn't very nice to live with. He'd bring his job home with him, so he could never sleep properly. He ended up in MI5 for about nine months, and then had a stroke. He'd been a detective in the police and that's why he got the gig. He was a 'foot soldier' in MI5, the kind of guy who went into the local paper shop and asked if people paid their bills and what kind of papers and magazines they bought. It was basic investigative work because he'd been a police detective and I guess that's why they figured he was safe. The *Spycatcher* book was banned in the UK but it came out in the US and I read it. My mother rang me up and said, 'Do they mention who the fifth man was in the book', and I told her, 'Yeah' and she asked me, 'Who did they say it was?' I said, 'Roger Hollis' and she said, 'That's who your dad worked for.' I remember years later I could have killed my mother, because she had a box full of dad's 'Top Secret' stuff and when he died in 1980, I rang up my mum and said, 'I've got to see what's in that box,' but she told me she'd burned it. She had promised my dad that she would destroy it all if anything happened to him, out of a sense of loyalty, but I was upset."

In the summer of 1957 Ian decided to "escape" from Shrewsbury and travelled to Butlin's at Pwllheli on the north coast of Wales. The Butlin's holiday organisation ran brightly painted entertainment camps in the UK, promising a world removed from the normality of drab post-war Britain. It was here that Ian chanced upon two young guys playing guitars one day and, as a trio, they entered The People National Talent Contest, sponsored by *The People* newspaper. They won the camp competition, a free holiday and a place in the next round but, whilst York, Broom and Patterson didn't advance beyond the semi-final, suddenly, Ian could see a musical road map.

> **IH:** "I went to Butlin's, a holiday camp for poor people which was also the biggest legalised brothel in Britain. One day I went past a chalet and I heard some people playing guitars. I knew how to play the chords C, F and G, so I banged on the door and there were these two lads from Northampton, Colin York and Colin Broom, who were in a band called The Apex. I told them I played guitar and the three of us entered the Butlin's competition, singing 'Blue Moon' with Spanish guitars. Colin Broom and I did the 'ooohs', while Colin York sang the song. We won our contest and it was a

big deal, because the prize was a free week's holiday back at the camp with all the other finalists – the *Miss Titbits* and *Miss Reveille* competition winners. We went back for the final but the three of us got the flu. There were a lot of girls at Butlin's and it was all starting to tie in. It looked like the beginning of the end with this girl I was going out with in Shrewsbury, Margaret Oliver, and I was in a bit of trouble, so I decided to make a move. I went to Northampton, which was considerably closer to London!"

Colin York worked as a toolmaker in Northampton and Colin Broom was an assistant in his parents' grocery shop in nearby Spring Boroughs, where Ian stayed when he first arrived in the town, in August 1957. Hunter later had lodgings in Bailiff Street and having been an engineering apprentice fitter at Sentinel Rolls-Royce in Shrewsbury, he continued his training in Northampton as a toolroom apprentice at British Timken's steel bearings plant in Duston.

> **IH:** "I was skint but, away from Shrewsbury, I was free – and it was fabulous. Freedom is the best thing in the world. I'd started off at Sentinel building diesel engines and that turned into Rolls-Royce and then I was at British Timken which made ball-bearings, and very good ones too. I tried everything including milling, turning and grinding in factories, but I hung out in pubs and got into music via jukeboxes. I was wandering aimlessly and had no idea of being a singer – until I heard Jerry Lee Lewis."

Like many British youngsters, Ian had first been alerted to a new musical dimension in 1956 when he heard Elvis Presley's 'Heartbreak Hotel' – but a year later he became absolutely hooked by Jerry Lee Lewis's 'Whole Lotta Shakin' Goin' on'. Now, Britain's ramshackle DIY skiffle music couldn't compete with its American cousin – rock 'n' roll. "Out" was Dickie Valentine and Lonnie

Donegan – "in" was Elvis, Bill Haley and 'The Killer', Jerry Lee. There had been nothing like it before, and as Hunter consistently remarked, this *was* a *real* revolution. It lit the blue touchpaper for Ian and his fondness for "the original rockers" has never waned: a love for Americana, Chuck Berry licks and Jerry Lee's piano playing. Ian's other inspiration became Richard Penniman – Little Richard – the electrifying and dynamic figure who Hunter still regards as rock's greatest-ever entertainer and singer. Little Richard's first hit single 'Tutti Frutti' landed like a musical missile and, for Ian, his two-year run of classic records has never been surpassed. 'The Sheik of Shriek' pounded piano and turned a monochrome world into instant Technicolor. The power and arrogance of this music affected Hunter deeply and he would perform several Lewis and Penniman songs over the years, including 'What'd I Say?', 'Whole Lotta Shakin' and 'Keep A-Knockin'.

> **IH:** "I didn't really fit in anywhere as a youngster and wondered what the point of my being here was – then I heard Jerry Lee Lewis – and I realised why. Music opened up the door of my life. I first heard rock 'n' roll on Radio Luxembourg and it was fast and furious – Gene Vincent, Fats Domino and Chuck Berry. 'Whole Lotta Shakin' was an absolute revelation though: the slow left-hand piano got me because it's not easy to play. That was the track that sold me. Jerry Lee Lewis blew me away. It was incredible because British pop music had no passion. A woman called Winnie Atwell played boogie piano and I thought that was good, but the only thing that was happening was American movies. That was my escape, then American music came too, and the showbiz attached to it impressed me. I became a rock 'n' roll fan but that was as far as it was meant to go. Music was my salvation and I would have probably ended up dead or in prison otherwise. I had an over-riding feeling that I was no good at anything, so I started going to gigs and developed a desire. It was so exciting because before that

40

I had no personality. I had no way of expressing myself and had nothing going for me, but I got into music – firstly as a fan – and then playing it.

"Little Richard was the Governor, the greatest of all time and has the best natural voice ever in rock 'n' roll, in my opinion. Maybe Paul Rodgers is close, but Little Richard is the guy for me. I've still never heard a voice like that – not bad for a dish-washer from Macon, Georgia.

"I was still a fan the night I saw Jerry Lee live, in 1972 at The London Palladium. His eleven-piece band came on and played the whole of the first half for forty minutes without him. Then there was a break and the band played four more songs – still no Jerry Lee. Finally, he appeared wearing a red shirt and red trousers, with a brandy in one hand and a cigar in the other, and the place went nuts. He told us the Palladium was sold-out "cos The Killer's in the house' and they went mad again. It's three-quarters of the way through the show and he's done nothing. Then he stood and combed his hair as the crowd went ape. Eventually, he sat down at the piano, did four songs, then turned to the audience with sincerity and said, 'I've done just about as much as a man can do' – and walked off. It was unbelievable and the best showmanship I ever saw in my life. I learned absolute arrogance from Jerry Lee and would use a lot of that style with Mott the Hoople.

"I saw Little Richard in 1957 at the Kettering Grand. Sam Cooke opened that night and was amazing, and Little Richard was at his height and was absolutely astonishing. I also saw Buddy Holly and the Crickets in 1958 at Leicester De Montfort Hall. I'd never seen a Stratocaster guitar before, but there were six different coloured Strats on stage that night. We'd only heard Hofners and five-watt amps, but Holly had a tall, narrow twenty-watt amp and we thought the roof was coming off. The volume was shattering, and all the guitars looked like something out of *Barbarella*. I saw

The Ike and Tina Turner Review and it had everything. I went to gigs in the Fifties where I was blown clean out of my seat; that's rock 'n' roll – not watching the fuckin' Pet Shop Boys!

"Those early rock 'n' rollers had such great natural ability and to this day they are the only thing that gets me. I guess that's true for a lot of musicians because what you hear when you're fifteen and sixteen is the stuff that stays with you. I was very drawn to American musicians. The US guys were 'rockers', whereas we had 'pop stars' like Adam Faith and I always thought that the English stuff was rather stiff. Adam Faith was a nice guy, but we didn't like his music, or Cliff Richard's. Music was more remote then and that was a great thing. You had to go and see singers perform and it was an event. Today music is instant, expendable and downloadable, and that's sad. I loved P.J. Proby and Screaming Lord Sutch live. Sutch's timing was perfect and I learned some stagecraft from him. I felt he couldn't sing that great, so I thought there's got to be a way to get into show-biz and that prospect seemed exciting and more fun than real life. The thought of going backstage and the showmanship of it all intrigued me. I fell in love with the whole thing. I'd lie awake at night and imagine being in a band – that, for me, was the living end. The Fifties and Sixties were amazing times – not at all like now. The minute rock 'n' roll arrived I finally realised that's what I was for – and it's what I'll do until the day I pop off."

Through Colin York and Colin Broom, Ian decided to join The Apex Group, led by Frank Short. Like Shrewsbury, Northampton was not a rampant rock 'n' roll town, but The Black Lion pub paraded a live band most Sunday evenings and The Apex often played there. Colin York was their blonde-haired, "handsome Scandic" vocalist and he had seen potential in Ian. York and Broom had teamed up with Short and his chum Tom Dawkins to form a band, known variously as The Apex, The Apex Group, The Apex Six and The

Apex Skiffle Group – even though their music was not exactly skiffle. Ian and the band often played at The Old White Hart Inn in Northampton where Hunter adopted wild on stage antics to the amazement of audiences *and* band members.

> IH: "My first TV appearance was in The Apex and it was a one-camera job filmed at The White Hart. I was singing 'Western Movies' and for some reason I was bouncing up and down, and the camera was stuck, so I would appear and disappear, then reappear and disappear on the film. We never saw what they'd shot, and I remember going into the local pub thinking I would be greeted like God, because I'd been on TV – but I was viciously ignored and then somebody told me I continually went on and off camera. I nearly died. You live and learn. The Apex was composed of enthusiasts more than an actual group and they were guys who were all older than me. I just played rhythm and didn't sing but I jumped around on stage like a total lunatic. The other guys in The Apex stood there and looked on me as a bit of a novelty. I just went nuts as music energised me in a weird way. It was funny because I had kids who came to watch and just stood and stared at me. I think I was doing what a lot of people did later on, jumping up and down like a maniac and playing C, F and G, which was the basic punk-thrash."

On Boxing Day 1957, The Apex Skiffle Group appeared on the TV show *Roll Back the Carpet* performing the American skiffle and folk songs 'Streamline Train' and 'Wabash Cannonball', with "Ian Patterson on Spanish guitar". On 3rd February 1958, a Pye Demo Session was held for skiffle groups at The Grand Hotel in Northampton and The Apex won. The Apex Skiffle Group started playing club nights at The Black Lion in St Giles Street, but Ian made his own impact on 6th March when The Apex appeared at The Northampton Press Ball and "Patterson broke free," injecting rock 'n' roll into the set and singing 'Great Balls of Fire'.

The 7th March 1958 edition of *The Northampton Chronicle & Echo* featured a short article about The Apex Skiffle Group. They had started to feature in more talent contests including The Daily Sketch National Skiffle Competition, playing at Wellingborough's Lyric Cinema in the Southern Area Final and winning with their rendition of 'My Dixie Darling'. Ian and the band qualified for the London final at the ABC Commodore Cinema in Hammersmith and The Apex's prizes, presented by Joe Loss, included 14" televisions, a Vogue Tempo recording contract, ABC summer bookings and a Radio Luxembourg appearance. Ian sold his telly for £45. In May, The Apex taped 'My Dixie Darling' at Star Sound Studios in Besant Hall near Baker Street in London's West End and, in July, the band played a one-week residency in 'The Pot Luck Show' at Great Yarmouth's Regency Theatre plus a further week in 'The Dorothy Squires Show' at Kettering, winning an appearance on *Cool for Cats,* one of the first British TV shows to feature teen music.

Ian lived back in Shrewsbury for a while and travelled to and from Northampton, taking a job as an apprentice draughtsman at Sentinel. In the latter half of 1958, The Apex Group played on *Women's Hour,* won the Radio Luxembourg Skiffle Club contest and appeared on Radio Luxembourg's *Opportunity Knocks,* hosted by Hughie Green, reaching the semi-final. In December, The Apex Six appeared on ITV's *Bid for Fame* with prize money of £1,000. The Apex also featured on the BBC's *Music Makers Show* but, in 1959, Colin York was called up for National Service. York returned to Northampton but left The Apex in 1965 turning professional as Dane Hunter and recording three singles for CBS and Oriole Records.

Ian came back to live in Northampton with his girlfriend, Hazel, in St James End, known locally as Jimmy's End. Working by day as a draughtsman, Ian Patterson had an onstage spot in The Apex, still singing lead vocal on The Olympics' hit, 'Western Movies'. As the skiffle boom faded, The Apex began to turn out middle-class R&B in pubs and sometimes the officers' clubs of Northamptonshire air bases.

IH: "The music we played in The Apex was pretty naff, but it was innocent then – modern-day TV talent shows are professional blow-jobs by comparison. Frank Short, the Apex's singer, was a very clever businessman and he had the whole American air bases circuit tied up as they paid well. I loved going out to the Northampstonshire bases – you could get different brands of cigarettes, the cars were incredible and sometimes you'd get a girl, so all in all they could be very profitable evenings. I can't say I was happy in The Apex though, as it became an R&B-styled band – not great for a hardcore Jerry Lee Lewis fanatic and a Little Richard and Screaming Lord Sutch fan. I also didn't like hanging out with the guys in The Apex and some of their friends who they'd introduced me to, so I gravitated towards the bottom of the barrel and started mixing with the rogues in Northampton. They became some of the best mates I ever had but I found out that people who were like me were, in the main, villains. Most people lived by the book and observed the rules. With the villains, there were no lines. It was loose, and it was easy, but I'd fallen in with what my dad considered to be the wrong type of people – people who got into spats and some criminality, although they did it more for the craic. One of my acquaintances did have 'sufficient fun' to get ten years in prison. I never got directly involved but my dad was advised by the Northamptonshire Constabulary to get me to go home, because I was in the wrong company.

According to future musical collaborator Freddie Lee, Ian considered working under the name Rusty Hunter at one stage and he also became friendly with a band called The Homelanders.

IH: "The Homelanders were three albino brothers whose family owned a dry-cleaning business on Abingdon Square in Northampton. They say I played with them, but I don't recall playing with them. We used to hang out sometimes and I do remember going to Leicester De Montfort Hall to see Buddy Holly with them."

In the autumn of 1959, assenting to his father's pleas, Ian left The Apex and returned to Shrewsbury to find work.

IH: "There was a spot of 'bother' in Northampton and my dad came down at one point and gave me strong advice. He was no saint and could let you have it between the eyes, but my friend Barry Parkes from Northampton was extremely hard, so I always took Barry along, just in case. My dad got heavily involved in the end and dragged me back to Shrewsbury. I wasn't making my hire-purchase payments and was a total whacko. I didn't wear any kind of underwear and my clothes would stay on me for months, so I must have reeked a bit. I never noticed though and had no shortage of willing ladies, but I was a bit of a mess. I couldn't really look after myself. I found that impossible."

Back in Shrewsbury, Ian formed a harmonica duo with Tony Wardle and took up employment with Brown Brothers & Co, iron-founders and engineers. He also met and courted a local girl, Diane Coles, who was three years younger than him, but when his hire-purchase obligations had been discharged, Ian returned to Northampton and Diane followed. The couple wed in June 1960 and had two children: Stephen Patterson, born in March 1961 and Tracy, born in September 1964.

IH: "Diane and I got married and I had two children by the time I was twenty-five. I'd lived near the racecourse in a flat, then somebody got us a place in Fife Street in St James End. My eldest son, Stephen, was born in 13 Fife Street where the rent was three quid a week. Diane was a real nice girl and the kids grew up great, but she married an average working bloke who turned into this other thing, 'in music', and it didn't work out. A lot was going on in my life. There were American servicemen in the area from all the air bases and I was buying and selling cigarettes and cars, and I didn't even have a driving licence. My mates were wide boys too – people like my first Northampton acquaintance Johnny Facer and great guys like Alan Manship, Johnny Ayres, Jimmy Taylor, Barry Parkes and Tony Perrett who went on to become a successful scrap metal merchant. We were all nutters."

Hunter returned to The Apex Group briefly and dodged in and out of different bands at different times including The Cadillacs, Johnny Cave and the Cave Dwellers, The Ian Patterson Vocal Group, Ian Patterson and the Acoustics and The Skyliners. Graham 'Wiggie' Worley of The Skyliners recalled that Ian Patterson was always keen to get involved and loved to get up on stage and join in with his band.

Ian does not remember precisely what he recorded in the Sixties but contrary to popular belief, he was absent from The Apex's two record releases. The band's drummer, Johnny Lever, was the owner of a music shop in Gold Street, Northampton, and arranged demo recordings there. An Apex single 'Caravan' and an Apex Rhythm & Blues All-Stars EP were issued on John Lever Records, pressed up as promo discs in Johnny's shop, but neither disc featured Ian Patterson.

Though Hunter was back with The Apex, Frank Short's band had become too safe and musically unadventurous. Ian had seen Screaming Lord Sutch, Nero and the Gladiators and Johnny Kidd and the Pirates, and was now thinking in terms of that performance, presentation and style.

Ian Patterson wanted to front a group playing "out-and-out rock'n'roll".

CHAPTER TWO

Blood Flowed from My Fingers

I knew the face. It was Freddie 'Fingers' Lee.

In 1963, Ian Hunter Patterson formed his first rock 'n' roll band: Hurricane Henry and the Shriekers.

Often rehearsing in a prefabricated war-time Nissen hut behind the Drill Hall on Northampton's Clare Street, the Shriekers line-up included The Jetstreams' lead guitarist Julian Coulter and drummer Tony Marriott from Dave Crane and the Strangers. Tony became a good friend of Ian's, as the pair worked together for the local council at one point, laying tarmac and erecting fencing. Hunter would still gig with The Apex making good money, but Frank Short was unimpressed when he caught Ian trying to book shows for the Hurricane Henry band.

> **IH:** "We had to wear jackets in The Apex, and I refused to wear mine one night and Short had me by the throat, up against a wall. I put the jacket on! Frank, who was twice my age, ran the Apex band and managed it. I remember he said to me years later that he should have managed me and Colin York. The Hurricane Henry group wore sacks and Viking

horns on their heads and there was many a crazy situation with that band. A lot of people came to see us, and I think Frank Short fired me from The Apex, but I kept working and playing. I was out most nights and had little time to spend with my family. My daughter, Tracy, arrived in 1964 when we were living in Alcombe Road in Northampton."

Ian now adopted Screaming Lord Sutch's rock 'n' roll style onstage, making Hurricane Henry's music almost secondary to showmanship. The Shriekers were advertised variously as 'The Midland's Own Maniacs, The Boys with the Noise' and 'Hurricane Henry and his MAD, MAD, MAD, Shriekers.' At an early gig, Ian dislocated his thumb jumping off the piano and wrote optimistically on a promotional card to his mum, "Let's hope this crew go down very well as your eldest is getting on a bit and it's probably his last bloody chance!"

IH: "Hurricane Henry and the Shriekers was formed out of my frustration at The Apex who were kind of straight-laced. The Apex band was very adult and conservative, and played 'Kansas City'. I didn't like the music much or the uniform jackets, so I had some off-shoot bands. I wanted to cross over and get into rock and roll. Hurricane Henry and the Shriekers was a silly title but we were fully booked with gigs. The group was great fun and was largely based on Screamin' Lord Sutch – *total* rock."

As music captivated Ian and his life became frantic, he is the first to confess that he neglected his marriage. He also lost his job at British Timken in Northampton because he was supposed to attend technical college one day a week, to learn theory as an apprentice, but played truant for a year and was duly fired. Ian once calculated that he'd had forty-four jobs in his early years, to keep some money flowing while he played in the evenings in pursuit of his musical dream. Hunter's employment history variously included bottling milk, cleaning bottles, goods inwards, goods outwards, factory apprentice, council worker, road digger, building demolition, labourer, hod-carrier and driver, although he had no licence and so would take work for a couple of weeks, saying his licence was in the post. Then there was a string of semi-skilled engineering jobs – milling, grinding, drilling, centre-lathes, engineering apprentice and capstan operator. Ian found all employment "dismal", but fortunately music was a constant throughout.

> **IH:** "I'd thought my parents were stupid, I'd thought my schools were stupid and now I thought my employers were stupid. A guy at Brown Brothers in Northampton employed me three times. Three times I managed to convince him that I was going to spend my life with Brown Brothers, and he went for it. I had to work because in those days welfare and benefit was not what it is now. It was frightening. Employers would give you a card and map out fifty years of your life in about a minute. They always thought they could make a good man of me and that I might have been a foreman. I did anything to do with engineering, having done a three-and-a-half-year apprenticeship and that's where I got a lot of the lyrics from for Mott, later on – because I'd been eight years in various factories."

Ironically, it was another Jerry Lee Lewis fan and rock 'n' roll pianist who helped Hunter shape his musical future: Freddie 'Fingers' Lee. Ian first saw Fred Cheeseman in 1963, playing piano in Sutch's Savages and Fred had witnessed The Apex and marvelled at Ian's friends, who "guarded" the area in front of the stage with sledgehammers. Nearly two years older than Ian, Freddie was a wild persona on stage, who discovered early on that the music business was tough and sometimes brutal. Lee had several non-musical jobs too, working in construction as a steel erector and scaffolder. Forced to wear a glass eye after a fight in Newcastle, when a guy stuck a dart in his right eye, Freddie became known as 'The One-Eyed Boogie Boy'. Inspired by the music of Lonnie Donegan, he was a guitarist in skiffle groups initially but, when Jerry Lee Lewis released 'Whole Lotta Shakin', like Ian, Fred was floored. He went to London in 1959, learned Jerry Lee songs on his landlady's piano and joined Screaming Lord Sutch whose 'Savages' mainstays included bassist Tony Dangerfield. Fred said he would be a pianist for Sutch, but he could only play six numbers and was sacked. Lee moved on to The Citizens and worked in Hamburg, eventually re-joining Sutch's group on piano and adopting the name Freddie Lee as a tribute to Jerry Lee Lewis.

"Sutch wanted a name for me and used to call me Humping Jerry Lee," said Fred. "We had this routine where I'd run around the theatre dressed in a leopard skin and he chased me as Jack the Ripper. He strangled me in Hamburg and knocked me into an orchestra pit once. I ran on stage one night in Sheffield and jumped on to the piano, which rolled off into the pit – with me on top. Sutch ran to get me but shouted to the roadies, 'Quick, phone the papers... after that, phone for an ambulance.'"

Lee once demolished a rare Steinway at Birmingham Town Hall, so promoters started to provide cheap pianos for Fred to take apart with an axe at the end of his sets. Buzz-saws and paint rollers were also utilised on stage and he would sometimes set fire to his headgear using paraffin, leading to partial destruction of ceilings and curtains. A bag of loose keys was often hidden in the lid of Fred's pianos so that he could throw them into the audience, and he would make light of his visual disability by placing his glass eye in a tumbler of water, taking a drink from it and inviting audience members onstage "for a swig".

IH: "The Hurricane Henry band was moving forward at full throttle and I used to go out and get gigs. I was about twelve miles from Northampton one day and there was a guy in this pub leaning against the jukebox, dressed in steel erector clothes, covered in dust with hammers and things hanging down from his leather belt. I knew the face. It was Freddie 'Fingers' Lee who I'd seen with Sutch, so I went up and said, 'Excuse me, are you Freddie Lee?' and he replied, 'Yeah. Why?' It turned out he thought I was going to hit him, because he looked distinctly nervous when I spoke to him. I said, 'I'm a big fan of yours. What are you doing here?' It transpired that Sutch had just let Fred go after he'd fallen into an orchestra pit during a show, so he'd gone back to steel erecting and was doing a job nearby. I said, 'Fred you can't do this. You've got to come back to Northampton and be a local star. Why don't you join my band?' He said, 'Great' and moved in at Alcombe Road with Diane, Stephen, Tracy and me. I remember Tracy used to poke his glass eye out every morning! Fred was a character. He had a huge collection of country records, was a good singer and played great piano and left-hand boogie, but he was unlucky in that he was quite naturally a ringer for Jerry Lee Lewis – and he copped him. I vacated the singing spot in my band, and it became Freddie Lee and the Shriekers, with me moving over to bass. I played bass more in hope than anything. I just played along with Fred and went up and down the bottom E string and picked things up."

Lee stayed with the Patterson family until he found his own flat and remained eternally grateful to Ian and felt that he owed him a lot given his personal circumstances. "I'd had a bad drugs scene in London," recalled Fred. "I was busy getting out of it all and had gone back to work to pull myself back to reality when I met Ian. I had a very, very soft spot for his son Stephen – I loved the little kid and used to take him everywhere with me – and Diane was a really beautiful girl with a heart of gold. The Shriekers were a very rough-and-ready band which suited me down to the bloody ground, and they had a reputation for doing wild shows so, naturally, I was interested. I did encourage Ian, because I used to write a lot and had worked as a songwriter for

Southern Music at one time. It wasn't that I saw things hidden in Ian – it was just his burning ambition to be famous. He always wanted to be famous and be recognised. It would take some time, but he got his wish."

Ian had learned rhythm guitar and dabbled with piano and now he was becoming reasonably proficient on bass. Hunter wanted to "turn pro" and with Lee it was possible, because Fred had contacts in Germany. In 1965, the Shriekers played over thirty gigs appearing at Bremen's Beat Club, The Star-Club in Hamburg and The Star Palast in Kiel, a converted cinema with a dance floor. Hamburg's Reeperbahn with its sordid drugs, prostitutes, transvestites and gangsters developed into a rock 'n' roll centre for British and American musicians. Hundreds of beat-orientated German clubs had been established and the landlords of many establishments earned fearsome reputations.

"The Shriekers band went down a storm," remembered Fred, "but there was one problem – we often didn't get paid. We were often stranded on the docks in Hamburg without our fares home and if it hadn't been for the sympathy of various fräuleins, we probably wouldn't have got back to England. All I can really say of the days in Germany and the early Sixties is that it truly was sex, drugs and rock and roll – and we made a meal of the whole bloody lot while we were there too."

> **IH:** "The German gigs were packed, and the trips were a great musical grounding. We often slept on horrible bunks and mattresses in boiler rooms at the clubs and played seven nights a week. One minute you were stars in Germany and the next you were back in Northampton, working in a factory or selling clothes. Hamburg, in those days, was totally unbelievable. I slept once every three days and I remember a club in Rendsburg where we played for thirteen hours, non-stop. The sets were so long that our drummer's ass would often be cemented to the drum seat and he couldn't get up because it was

too painful. You could always tell if you were playing well because the lanterns behind the bar would start swaying. I just missed seeing my big influence, Jerry Lee Lewis, at The Star-Club but I was Tony Sheridan's fetcher for a while in Hamburg, running up and down the strip fetching wine, out of the automats. You didn't really want to get on the wrong side of Tony or be in the room when he finished the wine as he always smashed the bottle. I was scared stiff of him.

"The downside in Germany was that sometimes you got paid by the club owners and sometimes you didn't. We were ripped off in Kiel when our van broke down and the guy who ran the club knew we were stuck and wouldn't pay us. As bad as it was, I always wanted to go back because I realised it was what I was made to do. The little I got I spent on food and drink and I used to get very depressed at the time. You'd go to Germany for four weeks work, get ripped off, come back home and do six to eight weeks at regular jobs until you got the next gig. At The Star Palast in Kiel, I went into the club owner's office with a knife one day and threatened him and demanded some cash. The owner went up to his flat to get money but returned with his number one heavy and gave me 10 Pfennigs, saying, 'This is for the stamp, to put on the card, to send to your wife, to tell her you send her *nothing*!' A band from Stockport, on the bill with us in Kiel, offered to take us to Duisburg in their van, because they were getting paid and we weren't. I thank that band to this day."

The Stockport outfit that helped Ian and Fred was The Estelles, and their lead guitarist, Dave Richards, described Freddie Lee and his musicians as "a top-class band". The groups lived on bread and jam, and, if the bar staff were amenable, Brockwurst and Brockfurst (fried and boiled sausages). It was quite a journey with Freddie and Ian, but Dave remembered the British camaraderie and how they never stopped laughing for the whole trip. Freddie gave the

Stockport band petrol money out of their "expenses-on-arrival" arrangement from the next club and The Estelles' vocalist, Colin Reeves, sagely recalled: "We did help Freddie and Ian's group, but I remember we borrowed transport from a band called The Jangles. Whatever happened in the Sixties, we always managed to get through. I used to buy vans for £25, just to try and get us to and from Germany."

"The Kiel club owner was a gangster and I took out revenge for non-payment on his pets," said Freddie Lee. "He had a parrot and a cat which he loved dearly. Before we left, I put a gas gun through the owner's office keyhole, and I killed his cat and nailed it to the office door. I'm very sad to say that, but I was young, angry and stupid."

In Duisburg, Freddie and Ian played at the New York City Club, an establishment that was part of a turf war under frequent assault from racketeers who could re-model glass doors with sledgehammers. Encouragingly, Ian was encountering many musicians, like sax player Howie Casey who played in The Krewcats, and who would later feature as a session player for Mott the Hoople.

> **IH:** "The owner of the New York City – Adolf Palffy – had a nice club, but few people would go in there, so he would sometimes pay us with watches. We would then go around restaurants and exchange the watches for food and that was how we lived. There's not a guy running any of those clubs that isn't dead or in jail for life. I know them, and I know what happened to them, and a couple are justifiably dead. Despite often not being paid properly in Germany, you couldn't wait to go back. You'd play pubs in England and then get offered a contract at The Star-Club, but somehow the contract always got lost and you were so enthusiastic you just went – then you'd be there, in Hamburg, at their mercy. I'd started to write by this point, and I'd play Freddie a song now and again. Fred told me, 'You can write songs Ian – they're good songs, and you might have a future as a

songwriter – just don't sing ever 'em.' In Hamburg, I learned there was more than one string on the bass, and I started to think I might be able to make a living out of music. It was blind enthusiasm."

Ian took his first steps into a recording studio playing on a novelty single titled 'The Friendly Undertaker', credited to "Fingers Lee" and Fred confirmed that Ian also played bass on several demos, some of which were cut onto acetate discs. Freddie and the Shriekers recorded at Regent Sound, a small but affordable studio at 4 Denmark Street in London, sited in a cramped, make-shift basement. 'Little Regent' was used for voice-over jingles, welcomed producer Shel Talmy, The Kinks and Jimi Hendrix and had a house engineer, Bill Farley who had worked at Tin Pan Alley Studios. Farley became an important figure in Hunter's musical advancement.

"Bill Farley did all of us a lot of favours in those days," recalled Freddie Lee. "Regent Sound helped us too because none of us had any money, but the funny part about it is, we never got any money either for all the records we made – so therein hangs another tale!"

Ian quit the Shriekers in late 1965 and joined The Homelanders – a "sedate" outfit – but only for three months. He admitted he played in The Homelanders because some of his friends were in jail and all he wanted was to be in a band. The Shriekers recruited another bass player, but Lee recalled it wasn't the same without Hunter because whilst the pair often fought and argued, Freddie had a camaraderie with Ian that he never found in any other band. As things shifted for Hunter musically, his domestic life was affected.

IH: "Diane thought she'd married a bloke who was just a normal guy, who was going to get a job and have kids and settle down. Then I started turning into this other person all together because music was really getting to me. I was also thinking I had to get out of Northampton because I'd taken things as far as they could go. I'd been in three of the biggest local bands, but I'd still got no record deal and we were not getting nationwide work. So, I decided to sell up and move down to London."

Ian headed south in 1966 to find the Midas touch in the glamour of London, Diane taking their two children back to Shrewsbury temporarily while Hunter looked for accommodation. Ian rented a flat for £5 a week and his family re-joined him but after a year Diane thought the rent was excessive, so they moved to Cheverton Road in London, just north of the Archway.

IH: "I had that flat for two pounds, ten shillings a week, so you can imagine what it was like. I'd tried to get down to London and had stayed in a van in Soho Square a few times and never been able to make it stick. London rent was double the rent in Northampton; it took me twenty-six years but at last I stayed in London, which is where I'd always wanted to be. I felt very proud walking round the streets. I always felt jealous of those guys who were born in London because they didn't have to go through all the drama to get there. You had to live in London before you got a shot in music. I was Jimi Hendrix crazy at one point. I loved Hendrix and wrote down all his lyrics, like 'The Wind Cries Mary', which I thought was amazing. I went back to Hamburg trying to get something going for myself, doing Hendrix covers, but that wasn't happening at all, so I returned to London and starved – literally. They talk about starving nowadays, but starving is eating fucking toothpaste."

Mirroring his Shrewsbury and Northampton days, Ian reverted to yet another factory job in London, this time with Fryer Brothers Engineering who manufactured bolts, nuts and fixings. Hunter also kept in touch with engineer Bill Farley and started to tape demo tracks at Regent Sound. Ian learned about making money via publishing when Farley approached him one day, laughing heartily and brandishing a cheque.

> **IH:** "Farley was a real Dalston boy, who looked both ways before he said anything. He'd never written a song in his life, but one day he showed me a royalty cheque and I asked how he got it. Bill said, 'Well I co-wrote 'Rosalyn'. I was in the studio with The Pretty Things and they were doing this really good riff, but they had no words, so they said, 'Bill, what shall we call this?' And I said, 'Sounds like Rosalyn to me.' And they said, 'Well what's the lyric?' So, I said, 'Well the lyric is... eh... Rosalyn where ya bin? Where ya bin Rosalyn?' For a 'co-write' with The Pretty Things' producer Jimmy Duncan, Bill had a cheque for £1,800 – for that lyric! The Stones did their first album at Regent Sound and their manager Andrew Oldham went in to see Bill and said, 'How much?' Farley said, 'Four pounds an hour.' Andrew said, 'Two quid an hour and I'll give you half the proceeds from the album' – but Bill told him to fuck off. Jimi Hendrix recorded there too. Bill said to Jimi, 'You're too loud. Get out.' Hendrix said, 'I thought this was a studio?' Bill said, 'It is. Get out.'"

It seemed inevitable that a new band would materialise for Ian and he soon met a guitarist and apprentice engineer from Scotland who would become a life-long friend. A fan of Gene Vincent and Chuck Berry, Miller Anderson was born in Houston near Glasgow and had moved to London in 1965 with Scottish R&B band The Royal Crests. The group evolved into Karl Stuart and the Profiles then The Voice, a psychedelic house-band for a religious sect called The Process, who represented the apocalyptic side of Sixties flower power and believed that God would become an amalgam of Jesus Christ and Satan. With such a backdrop, Miller did not hang around!

"The Process wanted us to change into something more in keeping with their message, so they came up with The Voice," says Anderson. "They liked the lyrics that I was writing as they said they were close to their beliefs, but I don't know how they worked that out. I left the group when they went to Mexico and lived in a commune, but I auditioned candidates to replace me. A lot of people tried out for the job and I chose an excellent guy and shared the guitar job in the band with him for a month. The guy came from Hull and was called Mick Ronson."

The original drummer from The Royal Crest had been replaced by Londoner Dave Dufort, who later played with East of Eden and Kevin Ayers. After quitting The Voice, Miller and Dave decided they would combine as a duo and look for a bassist, and Ian Patterson attended an audition.

"I first met Ian in 1966 when we were auditioning for a bass player," says Anderson. "When he turned up, I felt right away that he was special. Ian was solid as a rock with great timing. He was six years older than me so Dave, who was very image-conscious, immediately thought Ian was far too old, but I liked him and could see something you couldn't really describe. Ian got me a job at Fryers factory, and we worked on capstan machines, standing side-by-side making small screws. It was like being in hell. Ian was there before me, so it pissed me off later on when he got another job and left me stranded in Fryers. I never had a problem with Ian. He had a couple of kids and I had one baby, Miller (Junior), so we got on well and remained friends for life."

IH: "I met Miller at an audition one day and it turned out he was living two streets away from me in North London. 'Mill' was also very serious about music, had a great voice and played great guitar – and I played bass – so we gigged."

Anderson, Hunter and Dufort formed The Scenery in June 1966 with Miller and Ian as vocalists. The trio recruited keyboard player Dante Smith and then found another drummer, John Vernon Smith. The Scenery became a house band, "of sorts", at Regent Sound Studios but were always broke. One night, Miller took Ian to see

The Voice play at The Swan pub in Tottenham and it was here that Hunter first saw Ronson, the band's guitarist. Ian does not recall that evening, but remembers meeting Mick "properly" when The Scenery played on the same bill as Ronson's next band, The Rats, at London's Flamingo club.

"The Scenery were a really good group and Ian became a fine bass player," says Anderson. "We did studio sessions on the cheap in the Sixties so were working all the time. Sometimes we included Dante Smith on keyboards, and we had Mitch Mitchell on drums for one session; he had just left Georgie Fame and said he was starting a new band with a black guy that Chas Chandler of The Animals had discovered in the States. 'I think he's a piano player,' said Mitch. I never saw Jimi Hendrix on piano. The Flamingo venue was a big deal then, even if you didn't get paid, because people like Georgie Fame performed there. Mick Ronson was coming down the stairs one night, having just finished his set and we were going up and I said, 'Mick, this is my friend, Ian Patterson' – and that's where Hunter first met Ronson – on the stairs of The Flamingo in Soho."

With Bill Farley's support, The Scenery cut various tracks at Regent Sound. A 1967 single on French-Belgian label Impact, coupled 'To Make a Man Cry' with the rough and raw 'Thread of Time'. Both songs were written by I. Patterson, M. Anderson and J.B. Antrobus (a Farley pseudonym). Ian's memory is not clear about The Scenery sessions for whilst he and Miller remember writing and recording the A-side, neither recalls 'Thread of Time'. The single's picture sleeve features a photograph of Ian, Miller and John Vernon Smith, but the drummer on the session was John Banks from The Merseybeats.

"The Scenery made a few demos at Regent Sound for Bill Farley," says Anderson, "and one of them was a song called 'Queue Jumping', which Ian mostly wrote with help from me. We composed another song which I later stole for The Keef Hartley Band called 'Waiting Around', although it was inspired by something we'd been writing together. We never saw any money from 'Queue Jumping' and I don't think we ever realised it was released in Japan until somebody showed me the cover years later."

During The Scenery era, Ian and Miller worked as a backing band for Mike Berry and British pop act The Young Idea, a duo comprising Tony Cox and Douglas MacRea-Brown who scored a 1967 hit with Lennon and McCartney's 'With A Little Help from My Friends'. The Mike Berry work was "by the gig" but The Young Idea appeared on a March 1967 package tour with The Hollies and The Spencer Davis Group.

> **IH: "The Young Idea was my first brush with teenage hysteria. The curtains would open, and the young kids would just go nuts. I'd never experienced that before. Miller and I also played with Mike Berry – England's answer to Buddy Holly."**

In The Scenery, Ian started to develop songs and he took up a short-term role with a music publishing firm. On 10th May 1967, Ian Patterson signed a songwriting agreement with Sandie Music Limited, represented by Kay O'Dwyer (Publicity) Limited; the deal was an initial twelve-week contract paying Ian £15 per week from 26th May to 18th August 1967. Sandie Music would have first refusal on any assignments of Ian's songs plus an option of two one-yearly extensions to the arrangement but, on 1st December 1967, they released him. Ian Patterson was then contracted to the publishers Francis, Day & Hunter Limited. Two early Patterson compositions were 'Broken Dreams and Promises' and 'Lucinda Brown' although these were not picked up by any artists. The first of Ian's songs to be covered was 'And I Have Learned to Dream', recorded by Dave Berry as a Decca B-side. Ian also penned 'Gilbert the Ghost' and whilst it was never released commercially, a publicity photograph was issued, showing Ian seated in dark slacks and sweater in front of a white-sheeted spectre with outstretched hands.

> **IH: "The first complete song I ever wrote was called 'Lucinda Brown', I think. I'd come home from work every day and**

battle away at it. I do remember writing 'Gilbert the Ghost'. Some discography suggested years later that I may have written that for Gerry and the Pacemakers, but I doubt that, and it's another question entirely as to whether Gerry might have wanted to do it. I spent a bit of time on 'Gilbert the Ghost'. I started buying old upright pianos in the late Sixties. They were thirty bob – one pound and fifty pence – and I could not stop playing them. I would really annoy the neighbours. I later wrote some Mott songs on piano using sharps and flats, as I used to wear out the white keys!"

Bill Farley continued to help Ian and placed The Scenery on a 1967 British tour as the backing band to Northern Irish singer-songwriter David McWilliams. The Scenery were the only electric group in the show, which featured Irish folk band The Dubliners and Scottish quintet The Kerries. The package appeared at nine venues including London's Royal Albert Hall, Newcastle City Hall and Glasgow Concert Hall, often with two shows played each day. "Ian, John and I did live gigs all over the UK as The Scenery," recalled Miller, "including a tour backing David McWilliams. We played at The Royal Albert Hall and I had a Telecaster and Vox AC30 amp while Ian played a Fender bass. Some of the purist folkies in the audience hated the electric sound."

The Scenery played gigs and provided backing to recognised pop acts, but Hunter and Anderson also attended odd auditions in search of more fertile pastures. One try-out was with a wannabee singer who would soon find major fame.

IH: "Miller and I went down to an audition one day in South London, in this horrible little room covered in dirt with a tiny gas fire. We sat on this filthy sofa and a guy called Paul Raven came out in a blazer and flannels and started jumping around in front of us with no music – no backing – just singing. Miller and I were sitting there trying to keep straight faces and when we left and walked down the road, we pissed ourselves laughing. Paul Raven later became Gary Glitter. We thought it was a joke at the time and it was a joke, until he got with producer Mike Leander who was a very clever, talented guy. Bill Farley was our only hope really – he called me 'Ginge'. He used to say, 'You know what I like about you Ginge – you've never had a hit!' Miller and I kept playing various gigs and got conned by various agencies who wanted to sign you for ten years, purely to sell you when you caught the eye of a more reputable agency. Mill and I worked together in Fryer Brothers factory and I hated every minute. It was dismal, but I found the harder I went at it, the quicker the day went. When the siren sounded on Friday, I was the happiest chap in the world."

In late 1967, The Scenery morphed into The Freddie Fingers Lee Band, but Miller left in early 1968 to re-unite with Dave Dufort. Anderson also joined the trippy-sounding quartet, Paper Blitz Tissue who changed drummers and brought in Bill Bruford, later of Yes and King Crimson. Ian wanted to join Miller and play bass, but Paper Blitz Tissue achieved little so Miller left and formed a duo with Ian.

Freddie Lee, meanwhile, noted that a rock 'n' roll resurgence had begun to take hold in Britain. This renewed popularity of Fifties music appeared to be a window of opportunity, so Fred and Ian formed At Last the 1958 Rock and Roll Show. The lengthy name derived from ITV's satire show, *At Last the 1948 Show*, featuring future 'Pythons' John Cleese, Graham Chapman and Eric Idle. At Last the 1958 Rock and Roll Show comprised Lee on piano, Hunter on bass, plus guitarist Chris Mayfield and drummer Pete Phillips. Pete had played with Del Shannon and Screaming Lord Sutch and got the job because Fred and Ian's chosen drummer, Johnny Banks from The Merseybeats, had his kit stolen. By now, Fred had left his wife and children in Northampton and moved down to London to live, once more, with Ian and his family in Cheverton Road.

"There was a massive upsurge in rock 'n' roll and there weren't any real rock 'n' roll bands except us, who were already playing," recalled Fred. "We had a residency but the whole thing was a short-lived fad. The idea for our band, At Last the 1958 Rock and Roll Show, was dreamed up by our agency."

"At Last the 1958 Rock and Roll Show played sped-up Fifties-style Jerry Lee Lewis," says guitarist Chris Mayfield. "Freddie once broke his foot doing a somersault to play the piano upside down, as he hadn't noticed a cross-beam. Fred had two speeds – fast and faster. I found Ian to be a formidable persona. He and I did not get along that well and I was soon 'out', as I think Ian was keen to get his mate Miller into the band."

"Ian and Fred were recording with another guitar player but got me to come along to the studio to record on a single called 'I Can't Drive', having tricked the other guitarist into not being at the session," says Miller Anderson. "Soon I was 'in', because Fred liked my Chuck Berry style, the record worked out well and management wanted me to join the band. I was taken to Carnaby Street and was in a fitting room trying out clothes that Ian had picked – a green-and-gold shirt and a pair of pink flares – and their guitar player walked in. I was told to hide in the changing room while they dispersed and left me stranded."

"We got Miller in because he was really good and phenomenal to work with," said Freddie. "We ended up joining NEMS Agency because we didn't have any money and they said they'd buy us a van, new gear and stage clothes. So, we had top of the range stuff, playing top of the range gigs."

> **IH:** "We played a lot of gigs and Fred was bringing the house down. I remember Chrysalis wanted to sign us, but we went with NEMS and Colin Johnson, who later managed Status Quo. NEMS impressed us. I was sitting in their office one day when Jimi Hendrix ambled in. Incredibly, he couldn't quite make up his mind whether to go to an upcoming party in London – or New York. That was a big

deal in the Sixties because America was so far away. I was duly awed."

At Last the 1958 Rock and Roll Show recorded two songs for NEMS at CBS Studios, produced by The Pretty Things' manager Jimmy Duncan, with backing vocals provided by Grapefruit, a group with Apple Publishing connections. Peter Swettenham of Grapefruit would later act as a tape operator on some Mott the Hoople sessions. In March 1968, CBS Records released 'I Can't Drive' backed with 'Working on the Railroad', the first and only At Last the 1958 Rock and Roll Show record. Freddie had already recorded the A-side in 1966, but 'I Can't Drive' had now become a speedy, tongue-in-cheek rocker, laden with Fred's boogie-woogie piano. Cashing in on the rock 'n' roll revival, the single was issued as the band appeared in a documentary with Bill Haley. Ian recalls that Fred wrote the twelve-bar 'Working on the Railroad' in minutes and that when Tom Jones covered the song Freddie made great money. Lee admitted they re-recorded 'I Can't Drive' because he couldn't write anything else that was good enough at the time. The band toured in Germany, played Hamburg's Star-Club and performed 'I Can't Drive' and 'Great Balls of Fire' in Bremen for the television show *Beat Club*. Surviving black-and-white film footage shows a shadeless Ian brandishing his Fender bass and Miller Anderson, with white Telecaster, whipping up a storm.

On April Fools Day 1968, Freddie 'Fingers' Lee hit the British press. Having accepted a bet and a challenge from the Rock 'n' Roll Appreciation Society, Fred employed his steeplejack skills and scaled London's Nelson's Column monument on 31st March, climbing to the top via metal scaffolding that had been erected by a stone cleaning company. Within two minutes, Lee had reached the Horatio Nelson statue and was waving his jacket to the crowd below. Fred was taken into custody and appeared at Bow Street Court where he was fined for conduct contrary to Section Two of The 1952 Trafalgar Square Regulations. Having previously broken a toe in a stage antic gone wrong, Fred re-fractured the digit during his Nelson Column descent. He paid his 30 shillings fine – but won the £10 bet!

"Climbing Nelson's Column was supposed to be easy as a steel erector, but I've never seen anything like it," says Miller Anderson. "Fred was up there in sixty seconds. He was amazing. Fred only had one eye but that was firmly fixed on publicity. We did a gig at a South London college on a bouncy stage and the PA column toppled and fell on our drummer Pete Phillips. He was lying on the stage unconscious and before anybody could do anything, Fred's first reaction was, 'Quick – somebody phone the press!' The word 'publicity' was always a laugh for Ian and me. If you tripped up a kerb, Ian would say, 'Call the press!' It was a standing joke."

At gigs, Hunter, Anderson and Phillips would appear onstage ahead of Freddie Lee and open the set with Miller singing 'Lucille' and Ian taking the lead vocal on 'Keep A-Knockin'. Miller described Ian as "mein host" and noted how he could get the audience animated ahead of Fred's arrival. It was Lee's show, but Hunter and Anderson were writing unused songs and had other ideas. They wanted to be more than a backing band, playing rock 'n' roll covers. In April 1968 they toured Ireland, but Ian and Miller were also becoming increasingly worried about the long-term future of the group.

> **IH:** "I remember Fred got some dates in Ireland and Rory Gallagher opened for us. Rory was in the band Taste at that time and was a lovely chap. The Irish promoter met us off the ferry at 6am and took us to seven pubs before we arrived at the bed and breakfast house. Fred used to say to Miller and me, 'It beats me why you fuckers bother to turn up.' Fred thought he was the whole show, which he was basically, standing on his head, playing the piano. We were getting unsettled, but it was good money. Then Fred wanted us 'on wages' but Colin Johnson wouldn't have that because he could see we were getting into something else and thought the future might lie more with Miller and me. We were all paid

equally but Fred couldn't understand that. He thought that we should get three quid a week and he should get the rest. It made us think about altering things a little. I said to Fred, 'This is going to go out of style and die a death and we're not going to have a gig. We've got to progress' – so, then Miller came up with the idea of changing the group name."

Anderson's suggestion was taken from an early Fifties Western, *The Half-Breed*, a tale about an Apache Indian named Charlie Wolf. Adapting the spelling, Miller, Fred and Ian's group became Charlie Woolfe and they soon had promotional pictures taken displaying a new style.

"You really had to have some kind of image then and I figured pseudo-Native American clothes would be better than green-and-gold shirts with pink flares!" says Miller. "We'd kept those horrible stage clothes in hanging bags in the back of the '58 Rock and Roll Show's van and our roadie ran up one day, ashen-faced, shouting, 'Miller, Miller, your clothes have been stolen' – and my reaction was, 'Thank fuck.'"

Charlie Woolfe was signed to the NEMS label, distributed by CBS and they recorded their only single at Olympic Studios, with producer Jimmy Duncan. Released in August 1968, the A-side was a cover, 'Dance, Dance, Dance' backed with 'Home' penned by Lee, Patterson and Anderson. Miller said the song was predominantly written by Ian and him, but it mattered little as the band was already falling apart. The single was a last-ditch effort under a new guise, but Anderson remained restless and opted to join The Keef Hartley Band, whose debut album would soon be titled, *Halfbreed*!

IH: "Charlie Woolfe didn't last long. We more or less used Fred the second time around to get our thing started. Colin Johnson was looking at Miller pretty hard, thinking the blues was coming in and Miller looked the part – he looked great, played great and sang great – so we decided to leave and

> started doing colleges, playing the blues. Miller liked my voice and let me sing a bit. He remains a seriously great guitar player to this day. I can't say enough about Mill."

"We made the 'Dance, Dance, Dance' single and then things started to peter out," says Anderson. "NEMS dropped us, so we ended up doing the pub scene again. From there we got John Vernon Smith back and did a few gigs as The Scenery once more. We supported Rod Stewart and the Faces at one venue. Then I saw an advert in the *Melody Maker* seeking a singer for a blues band, so I auditioned and left Ian."

After a tenure in The Keef Hartley Band and Dog Soldier, Miller went on to play with T. Rex, Donovan, Mountain, The Spencer Davis Group and Jon Lord, but he and Ian have always remained friends. Freddie Lee joined The Wild Angels, eventually returned to his native County Durham but continued gigging throughout Europe for years. He released a 1973 single as 'Hurricane' and issued material through his own record, publishing and production companies. "Nobody will rip me off anymore, like they used to in the old days," he said in the Nineties. "I can't even rip myself off!"

> **IH:** "Fred was a great showman and I guess I served my apprenticeship with him, but in all honesty, I don't think he was that much of an influence on the music that was going on in mine and Miller's heads. Fred had a great live act though, a great voice and was no slouch on piano."

By the time he split from Fred and Miller, Ian was a reasonable bassist and he took up an opportunity to work "the club circuit" with Billy Fury. Originally a tugboat worker from Liverpool, Fury had leapt into the rock 'n' roll limelight in 1959. With a kind persona, great looks and a quintessential quiff, Fury clocked up twenty-nine British hit singles and Hunter played in Billy's backing band in early 1969.

IH: "Billy Fury was a lovely guy, but kind of nervous. He was very quiet and polite and always came into the dressing room ready-dressed and looking as good as Elvis. Billy was winding down when I joined him, so half the gigs would be working men's clubs where they'd queue up for miles and he'd go down a storm to total adoration, while the other gigs would be 'groovy hip' venues where Billy wouldn't mean much. Times were changing! I remember Fury could only put his arms up to shoulder height and no more. I used to watch him on stage with his arms outstretched at his sides each night, looking like he was ready to take off. He'd arrive a minute before we went on stage, looking amazing, he sounded incredible and he would leave the minute we went off. 'It's Only Make Believe' used to bring the house down. I went to Billy's parent's home in Liverpool once and I couldn't believe the number of gold discs and platinum records on the walls. I remember going to his house too and there were tons of the things all over the place. I had no idea that he was that big. Billy was a very nice man, but he wasn't keen on our guitar player. He'd hired us as a band and when we couldn't find another guitarist, he fired us."

Domestically Diane and Ian were now drifting apart, and he was becoming fairly desperate in terms of his musical advancement and continuance. Hunter had always had problems with his parents, but he decided to talk to them about his rock 'n' roll passion.

IH: "I looked at myself in the mirror one day and there wasn't much left, so I thought why don't you go and see your mother and father? I got a ride to Blackburn and then hitched to Blackpool where my parents were living. There were problems because Diane wanted to go back to Shrewsbury. She thought I was crazy. We had two kids and I felt terrible that I wasn't really supporting them like I should be. Diane had said, 'It's the band or me, make up

69

your mind.' There was no hope. So, I told my mum and dad about it all and said, 'I just believe my future's in music. I feel I've got to do that.' They went into another room and came back and my dad, who had never given me a dime in my life, said, 'We'll give you £200.' I nearly died. My dad was a very individual man who believed you should do what you felt strongly about. That two hundred quid gave me some leeway until I got the call from Mott. I could give Diane money and stay in music. For once in my life, when I was at an all-time low in every department, I went to my parents as a last resort and they came through for me. I never, ever forgot that."

Ian was still writing and recording at Regent Sound and, one day, Bill Farley played an Ian Patterson demo, 'Season's Song', to Mike Smith, Head of A&R at CBS. Smith decided to record the song with Shakespearean actor-turned-singer Nicol Williamson, but a consent faux pas led to a permanent staff songwriter job for Hunter.

IH: "Mike Smith was the guy who turned The Beatles down and signed Brian Poole. Mike had recorded 'Season's Song', but they hadn't got my permission first. They'd recorded it with a forty-piece orchestra and had spent a lot of money, so they quickly had me down at Francis, Day & Hunter, asking me to sign 'a bit of paper' – a contract. Now I was in this factory at the Archway and playing live at weekends – and they were in a hole. Even as dumb as I was at the time, I realised it was my chance. So, I said, 'I don't want to sign anything unless you give me some money.' CBS said, 'What do want?' I said, 'Well, I want a retainer.' So, there was a bit of a flap around Francis, Day & Hunter and the upshot was they took me on a three-month contract, for £15 a week. It was a fluke, but funny. The retainer turned into a year – and I got out of the factory!"

Published by Peers Music, Ian's 'Season's Song' appeared on *Nicol Williamson*, an LP featuring keyboard player Roy Young who would tour with Hunter in the Eighties; Louisa Jane White would also cover 'Season's Song'. Francis, Day & Hunter's roster included Tom Jones, Engelbert Humperdinck and Tony Macaulay and, as a staff songwriter, Ian was expected to compose to order. He also wrote for Leeds Music and Peers Music but felt guilty collecting his wages each Friday when Francis, Day & Hunter kept picking up his option.

> **IH:** "I wasn't completely bereft when Miller joined Keef Hartley as I was still writing for Francis, Day & Hunter. I got a weekly wage and was meant to be writing songs for people like Tom Jones, but I never got 'a big song'. There were other musician-writers at Francis, Day & Hunter, like Roger Glover, who joined Deep Purple. We took solace in each other and, in fact, we both left Francis Day at the same time. Roger was in a similar position to me; they liked the songs, but they couldn't really get them recorded. I think I wrote two songs a year at Francis, Day & Hunter. Kay O'Dwyer, later an EMI executive, was my 'boss'. Kay was a lovely lady with a great sense of humour who kept me on, but it became increasingly embarassing picking up my paycheck. I had regarded it as a summer holiday, but they employed me for a year. Kay kept paying me, but I used to sneak in on Friday afternoons for my wages when they were all out to lunch. I wanted to find a band that would pay me the equivalent – £15 a week – which is the amount I would ask for to join Mott the Hoople!"

Ian decided to pick up his bass guitar once more and became involved fleetingly with a version of The New Yardbirds. The original blues-based mid-Sixties Yardbirds of 'For Your Love' fame had hired a new manager, Peter Grant and engaged producer Mickie Most for their 1967 *Little Games* album. Most was positioning the group for pop radio success with short tracks, while the band's live shows were moving in a heavier musical direction. The band split in June 1968 and guitarist Jimmy Page formed The New Yardbirds to fulfil live commitments, finding Robert Plant, John Paul Jones and John Bonham for the tour. Most had shared a production office with Grant and Mickie tried to prolong The Yardbirds ride by assembling "another" New Yardbirds, planning that his band would play venues where Page's group would not be appearing. The "Ian Hunter version" of The New Yardbirds included drummer Dave Dufort, singer Johnny Gilpin and guitarist Mick Strode who had played in Band of Joy, with Robert Plant and John Bonham. Ian and The New Yardbirds rehearsed for a few weeks, but Most's project fell apart.

> **IH:** "The New Yardbirds had nothing to do with any real Yardbirds. I knew Mickie Most when he sat in an office above Peter Grant in Oxford Street and was paying wages for Grant. Most was on about doing a Yardbirds re-union and they were going to travel to the Midwest because no one there had seen The Yardbirds. So, we would be The New Yardbirds. Our band was very good, but it was just a scam. Mick Strode used to play with picks on all his fingers and our singer, Johnny Gilpin, was a delicate kind of guy who couldn't make his mind up if he really wanted to be in music or not, but he was a great singer. Grant never saw us because while he had Jimmy Page over in America saying The Yardbirds were still going, which they were, I think there were three sets of New Yardbirds in London. I remember Mickie Most came to see us rehearse in an old church hall. There was a football there that he was kicking around but when we started playing, he stopped and took notice. Mickie liked us, so he started giving us wages for about a month until Grant's New Yardbirds came back to London. Peter nixed Mickie's New Yardbirds idea, our payments stopped and the whole fiasco aborted."

During this period, Ian encountered Richard Anderson who would soon become the fulcrum of Mott the Hoople's road crew. Richie had been a roadie for Tangerine Slide and the "in-charge organiser" for Portsmouth group, Harlem Speakeasy. In 1968 the band turned pro but found life tough logistically and managerially, so, when they split, Richie headed to London.

"I first met Ian Patterson in early 1969 when Mickie Most had tried to form a New Yardbirds band," said Richie. "I was living in Chiswick in the same house as their guitarist, Mick Strode. I think they'd placed an ad for a bassist and Ian came along one day and played – then it all fell apart fairly quickly. I recall that this would be around March 1969, as it was my twenty-first birthday – and we did a midnight flit from our flat!"

In early 1969, Ian was still toiling, writing songs for Leeds Music, but he felt his options and opportunities were almost totally exhausted. However, stalwart Bill Farley at Regent Sound Studios had faithfully supported Hunter in his pursuit of musical recognition – and Bill was about to play his most valuable role yet – in helping Ian achieve his goal.

Following an early life full of personal frustrations, the earth-shattering arrival of American rock 'n' roll music and a tough musical apprenticeship in Britain and Germany, young Ian Hunter Patterson was primed... and ready!

CHAPTER THREE

Two Miles from Heaven

Mick Ralphs was a born hustler.

As Ian Hunter was taking his first musical steps in various Northamptonshire groups, two youngsters were forming a school band in Herefordshire. From basic beginnings at Ross Grammar School, a series of pre-Hoople Herefordshire bands was formed including The Buddies, The Doc Thomas Group and The Shakedown Sound. Finally, there was Silence, comprising lead singer Stan Tippins, guitarist Mick Ralphs, organist Terry Allen, bass player Peter Watts and drummer Terry Griffin. In 1969, a driven Ian Hunter Patterson would meet Silence at "another audition", before the new ensemble magically morphed into Mott the Hoople.

Born in Ross on 24th October 1948, Terence Dale Griffin had worked as a brush salesman and PR man for an electrical firm, while his part-time musical career developed. Inspired by his parents' Frankie Laine and Johnny Ray records, Dale's boyhood hero was John Leyton, a British actor who recorded the No.1 hit, 'Johnny Remember Me.' After some 78 rpm discs by the oddly named Elvis Presley began to appear in the Griffin's living room, Dale was soon interested in drumming, using knitting needles and metal fruit servers at first, before graduating to a snare drum and cymbal.

Terry Griffin met Peter Overend Watts in 1961 at Ross Grammar School. Pete was born in Yardley, Birmingham, on 13th May 1947 to Ronald Overend Watts and Joan Aylwin Lineker, who was distantly related to footballer Gary Lineker's family. Ronald was a college lecturer in metallurgy and applied mathematics and unearthed the Lineker connection, discovering that Overend probably originated as the family surname in Westmorland. "My father was something of a musician," said Pete, "and he'd written a song called 'I've Got a Cow That's Got Three Legs', which was brilliant."

Pete was known as Overend during most of his Mott career and hated to be called Peter 'Overend' Watts – with his "real name in fuckin' inverted commas." The bassist developed devilish dexterity at corrupting names and generating amusing spoonerisms and derived Dale's alter ego when Sniffin' Griff Griffin became that Little Bugger Sniffin', then Buffin. Watts would also craft the nickname for Terry Allen, Mott's organ player and devise group identities such as The Natalie Tokered Band, as well as working titles – "Why King Turtles" – for group songs.

As a kid Pete sang along with show soundtracks and pop tunes on the radio. He mispronounced titles, singing "Glory to the Newport King" in 'Hark the Herald Angels Sing' at Christmas one year, and asked his parents if he could go to Newport to see the King. Then young Peter was "blown away" by Tommy Steele playing 'Singing the Blues' on TV, an Elvis cinema poster and the sounds and attitude of Little Richard, Chuck Berry and Jerry Lee Lewis. Watts adored music, his favourites extending from Lonnie Donegan ("probably the most underrated person in the history of British pop music") to The Beatles ("the greatest band of all time") and The Who ("the greatest live band"). Other fanaticisms included Nils Lofgren, Grin, Warren Zevon, The West Coast Pop Art Experimental Band, Love and The Easybeats.

When Pete heard The Shadows' 1960 instrumental single 'Apache' and saw a Hofner V3 electric guitar in a shop, he was really hooked. Ronald Watts bought his son a Hofner Colorama six-string, for thirty-two guineas (four weeks wages) and at fifteen, Peter started playing "wild guitar" with Ron Rudge and his Ploughman Band – then The Hawaiian Airs, The Crystals and The Sandstorms. At local dances "The Boy Watts" played his Hofner but was continually required to "turn it down". At one venue an exasperated patron gave Pete 1/6d to, "Go and have an orange juice and give my bloody ears a rest!"

One lunchtime at Ross Grammar, Griffin heard Watts playing blues and guitar instrumentals with some chums in a form room and as they had no drummer, he wangled an upgraded kit from his dad and made sure that his latest acquisition became known to Pete. "I'd seen Buffin around the school and he seemed an odd sort of kid," said Watts. "One day I saw a group of kids laughing in the playground and I went over and Buffin was doing a silly walk and crashing into posts. Then he'd fall into a big puddle on the floor and roll around and everyone would be laughing. I liked him and used to call him 'my friend'."

Buffin appeared one day with a "Premier" ticket. Pete thought Premier was a new pair of shoes, but Dale explained he had a set of drums, so Watts arranged a practice and with his incredible blue-sparkle professional kit, Buffin was "in". Pete suddenly felt inadequate with his Watkins Westminster amp and Colorama, but a summer residency began for the hurriedly christened Anchors. Dale felt the band name was a mistake as people could add a 'W' in front of Anchors. With a repertoire that embraced Beatles, Shadows and Ventures songs, The Hope and Anchor pub on the edge of the River Wye in Ross became a regular date for the group. Although they were under-age, they were paid £2 a week and two pints of beer each night.

The second incarnation of The Anchors included Fred Fishpool (aka Robert Fisher, "rock 'n' blues bawling"), Peter 'Dog' Watts (lead guitar) and 'That Little Snigger' Buffin (drums). They had no bass player and various singers guested, including Mike 'Jeambers' Chambers, the brother of future Pretenders' drummer Martin.

The next Ross Grammar group was Wild Dog's Hell Hounds, named in part after a rotary switch setting on a Burns' tri-sonic guitar. 'The Hounds' were led by Pete 'Wild Dog' Watts and Moanin' Cass Brown (Robert Fisher) but they had a short and inauspicious career playing school dances. Watts sported a gold lamé waistcoat made from curtain material with Marks and Spencer's see-through shirts and borrowed string vests underneath; the band used to wear Beatles wigs and leap around the stage playing 'Lucille', when everybody wanted to hear 'Twenty-Four Hours from Tulsa'. The school stage had a trap door where Watts used to hide a rubber bone, pre-gig; during their performance, Pete would go down on all fours, open the trap, remove the bone, and bite it, before drinking water from a 'DOG' bowl. Watts also wore "the hat of many horns" – a bowler pushed over a smaller bowler hat with two horns wedged out of the sides – as he "went berserk" playing huge guitar bends. The headmaster didn't like Wild Dog's Hell Hounds!

The Hounds soon became The Soulents because they played "with soul" and because, unlike The Anchors, this wasn't a name that could be turned into something rude – unless prefaced with 'Ar', which the band failed to notice. The Soulents turned semi-pro and secured support slots with The Zombies and The Yardbirds. Utilising the Griffin family's Arbour Hill Farm near Ross-on-Wye as their rehearsal base, Dale's dad generously gave the group encouragement, and a van. With their name emblazoned on the side panels and the van's paintwork covered with shameless lipstick messages from young girls, the group drove around like arrogant lords, oblivious to local lads who wanted to drag them from the vehicle and beat them up.

Herefordshire produced several good groups at this time and The Soulents spotted The Buddies at some gigs – a Bromyard band featuring guitarist Mick Ralphs and "heart-throb" vocalist, Stan Tippins. The Soulents also enjoyed friendly rivalry with The Tyrants and The Ups 'n' Downs who featured Phil Tippins, Stan's cousin, and Richard 'Dicky' Weaver, who would later direct some promotional videos for Mott the Hoople.

In 1965, The Soulents changed their name to The Silence and adopted the pop-art image of the time. They supported The Merseybeats at Hereford's 1600 Club and The Who at Cheltenham's Blue Moon where they used the Londoners' equipment and played some Who songs, much to their annoyance. "Moonie" glared at Griffin, Watts blew the borrowed amps and The Soulents fled from the venue after Fishpool sat on a Townshend Rickenbacker backstage and snapped it. Pete Watts was training as an architect by day but had been impressed with Mick Ralphs' Rickenbacker guitar and hairstyle, and Stan Tippins' persona, so he decided to turn professional with the "clean-cut" Buddies.

Stan and Mick both hailed from rural Herefordshire. Stanley William Tippins, born 14th May 1945 in Sarnesfield, enjoyed English, history and football, and played centre half for the school team. After working at Henry Wiggin & Co's metal-forming factory in Hereford, Stan became a professional musician in 1965. Tippins was influenced by P.J. Proby and the image-drenched rockers, Johnny Kidd and the Pirates, whose 1960 hit 'Shakin' All Over' he regarded as the first authentic rock and roll record originated by a British artist. "I saw Johnny Kidd live, eight times," recalls Stan, "and he was probably the best mover I've ever seen and the best rock and roll singer of all time, both British and American. My other interests included Jerry Lee Lewis, Sam Cooke and Little Richard. In those days it was all singles. I was keen on music and used to do some singing at school – my specialities were 'The Man from Laramie' and 'Davy Crockett'."

Tippins had formed his first group, Jet Black and the Stormraisers, in 1963, arriving onstage in leather as Jet Black, long before Ziggy Stardust was conceived. Jet soon morphed into Billy Thunder (and the Stormraisers) but Stan was tempted away to Mick Ralphs' group, The Buddies. Tippins joined the band then "changed them a bit" because he felt uncomfortable with some of their material.

Stan's fellow 'Buddie', Michael Geoffrey Ralphs was born in Hereford on 31st March 1944 and was brought up in the village of Stoke Lacy, near Bromyard. Mick was an only child and his father

Geoffrey was a keen writer and poet, who penned press articles and live reviews on The Buddies. Mick described his educational interests as "leaving school" although he later attended Keele University where he studied electrical engineering. "I used to work for the Midlands Electricity Board in Bromyard," says Ralphs, "as an apprentice electrician, and that entailed cleaning the showroom windows and making tea – which was *very* electrical!" Mick's musical influences would include Chuck Berry, Ricky Nelson, Buffalo Springfield and Mountain guitarist Leslie West, but the world first stopped for him when he heard the 1962 instrumental 'Green Onions' by Booker T & the MG's. Ralphs had not been a lover of rock music initially and was a "late-starter" playing "standards" in dance bands, picking up chord changes and learning by ear.

"I only started playing when I was about eighteen and was self-taught," says Ralphs. "Before that I couldn't afford a guitar. My first instrument was a horrible Rosetti Lucky Seven guitar and an amp that looked like a radio. I never really liked pop music much but when I heard 'Green Onions' that really grabbed me. Overnight, I wanted to play, and took an interest in the guitar. Chuck Berry was one of my main heroes and I adored Chicago blues. I've always enjoyed records like The Righteous Brothers' 'You've Lost That Loving Feeling', 'My Baby Left Me' by Elvis Presley and Don McLean's 'Vincent' – anything with feeling really."

Ralphs' first groups were The Mighty Atom Dance Band and The Melody Makers but then Mick saw The Buddies play and convinced lead singer Les Norman that he should join, auditioning on the fire escape staircase outside Hereford's YMCA building. "In those days, whoever had the reddest guitar was the leader," says Ralphs. "I never differentiated between rhythm and lead – it was just guitar – so I guess I was a guitarist at that time."

In 1964, The Buddies recorded four songs at Hollick and Taylor's studio in Birmingham and a hundred discs were pressed-up featuring two of the session tracks. Hollick produced Gerry Anderson's *Thunderbirds* soundtracks and was linked to Pye Records but an official Buddies single release never materialised.

The band, "styled on James Brown and Cliff Bennett," was described on promotional cards as 'The Buddies – The Entertainers You'll Like.' Soon they were playing a month of German gigs at a Konstanz club and although they taped four more songs at Decca Records in Hamburg, again, no single was issued.

When The Buddies came home from Germany and their bassist quit, Stan decided to "make The Silence's guitarist play bass" and visited the Watts household, masterfully charming Pete's parents to get him in the band. "Stan put his suit and tie on and came to my mum and dad's house," said Watts. "He was like a bank manager saying, 'Now listen Mr and Mrs Watts, it will all be alright. Peter will earn £30 a week' – and they were very impressed with it all. Mum and Dad thought Stan was amazing and that's why they let me go."

The Buddies identity seemed vague and tepid to Pete but at least they offered the chance of work in Europe. Watts was full of anticipation after Tippins' heavenly tales of Konstanz, but, back in Germany, the "low or no pay" gigs were hell. Hundreds of British bands had played there by then and the novelty was evaporating. Sleeping on burnt-out mattresses, it was hard to get money from promoters and Stan was losing weight – and his voice. Playing at The Pferdestall (The Horse Stable) in Hagen, in December 1965, was a nightmare for the group.

"It was real tough," Pete Watts recalled. "The Horse Stable was full of prostitutes and gangsters. We played eight hours a night – all night – and you were allowed two free drinks. There were some horrible fights, so we used to play as quietly as we could, looking at the floor, so as not to attract attention. One night in The Horse Stable, a guy wearing a camel hair coat walked in with two other blokes. Suddenly, he whipped this sword-stick out and ripped the Turkish owner's white shirt wide open. There was blood everywhere, but the three intruders were too slow, and the owner's staff almost murdered them with bottles. We thought they'd killed this bloke because the camel hair coat was completely covered in blood. A few days later, we were sitting in a café along the road when somebody nudged me. I looked up and this same bloke was walking in the door wearing *another* camel hair coat. I thought, Christ, he's still alive. He looked like The Invisible Man. He had bandages all round his face and head and all over his hands, and he must have had slits in the bandages because he had dark glasses on. He still had a walking stick and sat down not far away from us, and then he got up and went to the jukebox and put on Jim Reeves' 'He'll Have to Go.' In the German clubs, the type of music requested by audiences would change several times each evening. I remember one demand was, 'Play jazz, or die'."

Gigs at The Big Apple and Crazy Horse clubs in Hamburg were happier locations but The Buddies saw gangsters, guns, prostitutes, pimps, hard drink and drugs at every turn. They emerged shaken but unscarred and had played alongside The Sorrows, The V.I.P.s and The Monks – a quirky band of ex-American G.I.s who wore habits, ropes round their necks and sported short hair with the top shaved out. Watts would "rave" about The Monks for decades.

Back in Herefordshire The Buddies became known as 'The Ambassadors of Beat' and hard gigging had made a vast difference to their playing. On a revisit to Hereford's 1600 Club the local press described them as "smooth professional musicians" – the journalist was Ralphs' dad. During some British dates the band's van crashed and their road manager, Vivian Phillips, was injured. Viv was The Buddies' "pyrotechnics bloke", who made bombs from sugar and weed killer, using them to explode TV sets on stage. During long journeys, the band also staged "happenings", placing sets at the side of the road and blowing them up, causing passing drivers to "flip". Believing that The Buddies was no longer a suitable name for a professional outfit, when a local newspaper reported Viv's road accident under the headline, 'Problem for The Buddies', another new identity was employed.

Group names were starting to become "flags of convenience" according to Ralphs. "Problem was just one of those names that we had when we used to go back and forth to Germany and Italy for a month at a time," admitted Mick. "We'd always have to leave under dodgy circumstances – then we'd re-appear a week later under a different guise."

Playing in Nantwich with Kenny Ball and his Jazzmen was now unexciting after the thrill of Europe so, in the summer of 1966, The Problem drove to Milano Marittima, an Italian seaside resort. They changed identity again when Dave Mason from The Hellions mentioned he would like to form a group. Watts thought Mason would try to take over their band, so Problem declined Dave's collaborative offer but adopted his idea for a new band name instead – The Doc Thomas Group.

Back in Germany, The Doc Thomas Group met a waiter who said his father was an agent in Italy and that he could secure gigs there. The band took this claim with a pinch of salt, but a contract duly arrived, so they headed to the Adriatic coast and ended up visiting the Italian Riviera every summer until 1968. Based at Riccione, just south of Rimini, The Doc Thomas Group first performed at Milano Marittima and their local agent, Signor Ricci, introduced them to a record producer, Gian Stellari. The band was offered a contract by Interrecord and travelled to Milan and recorded some twenty songs with Stellari. Twelve tracks were selected for *The Doc Thomas Group*, an LP released in January 1967 on the Dischi Interrecord label. The album content was based on the band's stage repertoire, recorded live in the studio and a single was also issued – 'Just Can't Go to Sleep'. "I thought we'd gone into the studio to do demos," said Stan, "but we recorded twenty-two tracks in two evenings – all cover versions – and it was hard work: we were even dragging people in off the streets to sing on the choruses of Sam Cooke's 'Shake'. Back in England, again, I couldn't believe it when, a few weeks later, our 'album' arrived through the post."

After the Italian sessions, Dale 'Buffin' Griffin joined Watts, Ralphs and Tippins in The Doc Thomas Group. Dale had been working semi-professionally with The Charles Kingsley Creation, playing on sessions at Future Sound Studios (soon to be known as Rockfield Studios), set up by farming brothers turned pop impressarios Charles and Kingsley Ward in their parents' Monmouth granary.

Buffin appeared on two 1966 recordings by Welsh artists, released as singles: 'Is It Really What You Want?' by Parlophone pop group The Interns and 'Black is the Night' by Yemm and the Yemen, featuring singer Bryn Yemm. Griffin recalled the aftermath of an Interns session at Future Sound when he accidently fell over a pile of albums marked 'Bert Jansch' and took a copy home to Arbour Hill Farm. Playing the LP, Dale thought Bert had the future of rock music all sewn up – but the LP turned out to be Dylan's *Highway 61 Revisited* – with a 'Jansch label' factory error!

Following frantic rehearsals, the re-vamped Doc Thomas Group set off for Milan in April 1967 to record two shows for RAI-TV, aimed at promoting their album and single. On one of the programmes, *Diamoci del Tu*, the group played 'My Babe' and 'Shake' with Ralphs and Watts comically attired as "very young dudes" in top hats and long coats. On the other show, *Bandiera Gialla (Yellow Flag)*, the band performed 'Just Can't Go to Sleep'. Stan had a great voice and presence, and a critic, James Paine, described Tippins as 'The Sinatra of Beat'. The group was soon deported, however, thanks to one of their touring party.

"A friend of ours nicknamed Chopper had come abroad with us as a sort of mechanic-roadie-helper," recalled Pete. "He was a lot older than the rest of us and was a hard man from Bromyard who started to bully the group, drinking whisky in the clubs we played, quicker than we could earn the money to pay for it. We couldn't tell him to stop. Chopper was extremely strong and would pull lamp posts over at a forty-five-degree angle into the road and Stan would run along behind him trying to twist them back. Chopper terrorised the owner of the hotel where we stayed by forcing wine down his throat – and we were *out!*"

Another Herefordshire chum, Robert 'Jona' Jones accompanied the band to Italy for the 1967 season. A deep character from the darkest depths of Bromyard's farming stock, Robert's interests ranged from "ancient magycke" and Aleister Crowley to the latest in shaggy-chic fashions of the day. He was influential on Pete and became a style guru to the band. Watts admitted that Jona helped them greatly, procuring American catalogues and ordering wild clothes and strange fringed jackets.

Sneaking back to Italy and a four-week engagement at The Titan Club in Rome, the group stayed in a hotel staffed by trans-sexual and transvestite maids – a rarity in Hereford – but they were soon arrested after Tippins got into a "strada-rage" incident with a huge American, Stan flooring the fellow with a single blow. The Doc Thomas Group also attracted attention at The Titan when they smashed their stock of televisions onstage (Move-style) and set off smoke bombs. The TV-smashing carried out by the axe-wielding Tippins, and the band's end-of-set freak-out, left the club's customers astonished. During a Milano Marittima beach gig, the group also set off a special "Gaz" container converted into a bomb that blew an enormous hole in the sand, triggered burglar alarms and set Italy's military police, the Carabinieri, into frantic action.

Milano Marittima and Forli became regular venues for The Doc Thomas Group as did The Bat Caverna Club in Riccione, a venue that would feature in Mott the Hoople's early history. They also played at an Italian ski resort where bands had to perform for hours every night, until the last customer had departed – Tippins endeavoured to "get them out early", by wearing a hat and coat on stage.

Stan was described by fellow band members as a forceful character with the sheer brute power to make others do what was necessary. With several sets a night, numbers often had to be repeated and Griffin later recalled Tippins introducing 'My Girl' for the third or fourth time one evening, but Watts refusing to play the number "AGAIN!" The song opened with a bass riff and it relied on Pete to commence proceedings but the two stubborn Taureans stood their ground.

"After introducing the song again and again," said Dale Griffin, "Tippins turned to Pete and said, 'If you don't start this fucking song now, I'm going to break your fucking nose.' Lo and behold Wattsy played the riff instantly proving that if push comes to shove, you don't say 'no' to Stanley – you do what you're told!"

"The gigs in Italy lasted on and off for a couple of years," Mick Ralphs says, "and gave us a great deal of experience. We used to get 1,000 Lira a day, which was about seven-and-a-half new pence. The food there was cheap though and included Spaghetti Bollocknose for about eighty Lira. Good English groups were very popular over there at the time, but we got sick of pandering to the pop crowd. We really wanted to play our own music."

The band sometimes swapped instruments on stage and played quiet "awful jazz" which the audience preferred to The Doc Thomas Group's repertoire of 'Sgt. Pepper's Lonely Hearts' Club Band', 'Hold On, I'm Coming' and 'Get Ready'. Mick's latest ambition was to join Tony Rivers, later a backing vocalist to Cliff Richard, whose band The Castaways played Beach Boys and harmony songs, while Watts tried to get The Doc Thomas Group to adopt a more powerful sound and image. Restless Ralphs was soon offered a job in The Shakedown Sound, a backing band for Jamaican singing star Jimmy Cliff during his pre-reggae "soul man" days.

The future Mott the Hoople began to take real shape at this juncture as Terry (Verden) Allen played keyboards in The Shakedown Sound. Allen was eventually persuaded to join The Doc Thomas Group in early 1968, providing the final component in the ensemble that would meet Ian Hunter Patterson. Known simply as Terry at this time, the name Verden would be chosen in Mott, based on his father's middle name, Verdun – but Terry was soon nicknamed "Phally" by Pete – a unique and interesting title for an organ player and another infamous Watts corruption. In the canyons of Pete's mind, Terry Allen became "Hairy Talon", then "Hairy Phallus" and, finally, "Phally".

Terence Allen was born on 26th May 1944 in Crynant, a small village in the Dulais Valley of South Wales. He was an only child who went to Neath Technical College "for further education" and Mott the Hoople "for even further education". As a youngster, Verden received classical piano tuition and passed five grades through The Royal Schools of Music, and he was always regarded by Ian as the best musician in Mott the Hoople. Influenced by Liberace, jazz albums, "organ players like Jimmy Smith" and ultimately R&B/ Soul artists "like Booker T & the MG's, and The Animals," Verden expanded his musical interests by night. By day, he trained and worked as a car bodywork repairer in Hereford.

"After leaving South Wales with my parents to live in Hereford in 1959," says Verden, "I was re-attracted to the piano by my uncle, Colin Thornton, who was a great pub pianist. He took me away from the classical approach of my previous tutors to an uninhibited, ad-lib style of playing. I loved watching him hammer out all the old sing-along songs in the pub but, better still, was how all the punters would queue up to buy him drinks afterwards. The minute I saw that, I knew music was the life for me!"

During his time with The Anchors in 1963, Dale Griffin recalled that they were glared at during some gigs by two threatening "Teddy Boy-types" who turned out to be Terry Allen and his cousin John. Verden played in a rival Hereford group and had simply been watching The Anchors to pick up hints. Switching from piano to organ, Allen played in The Inmates then The Astrals but when The Doc Thomas Group asked Verden to accompany them to Italy, he declined initially and auditioned for The Shakedown Sound instead. Allen made his recording debut on a Jimmy Cliff LP, playing a cover of 'A Whiter Shade of Pale' and, with The Shakedown Sound, Verden accompanied Jimmy playing gigs in France. Then, Ralphs joined Cliff's band at Allen's invitation, but Mick told Pete and Buffin that via The Shakedown Sound he would get a foot in the door in London, where he now shared a flat with Verden and John Best, the Shakedown's bass player.

Watts, Griffin and Tippins attempted to find a new guitarist when Ralphs joined Allen and Jimmy Cliff, and Pete remembered auditioning Len Tuckey, Suzi Quatro's husband-to-be. Meanwhile, Mick kept ringing Pete telling him how useless most of the London groups were and when Ralphs eventually left Jimmy Cliff, he brought Allen to Watts, Griffin and Tippins. Dale had also auditioned for The Love Sculpture with Dave Edmunds and was offered the job but, after the session, the drummer said he wanted to "think things over" and Edmunds was not pleased. Griffin opted instead to work with Ralphs and Allen for the final weeks of the Shakedown's Jimmy Cliff contract.

Finally, Ralphs, Tippins, Watts and Griffin formed a band with Allen thus completing "the merging of the Motts". A "new" Shakedown Sound was established, playing gigs where the previous Shakedowns had a reasonable following, as the name was a useful key to live work over a wide area – and the band needed the money. As Verden's musical knowledge developed in these early groups, he was already starting to devise a playing style and sound that would later distinguish Mott the Hoople's material. Allen was one of the first rock musicians in Britain to own a Leslie tone cabinet and he contributed a musical component for Mott much admired by rival bands, employing an American Acoustic amp and speaker with fuzz facility. Verden's keyboards history included a Hohner Pianet, a Vox Continental ("like The Animals") and a Hammond M100 ("like Booker T").

"My first pro gig using the Hammond M100 was with Jimmy Cliff in Paris." says Allen. "I didn't have any amplification, so I shared a Selmer Goliath bass system and speaker with John Best. It sounded like a distorted fart! Returning to Hereford I purchased one of the first Leslie speaker cabinets imported into the UK. I later used a direct sound from the Hammond through a Marshall system and then switched to a HiWatt head and Marshall cabinet, combining it with the Leslie. I would use the Hammond M100 on the first three Mott the Hoople albums."

"The M100 was quite a medium-sized Hammond – wooden and immaculate," said Pete Watts. "The Leslie tone cabinet was cubic and French-polished with slats in it – very posh. When Phal wasn't on the road, his mother would polish these and put mats and flowers on them using them as furniture around the house. Everybody else's Hammonds were either beaten-up looking or painted matt black – not Phally's."

The Shakedowns continued gigging and made some demo recordings at Rockfield Studios, but as the summer of 1968 approached, the band was offered more Italian dates as The Doc Thomas Group. They played outdoors on the outskirts of Milan facing a turkey farm that stank and whilst their Milano Marittima gigs were not a success, The Bat Caverna in Riccione was fun-filled for the band. During this time, Watts became engaged to a beautiful Italian artist and was "in discussions" with an Italian progressive rock band. "Watts agreed to join major stars, I Giganti," recalled Griffin, "having been lured away by their leader, Checco, with promises of money, fast cars, villas and fame."

The Doc Thomas Group was forced to take a taxi and caravan back to the UK with their equipment, but without Pete. They played some "poor" gigs and auditioned bassists, but the drama was damped down when Watts came home; Checco's great promises and the Italian "super-group" had failed to materialise but Pete had written his first song – 'Shades of Life'. Ralphs, Watts, Griffin, Tippins and Allen decided to resurrect the 1965 band name, Silence, but there the similarities ended. Now, new and important changes lay ahead.

One of the group's entourage at this time was Mick Hince who would later become part of Mott the Hoople's road crew. Mick was given the nickname "Booster" and Tippins thinks this came from the Herefordshire farming term "Master", which Pete didn't like, so he applied another of his variations. "Mick Hince got his thumb cut off at work and with the compensation he got, we made him buy a van which we pinched off him on the condition he became our roadie," recalled Watts. "He nearly became The Silence's bass player for a while when I stayed in Italy. He played a couple of gigs and was horrified when I came back."

During early 1969, while Ian Hunter Patterson was employed as a staff songwriter in London, The Silence gigged without any greater success than before. They decided to up the ante, acquiring a new PA system and amps. They were also signed to Jay-Vee Entertainments in Swansea, but this was the beginning of the end as they wanted to play their own material and no covers, which the agency resisted. Jay-Vee demanded a pop approach and suggested Silence add a small brass section and play Blood, Sweat & Tears material. On stage, Silence would swap instruments performing a Buffalo Springfield number, 'Child's Claim to Fame', where Phally played bass, Mick went on to slide guitar and Pete used Ralphs' Gibson SG Standard; Watts described the SG as, "very nice... with a sideways tremolo and a front-ways neck." Silence also played Buffalo Springfield's 'Mr Soul', The Byrds' 'My Back Pages' and Elmer Gantry's 'Flames' – and two songs that Mick had written – 'Yellow Van' and 'Wide Asleep'. "We would sneak one or two of our own songs into the set," admitted Ralphs, "and pretend it was a Stones B-side, so we wouldn't get dragged off stage and beaten up."

Suddenly former roadie Vivian Phillips re-emerged as a tour manager for Traffic. Silence knew Traffic's drummer Jim Capaldi from his Hellions days with Dave Mason, so an Island Records "connection" was formed. Silence was invited to Olympic Studios in Barnes to see Dave Mason, on a day when The Move was recording, and The Rolling Stones came in to work on 'Jumpin' Jack Flash' with producer Jimmy Miller. Future Sound Studios was also trying to support Silence behind the scenes. "The Wards" assisted the band, taping demos including 'Transparent Day' and 'The Rebel', the latter submitted by Kingsley to Malcolm Jones, his A&R contact at EMI Records. Dale claimed that Malcolm wanted to release the track but was over-ruled by Tony Hall, a respected figure in the British music scene. "We were hugely pissed off, but he was quite right of course," said Griffin. "Our performance was pretty rough and ready, with the exception of 'The Paul Newman of Pop' – Stan Tippins."

During early 1969, Silence considered splitting but hedged their bets and came to London collectively, but also to attend individual auditions. They started going to different agencies and got involved in "ridiculous projects", backing Tommy Steele's brother, Colin Hicks and two girl vocal groups, The Pearlettes and The Paper Dolls who recorded for Pye and RCA. Silence rehearsed 'Yakety Yak' with the Dolls and their Top Twenty hit, 'Something

Here in My Heart (Keeps A Tellin' Me No)', but when they confessed to the girls' manager that they didn't read sheet music, the game was up. Silence also chanced upon The Searchers' drummer Chris Curtis, in the West End one day, but Chris's plans to re-name their band Roundabout, and a deal with Polydor Records was another dead end. Silence even trudged along to see an Apple Records' A&R man.

"The A&R guy was Mike – a gay bloke – and he 'liked' us – well he would at that time, wouldn't he," said Watts. "He thought our Herefordshire accents were incredible and he wanted to sign us and call us The Archers. We came out of Apple feeling that something might happen, but it never came off in the end. I recall seeing him a lot later, when we were in Mott and goading him about it. I remember saying, 'Ha ha, you missed us, didn't ya? You didn't get us, did ya?' And he said, 'Yeah, I will in the end though luvvie!' – and I thought, 'No you fuckin' won't mate!'"

Immediate Records was another label that seemed keen on Silence, but Watts was amazed, on reflection, that the group drifted around record companies simply "hoping" for a deal. The band became desperate and Pete and Mick resorted to busking. Outside the ABC Cinema in Muswell Hill, two girls took pity on their version of Don Partridge's 'Rosie' one rainy afternoon and paid for them to see the Sidney Poitier movie, *Guess Who's Coming to Dinner?*

Gigging between London, Herefordshire and the Welsh borders, Silence supported The Small Faces at the Top Rank Suite in Swansea. Mick Ralphs and Steve Marriott enthused about guitar playing together, before the show, and took to the empty stage to experiment in front of the gathering audience. Joined by Dale, bassist Ronnie Lane, then Ian McLagan and Verden on keyboards, this odd combination jammed for thirty minutes before Silence's set and Marriott was full of praise. "The Small Faces were a nice bunch of lads," recalled Stan Tippins. "We went out for an Indian meal with them after that gig and they even paid the bill, which I thought was amazing as I think they were getting ripped off left, right and centre. We took them to the railway station for the train back to London at 5.45 in the morning."

Fortunes improved for Silence when Ralphs started pursuing an A&R figure at Island Records who might aid their quest. Watts had also noted an interesting advertisement in *Melody Maker* that read, 'Tough, aggressive bass player required for Island Records group.' Pete phoned and was told the band was Free, so he ventured to London accompanied by Mick, who would provide "moral support".

"When I arrived at the Free audition there were hundreds of 'tough, aggressive bass players' in the street, dressed in German metal helmets, chainmail waistcoats and tattoos – horrible looking blokes – all waiting to audition," said Watts. "Mick was with me and said, 'I met Guy Stevens from Island, with Dave Mason. I wonder if he's here because if he is, I might be able to get you in ahead of this lot.'"

Ralphs pushed his way in and Watts jammed with Free. As they played, guitarist Paul Kossoff and drummer Simon Kirke shook their heads, and Guy kept putting his ear in Pete's bass speaker. Stevens liked Watts' buckskin fringed jacket, lace-up knee-length boots and long hair. Watts would not join Free, but Mick's visits to record companies in London bore fruit. Later, at Island Records in Oxford Street he had waited "like an idiot" again, outside Guy Stevens' office, before "barging in". Ian Hunter later acknowledged the importance of Ralphs' determination in getting a break for Silence.

IH: "Mick Ralphs had gone to Guy Stevens who was head of A&R for Island Records. They were reputedly the best label in England at that time and Guy had been impressed with Mick. Guy had ignored him a couple of times apparently, but one day Mick just banged on the door and walked straight back in demanding, 'Listen to our stuff.' Mick Ralphs was a born hustler and he hustled for the original group. He kept on going to see Guy. Jim Capaldi of Traffic had also put a word in apparently. Mick knew a lot of people. He knew Luther Grosvenor of Spooky Tooth, back in Evesham as kids, where they used to practise guitar together in the relative quiet of a telephone box – because they had no amplifier."

"We got Guy to hear Silence at a small rehearsal studio and he really dug us," says Ralphs. "My initial impressions were that he was a record company person, but I didn't realise how great he was then. Island was the first real independent record company. Guy Stevens found most of the bands and if it hadn't been for him, I don't think Island Records would have lasted five minutes. Island boss Chris Blackwell had the money, but he didn't possess Guy's vision. Guy was quite a character and a fantastic bloke."

About to become Britain's most influential label, Island Records had been founded by Chris Blackwell, the son of one of Jamaica's most prominent families, linked to the Crosse & Blackwell foods and Wray & Nephew rum businesses. Chris spent his childhood in Jamaica but was educated at Harrow in England and was a charismatic, creative figure. In 1959 he started importing discs into Jamaica, travelling to New York buying cheap records for re-sale. From his first bluebeat label, R&B Records, he formed Island, inspired by Alex Waugh's *Island in the Sun* novel and Harry Belafonte's hit of the same name. A mountain area of Jamaica would even provide the name for Island's publishing company – Blue Mountain Music.

As Jamaica became independent in 1962, Chris moved Island Records to London, peddling records from his Mini Cooper, running a stall in Portobello Market and later operating from a rented flat. Initially, Island was an import business, but they promoted reggae music and became influential in the development of British R&B, signing a distribution deal with American label Sue Records in 1964. Blackwell tapped into Guy Stevens' energy and musical knowledge at that point and put him in charge of the Sue UK imprint to release hits by James Brown, Bob & Earl and Inez & Charlie Foxx. Chris had early record success with Millie Small, Desmond Dekker,

Jimmy Cliff and The Spencer Davis Group, whose offshoot, Traffic, became Island's first rock signing. Blackwell decided to originate his own recordings instead of investing in finished masters and he devised a pop image to boost Island's changing catalogue. With striking vivid pink record labels and intriguing album artwork, music collectors were encouraged that interesting music must be nestling on the vinyl within lovingly presented gatefold LP sleeves.

Island soon snared King Crimson, a sensational 'prog' band coveted by all the major UK labels and they attracted Jethro Tull, Spooky Tooth, Free and Emerson Lake & Palmer too. Rival record companies struck back with progressive house labels such as Harvest, Dawn and Vertigo but they could not compete with Island. A "savvy Svengali", Chris Blackwell surrounded himself with key people like David Betteridge (Island Sales Manager), Muff Winwood (A&R Chief) and Guy Stevens. Broadening Island's menu with acoustic acts like Fairport Convention, John Martyn and Nick Drake, one employee described Blackwell as an amazing businessman who walked in, made the deal on his terms and walked out. Island possessed a libertarian spirit and appreciated that signings needed time to grow. They also threw the dice with artists that were unknown but might be the next big thing. Not all the Island team agreed all the time however, and King Crimson (and later Roxy Music) were not universally embraced within the company, but they became two of Island's greatest acquisitions.

Blackwell would move Island from Oxford Street to Basing Street in Notting Hill, where a new corporate headquarters was constructed within a former chapel building; they later acquired a former laundry property at St Peter's Square, creating a first-floor recording facility and basement studio christened "The Fall-Out Shelter". They would also net more classic acts, signing Sparks, Bad Company, Robert Palmer and U2, and "oddities" like Dr Strangely Strange, Grace Jones and The Slits, although 'punk rock' would be conspicuous by its absence, Blackwell admitting that he appreciated the attitude of punk but not the non-musicality. Unquestionably, Island Records created an influential shift in popular music and became rock's most important independent.

In 1969 Silence joined Island's astonishing stable and the catalyst was Guy Stevens. The band's demo tape, that Mick had thrust upon Guy, contained 'Find Your Way', 'The Rebel' and an instrumental, 'The Silence'. Although he liked 'The Rebel', Stevens wasn't particularly impressed, but he told Ralphs he would like to see the group and arranged an audition at Spot Studios, located at 64 South Molton Street in Mayfair. The third-floor studio had been used to record *Top of the Pops* budget compilation albums and Silence was nearly crushed to death carrying Allen's Hammond organ upstairs. Guy Stevens claimed that he now knew the band had to be "right", before they even played as they had transported the enormous musical contraption up three flights of stairs!

"I remember wrestling the Hammond upstairs at that first audition," says Verden. "Guy said, 'Anyone who carts that bloody big thing upstairs deserves a record deal.' They were complaining like hell across the road about the noise when we played and that turned Guy on – he was leaping up and down."

There was one problem for Silence at the audition, but it would prove fortuitous for Ian Hunter Patterson. Tippins was unable to sing at the session as he had recently tried to break up a fight in Hereford and was punched from behind; Watts stressed that nobody could punch Stan from the front. The next night at a Liverpool Cavern gig, Tippins struggled through the first set but could not appear for the second. At Spot Studios, sans vocalist, Watts recalled his audition for Free and their head-shaking and prompted Silence to do the same. The band agreed that they should just play full on in the tiny studio and hope for the best. They delivered the songs with madness but had decided to split if they failed the audition. Stevens was their last hope, but Guy loved them. Silence's songs included Watts' 'Mystic Balls' and Ralphs' 'Lena', 'Yellow Van' ("a Move rip-off"), 'Find Your Way', 'Wide Asleep' and 'The Silence' – Pete likening some of the numbers to early Yes.

"Most of my early efforts were pretty awful," says Ralphs. "But when you start to write songs that's what happens really. Songwriting, I've learned over the years, is a bit like building a bridge or knocking up a chair – you learn after a while there's a way of doing it that works. In the beginning, the construction of your songs is usually dreadful, but you've got to begin somewhere. It was a good start. They were early attempts at commercial songs, but with a wild side!"

Having heard Silence play, Stevens agreed to hold another audition at Regent Sound, but there were two conditions for their potential signing with Island Records: a change of name and a new lead vocalist. Ralphs recalled that Guy felt Stan didn't have the right look, so Tippins magnanimously agreed to leave, encouraging the band to find another singer.

"Stan didn't want to stand in anyone's way and said he'd leave the group," admitted Watts. "We didn't know what to say. We hadn't even asked him, and we hadn't even talked about it. He just sold his PA and gave up on the spot. Guy had got this thing in his mind about Dylan and the Stones and he didn't want the long drawn out progressive stuff like 'Mystic Balls' that I'd been writing. He wanted to go back to basic rock and a cross between *Blonde on Blonde* and 'Jumping Jack Flash'. Stan had a big powerful voice, but it wasn't what Guy had in mind. It left us in a horrible position, but Stan said, 'There's the chance of a deal. You can't turn it down' – and he left."

Tippins admits that he wasn't happy with the musical direction of the group by this juncture: he had "hated" 'The Rebel' and felt the band's songs weren't strong enough, so he played his final gig with Silence in Herefordshire. "I was very apprehensive about the Island audition in the first place," admitted Stan. "I wasn't enjoying the music and Guy Stevens didn't really like me and felt it was better to have someone who could play an instrument rather than a solo singer. At the end of the audition he said, 'Well, I can take the band, but I can't really take the singer. You need to find someone else or there will be no band.' It was a mixture of sadness but also relief when I finished."

"Tippins leaving Silence was sad because Stan had been with us for so long," says Ralphs. "He was an excellent singer with a really good voice, but he realised we had a real chance with Guy, so he graciously stepped aside. I said to him at the time, 'If and when we do have any success, we want you to come back with us in some capacity.' I'm glad he did too because, of course, he went on to become a very successful tour manager with Mott and several large name bands after that. In hindsight, Guy saw something in our band and felt that we were relatively accomplished, but he wanted to hone it."

Walking away with grace and good heart, 'The Sinatra of Beat' soon accepted offers for shows, television and film work in Italy but, after a year, the Italians had botched Tippins' career and he returned home becoming Mott's on-the-road manager, accountant and shepherd for life. Stanley was described through the years as psychotherapist, mother, father and fixer for Mott the Hoople. He would be widely regarded as a "diamond", devoted to his charges and heroic in the lengths that he would go to, just for them.

On 13th May 1969, Watts' birthday, Guy Stevens took Silence into London's Morgan Studios for a recording test, to *finally* decide whether he would sign the group or not. The band played 'The Rebel' with Mick on lead vocal and an instrumental version of 'Find Your Way'. Silence was enthusiastic at the end because Stevens appeared to want them: he liked their accents, provincial naivety and unusual clothes – but they still had no lead singer. Silence returned to Herefordshire and Ralphs decided that if no Island record deal was forthcoming by June, he would move on. He began casting around for other groups, amongst them Scottish band Cartoone, managed by Peter Grant.

"Mick was thinking of joining Cartoone," said Watts, "In fact he was thinking of joining everybody. They were usually putrid groups too, like Tony Rivers and the Castaways – a middle-of-the-road, polite, poor man's, British Beach Boys. Who would want to be in a group like that? It was funny because Ralphs always ended up back with us no matter who he tried to join. Cartoone were great blokes though – Scottish guys, who shared everything they'd got with us – and they'd got next to bugger all."

Whilst Mick Ralphs remained restless and impatient, Guy Stevens was pondering over the missing jigsaw piece for his charges and placed an advertisement in *Melody Maker*... with a clear picture of the central character that he needed.

CHAPTER FOUR

The Twilight of Pain Through Doubt

Guy liked me, so they took me on.

Guy Stevens had a vision: the ultimate band – a unit that would directly fuse the rock 'n' roll flair of Jerry Lee Lewis, the power of The Rolling Stones and the lyrical prowess of Bob Dylan – with a dash of Procol Harum keyboards thrown in for good measure.

Guy was central to Mott the Hoople's conception and development. Razor thin and driven by pure passion, he ran on high octane and, in a recording studio, was the sworn enemy of moveable furniture. Once described as, "A&R man, talent scout, art director, producer, image maker and provider of joints – an amalgamation of mushroom hair, sheepskin coat and rainbow scarf," Guy was a catalyst and instigator who became Mott's mentor.

Stevens' history is shrouded in some mystery. Mott the Hoople claimed Guy was always vague about the past and they never enquired about his background. Maverick, whirlwind and psychic puppeteer were all used to describe a creative and zany personality but, hidden from view was Guy the football fan and family man, playing with his young son or reading his daily newspaper over breakfast. He was a complex and dysfunctional character but his wife, Diane, always felt that the tales about Guy painted a crude, inaccurate picture. Whilst some described Stevens as "a maniac" and "a nutter", Ian Hunter would discover Guy was clever, not only in terms of creative contributions, but business too.

Guy Stevens was an emotional and colourful firecracker who appreciated music, movies and literature. He adored Jerry Lee Lewis, Bob Dylan and The Rolling Stones. He was drawn to the writing of Kerouac, Burroughs and Baudelaire. He loved records, language and word play. This inspired him to propose some bewildering band names – Procol Harum, The Heavy Metal Kids, Frosted Moses, Savage Rose and Fixable, Griff Fender, Brain Haulage, The The, Violent Luck and Mott the Hoople – as well as astonishing titles – *Tons of Sobs*, *Talkin' Bear Mountain Picnic Massacre Disaster Blues*, *Sticky Fingers*, *Mad Shadows*, 'Backsliding Fearlessly', 'Wrath and Wroll', 'Death May Be Your Santa Claus' and 'The Wheel of the Quivering Meat Conception'. As Ian Hunter once remarked, "Guy was full of it!"

Born on 13th April 1943 in East Dulwich, the Stevens family lived in Sydenham Hill, an affluent area of south-east London. Guy's father died when he was only six years old and the loss had a marked effect on his personality.

Guy attended Woolverstone Hall School near Ipswich, a London Education Authority experimental boarding school for disadvantaged, inner-city children. Referred to as the poor man's Eton and described by one former pupil as having "a left-wing Socialist bent", Woolverstone taught the sons of single-parent businessmen, diplomats and forces personnel. The school became well known for its sporting achievements and practised corporal punishment. Guy left at the end of his fourth year and it had been an unhappy time for him, not least because it was a rugby school and he was an avid soccer fan, later becoming a season-ticket holder at Arsenal Football Club.

Like Ian Hunter, in his teens Stevens heard Jerry Lee Lewis's 'Whole Lotta Shakin' and underwent an almost religious conversion to the cult of the American rock 'n' roller. He claimed he was never the same person again and became obsessed about music, running a record group at Woolverstone. Stevens eventually left 'Woolvo', "by mutual consent" and went to work for Lloyd's brokers in London. Alan Baguste was a schoolmate of Guy Stevens at Woolverstone.

"Guy was a bright kid who was always in the high stream," says Alan. "He was fine at school – a touch rebellious, but a clever boy who was always interesting and made his point very clear. Guy ran 'DJ sessions' at Woolverstone but was almost tone deaf in that his sense of pitch was not too clever. Although he played rugger pretty well in the first and second forms, he got into trouble by going out on the pitches to kick a soccer ball. Guy never spoke about his dad who was an industrialist. The Stevens family lived at Whitewalls, a sizeable pile on Sydenham Hill. In the summer I'd join Guy and he would monopolise the juke box in the local coffee shop constantly playing Jerry Lee Lewis, Chuck Berry and Platters records. Guy was not expelled from Woolverstone but, by 1958, a parting of the ways was inevitable. Money was left in a trust for Guy by his father and after he convinced the trustees to release funds when he was eighteen, rather than twenty-three, he went to the USA to buy mountains of records. He was harmless, extravagant and very funny, with extraordinary mannerisms but no maliciousness. I remember he returned to a Woolverstone Open Day once, appearing like a dandy in a heavy striped jacket. A few years later, there had been a dramatic change in his persona."

Stevens first saw Jerry Lee Lewis live in 1958 at the Gaumont State cinema in Kilburn. Two years later Guy was introduced to his future wife Diane Cox on London Bridge, through a mutual friend. Diane was the same age as Guy and he was impressed because she had seen a Buddy Holly show, so the couple dated and attended Jerry Lee concerts. Guy and Diane married and had a son James, and acquaintances described their partnership as an energetic, electric relationship. Diane recalled Guy's absolute mania for Jerry Lee Lewis and later Bob Dylan, and that he was obsessional over records, storing his collection in long boxes and then a purpose-built chest on legs. Stevens was enthusiastic about vinyl and label numbers, procuring singles by mail order from America. His other manias and discussion points included clothes and he recorded movie details in notebooks, his favourites including *On the Waterfront*, *Psycho* and actors Marlon Brando, Anthony Perkins and James Dean.

In 1963, Guy became a king-pin disc jockey at The Scene, a basement underground club in Soho. Located in a corner of Ham Yard, The Scene was small, seedy and doubly dark with matt black painted décor and here Guy DJ'd with two turntables and his boxes of treasured, hard-to-find 45s. The Scene's 'R&B Disc Nights with Guy Stevens', held on "dead-spot" Mondays, created great interest. Guy spun London's coolest mix of Soul and R&B for his drinamyl-driven audiences. He adored 'Let's Stick Together' by Wilbert Harrison and would play new Sue releases and sell vinyl. 'I Put a Spell on You' by Screamin' Jay Hawkins would blast from the club's massive speakers and the punters had never heard anything like it. Tony Brainsby, who became Mott the Hoople's publicist, recalled how Guy was one of the first "names" he ever met in the music industry. "I worked with Guy at The Scene," recalled Tony. "We used to give out cards at Piccadilly Circus with our initials on the back and anyone who turned up with an initialled card earned us two pence commission. Guy was always an instigator and he turned me on to Chuck Berry from the very early days."

Stevens became a stalwart of London's R&B world, even turning The Rolling Stones on to some of the music in their early repertoire. A fount of knowledge, Eric Clapton and Steve Marriott were visitors to Guy's flat to listen to his records and he became a rabid publicist for the music that he adored. Stevens eventually moved on from The Scene and embraced the Middle Earth club, but in 1964, he was invited by Chris Blackwell to run Sue Records.

Blackwell had witnessed Guy at The Scene and wanted to harness his energy to drive Sue's releases and fan the flames of the British rhythm and blues fire that he had helped to ignite. If Stevens liked a song and believed it carried musical relevance, it was issued – though it turned out his releases often only made money on every fifth single. Anthology albums were successful though, with Guy curating and conceiving sleeve notes and covers for *The Sue Story*, *50 Minutes 24 Seconds of Recorded Dynamite* and *Guy Stevens' Testament of Rock 'n' Roll*. He also became President of the British Chuck Berry Fan Club and succeeded in bringing Berry over from the US for his first British tour.

> **IH:** "Legend has it that Guy and promoter Don Arden met Chuck, and that Arden offered Berry £10,000 to tour Britain. Guy immediately offered 'twenty grand' – and an astonished Chris Blackwell was soon enquiring why Guy had not bid eleven!"

Diane Stevens often emphasised that Guy could be a measured and considered man; he wrote meticulous features for *New Musical Express*, *Record Mirror* and *Jazz Beat R&B Supplement* but eventually mogul-extraordinaire Guy tired of the clerical aspects of running a record label and the reins that were placed on his eclectic tastes – taste that he regarded as unquestionable. With the R&B cult fading in 1967, Sue Records UK was shelved but Muff Winwood recalls Guy's elation when he was offered an A&R role at Island's Oxford Street offices.

"I got a job with Island as an A&R man and booking agent," says Muff. "At the top of the Island building was a big office with a huge round table and Blackwell and the rest of us would all sit around this table and work. One day, Chris came in and said, 'Great news. Guy is joining us tomorrow.' And we're all going, 'Fucking hell' – and holding our heads in our hands. The next day, we're sitting there, and you can hear this kerfuffle getting nearer and nearer, and the door bursts open, and Guy leaps up on to the table, hair everywhere, dressed in these amazingly tight trousers and suede creepers and shouts, 'We're going to make this the best fuckin' record company in the world!' And he just continued to jump around from then on."

Skinny, gangly, larger than life and hyperactive with a large frizzy hair style, Stevens could combine the rolling, bulging eyes of a speed freak with the slur and lurch of an alcoholic. He could be charming and urbane but was also unpredictable and his enthusiasm, at times, could take him to extremes resulting in chaotic recording sessions. Becoming a house producer for Island, one of his first projects was an instrumental album by a young Billy Preston, titled *The Most Exciting Organ Ever*.

Guy signed Cumbrian band, The V.I.P.s saying that he liked them because they were incredibly heavy and took "500 blues a week". The V.I.P.s were re-named Art and Stevens produced their album *Supernatural Fairy Tales*, then used Art as backing musicians for a free-form improvisational LP, snappily titled *Hapshash and the Coloured Coat Featuring the Human Host and the Heavy Metal Kids*. Described as "an LSD opera", one of Guy's co-writes was a track called 'A Mind Blown is a Mind Shown'. Art included Luther Grosvenor, who would eventually appear on Mott's horizon, and the guitarist marvelled at Guy's behaviour.

"Apart from being a great bloke, Guy Stevens was a great motivator," says Luther. "If you had an eight-hour session, he was excited from the first minute to the last minute. He was very energetic, speedy, inspirational and extremely good at drawing you out of yourself. Unfortunately, with Guy, he did tend to be off his head more than he was sober and, sadly, drugs became a burden for him. The Sixties were amazing, and I didn't meet a lot of people that were totally straight – it was unheard of. Guy did a lot for Art, Spooky Tooth, Mott the Hoople and lots of other people, but he was strange and had a dark side as well. He was a genius – but geniuses are lunatics really."

As Art evolved into Spooky Tooth, Guy did not stay around to complete production of their debut album, but he did guide lyricist

103

Keith Reid to Gary Brooker of Procol Harum and proposed the band's name.

> **IH:** "Guy found and invented all sorts of names. Like Mott the Hoople, everyone thought that Procol Harum was odd and all the music papers were trying to figure out what it meant, including the Latin derivation. It turned out it was just a name on a cat's pedigree."

According to Diane, Keith Reid also picked up the title of Procol Harum's biggest hit at the couple's Gloucester Avenue flat when Guy turned to her during a boozy, pill-popping party and remarked, "My God, you've just turned a whiter shade of pale."

Chris Blackwell invited Guy to work on Traffic's first Island album, *Mr Fantasy* and Stevens joined the band at their country retreat on Sheepcott Farm near Aston Tirrold in Berkshire. When a neighbouring cottage was broken into and the police trapped the culprit, it was a Mr G. Stevens who had been entering, eating, drinking and lounging around; *Mr Fantasy* was produced by Jimmy Miller. Diane Stevens noted that Guy did not have any major involvement with drugs in the early Sixties, despite the mania of The Scene club, but when he discovered speed one weekend in 1967, his compulsive and addictive nature unlocked an uncontrollable side of his personality. In a short space of time, Guy started to ingest large quantities of drugs and drink, and his general behaviour became extreme. Island would continually lose him on binges but thanks to Blackwell, Stevens was not sacked. According to people like Tim Clark at Island, Guy was still considered a guardian of the label's musical taste.

"Guy was a one-man army – a whirlwind who was always eager to get things done," says Tim. "He was a dervish, full of gibberish, ideas and enthusiasm for music. His opinion was always sought on how the music and, increasingly, on how an artist should look. He used to keep a little black book with names that he'd thought of. If he stumbled across a band and thought they were great but didn't like their name, he'd consult his little list to come up with something better. My principal memory of Mott at Island was Guy's extraordinary enthusiasm for the band; he really did the best 'selling job' of any A&R person I ever met."

Steve Hyams, a close friend of Mott in their early days, experienced personal problems with drugs and remembered Stevens' involvement. "Guy was a kind of enigma, because musically he was cloth-eared," recalled Steve. "Personally, I thought he was pretty useless as a producer. Guy first got busted in 1967 – the Summer of Love – with Brian Jones, for having some cocaine – which was unheard of in those days and I think Guy took the rap for it. He was a speed freak and was always on uppers. You'd always get a messy sound with Guy and he'd switch moods depending on whether he'd had speed or coke or whatever. He'd generate this wildness and try to capture it on tape, but of course you can't really sustain that because drugs wear off and so does the enthusiasm. Blackwell really used to put good things his way like Spooky Tooth, Free and Traffic, then on things like Traffic's *John Barleycorn*, Chris eventually had to come in and take over. I'd often go around to Guy's flat with my girlfriend. People like Chris Wood would be with him and I remember Guy answered the door one day wearing nothing but a suspender belt and stockings. He had piles of bizarre magazines and he had cut out pages and stuck them on the wall with butter. The only furniture was an enormous television and there were masses of records everywhere. He could be sad and mad, but Guy had a humorous side too and was always fantastic with potential names for bands. I once asked him, 'Have you got a good name?' and he said, 'Two Grand!' – before he'd even tell me!"

Stevens extended his track record with a group that was to become one of the finest rock acts of the Seventies: Free. Guy immediately suggested a name-change to The Heavy Metal Kids, but fifteen-year-old bassist Andy Fraser refused to join Island unless they retained their identity. Free entered Morgan Studios to record their debut LP, *Tons of Sobs*, Stevens reputedly bringing the project in for a mere £800. Drummer Simon Kirke and bassist Andy Fraser acknowledged that Guy was instrumental in getting them off the ground. "Guy Stevens was a complete nutter," said Andy. "He functioned on 150 octane all the time, was probably on speed, which I hadn't given a thought to at the time but was a really nice guy and very supportive of the band."

"Guy wanted us to be called The Heavy Metal Kids, which was actually way before its time and *Tons of Sobs* was his album title," says Simon Kirke. "We were really nervous when we went in to record and didn't know what to do. They were partitioning us off and Guy came in and said, 'Get rid of these screens and just play your set.' Guy was careering around, and it was a fabulous vibe. He was very talented and was forever buzzing around the studio. *Tons of Sobs* was recorded in a week."

In the summer of 1968, Guy was arrested for possession of cannabis and given a twelve-month custodial sentence. He served eight months at Wormwood Scrubs Prison and found it horrifying, sharing a small cell with an Irish alcoholic and a life-term psychopath who kept pulling him off his bunk to fight. Guy tried to lay low by reading Jack Kerouac, Norman Mailer and Scott Fitzgerald books. Around this time his prized record collection was stolen from his home and he reputedly suffered a traumatic breakdown. He was subdued when he was released from prison one Friday, but he was instantly re-employed by Island Records, enthusiastically devising bands, naming them and inspiring them.

Not really a producer or manager and certainly not a musician, Stevens' contributions were ideas and motivation, drawing out and stimulating nascent talents to create something special. He could be an explosion of energy, enthusiasm, ideas and inspiration one minute, or a crumpled heap of despair the next. Tormented by his shortcomings, Guy could also destroy the things he loved and had nurtured, including himself and yet the members of Mott invariably recalled Stevens' positive aspects rather than any negative side. Guy later revealed that he was angry about the violence that society had perpetrated against him and explained that he used music to convey his fury, describing rock and roll as "the last place for madness to show its face". Verden Allen remembers Guy with affection but also the darker side of Stevens' personality.

"I respected Guy. I could never talk to him properly because I always thought he was superior in a funny sort of way. He was like a whizz-kid and something special, I thought. He pulled things out of people – not just us – because there were other great bands that he started off too. They just couldn't have happened without Guy. Guy had the power to sign anyone he wanted, and he liked our band. Guy was also destructive. He'd create then destroy. He would start something off and if it developed into something and slipped from his grasp, he'd demolish what he'd created before it had developed into anything."

"Guy was very, very strange to say the least," says Stan Tippins. "He had outlandish ways, but his main thing with Mott the Hoople was that he had this confidence in them, and, in football terms, he was a really good coach. On the other side of things like management, he wasn't good at all."

Alec Leslie, who booked gigs at Island Artists Agency acknowledged Stevens' importance through the early development of the company. "Guy would wander into the office with 'projects' then disappear," said Alec. "He convinced Chris Blackwell that he should produce Mott but when he started it wasn't a band – it was an idea. In spite of his 'genius', Guy was not really appreciated by the majority of the Island Records' people because of his unreliability and lunacy."

Muff Winwood, who became a senior figure at Island and later the producer of Sparks' *Kimono My House*, remembered Stevens as a fun-loving, mad figure and recalled the discovery of Mott, with Guy careering around the office, leaping on tables and chairs screaming, "Mott the Hoople – Mott the Hoople." Muff described the wild-card Stevens as a vibe for Mott – not a producer. "I loved Mott as a band, and they were lovely guys. Ian was older than the others and wasn't as daft. Guy was always way over the top, running around like a mad puppy dog. You couldn't settle down and discuss anything with him in a sensible way. He had outrageous ideas and was like a child with a new toy with them. Eventually, we would have to say, 'For fuck's sake Guy – we've had enough now – wonderful!'"

In addition to Spooky Tooth and Free, Guy worked with Mighty Baby and Heavy Jelly and claimed he auditioned over seventy bands in one year. His list of contenders included Newcastle outfit, Downtown Faction and drummer Ray Laidlaw described how Stevens gave them a recording test because he said they sounded like Credence Clearwater Revival, a group he had tried to lure to Island. Guy considered Downtown Faction had potential but were not ready to make records however, as they left, an engineer asked if the band would be interested in making an album elsewhere. They were interested – and Lindisfarne was born.

Ian Hunter was probably the first to spot that Guy lacked staying power in terms of seeing musical projects through to completion, but his passion and enthusiasm were contagious. Having agreed to sign Silence to Island Records and still aching from the loss of 'A Whiter Shade of Pale', Guy wanted to create a band that fused Procol Harum organ and piano, and a Rolling Stones rhythm section with a front man capable of delivering Jagger's vocals and Dylan's anti-establishment poetry. Stevens placed an advertisement in *Melody Maker*: "ISLAND RECORDS LTD. Need PIANIST/SINGER to join exciting hard rock band playing Bob Dylan influenced country rock music – Immediate album recording work – RING REGENT 6228."

Despite a limited response to the ad, on 5th June 1969 Guy and Silence held auditions for a vocalist at Regent Sound, where Ian Patterson had worked with Bill Farley. Dale Griffin recalled that only four people turned up: "An old rocker like Cliff Richard, an over-the-top gay guy called Max from One Stop Records, a total fool who whined about spending two shillings on a bus fare, and a non-descript bloke who was so shy that he took five minutes to tell us that he was there for the audition – he'd been hanging around, moving screens and cables – we thought he worked at the studio." Pete Watts described one candidate as "a piano player who looked like comedian Les Dawson with thick pebble glasses." The group was now regretting the departure of Stan Tippins but Verden Allen recalls Bill Farley saying he knew someone named "Ian" who might be interested and that he would phone him. Guy cheered up but had decided he would place another advertisement.

Enter thirty-year-old Ian Patterson who was now semi-veteran compared to the young lads from Herefordshire and a figure who had experienced frustration in his fight for musical acceptance. Bill telephoned Ian at his Archway flat and although Hunter hesitated, Farley persisted and called three times.

> **IH:** "Bill Farley was the only real music guy I knew in London and he rang me up and asked if I'd seen the ad in *Melody Maker* for a pianist-singer. Bill said, 'Ginge, there's a bunch of hairy geezers down here. I think they'll appeal to you. You've got to come down and see this band. They've been trying out people and don't like anyone, but they're weird so they might like you.' I'd seen the ad but hadn't bothered. Even though I was looking for a job, Bill had got me into auditions before and they'd never turned out to be any good."

Richie Anderson, who had met Ian a few months earlier, through Mick Strode of The New Yardbirds, remembered chatting with Hunter about the Island audition. "Ian had turned up at some pub for a bass player audition in The New Yardbirds, which didn't last very long and didn't do anything much, but Ian and I had got on really well and kept in touch," said Richie. "I think I called Ian to say 'hello' one day and he told me that someone at Island Records wanted a Bob Dylan-sounding singer that could play piano. I said it was worth him trying out for the band and that he might as well give it a go. I don't really think I was instrumental in Ian joining Mott – but I'm happy to take any claim to fame."

IH: "Bill Farley kept calling me and saying, 'It's Island Records. It won't hurt.' I'd never heard of Island, Traffic or Free at that time as I had no records. Somehow this band from Herefordshire called Silence had conned their way into an Island contract without a singer. When Bill rang me for a third time and said there was a retainer involved, I relented. I got two buses down to Denmark Street in record time and when I walked into Regent Sound there were these hairy people. I couldn't distinguish between them, but one person soon became apparent and that was Guy Stevens, who looked like a total madman, staring at me. He started off serious and there seemed to be some intensity between us straightaway. I had no confidence or ability on the piano, so it was a case of brazening it out. They asked what songs I knew, so we stumbled through Dylan's 'Like a Rolling Stone' and Sonny Bono's 'Laugh at Me'. I'd not really sung lead before and I hammered away at the piano, but it caught me at the right moment. I had nothing to lose. I didn't know that Guy was a Dylan freak as I was, and he was hopping about. The rest of them were saying nothing but Guy was cheering up. 'Laugh at Me' went down well with him so, emboldened, I played a solo bass opus I'd just invented which ruined the whole thing immediately."

"Ian looked horrific at his audition," said Pete Watts. "Guy explained, 'We're looking for someone like Dylan and the Stones – can you play anything?' Hunter could hardly speak and mumbled, 'Well, I can have a go at 'Like a Rolling Stone' I suppose.' He sat at the piano and started playing and singing. He wasn't a good piano player and he certainly wasn't a good singer, but there was something about him. The vocal meant something to him and he looked like he'd lived. Guy was standing behind Ian pulling horrific faces and giving the thumbs down, trying to get my reaction. I couldn't respond because Ian was looking at me as he was singing. After that we all got talking and Ian said he was a bass player and had an idea and could he borrow my guitar. I gave him the bass and he played this awful thing at the speed of sound, high on the neck. After Ian had gone, we said, 'Well he's better than everybody else, but he's not exactly what we had in mind is he?' Guy said, 'Let's just get him in so we can say to Island we've got a complete group.'"

Hunter had been nervous at his audition but reflected years later that he possessed a winning desperation on the day. The Silence band members thought that Ian didn't look the part with short curly hair and a corduroy fabric suit, but there was something about his voice. Guy didn't notice that Hunter only knew three or four simple chords, but the basic nature of his choppy piano playing threw small chunks of Jerry Lee Lewis and Little Richard into the musical mix, which Stevens liked. Watts and Griffin subsequently claimed that they were the most pro-Hunter and that Ralphs and Allen were wary. Mick recalls that Guy didn't really care what Ian played or sounded like – "he had the look" – so Stevens decided to weld Ian Patterson onto a rudderless band. Silence had found the dude they were looking for, although they didn't appreciate it at the time – or what Ian Patterson would bring.

IH: "The Regent Sound audition was a bit of a mess and my joining Mott was not as romantic as some of the band later claimed. I got the job because they'd auditioned good singers who couldn't really play piano, and good piano players who couldn't really sing. I was pretty crap at both, but I could function. Also, Guy was into Sonny Bono and Bob Dylan like me and we liked their kind of phrase singing, so I was 'in'. Well, I wasn't totally 'in' at first. I was a makeshift. The band's verdict was, 'Okay, he'll do for now, so let's try him for a few weeks until someone better comes along' – but Guy liked me.

"I was a bit overweight and I'd worn a brown corduroy suit and shades to the audition because I looked horrible. I had bought dark glasses because I'd discovered I had extremely weak eyes. I was driving in the sun once day, after I first got my driving licence and I started squinting badly, so I nipped off to Woolworths and bought my first-ever sunglasses – five shillings. My eyes are chronically weak, and I am almost albino, but when I wore shades, I didn't squint. Anyway, I was soon considered arrogant with shades – so that also encouraged me to wear them. The band wasn't impressed with me but Guy thought, 'We'll grow his hair, skin him down and get him a decent suit.' He rang me up a couple of days later and his first words were, 'You looked terrible.' I thought, 'Great! He's interested.' Guy said, 'We're worried about the way you look Ian.' So, I said, 'No problem. Whatever you want me to do, I'll do it.' Guy said, 'We'll take you.' I knew that this was my shot. It was them or the factory and working in the latter was like jail to me. I wanted music and I'd been waiting for Mott the Hoople, playing around in nothing bands for ten years. I guess I'm pretty optimistic by nature, but when you get 'the call', the desire is huge. Stan Tippins heard me talking about my view on the options a little later, so he would try and scare the life out of me in the early days of Mott. When Stan wanted something he'd say, 'Do it – or you'll be back in the factory.' It took years for the threat to be obliterated completely."

Ian joined Silence and, directed by Stevens, Hunter started to lose weight. Brown corduroy was *out*, Guy accompanying Ian to a Berwick Street shop to buy a black Dylan suit which was absolute affirmation that he really was *in*.

IH: "Guy took me to a West End tailor's and spent £100 on clothes, which was a lot of money then. As they were fitting me up, Van Morrison's *Astral Weeks* was playing in the shop, so it was a magic day. When I got home that night with my new suit, Miller Anderson came around to see me. He had *The Evening Standard* jobs pages and I said, 'We're not going to need that Miller. I think I've got a real gig.' I always thought he and I were going to do something together, but it never worked out. It was more timing than anything. I saw real commitment from Guy and just seized the opportunity. I told him I'd been earning £15 a week with Francis, Day & Hunter and he said he'd give me fifteen quid a week from Blue Mountain Music. So, I joined the band and started this strange relationship. I know Watts was worried because he didn't think I looked right, and the others said they liked me, but they were very shy. Guy told me they were living in Lower Sloane Street, so I went down there and saw the drummer, Buffin. He walked straight past me as I went downstairs and never even said hello. Nobody said a word to me for twenty minutes until this guy came over who happened to be Stan Tippins. I was worried, because I'd taken his job in Silence, but we got on great. Stan was an absolute gentleman about it, fortunately, as he had a wicked right-hook! He was the one who knocked all the barriers down. Tippins was an amazing guy who thinks differently so, as soon as Mott could afford it, we just had to get him back as tour manager."

"I do remember the band didn't talk to Ian much when he joined," says Stan. "I seemed to have more rapport with him than anybody else. I knew he was interested in football and I was, so we often talked football. He supported Shrewsbury Town and Northampton Town. I remember asking why he didn't come along with me and support Hereford United – a proper team. The others never said much to Ian, but when we started rehearsing, everything clicked."

Mott's basement accommodation at 20b Lower Sloane Street in SW1 would house the "Hereford ring" until they moved to 17 Stonor Road and later a flat on the North End Road, both in West Kensington, Hunter taking the smallest room in the latter at £4/10s, as he was paying maintenance to Diane.

Steve Hyams was a young lad who met Mott and later became a respected singer and songwriter, but would be best known in the music business, "frustratingly", for his association with Mott the Hoople. Steve exposed the band to great albums of the time through his job at the sleek Chelsea Drug Store, soon immortalised on celluloid in Stanley Kubrick's 1971 movie, *A Clockwork Orange*. Hyams admired the band's attitude and lived with them at one point. "I think Mott's rent was £18 a week but there were so many people living there," said Steve. "I took a basement bed above a structure that housed the heating boiler. There was a room out the back which had water sweating continuously out of the walls and everybody shared accommodation, except Pete who was always canny and made a 'den' in a tiny front room. They would all get up as late as possible and were naive in many ways. I smoked hash and occasionally took acid and they knew nothing about this. I put some hash on the flat table one day and they just looked at it. They even asked how to inject it! They were great guys."

IH: "Mott were the weirdest people and in the early days we didn't really become bosom friends. They were a very rural, insular mob who stuck to themselves. You couldn't keep them in London some of the time – they wanted to be back in Hereford – and when I said a few years later that we should go to the States – fuck – forget it! Watts spent most of his time 'raging' around the Kings Road, but they were a little band in the big city and seemed scared of everything and anybody. My first year with Mott was a real dodgy existence. Guy was always a Stones and Dylan fan, and wanted a group that was a cross between the two, so we tried our best to live up to it. When I started writing songs, they got really excited. I knew I was going to be the frontman in Mott but was still paranoid and wasn't singing very well so I kept wearing shades as a privacy and defence mechanism. If I took them off, the band would scream. I can remember Mick Ralphs howling at Stan, 'He's taken them off! He's taken them off! Get him to put them back on again!' Many years later, Ellie Greenwich who wrote for The Ronettes told me to put my shades back on one day because it wasn't me and she couldn't stand me without them."

The five members of Silence had to pen Island contracts, but it transpired that they signed with Guy Stevens, *not* the label. In the case of the youngest "Mott", Dale's father Fred Griffin signed the document. Guy was relieved that he had found his Jagger-Dylan figure. He had his perfect band and he would be their conductor. London rehearsals were booked swiftly at The Pied Bull at 100 Upper Street in Islington, commencing on 9th June 1969. The pub was used by other Island groups including Spooky Tooth and If, and was run by Mad Phil, a former ballroom dancer who still sported a 1930s hairstyle to prove it.

During early rehearsals, the group worked on a surprisingly large amount of material including 'The Rebel', 'Laugh at Me', 'At the Crossroads', 'Little Christine', 'Rabbit Foot and Toby Time', 'Half Moon Bay' and 'If the World Saluted You'. Other material which wasn't completed or didn't survive for their first recording sessions included Watts' 'The Wreck', Hunter-Ralphs' 'Back In The States Again' (a take on The Beatles' 'Back In The U.S.S.R.'), Ian's 'Lavender Days' (a song in waltz-time), Dylan's 'Desolation Row', Chuck Berry's 'Little Queenie', a bizarre reggae-flavoured piece called 'Yma Sumac', 'The Parrot and the Cat' (an ode to Freddie Lee's friendly club owner in Kiel), the "gothic and progressive" 'Jekyll and Hyde' and 'When My Mind's Gone'. 'Half Moon Bay' came out of their first rehearsal and Watts felt things didn't seem so bad after all.

"The Pied Bull was so boring," said Watts. "Ian would be there at ten in the morning, on-the-dot, writing stuff on the piano, all conscientious. The rest of us would arrive in the afternoon, with hangovers from the night before and couldn't give a shit about anything. Poor old Ian was really putting a lot into it and we didn't care. I felt sorry for him in the early stages because he was the only one trying. We didn't realise the significance of what was going on. Ian was writing stuff for Guy who was saying, 'We want Bob Dylan-type songs', so he'd come back to rehearsals with 'Backsliding Fearlessly' and 'Road to Birmingham' as he could write to order after Francis, Day & Hunter. Guy had his group all mapped out. The whole direction came from him, but he was lucky as Hunter could translate what he wanted into actual songs. Ian saw that the only way was to forge ahead on his own without listening too much to Guy."

Stevens developed the group's interest in American music, playing them the first Chicago Transit Authority album. He also loved the dramatically intense *Trilogy for the Masses*, by Ford Theatre, a band named after the Washington building where President Abraham Lincoln had been assassinated! Mott would listen to Delaney and Bonnie, Buffalo Springfield and The Beatles in the group flat, but Guy remained Dylan-crazy and at rehearsals made them play 'Highway 61 Revisited', 'Can You Please Crawl out Your Window?', 'Desolation Row' and 'Just Like Tom Thumb's Blues'. They also adopted 'Laugh at Me', because Ian adored Sonny Bono's song and Stevens suggested Doug Sahm's 'At the Crossroads'.

> **IH:** "Guy was just amazing. Musically, he couldn't do it, and we played and worked through him, but he had taste and played some classy records."

After eleven days of rehearsal, on 20th June 1969, Ian and the band entered Morgan Sound Studios on Willesden High Road in north-west London to cut their debut album with Guy as producer. Recording engineer Andy Johns, who had produced *Ahead Rings Out* by Island band Blodwyn Pig, described Mott as "so ready to go" and Johnny Glover of Island observed Guy's passionate vision for the band.

"Guy Stevens put the entire Mott album together, recorded them at Morgan Studios and went way over budget," said Glover.

116

"In those days Blackwell's budget for an album was about two thousand quid. Guy spent five, which was outrageous. It was all Guy's concept and Ian wasn't the dominating figure he later became. He was the new boy, didn't say too much and Guy's word was law."

Ian Patterson had joined Herefordshire four-piece Silence, but Stevens re-named the band Savage Rose and Fixable for their album sessions. The naming was further evidence of Guy's Dylan fixation as it was lifted from the sleeve notes of *Highway 61 Revisited*, but Stevens was soon forced to opt for another change of identity when a pre-existing Danish group, The Savage Rose, was revealed.

Guy had toyed with several identities for Silence including Blue Egg, Ball and Chain, Griff Fender and Brain Haulage. Another amazing name was Mott the Hoople – the title of a book that Guy had read during his first stretch in Wormwood Scrubs. The 1966 underground novel by New York author Willard Manus told the humorous tale of Norman Mott, a seventeen-stone, cigar-chomping, card-playing, wise-cracking scam artist who spent time in prison and later escaped attack in a hot air balloon, drifting off over Tulsa, Oklahoma. Definitions of the American term 'Hoople' include a misfit, a loser or an unsophisticated rural person. *Life* magazine considered *Mott the Hoople* to be one of the funniest novels ever written and it became Manus's best-known work. A Twenties US cartoon strip, *Our Boarding House*, featuring Major Amos B. Hoople and his wife Martha Hoople, had provided part of Willard's inspiration.

"The leading character in the strip was a large, overweight guy named Major Hoople," said Willard Manus. "He was forever hanging around the house, avoiding work and spouting a lot of nonsense interspersed with lots of 'ahems' and 'harhars'. I was fond of the strip for as long as it lasted. I worked on the Mott book on and off for seven years. The original version was much bigger and more ambitious. The book got rave reviews in England but got put down in a New York review and that killed it. Not long after that,

I heard that a rock group had named itself after the book. I was never asked for my permission, which I would have given, nor have I ever made a penny from any of the band's activities, which was not a problem. 'Hoople' is an old American slang word, meaning variously, fool, rogue, buffoon and even sucker. That's why my character, Norman Mott sometimes thinks of himself as a Hoople, because at different times in the book he is all of those things."

> **IH:** "The *Mott the Hoople* novel is a kind of cynical, very offbeat book but it's a good story about a hobo, or Hoople, who didn't fit in anywhere – and for two years at Island Records, neither did we! Norman Mott was an eccentric guy who ended up in a circus of freaks. Finally, he got in a hot air balloon at a fair and dumped the sandbags. He was last seen two miles from heaven. In retrospect, that seemed more-or-less right for us."

After reading the Manus novel in prison, Guy wrote to Diane asking her to keep the title secret. He thought Mott the Hoople would be a great band name and that it would look fantastic spelt out on a marquee – "with lots of Os and Ts." Stevens later learned that the young inmate who he'd lent the Manus book to had died, so suddenly the omens attached to Mott the Hoople were bad and Guy did not want the group to use the name.

> **IH:** "I remember Guy telling me that he had met this young guy in the prison library at Wormwood Scrubs. He was a good kid, but he was doing time as a heroin addict. Guy lent him the *Mott the Hoople* book and, apparently, gave him the name as he was going to be a solo act when he came out of jail. Then the youngster died, so Guy was backwards and forwards on the name when he met us. He felt that we were Mott the Hoople, but he thought the name might be cursed, because of what happened to the boy. He simply mentioned the title one day, off the cuff and the band went

118

ape. Mott the Hoople was odd and we thought it was an incredible name for a band. We liked the name Savage Rose and Fixable too, but we really wanted Mott the Hoople because it sounded so different. Anyway, we plagued and nagged Guy, and, in the end, he let us use it."

On 27th June 1969, seven days into the Morgan recording sessions, Guy relented and Mott the Hoople was adopted. However, it wasn't long before a Canadian group, Major Hoople's Boarding House, complained.

> **IH:** "Major Hoople's Boarding House were a band who sent us a note protesting about our name, so we had a spoof letter based on them placed as an advert in *Melody Maker*. One of them wrote to us and was disgusted about us using 'the Hoople', but in the last paragraph he said he'd written some really good songs lately and would we mind having a listen! I think Guy wanted to record us before Blackwell got involved or heard us because Chris's roster was full of talent and we were something else entirely. Suddenly, at Morgan Studios one day, we were Mott the Hoople and suddenly, I realised that I was with probably the best label in the country, so I got inspired. Pete and Mick wrote at that time, but when I started contributing, they encouraged me to do more. I'd been writing a song one day and it became 'Half Moon Bay'. The band was impressed and that's when they thought, 'Maybe he can write.' Pete said, 'You're a better writer than me, so I'll leave it to you.' Pete was good about it. It was very hard to imagine that in Watts, because Pete was a very selfish guy, but in other ways, not in musical ways."

When Mott completed their recording sessions in July, Guy enthused wildly about their forthcoming LP to *ZigZag* music magazine, explaining that the record was amazingly like Bob

Dylan. The album would be titled *Talking Bear Mountain Picnic Massacre Disaster Dylan Blues*, after an unrecorded Dylan song, and Stevens wanted a picture of Dylan inside the sleeve. Mott would soon have to resist several Dylan and *Blonde on Blonde* accusations, although musically, the album seemed more aligned to *Highway 61 Revisited*. Another potential title for Mott's LP was *The Twilight of Pain Through Doubt*, an "awful pseudo-rewrite" of 'A Whiter Shade of Pale' according to Dale and a literal translation of an Italian phrase lifted from a record that Mick Ralphs had found in 1968. Stevens loved this archetypal Hoopleism but, as he did not originate the title it was quietly discarded. In the end, the LP was released plainly and simply as *Mott the Hoople*, featuring eight tracks: 'You Really Got Me', 'At the Crossroads', 'Laugh at Me', 'Backsliding Fearlessly', 'Rock and Roll Queen,' 'Rabbit Foot and Toby Time', 'Half Moon Bay and 'Wrath and Wroll'.

'You Really Got Me' had been a crisp early-Sixties hit for The Kinks but, driven by Stevens, Mott's original recording was a highly repetitive eleven-minute bull-dozing take, with an increasingly frenzied ending and 'God Save the Queen' coda from Ralphs. Griffin termed Mott's version "very fast, very high-energy and very un-cool" and sensibly the monster take was confined to archive; sanity prevailed during the Morgan sessions when a shortened three-minute option was mixed with Ralphs adding a lead vocal, before an instrumental cut made the *Mott the Hoople* pressing. The band had struggled to write slow songs and 'You Really Got Me' was attempted by Mott after they saw The Kinks going into Pye Studios one day.

> **IH:** "Our version of 'You Really Got Me' on our album was a three-minute song like The Kinks, but a year later it lasted twenty minutes on stage. When we went to America supporting The Kinks, half our show was that song, so, we had to say to Ray Davies, 'If you don't let us play this, we can only do half an hour before you come on.' He let us do it but

at the end of their set Ray would say to audiences, 'We'll do a medley so Mott the Hoople can figure out which song to nick next time.'"

The remainder of *Mott the Hoople*, Side One, illustrated Guy's concept for the group so well – Doug Sahm's 'At the Crossroads', Sonny Bono's 'Laugh at Me', and Hunter's wonderful 'Backsliding Fearlessly'. 'At the Crossroads' had been recorded by Sahm's band Sir Douglas Quintet, to make the group "sound English", but Mott succeeded in taking the piece away from its American-centric roots, applying their own stamp and creating great intensity on the track's fade-out. Mott's 'At the Crossroads' cover was also included on an Island budget compilation LP, *Nice Enough to Eat*, which helped to widen the band's early exposure.

> **IH:** "The Doug Sahm cover was Guy Stevens' idea and something that he wanted us to do. I'd never heard of it, until he walked in with it. That was the first number we were ever known for because it was on Island's sampler; people started clapping before we did a song. I remember years later Mick Ronson and I went to a club in New York where Doug was playing. He invited us up to play – Ronno on guitar and me on piano. Doug sang and then said, 'Take it Mick' – but Mick had to put a melody in his head and form it – he couldn't jam. Several times Doug sang and said, 'Take it Mick' – nothing – and I was just holding the chords. We were probably half-cut at the time. Good fun."

Sahm may have been a Stevens selection, but the next two tracks were Hunter-driven. 'Laugh at Me', written by Sonny Bono and issued as a maudlin 1965 solo single, had been played by Ian at his Regent Sound try-out for Silence, and Sonny and Cher's 'I Got You Babe' remains one of Ian's all-time favourite tracks. Bono and Dylan possessed a similar vocal approach that had convinced Hunter he should sing, but Sonny's two-minute 'Laugh at Me' single was taken on a much longer trip by Mott the Hoople, clocking in at some seven minutes.

The Zimmerman influence on Ian was echoed and homaged on *Mott the Hoople*'s fourth cut, written by Hunter as 'If the World Saluted You', but re-titled 'Backsliding Fearlessly' by Stevens. Ian's composition comprised an appealing mesh of Sixties influences, some critics referencing The Kinks' 'I Am Free' intro riff, as well as Dylan's 'The Times They Are A-Changing' and 'One of Us Must Know' – but Hunter applied his own style with individualistic lyrical imagery that was a bright sign of a prolific writer.

> **IH:** "I thought when 'Laugh at Me' was released that it had a lot more to it than Sonny Bono put into it. All his songs were very strong and adapted well to changes of tempo, so we did 'Laugh at Me' much slower than the original. I just loved Sonny's great lyric and it applied to me at the time. It was a natural fit. I only ever went mad twice on image – one was Jimi Hendrix and the other was Sonny Bono. 'Laugh at Me' was a great song and people used to laugh at me because I wore shades when it wasn't fashionable. People used to think you had a big head if you wore shades and I did have a big head. I was extremely arrogant and I kind of liked it that way. A lot of people would laugh, so I guess it was appropriate. Sonny Bono and Bob Dylan couldn't sing that well, but I was lucky because Dylan had great delivery and they were both influential on my style. Bob had a personality way of singing, rather than the accepted sense of singing. He impacted on me because I could see it and I could sing like that, but I was only using my vocals to get the words across.
>
> "Whenever I think of 'Backsliding Fearlessly', Guy Stevens comes to mind immediately. It was originally called 'If the World Saluted You', but Guy gave us several amazing titles and had a big thing about names; he had all sorts of stuff and they weren't like anything else! I have always said if you

are going to be inspired, you might as well be inspired by the best and Bob Dylan was my favourite artist. A lot of people went into the influencing of how I act, and Dylan influenced my writing, as did The Rolling Stones. I started out with a very dull personality, so I filled it in with people I admired as I grew up. Once I got to where I thought I liked my personality, I stuck to it and that, apart from the genes, is where I am. Bob Dylan is a genius. He changed the world. He made music into a culture. He gave the whole rock 'n' roll syndrome validity. I should imagine he's an influence on nearly everybody. Anyone who says that they aren't influenced by someone else is a liar – and anyone who says they don't like Dylan doesn't understand rock 'n' roll."

Where Side One of *Mott the Hoople* comprised an index of influences and a colourful Hunter composition, Side Two contained original group songs. The opening track 'Rock and Roll Queen' was a golden moment but Mick Ralphs' song was an afterthought. Having completed the album sessions, Guy began to "panic", fretting that the record needed a "tough rock number" and so he instructed Ralphs and Hunter to "get something written QUICKLY!" To the band's amazement Mick composed 'Rock and Roll Queen' on demand and under the severest of pressure. "It was a fictitious story," says Ralphs, "written about being on the road in America using a load of clichés, but it was a good song – and the right song at the right time!"

Another of Ralphs' composition with lyrics, 'She's a Winner', was converted to an instrumental, re-titled 'Rabbit Foot and Toby Time' and placed before the stunning, pictorial 'Half Moon Bay'. Written by Ian and Mick and originally called 'Half Moon Bay, Part One', Mott's first *tour de force* had originated during rehearsals at The Pied Bull and showcased contrasting piano and organ from Hunter and Allen. The song was intended to be a crossbreed of 'Like a Rolling Stone' and 'At the Crossroads' but was reminiscent of Procol Harum. Verden's arresting sounds came courtesy of his cherished Hammond to provide a "swirling sea" effect while the fearsome "helicopter" chords in the central portion of 'Half Moon Bay' was reminiscent of *Trilogy for the Masses*, Ford Theatre's ominous album that was centred on multi-sectioned pieces of music. The dynamics, time changes and lyrics on 'Half Moon Bay' were astonishing from such a young band and, like 'Backsliding Fearlessly', the song was an early benchmark for Ian's developing songwriting talent.

> **IH:** "Guy got me writing by getting us to do strange things. I would play songs backwards and I just reversed the chords from another song. Guy was egging me on and Verden waded in – 'Moonlight Sonata' and all that – and before we knew where we were, we had our first ten-minute epic – it came out as 'Half Moon Bay'. I still believe it's one of the best things Mott the Hoople ever did. I always think of that as the essence of Mott because it had everything in it – all the jumbled ingredients of those early days, thrown together in one bizarre track. I remember Mick and I loved the riff. Many years later, we were going down that road between Los Angeles and San Francisco and there was 'Half Moon Bay' on a sign. At the time I'd just made it up. The whole song was simply visual words."

"'Half Moon Bay' was one of the most important tracks Mott did," opined Ralphs. "We didn't know about the Californian village at the time, nor did we know that a Hell's Angel Chapter lived there, which we found out later!" Says Allen: "I remember on that session, Chris Blackwell brought his new girlfriend along to the studio. When we did that grating organ bit, she said, 'What's that sound? I like that. Fantastic! What's it about?' I said, 'I haven't got a clue. I don't know.' She said, 'Well, it sounds nice anyhow.' So, Blackwell said, 'Carry on lads,' and walked out!"

Mott's debut ended with a frenzied fragment entitled 'Wrath and Wroll'. Credited to Stevens, Guy had simply swiped a section of tape from the chaotic climax of Mott's full 'You Really Got Me' take, to create an "instrumental track". In Guy's handbook, passion counted more than perfection and oddly, Ian said at the time of release that the lengthy "jam" was the best thing he'd ever played.

Mott the Hoople is fondly regarded by many longstanding Hunter fans but the band was largely filtering influences and following Stevens' direction, superimposing them on an infant style. The group did not really know where they were heading musically, so the album is as ironic as it is touching. Watts recalled that most of the tracks were recorded in one take and the sessions seemed so easy with Guy and Andy Johns, while Allen always retained fond memories of *Mott the Hoople*.

"That was the best Mott album for me really," says Verden. "It was recorded on eight-track and when we did it there was no messing about. We had one track each and that was it. We went in and laid it down and the feel was there and maybe something went on afterwards – like the vocal. It was all about the complete feel of the album. With Guy, the Dylan influence came in a little bit and there is something nice about that record."

Mott attempted other songs at Morgan Studios including Chuck Berry's 'Little Queenie', 'Find Your Way' and Ralphs' cowboy love-triangle tale, 'Little Christine'. Fragments of other tracks were shelved on Island tapes including Dylan's 'Like A Rolling Stone' but 'Desolation Row' was lost. 'The Rebel', Silence's audition number for Guy survives, with a Ralphs vocal, but Watts wished they'd cut the song "properly", with Hunter. Griffin recalled that Stevens' original plan was to collate a double album as Mott's debut release, containing the eleven-minute version of 'You Really Got Me', and that the band was "crestfallen" when Guy announced the idea had been shelved and a single LP emerged.

Mott the Hoople was promoted with an Island single – an edited cut of 'Rock and Roll Queen' backed with a non-LP track, 'Road to Birmingham' written by Ian and with Ralphs on bass. Alongside some earlier Hunter songs – including 'Don't

Make Any Promises' and 'Suddenly I'm Alone' – Ian had started composing 'Road to Birmingham' before he joined Mott the Hoople. Adjusted lyrically for the band, the song addressed the controversial topic of racial prejudice and related to Birmingham, USA, as well as Birmingham, England. The exclusion of 'Road to Birmingham' from *Mott the Hoople* has always seemed inexplicable given the strength of Ian's writing, though some initial mis-pressed copies of the LP contained Hunter's composition instead of 'Backsliding Fearlessly' and 'Rock and Roll Queen' with alternate running orders denied by pink Island labels and sleeves throughout. White label promos, with hand-written notation were also different and some tracks on early discs contained alternate mixes of several songs. The pressings puzzle had Guy's fingerprints all over it and arose because of the late capture of 'Rock and Roll Queen' although Stevens' "chemical assistance" was also cited as a reason by one band member.

Island promoted the group's arrival on the British music scene with a full-page press advertisement headed "Mott the Hoople Is Two Miles from Heaven" – a reference to the opening line of Willard Manus's novel. The band's first Island photo session took place at a rainy and windswept Kensington Gardens featuring Ralphs, Watts, Allen and Buffin, but with Guy Stevens as "stand-in" for Ian, who had missed his bus and couldn't afford to take a taxi.

Mott also captured some early publicity photographs on a gritty, soon-to-be-demolished site found by Guy. Located in West London, the derelict buildings in and around Testerton Street and Barandon Street had recently been employed as a gloomy slum set for John Boorman's powerful 1970 film release, *Leo the Last*. Peter Sanders, who had worked with Bob Dylan, photographed Mott the Hoople in front of a residential terrace where the brick façades had been painted black to make them look sinister for the movie. One of Sanders' frames from the shoot, was later employed as the cover for a Mott BBC Sessions CD.

Mott the Hoople was released by Island Records on 22nd November 1969 when The Beatles rode high with *Abbey Road*;

when Mott's debut LP finally entered the charts at No.66 on 2nd May 1970, The Beatles were at No.1 again with their swansong, *Let It Be*. *Mott the Hoople* only stayed on the chart for one week but the album received several excellent reviews. One journalist drew comparisons with Bob Dylan saying, "This is a collection of good sounds. I always wanted more of the *Highway 61* stuff anyway,"... while another writer noted, "Mott the Hoople play the type of heavy music that I was disturbed not to find on *Led Zeppelin II*. Mott the Hoople – too good to be believed – much too good to be missed." *International Times* considered Mott brought a sophistication to rock 'n' roll and that the band might be the threshold of a new musical era, their enthusiastic reviewer proclaiming, "It's like my favourite bits of Dylan have been cut out and preserved in a thick, spicy sauce."

For American distribution of their recordings, Mott the Hoople signed a three-year contract with Atlantic Records, a label that had also diversified into rock and was considered cachet by British bands. The Atlantic signing was reported in the press as a $125,000 deal but Hunter reflects: "I never heard of that sum... and I never saw a penny of it!"

In America, 'Rock and Roll Queen' was issued as a single coupled with 'Backsliding Fearlessly', but the release of Mott's debut LP was delayed until spring 1970. *Mott the Hoople* would be the group's only Atlantic album to chart in the US Top 200 but it attracted American attention for Hunter's "Zimmerman-like" vocals and the eclectic choice of songs. Like the Donovan-Dylan comparisons of the Sixties, it was an easy journalistic link, but one writer opined that Mott's album illustrated what Bob Dylan might have sounded like if he had travelled further down Highway 61, and most observers felt that the adoption of any influential insignia and the rough, rambling style of Mott's music was a happy discovery. Drawing references to 'Desolation Row' and 'From a Buick Six', *Mott the Hoople* was still seen as new music in a different form, with lead vocals from Ian Hunter that equalled the spirit of Dylan and the emotion of Sonny Bono.

IH: "We didn't get any action off the album at all. In England it sold about 8,000 copies and everybody hated it; no one seems to like what you're doing at the time – they always like it afterwards. I think it only got to about 185 in *Billboard* in America, but Lester Bangs wrote the most amazing thing about the record saying he ran around the block three times thinking Dylan had put an album out under somebody else's name. My career was really shaped by Dylan and the Stones and I was shameless on the first album. I couldn't sing, and it seemed to me Dylan couldn't sing, but there was something magical about the way he put words together so that's why I homed in. I still think 'Like a Rolling Stone' is probably the greatest rock song ever written. The lyrics are amazing. If you look at a book of Dylan lyrics, it scares you. I still love his music and listening to it is an intimate experience."

Mott the Hoople was presented in a gatefold sleeve featuring a coloured reproduction of 'Reptiles', a 1943 monochrome lithograph by M.C. Escher, the sensational Dutch graphic artist, renowned for inspired artwork of impossibly constructed geometrical repetitions and shapes. Using his imagination and choosing lizards, insects and birds, Escher created mind-bending illustrations that were fun. He termed some of his more complex work "brain gymnastics" and 'Reptiles' combined images illustrating structure and Escher's fascination for visual riddles and explorations of infinity. The pattern of eight small two-dimensional lizards with tusks, coming to life from the page of a sketch book and wriggling out in three dimensions, passing in a circle over a set square and dodecahedron, snorting and then heading downhill to re-enter a tessellated drawing, depicted a wonderous paradoxical effect. A tiny book labelled JOB in the artwork was not a reference to the Bible or Job's trials at the hands of Satan, but a book of JOB 'French White' – a popular brand of cigarette rolling papers.

Ian's mum and dad, Walter and Freda Patterson.

courtesy of Freda Patterson and Trudi Hunter

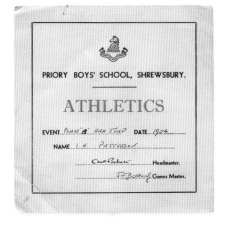

**Ian's Priory Boys School
Cadet and Athletics cards.**

courtesy of Freda Patterson and Trudi Hunter

**Ian Hunter Patterson,
apprentice engineer.**

courtesy of Freda Patterson and Trudi Hunter

The Apex Skiffle Group with Joe Loss, 1958.
Ian Patterson far left
courtesy of Freda Patterson and Trudi Hunter

The Apex, 1961.
Ian Patterson second from left
courtesy of Freda Patterson and Trudi Hunter

HAVE A CRAZY NIGHT

with

**Hurricane Henry
and the Shriekers**

Sole Agency   Mike Hill, 15 Alcombe Road, Northampton

**Hurricane Henry and the Shriekers
mid-sixties promo card...**
courtesy of Freda Patterson and Trudi Hunter

Mum, Lets hope this crew go down very well as your eldest is getting on a bit and its probably his last bloody chance! see you . xxxxx

...with message from Ian to Mum.

ACCEPTED & AGREED TO:

Ian Patterson

**Ian Patterson's songwriting
contract signature, 1968.**
courtesy of Freda Patterson and Trudi Hunter

AT LAST
The Nineteen Fifty Eight Show
With Freddy Fingerslee

At last it's the 1958 rock show
with At last it's the 1958 rock show

**Promo ads for At Last the 1958 Rock and Roll Show featuring Freddie 'Fingers' Lee,
with Ian Patterson and Miller Anderson.**
courtesy of Freda Patterson and Trudi Hunter

"Don't worry 'bout the shirt shine", Ian Patterson, 1968.
courtesy of Freda Patterson and Trudi Hunter

"Staff songwriter"
Ian Patterson with 'Gilbert the Ghost', 1968
courtesy of Freda Patterson and Trudi Hunter

**At Last the 1958
Rock and Roll Show,
1968.**

Pete Phillips (top),
Freddie 'Fingers' Lee (seated),
Ian Patterson (standing) and
Miller Anderson (crouching)

courtesy of Freda Patterson
and Trudi Hunter

Ian Patterson, Pete Phillips, Freddie 'Fingers' Lee and Chris Mayfield

Ian Tyas/Keystone Features/Getty Images

"Part of The Scenery"
Ian Patterson and Miller Anderson, 1968
courtesy of Freda Patterson and Trudi Hunter

overleaf
"The Twilight of Pain Through Doubt"
An early Mott the Hoople promo shot, taken on the *Leo the Last* film set, London, 1969:
Peter Overend Watts (in doorway), Ian Hunter (sitting on steps), Mick Ralphs (standing on steps),
Verden Allen and Dale 'Buffin' Griffin (in armchair)
Pete Sanders

Guy Stevens selected Escher's work but did not seek permission to use it, presumably as The Rolling Stones had tried – and failed! In January 1969, Mick Jagger wrote to the artist requesting an image for their album, *Through the Past, Darkly*. Jagger addressed the letter "Dear Maurits" and asked Escher to respond to two of his aides – but 'Maurits' said "No" as he had many commitments and could not spend any time on publicity. He also added, in his reply to Peter Swales, Mick's assistant: "By the way, please tell Mr. Jagger I am not Maurits to him, but Very sincerely, M.C. Escher."

> **IH:** "Mick Jagger wanted our album cover image, but he called M.C. Escher by his first name apparently and Escher got offended and wouldn't give it to him. It was strange because Jagger is one of the nicest people around and I'm sure he would have gone out of his way to be polite. Guy had picked the name Mott the Hoople for the band, and he selected 'Reptiles' for our album cover. I thought both choices immaculate. I had never heard of Escher before, but I soon had a few prints on my wall and wanted to know more about this man who was as unique as he was hip. Escher was extraordinary – hovering between analytic and creative."

For Mott's "Escher sleeve", Dale claimed that Guy blazed ahead, with no consent and arranged for a copy of the brain-twisting 'Reptiles' lithograph to be "coloured-in" for *Mott the Hoople*. The rear of Mott's cover exhibited a specially drawn green reptile, the lone lizard endeavouring to devour its own tail. The inner gatefold of *Mott the Hoople* featured black-and-white photographs of the five Mott members, in line, with each face superimposed on the same torso – Mick Ralphs – the five heads incorporating halo effects, facing in different directions against the backdrop of a London Transport bus. Verden recalled the day that Guy arrived with an enlarged 'Reptiles' print.

"We were in Morgan Studios when, suddenly, the door opened, and Guy was struggling to get this bloody great cardboard sheet through, and it wouldn't come in. So, we gave him a hand and had to bend it round the door, but he got it in and put it up against the wall. We said, 'What's this Guy?' It was huge. He said, 'Oh this is your album cover' – and somebody quipped – 'Not that size is it, Guy?' The inside photo was taken outside Island's studio. I remember Guy bringing in the sleeve mock-up later on and he said, 'Right, we're doing the sleeve now. Your name – Terence Allen – your name – we can't use that. You've got five minutes to think of one.' So, I said, 'Well, I can always use my father's name – Verdun with a "u" – put an "e" in instead – Verden Allen.' Guy said, 'Oh yeah, Verden. That's not bad.' He just walked off and the next thing I know, it's on the album sleeve. My mother went ballistic when she saw it saying nobody would know it was me."

"Buffin was Dale's nickname at school and Guy liked that," said Watts, "Then he got Verden to use his father's name. Hunter was Ian's middle name, but he didn't like Pete Watts at all. 'It doesn't sound big enough,' he said. So, I told him that my middle name was Overend and he started leaping about and shouting. 'That's wonderful! Overend Watts! Not for him the turgid bass riff!' And he began a long Shakespearean-style monologue. He was so excited, you couldn't help getting caught up in it."

> **IH:** "I wasn't having much luck with Ian Patterson, so I adapted my name in Mott to Ian Hunter. I thought it sounded better. I don't think my parents were disappointed when I dropped the Patterson name. My daughter Tracie has always used Hunter, but my second son Jesse has stuck with Patterson although I wanted him to change as well. It just sounds better to me."

John Glover at Island Records remembers Stevens and the band completing Mott's debut LP: "Once Guy brought the album in, he went missing on a drugs spree and we never saw him again for ages. He always went off on these benders, but Blackwell had put a deal together where Guy would manage the band. I don't think the management lasted long enough for the record to come out. He was off, so the agency took over. We all looked after Mott as agents, so the album did okay, and Ian began to get stronger within the band."

Mott the Hoople had joined Britain's most exciting record label, although Hunter would later express the view that the group stuck out like a sore thumb at Blackwell's organisation. Mott sat amongst "feel band" Traffic, "teen blues" group Free and "prog-rockers" King Crimson, but Island had been Mott's first and only signing offer and they gave no consideration to any other record labels.

The band was satisfied with their eponymous album and Mick Ralphs was soon telling the press that the follow-up would be recorded at Olympic Studios. "After you make a record, you always feel that it could have been improved on somewhere, that certain passages should have been re-arranged," said Ralphs. "But we're much wiser now, having done this first one. The next will be so much better." Mick was appearing in press quotes as much as Ian at this point, Hunter being conscious that Ralphs was the group's original captain.

> **IH: "I wasn't brought into Mott the Hoople as songwriter or leader. It was Ralphs' band, I guess. If we were all walking down a street in the early days and Mick turned left, we'd all follow!"**

The group had recorded their debut album, but they had not played live so, to kick-start their career, "away from the British press," they booked a get-it-together residency at The Bat Caverna in Italy. Inspired by *Batman* comics, 'The Bat Cave' was sited in the basement of Riccione's Hotel Nautico and had been the scene of some earlier Doc Thomas Group gigs with singer Stan Tippins. Mott the Hoople made their first-ever public appearance in The Bat Caverna on 6th August 1969 alongside two acts: experimental

Italian band I Nomadi, and British-based balladeer turned soul singer, Thane Russal. Dale recalled that Mott the Hoople's Italian debut was warmly welcomed, but subsequent performances were poorly received. In hindsight, Ian considered that the out-of-the-way location was fortunate.

"The opening night was remarkable," said Dale Griffin. "They loved us far more than we could justify. The next night nothing – why? The first night audience believed Ian to be blind and with all the stumbling, fumbling and bad chords who could blame them? When they realised that our boy was sighted they lost all interest and the Bat management was howling for the return of Stan – the Paul Newman of Pop."

> **IH:** "We went out to Italy and it was certainly an inauspicious start. The Bat Caverna Club was run by a bloke who drove a Batmobile and wore a Batman suit – ridiculous and daft! He hated us, and we only managed to continue playing there because he offered us either 'half-pay' or 'get out' – after only four days! Things were bad at the time, so we took the cut and treated it like a rehearsal. The Italians liked everything at break-neck speed in those days and we were a bit on the slow side. We died a death there – me, in particular – and all they wanted was Stan back. I think they liked the band, but they hated me because I was doing slow songs. I also had an electric piano which made more noise than it had notes, and I couldn't play it very well anyway. I remember sitting on the toilet there one night, thinking, 'You've got to do it – you've got to get through it.' I mean the gig really was hard and was certainly not our finest hour... or fortnight!"

Guy Stevens accompanied Mott to Riccione to "help" but felt absolutely alien and trapped in Italy according to Watts: "Guy was like a fish out of water over there, because he meant nothing to anybody. They just thought he was a nutter. Nobody could understand him, and I can remember him on the beach –

he weighed about six stone and was almost translucent with whiteness. He had this big ball of black hair and was as thin as a rake. He looked ridiculous. The club owner threw him out and they wouldn't have him back in The Bat Cavern because they thought he was disruptive. It was frightening, and we had no coherence as a band on stage – it just wasn't happening. We lasted about ten days and then they threw us out. I think all the rest of the groups thought, 'My God, how did a pile of shit like that get signed up to Island Records?'"

Mott's early live repertoire contained several un-recorded songs including Hunter's 'The Hunchback Fish', 'Rung from Your Ladder', 'Brand New Cadillac', 'Opus in Dm', 'Jekyll and Hyde' (an "epic" in 5/4 time) and a cover of The Youngbloods' 'Darkness, Darkness'. They also performed 'Half Moon Bay' with "a special introduction of drums and percussion". By the end of their trip the feeling was not good. Guy Stevens was depressed again, and Dale subsequently claimed that Ian wanted him replaced with drummer Terry Slade, who would soon join Island group, Renaissance.

Mott the Hoople made their first British live appearance at Romford Market Hall on 5th September 1969, supporting the new heralds of progressive rock and fellow Island act, King Crimson. Described by Jimi Hendrix as the best band in the world, the stunning "Crimson" had arrived on the music scene fully formed, playing inventive, dynamic and contrasting pieces that were fast and syncopated, or beautiful and symphonic. The group's unique debut LP, *In the Court of the Crimson King: An Observation by King Crimson* was universally praised upon release, not least by The Who's Pete Townshend who proclaimed it an uncanny masterpiece. The frantic and angular '21st Century Schizoid Man' was monstrous and King Crimson also possessed a light-show to die for, that was wonderfully in-sync with their stage performance.

Guy had switched on music business luminaries, "cornering" them with copies of *Mott the Hoople*. Recipients included *ZigZag*'s Pete Frame and disc jockeys John Peel, Andy Dunkley and Jeff

Dexter. Jeff described Stevens as obsessive with records, clothes and rock 'n' roll – an enthusiastic figure with an artistic, flamboyant air – and he termed the merging and gelling of Guy and Mott as "magic".

"Guy had got White Label copies of the album done and sent them exclusively to all the 'hip' DJs, who hung on to everything that he did," said Watts. "Because it was a Guy Stevens project, the name was weird, and nobody knew anything about the band, they all took to it. Guy already had it worked out that Mick and I would do the talking, and Ian would sit as a mysterious character in shades, not saying a word, playing the piano, in a black suit, like Dylan. And that's how we were on the first gigs – Mick and me all cheerful introducing numbers, and Ian sitting like an albino Ray Charles! We did this set at Romford and it was fucking diabolical. After every number, the audience looked at us in disbelief, while tables of DJs, invited by Guy, all gave reverent applause. Guy had told them that Mott was hot, so therefore they were going to clap.

"King Crimson was so great and halfway through watching their set I had to go glumly to the toilet. When I was standing, contemplating packing it all in, a guy four stalls along spoke to me and enquired, 'Hey mate, were you in that first group?' So, I said 'Yeah', dejectedly, to which he replied, 'You were better than this bloody lot!' I thought he was totally mental because Crimson's lights were spot on with the sound during all these complex numbers like '21st Century Schizoid Man'. I thought maybe there was some sort of hope for us, if he thought we were better than them. In fact, after this, Robert Fripp used to come and see us quite a bit in the early days of Mott. I was always quite surprised to see him there because I couldn't quite figure out what we had in common with King Crimson. They were such perfectionists and one of the most incredible live bands at that time. I got talking to Robert one night and asked him why he kept coming to see us. I said, 'We're kind of not your cup of tea really, are we, because we speed up and slow down all the time' – and

Fripp's reply to that was, 'Yes, but you all do it at exactly the same time. It's fantastic!'"

> **IH:** "Mott the Hoople's first British gigs were opening for King Crimson, who were monsters – and Free, who were gods! I wasn't too fond of progressive rock. I always thought Yes had songs that were intros and endings, with nothing in the middle. I didn't get 'prog' at all. King Crimson, who were scarily good, was an exception. We would pale beside these great bands and wanted to jack it in more than once, but strange things would happen. Rival roadies would come up and tell us we had something. Somehow, we stuck it out and began to learn to understand audiences. Music crowds like to be led. They don't like scared bands. We adjusted."

Mott were awkward and self-conscious at their initial gigs and Ian was "down" especially after supporting Free, when the crowds went wild for their Island label-mates. But, slowly, Mott developed, and Hunter found a confidence and stage presence. Ian started talking openly to audiences, drawing them in as if they were part of the band. Watts felt Mott the Hoople hadn't "clicked as a unit" yet and he knew they had a long way to go.

> **IH:** "I couldn't really see Mott happening at the time because I didn't think the band was very good and I was aware of my own inadequacies. It was ironic because I had worked hard at being a bass player and after five years of that I got offered singing and piano playing. In Mott's early days, they kept the PA and piano well down in the mix and some people used to come up after a set and say, 'The band's great but I can't quite hear you' – and that was fine, because it was exactly what we wanted. I'd not been playing piano very long, and I'd never sung before, so it scared me to death. I'm sure everybody wanted to get rid of us. Guy held the whole thing together quite honestly. I never saw any

hope for us. But Guy saw something hidden in me from the start really. He'd be in my face going, 'You are fuckin' great!' That made up for all the times other people had said, 'Don't sing, Ian!'"

Magically, in October 1969, Mott generated their first animated audience reactions in Oxfordshire and Hertfordshire. For a show at a small social club in Harwell, the band halved their guitar amplification for the first time and suddenly, they snapped into gear, Dale describing that gig as the first typical Mott the Hoople night. Short of material at the outset, the band played some songs twice and included their grossly elongated 'You Really Got Me'. Hunter wanted to make an impact and whilst he was restricted to his keyboard towards the side of the stage at first, as Mott's "five-man midfield" set up in line, suddenly, Ian adopted the persona of his Fifties rock 'n' roll heroes. As Mott became more powerful and ferocious on stage, Hunter climbed on to the electric piano like Little Richard or played the keyboard with his boot heel, Jerry Lee Lewis-style. At some gigs Ian would edge and tilt his keyboard towards the edge of the stage as Mott's sets reached a chaotic climax. Singular, wild and sporting the longest hair feasible, Mott the Hoople became a rabid concert experience, the band exhibiting a raw energy that later drew justified comparison with the punk rock experience.

IH: "They went spare at that Harwell gig and we couldn't believe it. Then the following night at Letchworth we did the same again. It was all over one weekend; it just suddenly happened. We started to develop 'You Really Got Me' and it went on for twenty minutes and got a bit crazy. I started moving around, kicking the piano over, stuff like that. Maybe it was in desperation to try and get a reaction. At Letchworth the lights were fixed in the middle of the stage and there was nothing on me. So, I stopped the show and shouted for lights – it was big-headed, but the place erupted and I realised, for the first time, that they liked the arrogance. I'd learned a lot off Jerry Lee Lewis. I started becoming a front-man, learning how to control an audience. I'd realised that the crowd is the masochist and you're the guy in charge."

Chris Blackwell witnessed Mott's intensity when he turned up one evening to watch the band live for the first time. Angry at the roadies over his faltering RMI electric piano, Ian hurled the keyboard towards the wings.

IH: "I broke toes with that fucking RMI. Up in the air it would fly – and I'd forget to take my feet away. I remember limping through airports miles behind the others. Chris came to see us and the flying RMI missed him by inches. Blackwell said, 'If they care that much, there must be something there. I'm glad we signed them up.' He didn't quite understand us – but he did understand our desire – and our desperation!"

Ralphs admitted that Guy instilled a commitment to cause uproar in Mott. "The point was to have style and image – to be an event," says Mick. "So, here was a polite little band from Herefordshire, going nuts, dressing up and overdoing everything. Everybody else was trying to be cool – not Mott."

Mott the Hoople was re-booked at Letchworth Youth Club and started to become an attraction at The Friars Club in Aylesbury. An alternative hippy venue outside the pop music domain, Friars was held on Monday nights in a 200-capacity, shoe-box-sized ex-servicemen's club. Mott the Hoople made their debut there in December 1969, on the New Friarage Hall's low, foot-high stage and the mammoth 'You Really Got Me' made Friars' "Leapers Corner" go mad. *ZigZag*'s Pete Frame, who had established his magazine in Aylesbury, championed Mott from the outset, describing them as "the greatest rock and roll band in the world, bar none." Pete looked up to the mad-ass maniac Guy Stevens and admired Ian as a Byron-Coleridge figure and a writer based in reality who wanted to be a serious rock poet. Frame said he used to watch Hunter singing, *"I'm just a rock 'n' roll star,"* during 'Rock and Roll Queen', and ponder to himself – "Not yet you ain't mate, but it's just a matter of time."

> **IH:** "Friars was ahead of its time and a great place to play. I think what was so special about Aylesbury was that you didn't expect so much enthusiasm and musical knowledge, in that area. Possibly because of *ZigZag*, Aylesbury was totally on it. The place was mobbed – and a good time was had by all."

In 1975, Hunter would say that he often thought about living in Aylesbury because it was like Toronto or Cleveland – a "weird one-off place, where everything seems to start." Mott "happened" in Aylesbury first and Hunter felt the people seemed to sense what was going to happen. Watts described Newcastle and Glasgow as fantastic crowds, and Mott felt the further north they went, the wilder they got. "You get off on them," said Ian, "and you always seem to deliver more. You get up and you think, 'Good God, look at them' – and then you've got to deliver." This enthusiasm contrasted with some of Mott's experiences in London.

> **IH:** "I never liked The Roundhouse. It was too hippy-ish – like Kensington Market – full of patchouli oil, joss sticks and filth. It was pretty disgusting really. I remember doing The Speakeasy early on and the whole Island record company was there. The power blew that night and we died the most abysmal death."

By the end of 1969, Mott the Hoople had the wildest of shows but they became concerned with Alec Leslie and Johnny Glover, Island's booking agents. The agency kept saying said they could get Mott the odd gig, but with no record deal Silence had played at least three gigs a week. "Island said, 'Well, you'll have to play

The Speakeasy for nothing, and we can get £10 for doing a club in Tooting'", recalled Watts. "And we said, 'But we got gigs for a £100 down in Wales' – and Alec Leslie would reply, 'But yeah, it's the law of nature isn't it – you've got to start at the bottom – it's the law of nature.' I wanted to stuff the law of nature up his arse!"

Diane Stevens recalled that her husband was infatuated with Mott the Hoople. She felt that the band gave Guy his first opportunity to create real rock 'n' roll and that Ian soon tapped into that as he had a similar psyche, albeit without Guy's problems. Hunter became aware of Stevens' vision for him within Mott, but also that he nearly fired him during the band's early days.

> IH: "Guy didn't see me as a frontman – he saw me as a keyboard player at first – sitting on the side playing piano. Then, after two or three months, nothing much was happening so the band wanted me out and Guy wouldn't have it – then Guy wanted me out and the band wouldn't have it – so I was living a very dodgy existence. At one point, Guy freaked saying, 'He sits on the left-hand side of the stage. I want a frontman!' But Mick and Pete turned around and said, 'No he's fine – we're right – in some strange way we're right.' So, we went through this thing that they didn't want me in the band – and I didn't want to be in the band – and it went on for about a year. When I started playing guitar in the middle, Guy loved that because Mott was really a faceless thing initially. I'd been out on a limb at the start, but things changed, and Guy got his frontman."

Without Guy Stevens there would have been no Mott the Hoople. He was their guiding light and svengali, but the band had little knowledge of their financial situation and royalty entitlement from Island Records. "Guy negotiated it for us," said Ralphs at the time. "We trust him and Island. The gig money goes straight into the office and they pay us £15 a week each." Ian subsequently clarified

Mott's arrangement with their label and learned that the band was originally signed to Stevens.

> **IH:** "It turned out that Guy was very big on ideas and good at beginnings, but not so good at carrying on or even ends. He was shrewd on the money side however and sometimes not quite as mad as people thought. Guy managed and produced us, and we were signed to Island through Guy, who was their A&R man. I think the deal we thought we had was 7 per cent, but then we found out Guy got 3.5 per cent and we got 3.5 per cent amongst the five of us. It sounds pretty stupid now, but at the time it wasn't that bad. I think Hendrix was on 3 per cent and he got less than one point because he was paying a manager and the other two guys in the band weren't. I think Island were a bit out of order with Mott the Hoople though because I don't believe it's right to manage, publish and record a band, and handle the agency. They should be separate, but they had individual sections and put simply, Island ran Mott totally."

'50 Years of Island Records' would be celebrated in 2009 and, in a review of their history, the label said of Mott's debut LP – "With its M.C. Escher cover, *Mott the Hoople* was a perfect 1969 product." Introducing further irony, *Classic Rock* magazine published 'The Real 100 Greatest Albums of the 60s' in 2019, placing *Mott the Hoople* at No.79. Guy's collision with Silence and Hunter had created a different and intriguing aggregation – a band with a frontman who harboured a special aptitude for songwriting, and an ensemble who were unusual and would not stand still.

> **IH:** "Mott went against the grain because it was all blues and then the hippie thing happened, and we didn't fit in to either of those categories. We wanted to be stars. We kept telling Chris Blackwell, 'We want to be stars,' and

Chris didn't know what we were talking about, because he had Traffic and people like that – but we wanted a different approach."

Mott demonstrated a different approach when they went into Olympic Studios in November 1969 with engineer Chris Kimsey to record Ralphs' heavyweight 'Thunderbuck Ram'. Hunter's 'The Hunchback Fish' was also taped and Stevens' cherished copy of *Trilogy for the Masses* came into play again as an influence. Ian had written lyrics, sung by Mick on rehearsal recordings and the number soon gained legendary live status with Mott's fans, but the track was never completed, partly because Guy became bored with the song. "'The Finchback Hush' was a nice old devil," said Watts. "Live, I could rest during this, before the onslaught on the unsuspecting audience. They had no idea of what was about to hit them."

Hunter's lyrics were his most obscure to date and Mott the Hoople's second album would be in a similar vein, representing the first of several curves on the band's road to commercial acceptance.

CHAPTER FIVE

Sticky Fingers

I began to see there was a strain in Mott that could happen.

In early 1970, Mott the Hoople secured their first British radio session, recording 'Laugh at Me', 'At the Crossroads' and 'Thunderbuck Ram' at the BBC's Maida Vale Studios. The corporation's recording facility for music and drama was built in the former Maida Vale Roller Skating Palace and the converted studio accommodation was dull, uninspiring and hardly conducive to creativity. A warren of rooms running off long brown-and-cream painted corridors were run by engineers who wore brown stock-coats and were "not keen on rock".

Stan Tippins, who had returned as Mott's "shepherd", found the BBC sessions boring and hated the entire experience because the band was asked to, "Keep the volume down!" Mott would tape three or four numbers at "The Beeb", as if onstage and then overdub vocals and lead guitar, all crammed into a four-hour session. Their first three radio tracks were taped on 3rd February 1970 at Maida Vale No.4 Studio and the session was broadcast on John Peel's *Top Gear* show on 21st February. Artists had to audition before they were accepted for broadcast and the first session was a try-out, played to an assessment panel. BBC record notes for Mott's debut gave "this Dylan-influenced group" a "unanimous pass."

> **IH:** "We always had to record at Maida Vale from 2.30 to 6.00pm and the engineers and BBC staff treated those sessions like a gardening or bricklaying job. John Walters, who worked with John Peel, was the worst. We came in and Walters was reading *The Daily Mirror*, spread over the controls, so we ran through a few things and asked him which songs he wanted us to do – to which he replied, 'The four shortest ones.' While we were recording them, he'd still be reading the newspaper. We were treated like scum at those early sessions."

"Generally, the sessions at Maida Vale were painless," said Pete Watts, "apart from the first one with John Walters who was being a prat. I felt very sorry for Ian then. We'd done the backing tracks and Ian was trying to do vocals and he couldn't hear himself. Walters was saying, 'Yes you can. There's plenty of level there. I've checked it.' And Ian was going, 'Look, I can't hear it.' Then Walters would say, 'Well try it now,' and he wouldn't do anything – it would be the same. Hunter went mad, screaming, 'I can't fuckin' hear it!' Walters was behaving like an absolute bastard. I got him back though on behalf of the band – and screwed his secretary!"

Mott the Hoople would play around 200 gigs in 1970 and produce four studio albums in two years at Island Records. Watts recalled that it was exceptionally hard work but considered that the Island Agency did not maximise financially on Mott's drawing power.

"A gig in those days was quite an event and all our live work tightened us up so much, unlike later bands," said Pete. "You could see Mott gigged constantly because we were spot on. If our agency had done their job properly, they could have booked us out seven nights a week for more money. We were going down incredibly well at all our gigs. The first time we played The Lafayette in Wolverhampton, we had about twenty people there, but they said we were the best group they'd ever seen and four months later they were turning people away for Mott, just through word of mouth from one gig. Island built things up gradually, but we saw all this potential. John and Alec never came to gigs and were like the rest of the Island label – 'musos' who loved serious musicians like Traffic – a nice safe group, bordering on jazz which gave them respectability. We were just kids, up from the country, that banged around a bit – that was their attitude!"

Mott the Hoople appeared on the German TV show *Beat Club* in March 1970 playing 'You Really Got Me' and 'At the Crossroads'. Taped at RB Studio 3 in Bremen, the colour film made use of special video effects on 'Crossroads' but the programme was not sold for transmission on any UK channel, even though the show was highly thought of amongst British bands. Mott had to use the *Beat Club*'s "Orange gear" for their session and kicked it over and smashed it.

"The Germans didn't know what to make of us," said Watts. "There was a small audience – probably producers' sons and mistresses – and after we stopped, there was a pregnant pause, then they went mad. Europe was challenging because they weren't used to groups like us. We went to Frankfurt's Zoom Club – supposedly a hard venue to play – and at the end of our set there was dead silence. They must've thought, 'Where did they get this lot from?' – but we didn't care, because now we knew we had something. We played a few days there and won them over in the end. We seldom failed to get a crowd going."

Mott's heavy concert work enabled them to build up a strong British following with an amazing stage act that included most of their first album, 'The Hunchback Fish' and a rock 'n' roll medley "rave-up" at the end. Importantly, Hunter saw that they were breaking through live and began to see the band's true potential as he got inspiration from within the group, via Mick Ralphs especially. Having had the steadfast and ineffably eccentric Mick Hince as Mott's "lone helper" since their early days, the band recruited Richie Anderson as a technical crew member in March

1970. Richie would stay with the group throughout their career, aided later by John Davies, Phil John and, as the band grew, supplementary hired crew. Ian had met 'Rich' briefly in his New Yardbirds days and Anderson had worked with John since 1968, after Phil advertised in *Melody Maker* for drivers with vans for road work. Richie had turned up at Phil's mum's house and his look, long hair and yellow Ford Transit convinced John that Anderson was the guy. The pair started their own adventurous journey together, working with different bands, from a house full of roadies, with a stream of females.

"Rich knew Ian before he moved in with me," says Phil John. "I have hazy memories of going into London with Richie to see Ian who appeared in a shabby towelling dressing gown and no sunglasses – not a pretty sight. I believe we took him for an audition with a band in a room above The Hope and Anchor pub in Islington. Ian had pretty naff hair and wore a navy-blue duffel coat."

Richie and Phil "roadied" for The Groundhogs, Free and other Island bands but went to see Mott the Hoople play in February 1970 and started working for them. Together, "the two good guys" would "cross the mighty oceans" aiding Mott; Anderson looking after "guitars and electrics" and John responsible for "drums, food, porn and cash flow", with Mick 'Booster' Hince on PA. Road life with Mott started in a red Ford Transit van and was more extreme than *Almost Famous*.

"I remember Ian hadn't looked great when he first auditioned for Mott the Hoople at Regent Sound," said Richie Anderson. "I didn't see him for maybe six to nine months after that. Then Phil and I went to see Mott live at Chelsea Art College and I was completely and utterly amazed. Ian had grown really long hair and wore big shades and was smashing the top of his piano with two fistfuls of tambourines. It was all rather manic. Ian was transformed and looked really cool – quite an eye-opener. He smashed the delicate bits of the piano so hard it said, 'Enough!' – and he had to play guitar for the rest of the show. It didn't matter – they were *really* good. I joined Mott's road crew when I was aged just twenty-two and we did six nights a week playing universities up and down the country."

"I remember being literally blown away by Mott's performance that night," says Phil John. "The sheer energy and power they generated was mind-blowing. The opening riff to 'Darkness, Darkness' was amazing – the stage blacked out except for a single spotlight picking out Ralpher on guitar – in his shadow Pete Watts with maracas – building ever so slowly towards the inevitable full-blown 'Mott Wall of Sound'."

"The purse strings were always tight with Island," recalled Richie, "but, as Mott developed, they acquired a Ford Zodiac for the band while the crew used two trucks and frequently drove 400-mile journeys through the night. Once, in one seven-day schedule, I got ten hours sleep. The European gigs were the worst. They were two years behind on the continent and they hated Mott the Hoople. I don't know why we went there at all. The border officials treated us like shit!"

> **IH:** "Mott had a great roadie in Richie Anderson. He carted two sets of gear all over the US in vans and on planes – and he *never* missed a gig. We tried various others, but Richie hated them all until we took on Phil John – and then there were two. Sound problems we had in abundance, but we never had crew problems. Richie was so great that after Mott the Hoople, some wannabees called Queen snatched him immediately."

Fashion became part of Mott the Hoople's image and appeal, with Watts dressed distinctively from an early stage. Griffin always maintained that "Bolan went electric" after witnessing Mott at The Roundhouse. "It's not something to boast about," said Dale, "but Mott the Hoople used to get boots made at Ken Todd's in Kensington Market and he started making them for us with double layers of leather on the soles. We wanted even bigger soles with stacked heels, and it developed from there with Ralphs and Watts getting taller and taller boots. Of course, Watts always got the tallest and then people like Slade, Sweet, Elton John and T. Rex picked up on this. They had them made even more tasteless with all the money they had – but it was Mott the Hoople's fault."

"Pete was the image one, who was always getting us to wear wild clothes," says Ralphs. "I think he did 'invent' the stack boots later adopted by everyone. Years afterwards, my wife had a clear-out and got rid of my multi-coloured leather platform boots to some thrift shop. A couple of months later I saw this drunk in Reading, tottering down the street in them, with his raincoat on!"

According to Stan Tippins: "Watts was *so* into clothes. Suddenly you got three-inch platform heels and then it was six-inch platform heels; in the end, they were so high Pete couldn't walk around the stage. If he fell over, which he sometimes did, a roadie used to run on stage and lift him up."

West Midlands rockers Slade took notice of Mott and observed the crowd reaction to them. The band watched a young fan at Wolverhampton one night run to the front of the audience and place his pork-pie hat on Mick's head, as the guitarist bent forwards on stage; Ralphs played his solo wearing the headgear, the audience was ecstatic, and Slade convened later and agreed that this was what they should do – "get the people involved" – subsequently adapting their act and embracing a barnstorming number like 'Keep A-Knockin' – Little Richard's 'Get Down and Get With It.'

> **IH:** "I remember I met Slade's lead-singer Noddy Holder, and we went out for a drink and he said, 'Do you realise you were the reason we started?' I said, 'No. How did that come about?' He said, 'Well, we went to see you at Wolverhampton Civic Hall, and we thought, if they can do it, anybody can.' I got charged at Wolverhampton for using 'rude and abusive language' and Noddy told me that the whole of Slade was in the front row that night!"

Hunter listened less to other artists at this juncture, ignored earlier accusations of being a Dylan soundalike and concentrated totally on his own writing. In early 1970, Mott the Hoople settled down to start their second album, provisionally titled *Sticky Fingers*, which would be recorded sporadically throughout February, March and April at Olympic Sound, a studio synonymous with many famous recordings including The Rolling Stones' *Beggars Banquet*, Hendrix's *Are You Experienced?* and 'A Whiter Shade of Pale'.

Ian recalls that while Mott the Hoople was camped in Olympic No.1 capturing an entire album, The Rolling Stones worked in Studio 2 and completed one track – 'Brown Sugar'. The Stones' LP would hit record stores in April 1971, but bearing Mott's original title, *Sticky Fingers*. Guy was credited on the Stones' cover for recording levels set according to standards suggested in the 'GUY STEVENS Producer Manual'. Having "given away" Mott's *Sticky Fingers* title, Guy proposed *Mad Shadows* to the band.

Stevens remained as 'producer' for Mott the Hoople's *Sticky Fingers-Mad Shadows* project, but he was really a puppet-master, creating a vibe and atmosphere to pull contributions from the band. Intimidation, mood-creation, frustration and elation were all key techniques in the *real* 'Guy Stevens Producer Manual' as he tried to maximise the passion that his boys delivered via mike to master tape. Under the loose theory that encouragement adds to the creative process, and that if musicians sense a producer believes in them, then those musicians often give more, Guy would challenge Mott, verbally *and* physically, probing and aggravating them to extract absolute commitment.

Recording engineer Bill Price, who later worked with Mott the Hoople and Ian Hunter, described Guy's technique as "direct psychic injection". Stevens would motivate Mott by telling them, "You ARE the Stones" or "You ARE Bob Dylan", as the mood required. He was almost a sixth member of the group now, crediting himself with providing 'spiritual percussion and psychic piano' on the *Mad Shadows* sleeve. "Working with Guy was vital," admitted

Dale. "Nobody else would have taken us on but Guy could see something in us. He made us feel good and made us believe we were the best band ever."

Verden Allen was a differentiating factor in Mott's overall sound but the logistics of transporting his beloved Hammond was frequently a fraught process and Watts recalled the outcome when Ian tried to help during the Olympic sessions.

"Phally's organ didn't split into two sections to assist handling, so it was extremely heavy," said Pete. "Taking it up and down flights of stairs was hell and Verden used to suggest we should throw ourselves under the organ to protect it if it started to slip. We manhandled this bloody thing for years until Olympic, where, halfway up the stairs it slid sideways and pinned Hunter's head against the wall, snapping his shades with a sharp crack. His skull was saved by the rest of us, but the incident caused much argument in the group car on the way to gigs – again and again – as things did in Mott! Verden never paid the 3/11d for the glasses, so Hunter refused to carry the Hammond anymore, as I did subsequently, when my fingers got badly trapped."

Guy Stevens decided that he would capture Mott the Hoople "live in the studio" for their second album. Andy Johns described the vibe on *Mad Shadows* as much more depressing and maudlin than *Mott the Hoople*, noting that there were dark songs, problems between Stevens and the band, and that Guy "was getting nuttier and nuttier". With its forbidding aura and oppressive cover artwork, the dark-hearted *Mad Shadows* featured seven tracks: 'Thunderbuck Ram', 'No Wheels to Ride', 'You Are One of Us', 'Walkin' with a Mountain', 'I Can Feel', 'Threads of Iron' and 'When My Mind's Gone'.

"Some of that album was recorded on sixteen-track," says Verden Allen, "and there was a lot of space and room to record different things, but I think we were genuinely a bit short of material. We were put in the studio to do something and it took a month or two. *Mad Shadows* was largely written in the studio, with Guy feeding Ian a lot of ideas and pulling things out of him."

Ian never recalled *Mad Shadows* fondly, describing the LP as very introspective, from a time when there were personal hang-ups within the group. Recordings were peppered over a period of six months, via only eight or nine studio sessions spread amongst the band's relentless live schedule. Guy Stevens once claimed that Side Two conveyed the kind of despair that taking drugs can lead to, particularly Hunter's song 'I Can Feel' and Ralphs' 'Threads of Iron'. *Mad Shadows* remains one of Mott's greatest statements for some hardcore fans and Ian later admitted that at least it was an honest record, describing it as a creative nightmare and a scream for help, although everybody was too embarrassed to say so. Hunter's trauma at the time related largely to his domestic situation, as his wife Diane had left him in London and returned to Shrewsbury with their two children.

> **IH:** "*Mad Shadows* was much more difficult to record than our debut, largely because Guy was trying to give the band speed to keep us awake. Instead of recording, we'd have twelve hours sitting in the studio control room talking. We were a bit unhappy with some of the record because Guy went purely by feel and he wasn't well when we did it. I was also going through my divorce and Guy was going through a bad time, so we were stroking each other's egos."

In 1970 Mott the Hoople taped two *John Peel's Sunday Concert* shows for BBC Radio One at London's Paris Theatre, a former cinema located on Lower Regent Street. Converted into a 400-seater venue for music and comedy broadcasts by the BBC, the hall had a one-foot high stage and provided an intimate setting. Mott's first show was recorded on 23rd April, shortly before they embarked on their first American tour. The set included 'No Wheels to Ride' and 'Walkin' with a Mountain' and John Peel introduced 'Wrong Side of the River' "from *Sticky Fingers*", which he intimated would be issued on 5th May. Re-titled *Mad Shadows*, Island would delay release until September and Ralphs' song was temporarily shelved.

Because of volume restrictions and the small seated audience, the BBC concert was subdued. Ralphs likened The Paris Theatre and the BBC to school or an institution. "I really didn't like working there," says Mick, "because they made you feel that you shouldn't be loud, and you shouldn't be wild, because it wasn't acceptable. We always felt a bit inhibited in those places."

"The Paris Theatre was a lovely little venue, but it was slightly restrictive," said Watts. "You really had to work on the audience, so we used to go in amongst them and goad them and poke at them a little bit. Worse was a live television show we did in Paris. They gave Ian some stick and somebody threw something at him, so I kicked one guy in the head. The audience grabbed at my legs and I was punching them. That got nasty and was in all the papers the next day. We didn't mind – it was great – but the French were just a bunch of bastards, they really were. England was different. I remember I knocked a bloke's teeth out one night in Cleethorpes Winter Gardens. He jumped up as I swung round, and I hit him with the head of the bass. He came to me afterwards with half his teeth gone and I thought, 'My God, here we go', but he praised me, with blood running everywhere, saying, 'Thanks Overend, it was wonderful. I'll never forget this.' He was pleased!"

In May 1970, Mott the Hoople made their live American debut, beginning a nine-week tour at the Eastown Theatre Detroit with dates running through to mid-July in Houston. Supporting Ten Years After, Traffic, Mountain, Jethro Tull and The Kinks, Mott played at The Fillmore East in New York, Chicago's Aragon Ballroom, the Whisky a Go Go in Los Angeles and San Francisco's Fillmore West. *Mott the Hoople* still had to be promoted in the States as Atlantic had delayed the LP's release until April and US reviewers were intrigued: an instrumental cover of a Kinks classic, a reinterpretation of an "un-hip" Sonny Bono single and Brits giving advice on Texas, admittedly via a Doug Sahm song? Was it a masquerading Dylan? Who *were* Mott the Hoople? Fortunately, *Rolling Stone* described Mott as "fantastically talented", the LP as "unbelievably good" and 'Rock and Roll Queen' as the best track, adding, "One might find oneself growing nostalgic for the old Dylan while listening to it."

The band's American live set included *Mott the Hoople* songs, two tracks from *Mad Shadows*, the unrecorded 'Darkness, Darkness' and their rock 'n' roll finale, 'Keep A-Knockin'. *Billboard* magazine carried a review of a Traffic-Fairport Convention-Mott the Hoople show at New York's "Church of Rock and Roll" – The Fillmore East – describing Mott as the surprise of the evening and highlighting 'Half Moon Bay' and 'Rock and Roll Queen' as stand-out songs. The band also performed at the second Atlanta International Pop Festival on 5th July, to a crowd of over 200,000 people, Spirit's Jay Ferguson frantically snapping photographs of Mott's performance from around the stage, much to Ian and the group's amazement.

> **IH:** "They met us at Atlanta airport with 'Mott the What' draped across the limo. I remember the driver got lost on the way to the site that day and I saw the other side of Georgia. The gig was miles and miles of caravans and tents. We played in the afternoon and then flew to Los Angeles and played the Whisky. That tour had its moments. When Mott opened for Mountain and Traffic in Fort Worth in 1970, I remember I went to the john and when I came back, I got lost and they wouldn't let me backstage – dramas!"

After the festival, it was arranged for Richie Anderson to transport equipment to Atlanta Airport with a local driver. In the middle of the night, the "American male groupie" pulled out a revolver and threatened to steal Mott's equipment: astutely offered a job on the next tour by Richie, the driver put the gun away and drove on. The road crew was always ready for violence of one sort or another at concerts and threw a stage invader six feet down some stairs one night on to his head – Anderson also described cowboy boots as "great weapons".

Guy Stevens was accompanying Mott the Hoople on the road, to a mixed response from Ian and the band. As their *de facto* manager, he decided to join Mott on a New York radio show with The Kinks: a promotional appearance centred round two concerts the bands played together in Westchester County. Ian found The Kinks a troubled outfit to work with but, off the road, Ray Davies was extremely nice, and he regarded Ray as a great songwriter. The radio event was devastating however, when Stevens lambasted The Kinks on air. Ian felt it was Guy's total commitment to what he was doing that ignited these passions, and his insistence that others should possess the same intense commitment.

"The Kinks, by this time, were a bit of a cult band over there and we were nervous on-air and didn't say much," said Pete Watts. "They seemed close-knit and insular, and Guy started getting on his high horse and began to goad them. When one of them said they liked football more than playing in a group, Guy went berserk and said, 'Well why don't you fuckin' leave the group and play fuckin' football then. You don't deserve to be in a group.' Guy went mental, Mott felt very embarrassed and The Kinks took it all. They just sat there, and to their credit, they didn't get up and thump him."

Mott also played Stony Brook, in upstate New York, but Dale felt their US label had no interest in the band after Atlantic chief, Ahmet Ertegun and Chris Blackwell came to a university gig where Verden's organ went out of tune with Ian's piano. Griffin described the show as a complete mess and a fiasco, but on a humorous note, Watts created another spoonerism, re-christening Ahmet Ertegun, "Urt his arm again". Ian vividly recalls the gig and being mesmerised when he encountered New York City for the first time.

> IH: "We were on Atlantic Records for two years and met Ahmet Ertegun and Jerry Wexler, but only briefly. Some people have said Mott stole that night at Stony Brook and overshadowed Traffic. I'm not so sure. I do remember Vietnam was still on and that somebody tried to stab me at that gig, and Stan Tippins saved my bacon. Going to America that

first time was a buzz, but it was pretty frightening when we came into New York City. Times Square wasn't square and the Manhattan skyline, driving in from JFK Airport, scared me to death. Everything was bigger, and we thought, 'What are we taking on here?' It really was a bit intimidating."

Mick Ralphs had favourable American memories as the band was judged on its own merits. *Mott the Hoople* was played often on FM stations and while people in England opined the group was trying to sound like Bob Dylan, Americans took the comparison for what it was and tried to understand Mott's playing. Ralphs was pleased that the knowledgable and critical Fillmore East crowd gave a bottom of the bill band the chance to play and they were happy with the US press and some incredible write-ups. "Ian didn't consciously go in and say, 'Right I'm going sing like Bob Dylan'," said Mick in 1970. "It just came out that way. I think Ian phrases and uses his voice as a sound, in a similar way to Dylan. Perhaps the numbers on the first album were more Dylanesque at that time, but on the next album Ian sounds more like himself."

> **IH:** "In England I was passed off as 'a copy', but in the States people accepted me and I couldn't believe that we were being heard. I was in the West Village and I saw a guy leaning up against a lamp post with his bike, with a little transistor radio in a leather case that he had strapped to his crossbar and I could hear 'Half Moon Bay' loud and clear. That just blew me away. I also remember some guy wrote to *Rolling Stone*'s letters page and said that on his new album, Bob Dylan was trying to sound like Mott the Hoople. We thought – what, us little chaps from England?"

Mott appeared in Texas with Mountain, a heavy rock outfit from Long Island, New York, featuring the colossal Leslie West on guitar, drummer Corky Laing and bassist/Cream producer Felix Pappalardi. West played with passion, precision and power and rival musicians would watch the group in admiration as they careered through soon-to-be classics like 'Nantucket Sleighride', 'Mississippi Queen' and 'Long Red'.

> **IH:** "I always remember Guy Stevens, right at the beginning of Mott, coming back and enthusing madly about this huge person who was playing the guitar around the New York clubs and concert venues. He said this bloke was about twenty-five stone – Guy was always prone to exaggeration – but we eventually saw Mountain live. Ralphs was in tears, because Mick was going somewhere with his guitar playing and he saw Leslie West was already at that journey's end – he saw the actual result. Leslie also turned us on to Les Paul Juniors – two knobs – and we loved the sound!"

"When I saw Leslie West for the first time I was blown away," says Ralphs. "His little Les Paul looked like a badge on him as he was so big, and the sound he had was huge. I became a big fan and a friend of his and a fan of the single cutaway Les Paul."

Verden Allen recalls: "It did poor Mick in when he saw Leslie West play with that sound that he got from his Les Paul Junior. It looked like a toy he was such a big bloke. I remember Mick saying, 'That's it. It's too late. I've had it. He's got the sound I want.' I said, 'Well, you'll just have to get that sort of sound, only better.'"

A Mott-Mountain connection was to develop over subsequent years. In 1971 Mott the Hoople covered 'Long Red', Watts and Ralphs recorded with West and Laing, and Leslie even approached Mott to join and augment their line-up. Ian would also work in the studio with Felix and Corky in 1978 and appear on a Mountain LP with Miller Anderson.

Mott started using heavier amplification in America and Allen plugged the Hammond direct into an Acoustic amp and horn. During one of Mott's quieter passages, at an agreed point in some shows, Watts would "rip" the horn off and push it into someone's face in the front row, while Phally "blasted" on the keys. Watts

ROCK 'N' ROLL SWEEPSTAKES

also ditched his 1959 Fender Precision bass switching to a "hard-to-find" Gibson Thunderbird. Pete first played a T-bird after The Hollies came to Hereford years before and he loved their stylish appearance. Watts found the Gibson top-heavy at first but procured six Thunderbirds in Mott, mainly from pawn shops. Pete broke the neck on every Thunderbird he owned as he often threw basses into the air on stage. He damaged three basses at a Newcastle gig in one night and the group always moaned about repair costs. Pete designed an elasticated strap so that he could "bounce" the guitars and catch them, but this invention was ditched when several rebounded and hit his face.

As Mott toured the US, some Americans assumed the group were "druggies" and saw a weird sexual connotation in Overend Watts' name. Hunter confessed he would occasionally take prescribed Mandrax tablets and a glass of wine to settle nerves or ease insomniac tendencies, but he was always scathing of younger bands who were cavalier about drug use.

> **IH:** "None of us would even have a joint in Mott but at The Fillmore West, Americans were asking, 'What do you want?' The name of the band was kind of strange and they thought we were strange. I remember this black girl sitting there and she went through all these abbreviations for illicit substances, trying to find out what we were on. I kept saying, 'No. No. No.' – and her eyes were getting wider and wider. She thought we had this great stuff that nobody had heard of when we were just sitting there terrified. Some people have addictive personalities, and some haven't. Some people can handle it, and some can't. That's why most artists, even if they do, say they don't. Some bands treated drugs as though they're oranges, and it makes good newspaper copy, but I wouldn't feel good making those kinds of headlines. I was never a dope fiend. Drugs are all rather romantic when you're young but boy, some of those guys paid for it later. Several of my friends aren't even with us."

Island held the completed master tapes for *Mad Shadows* in early June but released Mott's LP on 25th September 1970, after the band returned from America and were able to promote the album in the UK. The record contained some moving musical and lyrical passages in 'No Wheels to Ride' and 'I Can Feel', but it also showed Mott's tougher side, with sections of 'Thunderbuck Ram' and 'Threads of Iron' veering towards heavier rock. Stevens had directed *Mad Shadows*, but he let Mott have space and freedom. Several of the tracks ran for some seven minutes but deep down, Ian really favoured the three-minute rocker or four-minute ballad.

Mad Shadows kicked off with Ralphs' stunning 'Thunderbuck Ram', a five-minute instrumental, with two short vocal sections. Mick's composition was originally a piece with no title until Mott found the words *THUNDERBUCK RAM* scrawled on a toilet wall in The Pied Bull. It transpired the phrase was the name of a Transatlantic Records group who had also rehearsed at the Islington pub. When Mott played Ralphs' number at The Country Club, Watts recalled that Stevens "went pots" over 'Thunderbuck Ram'. Ian admitted he was not in good shape at that Olympic session.

> **IH:** "If you listen to 'Thunderbuck Ram', you'll hear me hit wrong notes. I was pissed out my head – didn't know what I was doing."

The other three cuts on Side One were all composed by Hunter including fan-favourite 'No Wheels to Ride' – originally titled 'Pale Ale' then 'The Coalminer's Lament'. 'You Are One of Us' was a reflection on Mott's relationship with their fans and a "thank you" to their audiences. By Take 9, the tribute was a 5 minute, 14 second song with an extended tail-out, Ian wrecking his voice in Lennon, primal-scream style. Eventually, the track was edited down to 2 minutes, 25 seconds, concealing some of *Mad Shadows*, mania and excess.

Watts recalled that in the beginning, Ian's role under Stevens' direction had been to write "Dylan-type songs" but Mick composed

'Rock and Roll Queen' and so Hunter offered 'Walkin' with a Mountain', written in direct response to Ralphs' effort on *Mott the Hoople*. Although Ian acknowledged he had trouble conceiving faster rock material, he composed 'Walkin' with a Mountain' quickly. Dale claimed an early Sixties LP by Spike Milligan, *Milligan Preserved*, featuring 'I'm Walking Out with a Mountain', had inspired Ian's title. Hunter's song became a live staple.

> **IH:** "'Walkin' with a Mountain' was a song about guilt, and a relationship that didn't work out. We were standing in the Olympic bar one day and Guy said, 'We need a rocker!' So, I immediately launched into this two-chord thing, which I thought was pretty obvious and Guy thought it was great, so, that was that. That night, none of the other Stones were in doing *Sticky Fingers*, so Mick Jagger came in with us and was dancing around. That's why it goes into the 'Jumpin' Jack Flash' line at the end. We were so knocked out that he'd come to a Mott session, that we did the Stones refrain purely on the spur of the moment. He was huge, and we were a little tiny band. It spurred us on to greater depths. 'Brown Sugar' is my all-time favourite riff and one of the best rock songs ever – and Jagger is one of the nicest persons I know. When he came by our session, it didn't bother me – I was so stoned, I just kept playing... but, when Stephen Stills appeared one day, I stopped – I couldn't play in front of him!"

Recorded with Watts using only two bass strings, Teardrop Explodes frontman Julian Cope later described Hunter's song as follows: "When they finish Side One with 'Walkin' with a Mountain', Mott is a Foden truck with the intentions of a Cadillac. Brutal, brash and totally without finesse, the bass and piano threaten to drive the whole tune into a lake at any moment, while Buffin's totally over-achieving ideas of drumming are matched only by his inability to achieve any of it. Startling upstart rock 'n' roll this is indeed, and their producer Guy Stevens would have made the worst politician ever. He can't even be bothered to do a cover-up of the most glaring errors."

Side Two of *Mad Shadows* contained some potent material, not least the gospel-tinged, majestic 'I Can Feel'. First aired live in December 1969, Hunter's song was originally nine minutes long. Ralph's gorgeous lead guitar tone on 'I Can Feel' was tastefully complemented by Watts, a melodic bass player who favoured harmony, rarely playing the root note of a chord. Ian's lyrics were also powerful and poignant but a squeaking foot pedal on Buffin's drum kit inadvertently added a sinister sound across the whole track. The careless oversight created a chilling effect, but the faux pas irked the group.

> **IH:** "If somebody had got hold of 'I Can Feel' with the right voice, it might have been great. It was like a basic declaration. I was a powerful lyricist then. I didn't notice the squeaking foot pedal on 'I Can Feel' until Buff told me afterwards. It never bothered me much, but he was angry. Once you notice it, you can never listen to that fuckin' album again without hearing the squeak. On 'Walkin' with a Mountain', Buffin broke a stick and missed a beat at one point so we said, 'We'll have to re-do that Guy. He's missed a beat.' But Guy said, 'No, no. It's fuckin' amazing as it is!' And, of course, every time you listen to it, that mistake just gets bigger and, in the end, you can't bear to hear it. The album was a very dismal affair."

Ralphs guitar-driven 'Threads of Iron' featured Mick and Ian sharing lead vocals on a song that swung from light verses, to pop-rock choruses and a chaotic conclusion. Hunter also throws in vocal snatches of 'Going Home', from a separate *Mad Shadows*-era song that was shelved, his tortured screams at the end of 'Threads of Iron' leading into the album's finale.

The LP's final cut, credited to Hunter – 'When My Mind's Gone' – was reputedly a spontaneous, stream-of-consciousness cut, recorded after Stevens had "hypnotised" Ian, but Mott had played a version of 'When My Mind's Gone' in some 1969 live sets. The lyrics were another cry of despair, while the piano comprised a simple contrasting three-chord arrangement from Hunter with muted bass from Watts, and Allen adding some delicate filigree on organ.

> **IH:** "That session was very weird. Guy was almost singing through me when I sang 'When My Mind's Gone'. He was very, very forceful. We more or less made it up as we went along and that was essentially the whole atmosphere of Mott the Hoople. A lot of it was scary. Guy believed that complete lunacy was the answer – so we would sit in the control room and he would start on a train of thought – and take it through the roof – through the clouds – through the ozone, and it was amazing to listen to him. Then, five minutes later, you'd be playing, and this stuff was coming out. Guy wanted to make you do something that you didn't know you could do. There was a telepathic thing going on. He couldn't do it, but I was supposed to do it for him. I was his channel. Phally and I didn't have the faintest idea what we were doing so we just kept going and made it to the end. When we'd finished there was silence, then Guy pushed the switch down in the control room and started screaming at the top of his voice. You felt like you'd got an A+ from the teacher. We just wanted to please Guy and to be great for him, because he was so excited when you were and if you weren't, he'd look at you with such a hurt expression. Guy would throw things around, cause mayhem and psyche us up. He was like a wrestling manager: 'You are the King! You are the King!' Guy would push his face into mine, close-up, and he would drag things out of me. That was a real compliment, because he was the first person that ever took a blind bit of fuckin' notice in me."

160

Leading up to the *Mad Shadows* sessions Mott had recorded three songs – 'The Hunchback Fish', 'Moonbus' and a six-minute Hunter-Ralphs instrumental titled 'The Wreck of the Liberty Belle', recorded with little Guy Stevens input. Other *Sticky Fingers-Mad Shadows* cast-offs were 'In the Presence of Your Mind', 'Enough Is Enough', Ralphs' country-flavoured 'It Would Be a Pleasure', a cover of Jerry Lee's 'The Ballad of Billy Joe', 'Going Home' and 'Keep A-Knockin'. A proposed cover of The Small Faces' 'Tin Soldier' was never committed to tape and 'Wrong Side of the River' was recorded but shelved as Stevens felt it did not fit with *Mad Shadows*' mood. Mott also rehearsed 'I'm a River' and another "Stevens-inspired epic" – an attempt at recreating 'When My Mind's Gone' with the entire band entitled 'Can You Sing the Song That I Sing?' Clocking in at almost sixteen minutes, Dale recalled that Guy wanted to release the complete track and having described the piece as "incredibly boring", the drummer was eventually involved with an edited five-minute version, issued as a bonus track on a 2005 live compilation. Like the extended take of 'You Really Got Me', the original 'Can You Sing the Song That I Sing?' was quietly archived, until the full, meandering labyrinth was exhumed for a 2018 retrospective.

In Germany, Island Records prepared some white label copies of the band's second LP as *Sticky Fingers* and any surviving pressings are now amongst the rarest of Hoople treasures. *Mad Shadows* had been first earmarked by Guy as a title for a Steve Winwood LP, aborted after only three songs were recorded because Stevens, rather typically, was pushing Bob Dylan and Jerry Lee Lewis covers. Winwood's solo 'Shadows' project morphed into Traffic's fourth album, *John Barleycorn Must Die*. Completing the circle, a pirate disc of Stones' Olympic sessions was released as *Mad Shadows* and a Mott bootleg LP was later issued as *Sticky Fingers*.

IH: "Mott's *Sticky Fingers* title must have been nicked by the Stones or donated by Guy, because he hung out with them as well as us. Guy always had lots of titles."

The artwork for Mott's *Mad Shadows* went through many drafts. One early design included a painting incorporating a Frankenstein figure driving a dragster, with *MOTT THE HOOPLE – STICKY FINGERS* on the sleeve. Also floated was a tartan shortbread tin effect and conventional band photo images. At one shoot, photographer Peter Sanders captured Mott dressed in druids' cloaks with silver foil obscuring their hooded faces. Another sleeve centred around a set of large scissors that chased and attacked the group, who were placed in a purpose-built room conceived as a visual deceit. The band was meant to be trapped in the space, but other than a strange situation where the walls appeared to be closing in on Mott with huge scissors attacking them, the concept wasn't clear.

"The druids photo session was a total disaster," says Verden. "The idea was for the foil to explode into light so that it gave off a certain effect, but it didn't. I remember the other sleeve where Guy had these massive cardboard scissors. The story was that the scissors chased us and caught us and were wrapped around the complete band, chopping us in half. Anyway, it didn't work out either and then Guy was driving around London for a month with huge scissors sticking out of his car. We used to do lots of photo sessions at Island, so somebody was making money."

Through Stevens, Mott worked with several photographers and designers, most of them his acquaintances including Peter Sanders, Richard Stirling, Richard Polak and Mike Sida, who had created Island's eye-catching sleeves for the *Nice Enough to Eat* sampler album and Free's *Tons of Sobs*.

Mad Shadows had Stevens' stamp in the grooves of the vinyl and across the final, dramatic gatefold sleeve. The front cover appeared as a black-and-white demon's head, but the image was a sideways reverse negative of a flaming fire, created by German photographer Gabi Nasemann, whose work graced East of Eden and Hawkwind LPs, book jackets and covers of late-Sixties *New Worlds* science fiction magazines. Gabi also photographed John Lennon, Jimi Hendrix at The Star-Club in Hamburg and took the last pictures of Brian Jones before his passing.

"I was not a music fan but the London flat I stayed in often had musicians visiting, people like Janis Joplin and Eric Clapton," says Gabi. "I was a shy individual and there were many musicians that I could have photographed but didn't. When I met Guy Stevens, he seemed quite crazy and, in fact, he almost scared me. I visited Traffic's cottage once to take photographs and Guy was crazy there too. I recall he had to get something from his flat one day and I went with him, and the apartment was something else. Guy saw these pictures that I had taken and adapted some months before; they included sand and a photograph of flames from somewhere. The fire photograph was a negative that had asked to be doubled-up and the mirror image suddenly took on human shape. Years later I did some photos of trees that I 'doubled-up' and I recall this man saying to me later that he had seen 43 faces in it. Guy saw the fire photograph and was very moved and shouted, 'This is it – this is it – mad shadows!' He was delighted and walked off with the picture – and I did get paid for once."

Mad Shadows' inner gatefold reproduced an 1896 religious painting by the 19th Century English artist William Strutt. 'Peace' depicted a lamb, calf, lion, wolf and child reflecting a prophecy from The Holy Bible and the Book of Isaiah. The painting conveyed an aura and message of hope because every creature co-existed peacefully with each other. With overall cover design by Peter Sanders and Ginny Smith, Mott's *Mad Shadows* received an ADC Award at The Art Directors Club's 50th Annual Exhibition in New York and the sleeve would later feature in *Classic Album Covers of the 1970s*. Peter Sanders took several studio and live shots of Jimi Hendrix, The Rolling Stones and Free but remembers Mott fondly: "They were one of the more interesting bands at a time when there was so much music that we couldn't really absorb it all."

Continuing his strange fascinations, Guy had re-named Mott's second album after a 1959 novel by French-Canadian author and playwright Marie-Claire Blaise, reflecting a Stevens obsession with the dark side of human nature. Originally titled *La Belle Bête (The Beautiful Beast)*, the book had been translated into English as *Mad*

Shadows. A hostile, strange and unsettling first novel, written when Blaise was only twenty, *Mad Shadows* was harrowing, depicting beauty and ugliness, love and hate, and vice and violence – the novel's main character possessing a destructive nature, setting fire to a farm and committing suicide.

Dark themes, fire, destruction... Mad shadows, a flaming album cover, Guy Stevens – this was Mott the Hoople's black album; a bleak chilling document shrouded in Nasemann's demonic picture with a further schizophrenic split-image of Ian Hunter on the back of the gatefold (the only band member photographed on the cover). The sleeve also quoted from Baudelaire's *Les Fleurs du mal*, that had been used as the preface for Marie-Claire's book. Baudelaire, Blaise and Stevens seemingly shared a propensity to write about or reflect on rage, eroticism and the oppressiveness of living.

Mad Shadows entered the British charts on 17th October 1970 and stayed for two weeks reaching No.46, while the upper regions of the Top Thirty were led by Black Sabbath's *Paranoid* and Pink Floyd's *Atom Heart Mother*. With music swinging from virtual silence to heavy thunder, Mott's album was considered an excellent package by the press, reviewers opining that the record offered deeply moving sounds and mystical, evil impressions. One British journalist commented on the tremendous power behind Mott's songs noting, "Musically, *Mad Shadows* is such a phenomenally tight, beautiful work that you can go mad happily and safely with it. Don't take it all THAT seriously, it's only music – but don't DARE underestimate it."

Rolling Stone wrote that the *Mad Shadows* cover resembled an ambiguous ink blot – a splattered spot that allowed any viewer to see in it what they want to see – reviewer Melissa Mills adding: "Mott the Hoople is itself something of an ink blot, this time around. Possibly the reason I haven't been able to decide whether or not I really like this album is that *they* haven't decided what they're going to be. Mott the Hoople has a lot going for it: competence, tremendous energy, a powerful dense bass-heavy sound and they know how to rock." The American press considered that *Mad Shadows* was not as Dylan-influenced as Mott the Hoople's debut and praised a fresher, less jaded sound, with one Hoople hoof planted in "insanity".

Although Ian had private reservations at the time, his public view was that *Mad Shadows* comprised original songs which were more representative of what they played live. By this stage, the volume of Mott's performance and Hunter's control of a live audience was receiving feverish press comment. Ian now had a confident onstage persona and a vocal style which started to rip and tear at lyrics with ragged exaggerations and pronunciations. Writing of a triumphant sold-out concert at London's Lyceum one journalist said, "What was amazing was that Ian Hunter was able to control the mass hysteria which prevailed with just a mere gesture of the hand, or a well-chosen command – it would have done Mick Jagger proud!"

"Mott was always wild in concert," says Ralphs. "We were a pre-punk punk band I think, who just went on and went berserk. We had the ability to bring out the wildness in people that was probably within all of us. We used to go and see bands play and people would sit and listen, but we always thought something was missing. We always went for contact with the audience from the minute we went on. Once you've won people over, you've got them for life, but we did it in a natural way. Mott was rough round the edges and we weren't the same every night. We were not particularly musical, but we were pleasantly acceptable and quite vulnerable. Crucially, Mott the Hoople was exciting and that's more important I think."

Internationally renowned promoter Mel Bush first saw Mott the Hoople at McIlroys in Swindon and then gigs in Devizes and Yeovil. "Mott was like an army on stage," observed Bush. "They generated a wall of sound and were incredibly impressive. I started to book them on individual shows and then, eventually, on a headlining British tour in 1973."

A year after release Ian declared that he couldn't listen to *Mad Shadows*, saying it was poorly produced, poorly mixed and that he and Mick had started writing things that were too medium-paced. Hunter is still disparaging about the LP.

> **IH:** "*Mad Shadows* was basically Guy and me stroking each other's egos and going over the top. We were allowed to go stupid and we did, but I think I single-handedly ruined the record. You can hear the poor guys trying to play but my singing is really bad. I was out of control at the time, my personal life was chaotic and so was Guy's. A lot was going on; incestuous relationships, things like that. Guy was in love with me by this album and the band was resenting it. There are some good songs on there and if somebody had got hold of 'I Can Feel' or 'No Wheels to Ride' and made them three minutes long, they'd be great. Everything I did in the early days of Mott the Hoople was over the top and the second album was the pinnacle of that. Guy gave me full rein and it was not a good idea as I wasn't ready for it. I was taking myself very seriously, but that's just a form of ego. *Mad Shadows* was my fault, not Mott's fault really. We meant well as a band, but we never had much expertise or confidence and we got so sidetracked at times. Our ideas and pure energy were good but at Mott's gigs people started going nuts, so we just played faster and faster. Nobody else was doing that at the time."

Ralphs believes that Hunter was finding it hard to deal with Mott's live success and that Ian got pretty serious about the rock 'n' roll experience. "We were very much into being us on *Mad Shadows*," he says. "We'd done the first album and Guy had got the Escher cover and it was all a bit avant-garde – avant-garde a clue – so, on the next album, Guy was into mood and delving into the mind. I think he was going through a mental state at the time and was unhappy, and he encouraged Ian to get dark. Guy ended up having more control than we wanted him to have."

Guy Stevens finally "explained" *Mad Shadows* in his essay for a 1971 Mott the Hoople tour programme, when he wrote: "Everybody involved in the making of it, including the engineer and the producer, and most probably even the studio walls, went to the brink of madness, but somehow none fell into the pit they all saw none too clearly beneath them. The songs on this record tell a story which will be clear to any who have been tempted by the forces of perversity and self-destruction, knowing or unknowing. Six months after the release of *Mad Shadows*, John Lennon came out with 'his' comparatively mild album which covered much of the same territory Mott had already explored and the phrase 'identity-crisis rock' was coined. Mott the Hoople was there first."

Dale Griffin recalled that Guy Stevens was very erratic after *Mad Shadows* and that he wanted to sack Ian. "Guy declared, 'Ian's out – he's finished' – but the rest of us said, 'If he goes, we go' and Guy backed down," said Dale. "He was like a little kid with building blocks. Guy would build this structure and then all he wanted to do was knock it over. I think there was a bit of a power struggle because Ian wouldn't submit to Guy. I would. Guy could scare the shit out of me!"

> **IH:** "Guy did want to fire me, but Pete and Mick wouldn't have it. At first, we didn't go down well at all live and apparently Guy would rave saying, 'Ian sits at the piano! We need a focal point! We need a Jagger! We've made a mistake with Ian!' But Pete and Mick had decided by this time that something was going on in Mott and they didn't want to change the band. After nine months or so Guy wanted me out again."

"Guy had tried to oust Ian after only a month or two, after we'd done 'Half Moon Bay', when he probably realised there really was something there," said Watts. "Guy also wanted Ian out of the group around the time of *Mad Shadows* and I believe Graham Bell of Heavy Jelly was a contender as replacement. I think he was considering other candidates because Guy suddenly took a dislike to Ian. He thought Hunter had got too dangerous and was maybe rivalling him in terms of being the main creative force. When Ian started writing good songs, I think Guy felt his hold might be slipping a bit, so he got hold of me and Ralpher one day and said, 'I think we should get rid of Ian. He's got to go. He's trying to take over the group.' Ian wasn't; he was only doing what he'd been asked to do by Guy. So, we said, 'No,' which surprised Guy, because we'd never shown that much affection towards Ian really. I felt very sorry for Ian in retrospect. He did take a lot of responsibility while I didn't give a shit. I just wanted to be out buying clothes and eyeing up girls, while poor old Ian was always trying to write songs. It must have been quite hard for him and then there was this business of Guy wanting him out.

"One day during *Mad Shadows*, when he was going through a bad drug period, Guy came in and he had a great big bump and cut on his forehead. He just looked like he was on another planet. He was obsessive and used to have hundreds of clothes all the same. If Guy saw a pair of trousers he liked, he'd buy twenty identical pairs. He always used to wear tight red trousers and striped jackets. This night when Guy arrived, he had a shirt on that he'd got from Stirling Cooper. It was an ordinary red shirt with tight sleeves and a tight body, but the collar had one point at the front and one at the back, and the open neck was on the side of the shirt. It just looked bloody ridiculous and Guy was gone. So, I asked, 'Are you sure you're alright Guy? Are you okay?' He just said, 'Who are you?' and turned around and walked off – it was quite extraordinary. I don't know exactly what had happened to him, whether he'd fallen over and got concussion, or it was drugs, or a mixture of both – but we didn't get much recording done that night!"

Now a rock and roll star, Ian was "wanted" by the music papers but when he met journalists, he was guarded. He did not discuss his Sixties years in Hamburg, early journalism, engineering jobs or staff songwriting on Denmark Street. "I was thirty years old when Mott the Hoople started," says Hunter. "Of course, I lied about my age. When journalists asked me later, I knocked off six years." Clearly, Ian had personality and was great copy, and independent publicist Tony Brainsby was introduced to Mott. Tony had already worked with Cat Stevens and Free and went on to represent Thin Lizzy, Steve Harley and Paul McCartney.

"I received a call from Guy asking me to go over and see Mott the Hoople, who were a raggedy rock band that could deliver live but were never able to capture it on record," said Tony. "That was their big problem. Whether it was the producer or the material or what I don't know, but they never caught their live show on record. So, I went along for a meeting with Guy and Mott and heard this sob story. But I could see something in Ian Hunter; he was a journalist's delight because you could wind him up, and away he'd go. He was good copy like Steve Harley and Phil Lynott, although Ian was ahead of them and the media always had time for him. I wanted to become their publicist and I soon learned that they really worked exceptionally hard. They were always on tour, virtually non-stop."

Mott was keen to release a single following *Mad Shadows,* to try and broaden their appeal and transport them to a wider audience. Label-mates Free had hit the jackpot with their 1970 hit 'All Right Now' but no Mott "45" was forthcoming other than seemingly pointless French and Japanese single releases of 'Thunderbuck Ram'. The band hit the road again, grinding through Europe with Grand Funk Railroad, a combination that contributed to a misconception that Mott the Hoople was "heavy rock". The tour also created some inter-band rivalry and the press tried to milk it, much to Mott's ambivalence. "Grand Funk never bothered us much," says Watts. "I never really looked at them and didn't know much about them. They didn't do anything for me at all because I didn't know what they were supposed to be – whether they were a metal band or what the hell they were!"

With a concert schedule that seemed endless, Mott maintained a live work rate which modern-day bands would term unthinkable and Ian felt it was excessive. "We toured too much," said Hunter. "Island Records tried to keep us from going into debt, but we were getting overexposed. After *Mad Shadows* the band was exhausted."

Mott the Hoople was selling out venues widely and was a dynamic band on stage, so a live LP was planned to try and bottle their essence. Mott played two shows in one evening with Free at a packed Croydon Fairfield Hall on 13th September 1970 and both sets were recorded using an eight-track machine borrowed from The Who. Mott the Hoople's feral Fairfield appearances captured the group in wild and provocative mood, Watts moving into the crowd with a long bass lead, clambering over seats, while Hunter invited audience members onstage, rendering the band barely visible to the crowd.

"I remember Traffic drummer Jim Capaldi was there and he was smashed over the head with a maraca," says Verden Allen. "He came on with a tambourine and suddenly someone jumped on the stage, picked up the maraca and bang – there were peas rolling all over the floor!"

"Croydon was always a good gig for us, although you can't imagine Croydon being wild," says Ralphs. "Status Quo came to see us there and that's where they learned to shake their heads and change their image from a pop group to an incredibly successful rock band. I think they were a great group, but they nicked the head-shaking business from us – and Elton John copied the outrageous boots and togs pioneered by Wattsy."

After fans had besieged the Croydon stage, according to Guy, little of the recorded material could be used. Stevens scrapped the proposed "Mott Live" LP but a fish-out-of-water 'Keep A-Knockin' would be spliced and slapped on the end of the band's third studio album. Later re-appraisal of the concert tapes revealed the canning of the Croydon recordings to be a misjudgement on Stevens' part, as the tracks had survived unscathed, intact and useable in Island's archives. With a set that included Neil Young's 'Ohio', 'No Wheels to Ride' (incorporating a portion of The Beatles' 'Hey Jude') and 'When My Mind's Gone', the concerts became something of a Holy Grail for fans. Following a Sony *Anthology* tape review in 1996, a

CD compiled from the two shows was finally released in 2007 as *Fairfield Hall, Live 1970*. Some attendees still regard the Fairfield Hall shows as the best Mott gig they ever witnessed.

Mick Ralphs had introduced the Crosby, Stills, Nash & Young single 'Ohio' into Mott's live set and the Croydon takes are Mott's only surviving record of the song. Neil Young's political protest had been composed in an afternoon, recorded by CSNY in fifteen minutes and released as a single within eight days of the Kent State University shootings. The controversial lyric pointed an accusing finger at President Nixon and was banned from US radio, but Ralphs had eagerly proposed it for Mott's repertoire. "I liked Neil Young, so I introduced 'Ohio' to the band," said Mick. "I thought it was great that he just reeled off this song about a news story. I ended up singing it for Mott because I had a high voice then!"

The piano sound at Mott's early concerts was restricted by the technology of the period when amplified grand pianos could not be used, and it shows on the Croydon recordings. Hunter was stuck with his "terrible" RMI electric piano which wasn't touch-sensitive and often blurted out discordant notes. It was a difficult instrument for Ian to play but later, grand pianos were specified on a rider in Mott's live contracts and things improved. The "RMI" piano took a major beating on the road and it was "Richie's job" to get it working again for the next night, even if the crew had to take it up to their hotel room for reparations after each gig.

As *Mad Shadows* hit the British album chart, Mott postponed an October American tour to consolidate on their domestic success. They were grateful to Free for the dates they had played together, as the shows had allowed Mott the Hoople to get across to a wider audience.

On 10th October 1970, Mott the Hoople made their first UK television appearance on *Disco 2*, a BBC show that plugged the gap between *Colour Me Pop* and the soon-to-be-famous *Old Grey Whistle Test*. The band played 'Walkin' with a Mountain' and 'Rock and Roll Queen' at Lime Grove Studios in Shepherd's Bush, where progammes such as *Hancock's Half Hour* and *Doctor Who* had been produced. The *Disco 2* show was filmed in colour and although the performance tape was wiped, some stills survived from the programme, one of which was used for posters in *Sounds* and *Pop Shop*, and later for a *Sticky Fingers* bootleg LP. Mott also taped their second *John Peel's Sunday Concert* at The Paris Theatre on 15th October. Aired on the 25th, 'Ohio' and a new Ian Hunter song entitled 'The Debt' was included but the BBC tape no longer exists.

Mott the Hoople continued to play regular UK live dates and Guy Stevens even decided to line up a special performance for the inmates at Pentonville Prison in North London. However, the band's touring plans to help their second album cruise up the chart were thwarted when Buffin was taken ill with glandular fever and their October-November live dates were scrapped. "No sooner was the prison gig announced than it was cancelled," said Griffin. "I was still dragged off for one provincial concert. The bastards took me to Bristol for a gig despite the pain I was suffering then took me all the way back to London, rather than on to Hereford which was closer."

Back on the road in November, Mott the Hoople played The Roundhouse, Birmingham Town Hall and Croydon Greyhound and four German live dates during December. They also frequented Island's newly converted studios in Basing Street during this period but a cooling in their relationship with Guy Stevens became apparent. Ian harboured reservations about *Mad Shadows* and his vocal performance, but Verden was unhappy with 'Thunderbuck Ram' as Stevens had placed Allen's organ track back in the mix by the time it appeared on the final pressing. The original version would be released on an Island sampler titled *Bumpers*, but the band knew that the organ had been forgotten. It was too late to argue about *Mad Shadows*, but Verden still exploded during an album playback at Stevens' Swiss Cottage flat, where he tried to destroy a copy of the record in front of Guy and the group.

"When Guy mixed *Mad Shadows*, he was on some sort of speed," says Allen. "I was annoyed and very upset. I actually failed to smash the album, but I bent it back and forth. Guy was sitting with his mouth wide open in disbelief. I couldn't tell him in words. I tried to tell them, but nobody would listen. So, I said, 'To tell you the truth, this is what I think of the mix on that track,' and I bent the album over on itself. I didn't snap it but after my rage somebody picked up the LP from the floor and it broke.

"After I'd buckled that LP, Guy wanted to get me out of the band and there were apparently discussions about this. Guy disappeared for about three days and then I had to go and see him and apologise. I went to Island Records because I had to meet the boys there and they said, 'Guy wants to see you upstairs.' So, I went and sat in this room and explained to him why I'd done it and my conscience was clear, because to me he'd done wrong. Guy's mouth was wide open, and I said, 'Well, really I think you were wrong actually. That was the only way I could express the way I felt about things and you should sympathise with my feelings as a musician. I was frustrated.' Anyway, the boys were outside listening to all this, but I didn't know that, and they came in and said, 'We've been having a good talk about this Guy and we've decided Phally's got to stay in the band and we're going to have to find another producer.' I turned around and thanked the lads and then we went in to do our third album without Guy – and that's why it's very laid back."

Mad Shadows would be Mott the Hoople's second most successful Island album in chart terms, but the band had started to feel overwhelmed by Stevens and considered that many of the *Mad Shadows* sessions had been unproductive. "We didn't record a thing some days," says Watts, "and just had big meals, and then we started to wonder who was paying for all this. Of course, it was us, but we didn't know at the time. It got to the point where we were going in and not recording anything. We got rid of Guy for a while."

IH: "*Mad Shadows* was the worst time of all in Mott the Hoople really. We had no money and we were always on the

clock. The Stones were in Olympic and piddled about with one track, while we did a complete album. Our style was 'get in there – and get out.' I'm not a fan of *Mad Shadows*. It was a chaotic record, slaughtered with bad vocals."

Guy Stevens had created and crafted Mott the Hoople, but a schism had developed between the group and their crazy, controlling producer. Having smothered his protégés, the psychic puppeteer would now fade from their orbit.

CHAPTER SIX

Original Mixed-Up Kids

There are some very truthful songs on Wildlife.

Mad Shadows had been dominated largely by Ian Hunter's writing, so Mick Ralphs was eager to see a change in direction and proposed a more modest manifesto for Mott the Hoople's third studio album, *Wildlife*. Guy Stevens was present initially for the odd session, but his personal problems and behaviour had resulted in Mott becoming tired of their increasingly erratic overseer.

> IH: "Guy was meant to be 'managing' us, but we were helping him to get out of bed! After the debacle of *Mad Shadows*, it was Ralphs, the voice of reason, who suggested we do some 'nice songs'. Mick said, 'Look, the hell with this, we're going in too deep, so let's do a nice quiet album. Let's produce the next one ourselves.' Mick liked country music a lot, so as much as *Mad Shadows* was towards me, *Wildlife* was Mick's. Neither of us was right. We were just searching around."

"During *Mad Shadows*, Guy's control had been greater than we wanted," says Ralphs. "He was overwhelming, and he'd taken things to extremes. Guy had done us in. We were shell-shocked, so we foolishly thought we'd do an album on our own."

The outcome of the schizophrenic *Mad Shadows* project and an unbelievably heavy tour schedule had left the band exhausted and Dale Griffin ill. The Island Agency continually hustled for gigs but in the two months that it took Dale to recover from glandular fever, much of the *Wildlife* album was written. Griffin once claimed that after *Mad Shadows*, Ian had not composed much in terms of songs "and no rock stuff" – and that Ralphs had "a muso-snob thing" that made him want Mott the Hoople to be serious musicians.

Whilst Guy Stevens had no connection with the actual recording of *Wildlife*, to supplement the album three previously recorded tracks were hauled in: Ralphs' unused *Mad Shadows* song 'Wrong Side of the River', the colossal 'Keep A-Knockin' from the Fairfield Hall live tapes and a cover of Melanie Safka's 'Lay Down' that had been considered as a possible single in September 1970. Most of *Wildlife*, however, was captured through a series of over-lapping sessions during a two-month period in November and December 1970. At this juncture, Ian Hunter also started dating Trudi Liguori, a beautiful, dark-haired, American-Austrian girl from Long Island.

Wildlife was taped at Island's Basing Street Studios, later known as Sarm West, after Chris Blackwell sold the site to producer Trevor Horn. Constructed inside a three-storey 1870s congregational chapel at 8-10 Basing Street, the building had previously accommodated Gems Waxworks, a company who manufactured life-size human figures for Madame Tussauds. Sculptured wax models created at Gems for the famous Baker Street museum included the Forties serial killer John Reginald Christie who had committed his crimes in nearby Rillington Place. Blackwell's first experience on viewing his future studio premises was freaking out when he suddenly found himself in a room full of dummies.

Mott the Hoople was one of the first bands to record at Island. In its infancy, the studio also captured Led Zeppelin's 'Stairway to Heaven' and Black Sabbath's *Masters of Reality*, while subsequent recording artists would include Genesis, Lindisfarne and The

Eagles. Jethro Tull's *Aqualung* was another early recording at Basing Street Studios and band-leader Ian Anderson would later reveal that he was not over-enthused with the newly constituted arrangement. The building housed Island's new head office, a penthouse flat for Blackwell who lived "over the shop" and two recording areas that were both used by Mott at different times – Studio Two in the basement and, above it, the more spacious Studio One.

Produced by Mott the Hoople and engineered by Brian Humphries, assisted by Richard Digby-Smith and Howard Kilgour, *Wildlife* is lightweight and as far-removed from *Mad Shadows* as it could be; it is also the only Hoople LP where Ralphs' songs are predominant. Untypically, Mott added strings to one track and whilst Ian has since described *Wildlife* as too safe and too tight in its attempt to satisfy Mick's aims, the lyrics, melodies and subtler songs certainly shot down one or two critics' claims that the group possessed musical limitations.

Wildlife featured nine tracks: 'Whisky Women', 'Angel of Eighth Avenue', 'Wrong Side of the River', 'Waterlow', 'Lay Down', 'It Must Be Love', 'Original Mixed-Up Kid', 'Home Is Where I Want to Be' and a live version of 'Keep A-Knockin'. A concert cut of 'Thunderbuck Ram' had also been slated for *Wildlife* at one stage but was dropped. Mick wrote and sang lead on half the studio tracks while Ian contributed an exceptional triptych of beautifully evocative lyrical ballads that glowed with melancholy, emotion and honesty. Hunter continues to rate the three songs amongst his best-ever work.

Many of Ralphs' musical inspirations are laid bare on *Wildlife*, notably his interest in American country rock with 'It Must Be Love' and his affection for Buffalo Springfield, Stephen Stills and Neil Young on 'Whisky Women' and 'Wrong Side of the River'. *Wildlife* also highlighted the different vocalising within Mott: Ian retaining his emotionally charged sing-speak charm in direct contrast to Mick's thin, tenor, West Coast style. The Nashville Rooms, on Cromwell Road in West Kensington near the group's apartment, had become a social haunt for Mott and they saw several country and western bands play there. Spotting pedal-steel player Gerry Hogan at the Nashville, Ralphs desperately wanted his sweeping glissandos to feature on some of his songs. Credited as 'Jerry' on *Wildlife*, Gerry appeared on 'It Must Be Love' and 'Original Mixed-Up Kid'. It was Hogan's first recording, but he soon became well known via albums by Albert Lee & Hogan's Heroes and Dave Edmunds.

"Mick Ralphs came to a gig or two when I was in Jan and the Southerners and we were playing at The Nashville Rooms," says Gerry. "He said he was looking for a pedal steel player. I'd heard of Mott the Hoople but was not familiar with their music at the time. Mick invited me to a session a few days later but I went around to the Mott flat that night and listened to some records; we both had the same taste in singers and guitar players. I recorded at Island with Mott for a day or two on a couple of Ian's and Mick's songs and I remember that they both seemed to be doing most of the work in the studio. I also went along to see Mott the Hoople live in London and was quite amazed at the power of the whole thing. Their sound was enormous and quite alien to me at that time. I hadn't heard anything like it. I liked Mick very much and always thought he was a great player and writer."

'Whisky Women', originally titled 'Brain Haulage', opened *Wildlife* in style, Ralphs' song having been inspired by the notorious Whisky a Go Go club in Los Angeles. Located on Sunset Boulevard, "The Whisky" was a focal point of the Hollywood music scene for the likes of The Doors, but the club also drew and became famed for its large contingent of jaded and faded first-generation rock groupies. "The Whisky was a horrendous place where people could go and pick up the odd lady," says Ralphs, "and then go to the doctor about three days later."

Mick also wrote the autobiographical 'Wrong Side of the River' which he described as "a lonesome, reflective song" about himself – and 'It Must Be Love', a straight country-rock track with Gerry Hogan's pedal steel guitar and shades of Poco, the

American band formed following the demise of Ralphs' beloved Buffalo Springfield. Mick's fourth composition, 'Home Is Where I Want to Be', was *Wildlife*'s penultimate track. The song, with its yearning-for-Herefordshire theme was admired by Ian for Ralphs' lyrics and Verden's "beautiful" organ playing. "I always felt very drawn towards home," said Mick, "especially when I was on the road, so the song's about missing your security and whatever it is you miss when you're away – a bit soppy really!"

'Angel of Eighth Avenue', the first of three stunning ballads that Ian composed for *Wildlife*, reflected on an encounter with a girl from The Bronx, written after a drunken evening at Nobody's in Greenwich Village during Mott's summer 1970 US tour. Soon to be one of The New York Dolls' favourite bars, Nobody's was a music hang-out on Bleecker Street patronised by the rock 'n' roll elite. Ian recalled that the "angel" from Manhattan weighed under seven stone and was one of the most beautiful girls he ever saw. They met for a second time, three days after the Greenwich Village encounter, when Mott travelled back through New York following the Atlanta Pop Festival.

> IH: "That song was about the first time I discovered New York. This girl worked in a bank and her whole family was a bunch of idiots – drunks, prostitutes – God knows what else. She was trying desperately to keep it together. I think I wrote 'Angel of Eighth Avenue' at Mott's flat on Stonor Road, in a bedroom that was eight feet by six feet with a mattress and wardrobe lying sideways on the floor. Ahhh, stardom!"

Wildlife's fourth track, 'Waterlow' would soon be termed Hunter's first great song by one music critic and it was a career high point, featuring Mott's first-ever string arrangement played by members of The London Symphony Orchestra conducted by Michael Gray. Originally titled 'Blue Broken Tears', Ian's lyric concerned his painful separation from Diane and his two young children,

Stephen and Tracie, who he used to take to Waterlow Park in North London. Set on a hillside the land had been bequeathed to the public by philanthropist and politician Sir Sydney Waterlow, as a "garden for the gardenless," a description that Ian would layer employ in one of his lyrics. The riptide of rock 'n' roll had been too much for Ian and Diane, and his daughter's "*blue broken tears*" and the evergreens of Waterlow Park were contrasted dramatically to convey the pain of Hunter's personal situation and the loneliness of lost love.

> **IH:** "I married young and had two kids when I was young. When I changed, and the hair got long, and I started going out to weird places and doing weird things – apparently, they were weird – Diane was dead against it. She hated London and it came down to the fact that if I stayed in bands, she left. Diane was a great girl, but she'd married a teenage apprentice and I'd morphed into something different. She didn't like the music. She wanted a different kind of life and I don't blame her, but sometimes there's a point in your life where you have to go for it – and I did. I wrote 'Waterlow' for Tracie and Stephen. I remember writing it in that small bedroom in the Stonor Road flat. It's about the park in North London where we used to go and feed the birds. I was going through the divorce from Diane about that time and that song was straight from the heart. To me, it's the best thing I ever did."

In November 1971, the Italian group I Nomadi, who had played alongside Mott at their 1969 Riccione gigs, released the song 'Suoni' ('Sounds'). Credited to Carlo Contini and Beppe Carletti and issued as a single from their album *Mille E Una Sera*, Dale Griffin claimed 'Suoni' was a straight musical "lift" of 'Waterlow' and reported matters to Island Music – but without reply.

Hunter's touching trio of songs was completed with 'Original Mixed-Up Kid', cruelly re-named 'Original Poxed-Up Sod' by

180

Watts. Ian's *"empty bed"* ballad was included on another Island compilation album, *El Pea*, and Hunter admitted the song was an example of where he truly "lived" his lyrics.

> **IH:** "I like *Wildlife* better than *Mad Shadows*. It is an uneven record but there are some very truthful songs on there. Every time we tried to do something decent like on the first album and on *Wildlife*, people would say it was crap. And every time we would do something completely nuts, they would say it was great, but it wouldn't sell. It sold more years later than it did back then. I know because I get the royalties. My life at the time of *Wildlife* was bittersweet. My first wife didn't want anything to do with our rock 'n' roll lifestyle, so my marriage was dying and there were a couple of kids involved. It wasn't much fun. 'Original Mixed-Up Kid' was written around that time – right in the middle of the whole mess. It was a terrible thing and I was in a bit of a state. I'd met Trudi and included a line, *'And Byron said happiness is born a twin...'* I remember Trudi saying the Byron phrase – she was a big Byron fan and it stuck with me. It made me look intellectual!"

Rounding out each vinyl side of *Wildlife* were two change-of-pace covers that sat in direct contrast to Hunter's and Ralphs' exemplary songwriting: 'Lay Down' and Mott's elongated rock 'n' roll tribute, 'Keep A-Knockin'. Melanie Safka's 'Lay Down (Candles in the Rain)' concerned the moratorium to end the US war in Vietnam and Mott's version featured Stan Tippins and Jess Roden of Bronco on backing vocals. Considered as a single release, the track originated with Guy Stevens although he soon abandoned it, leaving the group to complete production.

> **IH:** "'Lay Down' was the first decent piano part I ever put down, so I thought I'd push that right out front. I loved the song and by this time we had our eye on a single."

After the harmony of the preceding eight tracks, the peace is finally shattered as *Wildlife* finishes with ten minutes of mayhem: Mott the Hoople's rock 'n' roll medley, centred around a locomotive version of Little Richard's 'Keep A-Knockin', salvaged from their September 1970 Croydon live tapes. During Mott's musical madness, Ian acknowledges various influences with vocalised segments of 'I Got a Woman', 'What'd I Say' and 'Whole Lotta Shakin', and the rampage is also notable for Ian's policy statement that – *"rock 'n' roll is the best possible form of music there ever was"*. After nine minutes, and approaching the death throes of the band's improvisation, during a short pause Hunter gasps... *"This is a disaster area up here – I don't know what we're doing – alright, well we'll finish it now then"*... before Mott's final crunching chord, PA interference and animated applause. The insane energy and penetrating power of the band was regularly rewarded by absolute audience devotion but the pole-axing of *Wildlife's* peace with the inclusion of a lengthy live track was trademark Hoople schizophrenia.

> **IH:** "Croydon was pivotal for Mott the Hoople. Before that, we'd only played clubs and the Fairfield Hall was the first 'big one'. It was packed – and chaos reigned. I remember the BBC being at one of our Fairfield Hall gigs. They were going to show footage on *The Old Grey Whistle Test* but somebody historically significant died that week, so the BBC screened a programme about him instead."

Prior to the release of *Wildlife*, Ian was keen to explain that Mott's new record was much lighter than their previous two LPs and was – in their own words – "a lot less weird." Hunter said that they had tried to produce an album that wasn't too heavy, and this was the first situation where they'd had full control. Ian believed *Wildlife* would make people finally understand that Mott the Hoople had musical ability and expunge the misguided belief that they could not record as well as they played live. For Mott, Guy Stevens' strategy for recording a studio album was capturing their stage act – but *Wildlife* showcased new strengths, the group's musicality and increased sharpness and class in Ian's songwriting.

> IH: *"Wildlife* was kick-back time after *Mad Shadows*. It was largely Mick Ralphs trying to get some sanity into the proceedings and it worked, to a degree. Mick said, 'Enough of this drama – let's do a normal album with good songs on it.' Unfortunately, we only had a few good country-style songs and we put them down, but we didn't have enough for a whole album. 'Keep A-Knockin' seemed to be the only thing that was salvageable from Croydon. Whenever we'd play live, it seemed like half the audience would get on stage with us, so it was hopeless trying to record as the kids would be pulling leads out and knocking mikes over. What would have been a live album was now out of the question, but the live version of 'Keep A-Knockin' was stalwart and got stuck on *Wildlife* as a sort of P.S. It didn't quite fit.
>
> *"Wildlife* was meant to be all the melodic stuff we wanted to do, but we stuck on a live rock 'n' roll number and messed it up. That was twenty minutes of total stupidity that I had in me too and I loved doing that. We went down a storm live but somehow when we went into the studio, we always wanted to do quiet little songs. It didn't make any sense."

In the late Nineties, Dale Griffin described *Wildlife* as a low point in Mott's career. "I think the most-inept album we did was *Wildlife*, in terms of the engineer getting it totally wrong and insisting that we did it that way," he complained. "I don't know what's worse – that he insisted we did it that way or that we just let him get on with it. Unfortunately, it sounded just as crap. Things like 'Whisky Women', which was supposed to be a heavy rocker, just came out with what I call the 'flubadubba' sound – very prominent in the Seventies – no attack, no depth, no power to the drums or the track in general. It was very, very disappointing."

> **IH:** "I have more of a fondness for *Wildlife* than practically all the other albums because I really like the songs on there, but it was a total departure and the worst-selling album we ever did. *Mad Shadows* and then *Wildlife* illustrated that we were just a band trying to find itself – checking out different routes – marking territory."

On 19th January 1971, Mott played at The Big Brother Club in Greenford, West London. The property was the Oldfield Tavern where Keith Moon first met members of The Detours (pre-Who) and a venue played by the likes of early Genesis, Hawkwind and Status Quo. Mott's Greenford appearance was filmed by ABC of Australia for a TV magazine-style music series named *GTK*, an acronym for *Getting to Know*. A four-minute black-and-white film survives of live clips and a short band interview.

Later in January, Mott undertook their first headlining appearances on a five-date English mini-tour supported by Wishbone Ash. With their twin-lead guitar set-up and fine frontman, lead vocalist, songwriter and bassist Martin Turner – "Wishbone" would soon be voted Britain's most promising new act following their highly acclaimed third album, *Argus*. Watts recalled that Mott enjoyed their time with the band, and he liked Martin's taste in musical instruments. "We got on very well with Wishbone Ash," said Pete. "They were nice blokes and a really good group. I always liked their guitar styles and Martin Turner was a good bass player too. He bought one of my Thunderbirds and I saw him using that in many photographs."

"I remember I'd broken my Rickenbacker bass," says Martin Turner, "and I phoned Pete Watts to ask if I could borrow an instrument and he said to come around but gave me a sunburst Thunderbird that was an absolute dog. I think it had been smashed into a dozen pieces at different times and their roadies had kept glueing it back together. I rang Pete a week later and said he'd treated a great old machine disgracefully, so I was going to buy it from him and sort it. He said he didn't want to sell it and he'd just lent it to me, but I knew from Mick Ralphs that Watts was hard up, so I said the loan was appreciated, but unfortunate, as I was coming back over to his flat with a wad of crisp bank notes. We had a cup of tea and I threw cash on the table and Watts was fine. He had a few Thunderbirds, but it was sweet of him."

A concert recording from February 1971 presents a fascinating document of Mott's early live prowess – a show played at The Konserthuset in Stockholm during a five-day Scandinavian tour. The Swedish show was taped by local FM radio and circulated for years on bootleg cassettes until a 1990 pirate CD entitled *Long Red* was issued on the Oh Boy label in Luxembourg. The show appeared legitimately in 1999 on a 2CD set, *All the Way from Stockholm to Philadelphia* but then, on countless chaotic compilations. Mott's Stockholm set included 'Original Mixed-Up Kid', 'Walkin' with a Mountain', 'Laugh at Me', 'Thunderbuck Ram', 'Long Red' and 'Keep A-Knockin', but despite the band's best efforts, there was little audience response with each song receiving weak ripples of polite applause. It sounded as though Mott was performing in a retirement home and, at one point, Hunter jabs sarcastically at the crowd: "Oh, you're VERY exciting and kind... thank you!"

Mott recorded another BBC session at Maida Vale Studios on 8th March. Aired eight days later, the set for Mike Harding's *Sounds of the Seventies* radio show promoted *Wildlife* to the hilt and comprised 'Whisky Women,' 'Angel of Eight Avenue', 'Keep A-Knockin' and 'Original Mixed-Up Kid'.

Wildlife was released by Island on 19th March 1971 and would be the only original Mott the Hoople release ever to feature all the band members on the front of an album sleeve: a colour image of Mott in a woodland setting captured by photographer Brian Cooke on Carlton Bank in the Cleveland Hills overlooking Teesside. Echoing the musical contrast within, the inner gatefold comprised a shot of the group on stage at Croydon's Fairfield Hall. *Wildlife* entered the UK chart on 17th April but stayed for only two weeks reaching No.44. Mott had threatened to disband if *Wildlife* didn't out-sell *Mad Shadows* and "officially" it just managed to edge past it, so the band staggered on. Hunter couldn't understand it, claiming that the record had shipped 15,000 more copies than its predecessor. The LP did receive some very favourable reviews though – "*Wildlife* must be the clincher"... "A true labour of love, *Wildlife* contains a wealth of fine material"... "Mott is just about the best rock and roll band around"... "An excellent album" – were just some of the compliments offered by the British rock press.

Rolling Stone in the USA enthused: "The outcome of the battle has yet to be conclusively determined, but my scorecard gives the race for 'The Most Beloved Rock and Roll Band in All the English Isles' to Mott the Hoople by two full lengths over Free. Now that they have apparently captured the British crown, isn't it about time they were given a shot on this side of the Atlantic? There is more than enough solid music on this album to warrant it. Take Side One and the live cut for their well-defined and satisfying brand of rock, and then make up your own mind about the country experiments on Side Two. And fear not; Mott the Hoople has clearly gone beyond any Dylan comparisons you might have heard. Ah, had only Dylan this much fresh energy!"

At the time, Mick Ralphs believed Mott had possibly made *Wildlife* too soon, and that they weren't "big enough" to have adopted such a drastic stylistic change. Years later he considered that *Wildlife* was essential light relief after the intensity of *Mad Shadows*, but not without reservation. "We needed *Wildlife* to survive," says Ralphs. "Nice is a horrible word, but it's a nice album and it was the first time that the band got a say in what went on. On the previous two we were just told what to do. In the end I really wasn't too happy with the third album either. We used to call it *Mildlife*."

Mott also dubbed the LP *Original Mixed-Up Mott*. It had been produced with assistance from sound and recording engineer Brian Humphries who worked with The Kinks, Spooky Tooth, Free, Pink Floyd and Traffic, but Watts and Griffin were critical. "We produced *Wildlife* ourselves, assisted by Brian Humphries and it was grim," said Watts. "All Brian ever talked about was West

Bromwich Albion Football Club. 'Can you give us a bit more treble on the bass Brian?'... 'West Brom 2, Arsenal 3'... 'Oh shit!' You knew it would be a bad recording session that day. 'Can you get us some repeat-echo on the voice Brian?'... 'Oh no, you can't do that at this studio – it can't be done... West Brom 3...' In fact, repeat-echoes can be done anywhere, as we found out later, but Brian would just get out of things at every turn."

"Everything was a problem to Brian," said Griffin. "He limited the bass guitar on one track and made it sound pedestrian rather than try and make it rich and get full value from each note."

As with earlier Mott album sessions, some *Wildlife* outtakes were shelved, notably Ralphs' 'Black Hills' (originally titled 'Green Valley Monday') and 'Surfin' UK' (a sadistic re-write of 'Rock and Roll Queen'), plus Hunter's 'Growing Man Blues'. Engineer Richard Digby-Smith also recalls a rare one-man recording during the *Wildlife* sessions when Ralphs turned up one Saturday to a studio that was set up, but minus Mott.

"Mick said, 'I've got an idea I want to demo.' He went out and played acoustic guitar first, then put some drums on top, then bass, electric guitar, vocals, percussion and backing vocals. Then we did a little mix and off went Mick with his demo called, 'Can't Get Enough of Your Love'. I never heard that song again for years, until it came on the radio in Los Angeles – by Bad Company – and I nearly crashed the car!"

In early 1971, Mott played some live dates supported by Bronco, a band that featured vocalist Jess Roden and future Robert Plant guitarist Robbie Blunt. Mott agreed to help Bronco with two tracks on their Island album *Ace of Sunlight* and Hunter and Ralphs played organ and piano on 'Amber Moon', while Allen added organ to a song titled 'Discernible'.

ZigZag magazine continued to give Mott the Hoople support and in their 1971 'Reader's Rock Poll', Ian Hunter and Verden Allen were placed eleventh and seventeenth in the British keyboard players listing, with Overend Watts thirteenth in the bass players' poll. However, Watts was not afraid to show the human side of

Mott and recalled that whilst they seldom failed live, there were exceptions.

"One of the worst gigs we ever played was at Southampton University, with Brinsley Schwarz as support, who were a very good band. I don't know what happened that night, but the sound we got on stage was awful and we played abominably. What Brinsley Schwarz must have thought of us, I don't know. A student said to me, 'Was that some kind of joke? The group's like a spoof, is it?' And I replied, 'Yes, that's right, we just take the mickey out of groups a bit, you know.' We didn't have many gigs where we were diabolical – maybe three or four in the whole of Mott – but that was the worst. I make a formal apology to the members of Brinsley Schwarz, Nick Lowe included, because that was bad."

Mott the Hoople was now eager to issue a second single, Ian realising that the band could cut a "predictable twelve-bar" that might hit the charts, but there was no point as they would not be proud of it. Ralphs considered that a successful 45 was the way to become an established band like Free. As Mott's 'Lay Down' single release had been abandoned, they spent time in Island Studios between 11th and 21st April 1971, taping 'One of the Boys', 'Til I'm Gone', 'Long Red', 'It'll Be Me', 'Where Do You All Come From', 'Ill Wind Blowing', 'Downtown' and 'The Debt'. No single release materialised, and the band embarked on a six-week American tour. Playing support to Jethro Tull, Emerson Lake & Palmer, Edgar Winter and Albert King, Mott's trek was reported as "a farcical stab at the USA", where bookings disappeared, guitars were stolen, and the tour deficit ballooned.

> **IH:** "We opened for Tull quite a lot in the early days and they were nice chaps. Ian Anderson was tremendously agile on stage and a great frontman. Because they all had extended solos in their live set, we spent a lot of time with them back in the dressing rooms. The Fillmore West was wonderful. Albert King topped the bill, Freddie King was bottom, and we were in-between. There wasn't a white face in the

place, but we got an encore. We played and finished and survived. I remember Albert King with Bo Diddley's brother backstage in New York and Albert was sitting staring at my Maltese Cross guitar. He kept on looking at it. Albert never let anyone touch his guitar, but he asked if he could pick up the Cross and I said, 'If I can pick yours up, you can pick mine up.' He kept looking at the Maltese Cross calling it 'a mean mother!'"

Still craving an elusive hit single, it was decided that Mott would take time out in America to work on one track, with the legendary Shadow Morton, a producer suggested by Atlantic Records. For a period in the Sixties, the "East Coast Spector", George 'Shadow' Morton, had poured the frustration of adolescence into original hit songs and pop-operettas such as the Shangri-Las' 'Leader of the Pack'. Morton could not read music or play an instrument but claimed he conceived songs in his head. Songwriter Jeff Barry gave George the name Shadow because of his silent evanescent presence.

Mott's single was cut on 12th May at Ultrasonic Recording Studios in Hempstead, Long Island. Ultrasonic had been employed by Shadow for some years and would be used in the Seventies for live recordings by Peter Frampton, Little Feat and Lou Reed, broadcast on WLIR Radio. In the lead up to the Shadow session, Ian had been working on a song called 'The Hooker' that Mott subsequently re-titled 'The Road to Rome', then 'Midnight Lady'. Following a Milwaukee concert with Emerson Lake & Palmer on 11th May, the band flew to New York, but they were not in a good state having drunk through the night with their old Herefordshire friend, Fred Fishpool. Frequenting Milwaukee bars until 6.00am, Buffin could hardly play at the Ultrasonic session and lay across the drum kit, severely hungover. Humble Pie frontman Steve Marriott sang backing vocals for Mott on 'Midnight Lady' after a chance meeting, although he had to be isolated at the opposite end of the recording room because his vocal was so loud. 'Midnight Lady' was "live-sounding" in its overall performance, but Ian felt that Mott had failed to exploit the potential of the Shadow session.

> **IH:** "We met Steve Marriott in the coffee shop of the hotel we were staying at and asked him to pop into the studio with us. I sang on the mike and Shadow put Steve about forty feet away from me – that's how powerful Steve was. Marriott wouldn't take a cent and was a lovely bloke. We'd been five or six days on the road with Emerson Lake & Palmer and were shattered after a party the night before. The band played badly but the second verse makes it. Although Shadow never got a chance with us, we enjoyed his company immensely. He was an amazing guy. He had this crocodile shirt on when we met him, and I remember saying, 'I love that shirt, Shadow,' and he took it straight off his back and it was mine."

Hunter invited his new girlfriend, Trudi Liguori to the recording session on Long Island. Ian had first met Trudi in December 1970 in England, where she had dated friend of Mott and fellow-Herefordian Richard Weaver during her stay.

> **IH:** "I'd met Trudi in London and then again in New York. She was going to St John's University and working as a waitress in Greenwich Village at night, to pay for it. I was going out with several women and one of them was her mate. Trudi was horrified by this and thought I was a complete asshole. She didn't want to know and swore blind she'd never get involved with a musician. It took a little while to win Trudi, but I eventually laid it on her. I proposed to Trudi during the 'Midnight Lady' session... outside the gents bog."

Hunter harboured misgivings before Mott embarked on their second US trip and claimed that Atlantic Records did little in terms of promotion for their tour. Ian felt the band "came in through the back door and went out through the back door," as they lost 6,000 dollars, four gigs through Free splitting up and two shows that were stopped by the police before they played.

Mott's second Island single was announced in the press as 'Road to Rome' – "written by Ian Hunter" – but was released as Hunter-Ralphs' 'Midnight Lady' on 11th June in a picture sleeve. One reviewer remarked: "More an album group really, but they can also create a commercial touch without losing that powerful and authoritative style. A hit I'd say – possibly a sizeable one." Ray Fox-Cumming described 'Midnight Lady' as a straight chunk of instant rock and noted: "Rough 'n' ready and full of guts this record drives with all the ferocity of a Force-9 gale. Very live in its overall performance it has a lot of urgency so a few airplays and full support from their fans should be enough to push it up the singles chart."

Released in Europe but not America, 'Midnight Lady' was backed with 'The Debt'. Described by Watts as "puny and miserable", Griffin regaled how the band often laughed about the track because it was never a dynamic number and on vinyl the surface noise almost drowned out the song. Vastly underrated, 'The Debt' was one of Hunter's finest compositions. "I remember doing 'The Debt' at Island," says Allen, "and Chris Blackwell came in and said, 'That's a good title. Yes. There is a bit of a debt building up now.' So, we said, 'We're having strings put on the next album, Chris.' And he replied, 'Yeah, there'll be an even bigger debt then. Don't go over the top lads!'"

Ian commented at the time of the 'Midnight Lady' release that if the single charted, Mott would make another album. If it failed, they planned to record another single, the band's aim being "quality single success" like The Rolling Stones and The Who. Mott the Hoople received adverse reaction to 'Midnight Lady' however, from Radio One DJ Tony Blackburn, who branded the band conceited. Ian responded with humour during several concerts when they played 'Midnight Lady', telling audiences,

"Tony Blackburn says he'll hang himself if our new single is a hit... and I wanna be a fuckin' witness!" Ironically, Blackburn would soon select a Mott single as his 'Record of the Week'.

Initial sales of 'Midnight Lady' were so promising that Mott the Hoople made their first appearance on BBC TV's *Top of the Pops*. The programme was Britain's only national "singles-orientated" chart television show at the time and was watched every Thursday evening by some 15 million viewers. In a world of satellite and cable TV, it is now hard to believe that early Seventies Britain had only three channels and two music shows – *Top of the Pops* on BBC One, and *The Old Grey Whistle Test*, an album-orientated rock programme on BBC Two. Filming 'Midnight Lady' on 21st July, Dale recalled that the day after the TV programme aired, Mott's single stopped selling: a mammoth feat that he deemed fit for inclusion in *The Guinness Book of Records*. Due to the BBC's policy of deleting most programmes, the majority of the first decade's *Top of the Pops* broadcasts were lost, including the only live appearance by The Beatles. Of around 500 episodes from 1964 to 1973, only twenty complete shows are archived. Mott's 'Midnight Lady' film was wiped.

Mott the Hoople also recorded further BBC sessions in 1971. In April they had filmed 'Whisky Women' and 'Original Mixed-Up Kid' for *Disco 2* but the show was not transmitted. On 6th July they recorded 'Midnight Lady', 'Like a Rolling Stone' and 'Angel of Eighth Avenue' for John Peel's *Top Gear* radio show. This session is highly notable because whilst Ian originally auditioned for Mott with the Dylan song, they never committed an entire take to tape anywhere else.

The band had been rehearsing Dylan's classic especially for an 8th July appearance at The Royal Albert Hall, a gig that had been earmarked for 16th June, until Mott toured America. The 8,000-seater Royal Albert Hall remains best known for holding London's annual Proms concerts, but Mott's gig there became another landmark in Hoople history when their performance caused scenes that one reviewer compared to Beatlemania. Overzealous fans were blamed for damage to several seats and boxes at the venue, and future rock concerts were cancelled indefinitely at the Albert Hall as *Sounds* ran the front-page headline: 'MOTT BANNED – RAH CRACKS UP'.

In the lead-up to Mott's appearance, Marion Herrod, the Secretary and Lettings Manager of the RAH had written to Johnny Glover at Island on 6th April 1971 saying she was alarmed to hear on radio a description of the group Mott the Hoople... "as being one at whose concerts the audience habitually participate and one which often causes a riot." Glover replied to Herrod noting that the radio report was greatly exaggerated as "Mott the Hoople usually get very good receptions at all their concerts and as far as we know there have never been any riots or damage caused to any of the places where they have appeared." On 9th July, Herrod wrote to Glover again, protesting that... "in spite of your assurances, that there would be no trouble at last night's Mott the Hoople concert, some members of the audience in the second-tier boxes became so enthusiastic and jumped and stamped around so much that the ceilings in two boxes in the Grand Tier fell in. It is for reasons like this that we here do not like concerts at which the audience stamps and dances."

Increasingly, Mott was accused of "wreaking havoc" on British concert venues in the light of the Albert Hall damage. "Apparently a crack appeared in one of the balconies above the press which was just right," recalls Verden Allen, "and we had a nice bill and every venue wanted us then!" The band was denied a December re-booking at The Royal Albert Hall and was presented with an account for damages amounting to £1,467 – but Hunter was suspicious that Mott's payment was a contribution to the venue's restoration fund.

IH: "It was expensive publicity being banned and we couldn't afford it. A few boxes got broken and that cost us in the end. It wasn't violent at that gig and we weren't encouraging it, but we didn't get paid and then got banned there – and elsewhere. As far as I know, Mott the Hoople is still banned from The Royal Albert Hall."

Miller Anderson joined Mott for their Royal Albert Hall finale after Hunter brought his friend on stage to sing 'Keep A-Knockin'. "Ian's parents were there that night," says Miller, "and I remember he had a funny relationship with his dad who was a military man and was *very* strict. He never had much good to say about Ian. Coming off stage, his dad should have been so proud of him, but all he could say was, 'Just as well they had you up there, Miller – they needed a good singer.' I thought that was a terrible thing to say. I think that was part of the reason that Ian was able to write such good songs, because he had experience and angst behind him."

Mott's "big gig" and return to London after a long American trek had been highly anticipated but whilst the live reviews were favourable, the band sounded flatter than normal and gave a somewhat lifeless performance, while legend has them virtually demolishing London's iconic venue. One music paper proclaimed, 'THIS GROUP MEANS T-R-O-U-B-L-E' and Mott the Hoople was soon banned from gigs at Cheltenham Town Hall, Brighton Dome and Nottingham Albert Hall. A plan was hatched with Tony Brainsby and the group announced that rather than miss out on live dates at British concert venues, they would hire a 2,000-capacity mobile fibreglass theatre called The Caraivari, which would be erected on village greens enabling Mott to play. The spoof was fun and widely believed, and the NME reported: 'More Bans on Hoople, so Mott Buys Mobile Theatre'. But the publicity was something that the band could have done without, not least because some venues where they played reacted adversely and it cost the group financially.

IH: "We were banned from several venues in England after The Royal Albert Hall went down. I'm sure the building was up for renovation anyway but whilst our riot looked good in the press and was very romantic, it wasn't good for Mott.

Our 'lot' just wanted a good time and it was just a fun 'riot' at the Albert Hall. God, we even played badly that night! It wasn't dangerous because they loved us, and we always seemed to have it in control. Some nights we had more people on stage than we had in the audience but there was no problem. They worshipped us. It was more dangerous sometimes when you came out the back door after a gig and tried to get in the bus. The worrying bit was after The Royal Albert Hall when they brought dogs into the halls at some venues. Newcastle was always one of Mott's favourites and I remember a show there when Alsatian dogs appeared on stage. The dogs were scared, and I think that was the stupidest thing I ever saw a ballroom manager do. The kids were wild in Newcastle. They'd have the tour bus two feet from the stage entrance door and they'd still get you – shades smashed, hair pulled, clothes ripped. We did get booed off in Newcastle once though when Buff turned up legless – not a pretty sight or sound – the good old days!"

Mott's audiences were always receptive and enthusiastic. Scottish novelist and playwright Irvine Welsh, later famed for *Trainspotting*, recalled seeing the band at Edinburgh's Leith Theatre, describing the concert as, "A crazy, mental, mad gig." Some fervent fans were so loyally committed that legions of supporters formed, travelling UK-wide to see Mott the Hoople play. Early followers included Kelvin Blacklock, who later joined The Tuff Darts, and future Clash guitarist Mick Jones, a "skinny teen" and one of the "lieutenants" from the "Mott Lott". Jones described Mott the Hoople as the kindest, most welcoming group around and an underground band that was very connected to their strong, hard core following.

"Stan Tippins used to let us in to gigs sometimes," remembers Mick Jones. "That was a revelation to be treated like that. Their kindness stuck in my mind. I really admired the songwriting aspect of Mott. It struck me they were regular guys and we just got lucky with this band. I always admired Guy Stevens too. He was a great mover and shaker and an influential DJ who turned people on to things. Guy was always going on about Jerry Lee Lewis. I remember at early Mott gigs you'd see him come in, in a flurry of mad hair. We used to follow them slavishly – Tunbridge Wells, Welwyn Garden City, Liverpool – and we used to bunk the trains. We had a friend whose dad worked on the railway and he had a pass card that we used to hand round. We'd hide in the train toilets, then, just before the destination, as the train slowed down, we'd jump off. We'd sleep on town hall steps and bunk back the next day too. It was a fantastic education."

> **IH:** "I recall Mick Jones from the early days because he always dressed well. Mick was a fanatic at sixteen but grew out of it. He used to hang out in Mott days with guys like Kelvin Blacklock. They were a little rogue-ish, but nice lads. They felt that we were 'theirs' and that we belonged to them. We'd let our real fans leap up and sing on stage. I don't know what caused the frenzy. These legions formed and grew, then we had lieutenants with maybe thirty guys and the legions grew into an army. We had a great loyalty thing and I have had that through my solo career. Still to this day the people who follow me are fanatical and loyal, and I am very grateful for it."

In 1971, Mott were approached by Leslie West with an offer to produce, co-write and play gigs following Mountain's split. Even though Mott believed Leslie to be the best guitarist in America at the time, they agreed they had started as Mott the Hoople and that was how they they would finish. Ian used the West rumour as an opportunity to put people straight on Mott versus Grand Funk comparisons which had appeared in the British press. "If we were some potty little band trying to get banned and some cheap publicity as the next Grand Funk Railroad," said Ian, "why would a musician of Leslie West's calibre and status want to work with us?"

"Ralphs and I did a recording of 'Sail On' with Free and Mountain, and Leslie played lead all over it," said Watts. "He never gave Mick a lead-break, so he was just hanging around on rhythm. I don't think we'd have had Leslie West in Mott. We loved his playing, but Ralpher was our guitarist."

Mott played another live set at the BBC's Paris Theatre on 17th July for *The Rosko Show* and the session was broadcast in a week when they had no gigs – a rare occurrence. "This was live," said Dale Griffin, "real live, as it happened, with rioting skinheads in the audience and just a handful of dear old geriatric BBC commissionaires to keep order. They had no chance and Rosko was encouraging the brawling through his PA system."

Mott the Hoople had become one of Britain's most in-demand live acts: so much so that several more established groups refused to work with them. Now a natural on stage, Ian's witty, occasionally self-pitying remarks – including knocking the press and appealing to audiences not to upset their equipment as they couldn't afford any more – were embraced by fans. However, record sales remained weak and the group became increasingly concerned.

> **IH:** "They say on its night, Mott the Hoople was the best live band going – and Jagger said that he felt we would be the next ones up, which amazed me. But I knew if we didn't get a hit, we weren't going to be able to sustain this business of selling out everywhere. Somewhere down the line, people always want a record to hang on to – they want it on vinyl. So, I was beginning to really panic after *Wildlife*. I thought we'd had it. Island Records was pretty bland. I kept telling them we were Led Zeppelin – that we needed lots of hustle and push. They said, 'Alright, we'll do it,' but they never did. Then they said, 'You've got to do another album.' I had stuff and I didn't even want to record it, which was amazing to me, having wanted to record all my life. There just didn't seem to be any niche for us, yet we were one of the biggest concert acts in England. I guess people didn't

> like the records or they thought we were a live 'experience'. We were very honest live. It used to be a chaotic experience. We'd filled The Royal Albert Hall with no success whatsoever on record."

As Mott prepared to record a fourth album in August, Island decided to issue a third single. Guy Stevens had proposed that the band cover Crazy Horse's ode to West Coast drug culture, '(Come on Baby Let's Go) Downtown'. Stevens had "raved" about the song as soon as it appeared on the band's stunning eponymous debut album. 'Downtown' was written by Neil Young and Danny Whitten. Young would document Whitten's slide into heroin addiction via 'The Needle and the Damage Done' on his 1972 album *Harvest*, before Danny died from a drug overdose later that year. During their Island session, by "Take 17", Mott was still debating the most appropriate tempo for the song and Watts was never convinced by their recording. "'Downtown' was great by Crazy Horse," said Pete. "God knows what went wrong when we got hold of it. Definitely one of our worst efforts – I blame Muff Winwood – or anybody else!" Ian did not feel inclined to sing the Crazy Horse cover, so Ralphs delivered the lead vocal. "We were desperately trying to get a hit," confessed Mick, "but it was an ordinary cover of an ordinary song."

Verden Allen recalls: "Guy came in one day with the *Crazy Horse* album and said, 'Look, I think you ought to do this track as a single.' There's a good video of that filmed in the Basing Street Studios, but that single was mushy, and Ian wouldn't sing it for a start. It wasn't his cup of tea. It didn't really suit him – so Mick sang it."

'Downtown' had been taped along with Hunter's 'The Debt' on 21st April 1971, but Mott's Crazy Horse cover was not issued as a UK single until September, with Ralphs' 'Home', from *Wildlife* as the B-side. Like 'Midnight Lady', 'Downtown' was not released in America but Mott made their first promotional performance video, filmed in Basing Street. Stressing that the band's 45 was nothing to do with the Tony Hatch-penned Petula Clark song, one

British reviewer said: "Mott has waited relatively patiently and now they've got their hit. It's a blatant aim at the commercial market which works."

Mott's 'Downtown' failed to chart, but the single and 'Original Mixed-Up Kid' from *Wildlife* (included on another Island sampler, *El Pea*) caught the attention of a future rock star. Sheffield-born Joe Elliott, who would find prominence fronting Def Leppard, became a life-long Hoople-Hunter follower via the budget compilation album and 'Downtown', when the latter was played as Radio Luxembourg's 'Record of the Week'.

Mott the Hoople next considered recording an interpretive album of cover versions – long before Bryan Ferry's *These Foolish Things* and David Bowie's *Pin Ups*. Inspired by complimentary remarks about their treatment of Sonny Bono, Doug Sahm and Melanie material, some of the potential covers included James Taylor's 'Fire and Rain', Tom Rush's 'Driving Wheel' and Dylan's 'Watching the River Flow' – the spirit and tempo of the latter having been re-vamped by Hunter as 'Where Do You All Come From'.

Mott the Hoople wanted to promote their lighter side. "We'd love to do *Wildlife* live," said Ian at the time. "We even considered doing it at the Albert Hall, using The London Symphony Orchestra. We could have done it and got good reviews, but how can you kick 3,000 kids in the teeth for the sake of four or five reviewers?" Mott tried to frame their live set to feature quieter songs, and whilst fans clung on to the faster, tougher numbers and the band's rock 'n' roll finale, Hunter always considered that two or three compositions on *Wildlife* remain amongst Mott's best tracks and his finest writing.

IH: "*Wildlife* was a bit of a rebellion against Guy Stevens. We all wanted to do a musical album instead of hurtling head long through the Guy wind tunnel. You also get bored musically, so you do a fast record and get bored again, then do a slow one. I just wrote quiet songs and slowly the *Wildlife* album took shape. It was a breather from the craziness of *Mad Shadows*."

Feeling trapped in a hinterland between *Mad Shadows'* schizophrenia and *Wildlife*'s melancholy, and with fans always craving their harder edge, the band decided to adopt their stage persona in the studio. Mott the Hoople would cut an aggressive, energy-laden album that would be ahead of its time.

Enter the Brain Caper Kids!

CHAPTER SEVEN

Bizarre Damage

You can actually hear The Sex Pistols loud and clear.

Returning to Island Studios in August 1971, Mott the Hoople's fourth album would be a further attempt to come to terms with their live-studio quandary. The original working title for their record was *AC/DC* because the group was schizoid with songs that were "half-fast" and "half-slow" – they even considered having a 'Rock Side' and a 'Slow Side' for the LP. The *AC/DC* idea was soon ditched however when the band became worried about possible sexual connotations; Mott's move was ironic, because under Guy Stevens' eventual influence, the project became *Brain Capers* – with bizarre influences behind the re-naming!

Mott had worked on new tracks during April, including 'Ill Wind Blowing', 'One of the Boys' and 'Where Do You All Come From', largely penned by Hunter, plus Mountain's 'Long Red' and Jerry Lee Lewis's 'It'll Be Me'. Ralphs had also written a very personal song, 'Til I'm Gone'. Ian and Pete regarded this as one of Mick's finest compositions and Hunter remembered coming back to the group flat one night to find a distraught Ralphs playing the piece on piano, in tears.

IH: "Mick wouldn't let 'Til I'm Gone' come out at the time. I campaigned for it, but the content and lyric were still very raw with Mick, so he wouldn't release it."

"'Til I'm Gone' was one of Mick's best songs,' said Watts. "It made me come over all unnecessary and run away and hide. I think the others were quite affected by it too. I really felt for Mick and his split from Nina. I'll never forget the night he did the vocal. It got right through to me. I loved doing 'It'll Be Me' live – it just pounded relentlessly on – until it stopped."

Mott the Hoople's new album was to be self-produced with engineers Howard Kilgour and John Burns in support, and the band set to work on 4th August – one of the sessions being captured by *Wildlife* photographer Brian Cooke, who would soon direct Roxy Music's first video, 'Re-Make/Re-Model'. Privately, however, Ian Hunter was disenchanted with writing and after some eight days of recording, Mott became frustrated with the tracks they had laid down.

Twenty-five years later, during a review of Island's archive, it transpired that Mott the Hoople had captured three fine tracks under their own steam: two blistering rockers titled 'Mental Train' and 'How Long?', and a gorgeous Hunter composition, 'The Journey'. Mott was a volatile vehicle and often on the verge of fracture, and yet there were times when they found genuine harmony. This was encapsulated in their original performance of 'The Journey' where the sensitive arrangement of Ian's song created a moving, attractive atmosphere. In 1971, the band was in a troubled state and felt that their attempt at self-production was not happening. In 1998, Dale Griffin reflected differently.

"The original take of 'The Journey', recorded before Guy ever got involved with the *Brain Capers* sessions is staggeringly beautiful," said Dale. "Over nine minutes long with an elegiac pace and overpowering majesty, the dynamics and build up executed by the ensemble is, to my mind, the best of Mott the Hoople ever captured on tape."

Mott's initial recordings were good, but they had stalled after taping only three songs, and so they decided to call on their mentor. "We'd recorded those three tracks, but we were probably having trouble getting anything else together," said Watts. "We were a bit stumped, so we made the decision to call Guy back. He wouldn't have kept anything that wasn't initiated by him. Like 'Growing Man Blues', which Buff found later. That was a good track that we never completed. We probably did it without Guy and he would have come in and said, 'That's no good, forget that and we'll start again. He liked to have his mark on things right from inception to completion."

"Mott wanted to get some of the Guy feel back, but technically better," admitted Ralphs. "We went back to Guy and said, 'Okay, we give in.' It was like plugging in the electricity again. We just roared."

Prior to the second set of sessions with Guy, the group played at the Weeley Festival of Progressive Music alongside T. Rex, The Faces, King Crimson and Status Quo; Mott's live set concluded with Hunter pushing his keyboard over, Griffin demolishing his drum kit and a raucous standing ovation. Mott also appeared at Hereford United's Edgar Street football ground on 30th August supported by German band Frupp, Heads Hands & Feet and Amazing Blondel. The gig was scheduled for the British Bank Holiday weekend, so there was concern that attendance figures for the event might be poor, but the inventive Stan Tippins rode to the rescue.

IH: "I remember the tickets for that Hereford gig weren't selling fast-enough, so Stan went around every local pub saying he'd heard that Mick Jagger was showing up. The attendance swelled. I also recall Ralphs' grandfather telling me that we had to go on 'at 6 o'clock sharp,' as he didn't want to be late for his dinner. He was ninety-five years old."

On 18th September, Mott the Hoople appeared at *Goodbye Summer*, a concert for famine-stricken Bangladesh held at The

Oval cricket ground in London. Ian recalled Guy Stevens watching an entire set by Atomic Rooster in silence and, at the end, saying, "Why?", before walking away. One commentator described Mott at The Oval as "more ballsy and glitzy" than the bands that preceded them – successfully paving the way for The Faces and The Who. Mott was witnessed that day by rock photographer, Ross Halfin: "A packed Oval cricket ground, on a very warm day in 1971. A curly-haired figure dressed in black tells the masses – 'Unless you get your arses up, we're not playing another note' – and a crowd of 30,000 all rise. It was a command tinged with arrogance. He then started playing an Iron Cross guitar – it was one of the most powerful of rock 'n' roll images. Hunter had a street swagger you warmed to – and slightly feared."

Mott the Hoople "reconvened" at Basing Street Studios to record *Brain Capers*, but the band was granted only five days of session time by Island Records. From Sunday 19th to Thursday 23rd September, at Studio One, Guy Stevens was tasked with producing the band's fourth album, but he astutely demanded £1,000 upfront, before he would work on the project.

> **IH:** "Guy was a smart bastard with money. We were selling out all the big venues in the land, but we had no record success. It seemed that Island Records was losing patience with us, so we got Guy and Andy Johns back and went in – and got out! We didn't have the guts to do *Brain Capers* and produce it ourselves. I was so down at that time that I didn't want to do my own songs – in fact, I didn't even want to write anymore. We went into studios with very few songs because we toured endlessly, and I never wrote on the road. Guy was also pissed off because we hadn't asked him to do the album originally. We'd been looking for him but hadn't been able to find him because he was off on another of his binges."

Verden recalls that he was despatched by Mott to find Guy as the band had effectively scuppered their relationship following the

'Thunderbuck Ram' mix argument. Allen found Stevens but spent two days and nights with him and engineer Andy Johns, whizzing round London clubs in Guy's Volkswagen Beetle. The party would continue in Island Studios.

Back on the team, Stevens "started from scratch" and scrapped Mott's recent studio work, applying his own stamp to an incendiary album. During the sessions Guy procured cases of wine, drove the band to distraction again, and insisted that they record live – "first takes" – with vocals over-dubbed later. The result would be a complete contrast to the measured and thoughtful *Wildlife*. *Brain Capers* possessed a last-gasp energy and captured Mott in wild and manic mood. The first few days achieved little in terms of actual recording however, and Stevens was absent from one session leaving Andy Johns in the pilot's seat. With a couple of songs attempted over the first few days and the clock running down, some "direct psychic injection" was needed. Stevens obliged, his enthusiasm emerging in an extreme way, as witnessed by recording engineer Richard Digby-Smith.

"I saw Guy and Andy enter the Island building. The door to the Basing Street reception flew open and in crashed Andy Johns and Guy Stevens wearing capes and Zorro masks. They ran around with enormous water pistols and created absolute mayhem."

IH: "Guy did come into Island dressed like a highwayman. I remember about half way through the *Brain Capers* sessions we had no more material. It was kind of like Pooh, Piglet, Kanga and Tigger. Guy was Tigger and said, 'I know what we have to do, we've got to set fire to the studio. This will inspire us to greater heights.' So, we set fire to the studio – fortunately, not the control room. While the fire was in progress, I felt bad about it and I thought it was bullshit too. I wasn't the leader of the band until something happened, then I *was* the leader of the band, so I said, 'Look, somebody's got to talk to Chris Blackwell about this.' Chris was upstairs in the penthouse flat and his studio's on fire. By this time in our career I didn't talk to Chris because he upset me once, but I had to talk to him about this. So, I said, 'Chris, your studio's on fire,' and he said, 'Are you talking about the control room or the actual studio itself?' It was the recording room that we were in, so I said, 'The studio itself.' Then, Blackwell said, 'Was it really necessary?' I said, 'Yeah,' and he replied, 'Fine'... and that was it! When I left it was still going on and I felt disgusted. I mean Guy was nuts and the band was nuts, but I never felt the madness that Guy felt. A few things happened in studios over the years. It was difficult then and with the best will in the world we couldn't get it the way we wanted. I think it was just frustration, so the studio got damaged. What can I say? We were young... and stupid."

At one point during recording, an Island employee had entered the studio to warn Guy that they were running over time. Stevens screamed that he didn't care about time when he was "creating" and freaked, wrecking chairs, throwing glasses of wine in random directions and setting off several smoke bombs. Surrounded by mania and under pressure, Mott recorded much of the album on their last day but came up with their most consistent LP to date. To some original fans, it remains Mott the Hoople's finest hour.

Island's Johnny Glover recalled the fall-out from the destructive session: "Guy had a plan for a manic album. Blackwell had a soft spot for him and let him into Basing Street Studios. I vividly remember walking in one morning and they'd finished the album and gone totally berserk. Guy always incited them in to being outrageous and the whole place was wrecked. The band had played the album back and gone wild. The whole thing was total lunacy."

"*Brain Capers* was all done fairly quickly," said Pete Watts. "On the last day Guy got us drunk out of our heads, we put the tracks down and then we smashed up the studio. Guy and Andy didn't do any 'proper recording'. They just got us to play a bit each and set the sound levels, said, 'Okay. Go!' and pressed 'Record'. Then they left the desk and chased each other round while we recorded.

They didn't touch the desk; it was just left running. We'd finish a song and they would say, 'Right. That's it. Next one,' and the tapes just kept rolling. Nothing was adjusted during the recordings. Andy didn't stop to ask if we wanted a bit more guitar or anything like that. I think I bust a string in the middle of one song and just carried on without it. In the end, we stopped, because Buffin collapsed and fell into his bass drum case, unconscious. We were all out of our heads completely. Guy ordered meals in the end and chefs were bringing these trolleys in. There were big steaks but no plates, so I threw something at this large studio wall clock to loosen it and I remember laughing at it as it swung there – then I ripped it down and ate my dinner out of the back of it – steak and salad! I was going out with a school teacher, Jenny Morgan, and I recall going to her Hampstead flat at five in the morning, drunk and yelling to be let in, still clutching the clock. I was told to go home."

"I remember a big pile of chairs got slung all over the place and some of them were sticking in the walls in Studio 1 upstairs," says Verden Allen. "Guy wanted to start something off, but it went further than he thought. When you walked into Island Records there were pictures of bands and album sleeves on the wall – Mott the Hoople, Blodwyn Pig, Quintessence – and they got destroyed, except Traffic, because that was Chris Blackwell's band. The mess and madness were not contrived. Guy had got us tanked up on wine. We never touched drugs, but we got drunk at that session – and when Buffin got drunk, he really got drunk!"

"Guy went out into the lobby and tore down all the framed album covers," said Watts. "He'd pick up something like King Crimson and smash it on the floor. 'Fucking King Crimson,' he'd be going. 'They're shit. Mott the Hoople's the biggest band in the world.' Chris Blackwell came in the next day and asked Guy what was going on. Guy said, 'We were recording, and it got a bit out of hand.' Blackwell enquired, 'Did you get any tracks done?' And Guy said, 'Yeah, five.' And Blackwell said, 'Well that's not too bad then.' I can see in a way why hardcore fans like *Brain Capers* because it is the most aggressive album – the most panic stricken."

Andy Johns described Guy's "furniture projection technique" as inspiring – and in *Spinal Tap* terminology, rated the studio energy level under Stevens as "eleven". Andy recalled how Guy had managed to get involved in the *Free Live!* LP, throwing more furniture around the dressing room and smashing items while Johns was recording the band. "Guy and I were very close," said Andy. "He was best man at my first wedding and the first real friend I made in the record business. He was sort of the titular producer. Guy was mad – very entertainingly – sometimes dangerously. He had no theory. He didn't know an E string from a teapot, but he really liked rock and roll music. Chris Blackwell liked him because he was this really bizarre fellow."

Brain Capers (featuring the Brain Caper Kids) comprised eight tracks: 'Death May Be Your Santa Claus', 'Your Own Backyard', 'Darkness, Darkness', 'The Journey', 'Sweet Angeline', 'Second Love', 'The Moon Upstairs' and 'The Wheel of the Quivering Meat Conception'. It referenced death, darkness, a farewell ode to dope and drink, screaming angels and nightmare rides – and where Mott's earlier production of 'The Journey' featured acoustic guitars, sensitive vocals and swirling Hammond, Stevens' psychotic approach captured absolute aggression and frustration, best exemplified by 'The Moon Upstairs'. The record's attack was energising and special. Guy Stevens was back on the block. Mott the Hoople was wrathing and rolling again!

'Death May Be Your Santa Claus' was Hunter-Allen's first joint composition, Verden providing the riff and chords, and Ian penning the words. The song was originally called 'How Long?' and there is no reference to 'death' or 'Santa Claus' in Hunter's lyrics, simply because Guy re-christened the track by plundering the compelling title from a shocking and controversial X-rated movie. Filmed near Rillington Place, and released *and* banned in 1969, *Death May Be Your Santa Claus* was a thirty-eight-minute underground, art-house movie that consisted of fragmented, disturbing scenes, including an Earth-Mother breast-feeding black and white children and a gang who castrated a passer-by, and ate what they cut off! The movie flew over the heads of many, but it was an exploration of racial and sexual issues from a black perspective using victimisation and fantasy scenes. The film's pseudo-soundtrack was provided by The Second Hand, an obscure progressive group who recorded an LP, *Death May Be Santa Your Claus* in 1971. The band complained that Mott the Hoople was listed as the writers of *their* title song, but there is no such credit and Mott was not referenced in the movie.

Guy Stevens embraced some strange and shocking inspirations, and *Death May Be Your Santa Claus* was no exception. Adrian Rifkin, a professor of art and visual culture provided a voice-over on parts of the movie. Believed lost until it was shown at a 2012 London event, *Blasphemy and Redemption*, Adrian referred to the making of the film as a trip and the castration segment as the ketchup scene: "The movie was an articulation of black subjectivity and the inner voice of a black film-maker in late-Sixties Britain. Someone said once that it should have been called *Pulling White Chicks* or *Dating Black Men*." Rifkin confirmed that the title of the movie came from producer Frankie Dymon, but that he never gave any explanation for the phrase. The source was undoubtedly the Reverend J.M. Gates, an American preacher who gave a sermon in the Twenties repeatedly using "Death May Be Your Santa Claus" as his theme; he also recorded songs entitled 'Death's Black Train is Comin' and 'Will the Coffin Be Your Santa Claus?'

> **IH: "I wrote the words to the original song, 'How Long?' – the 'Santa Claus' title was Guy's. He *was* into some *very* weird stuff. 'Death May Be Your Santa Claus' was an okay song. It sounds like a band track to me, where we all pitched in. We all used to come in with riffs from time to time. Mott was pretty democratic that way."**

Mott the Hoople included two side-by-side cover versions on *Brain Capers* – Dion DiMucci's autobiographical and redemptive drug confessional 'Your Own Backyard' and The Youngbloods' neglected classic 'Darkness, Darkness', from their 1969 album,

Elephant Mountain. Writer Jesse Colin Young described the initial inspiration for 'Darkness, Darkness' as an acid trip that had a frightening end, evoking images of a soldier trying to sleep in Vietnam. New Yorker Dion had fought addiction in the Sixties and 'Your Own Backyard', a 1970 Warner Brothers single, was his honest reflection on the drugs, the delusions and the decisions that turned him around after he found religion.

> **IH:** "'Your Own Backyard' was brought in by Guy and he made a very strong case for the band to do it on *Brain Capers*. That was Guy Stevens. He would come in and go completely bi-polar over a song and you would *have to* record it. There was *no* reasoning with him."

The suicidal fantasy of 'Darkness, Darkness' showcased Mick Ralphs and his lead vocal is possibly the best that he recorded with Mott. The band had performed The Youngbloods song in their live repertoire in 1969, however they took Jesse Colin Young's country-style cut and applied a new thrust. Album reviews commended Mott's approach to covers, one critic crediting them with the panache to re-interpret other writers' material with feeling and understanding, on a track that featured prominent guitar work from Mick. "I recall that I didn't think 'Darkness, Darkness' needed organ when we came to record it and that it would make a change for me to step aside," says Verden Allen. "Also, Mick didn't have a track of his own on *Brain Capers*, so I let him do guitar. It was a guitar song really."

Side One of *Brain Capers* closed with Hunter's 'The Journey', a sad, introspective but masterful nine-minute epic. The recording began as a ballad with Ian at piano but caught listeners with a tougher-sounding middle section, before falling back to the gentler central theme and concluding with a frantic crescendo. Hunter noted at the time that Mott's music had always been schizophrenic and that whilst he and Mick had written "reasonable numbers", their stage shows usually became explosive. Despite

210

its widescreen drama, Ian would make apologies for playing 'The Journey' live and Mott soon dropped the song from their set.

'The Journey' originated as a poem about Hornsey Lane Bridge, a cast-iron structure spanning Archway Road on Highgate Hill. One of North London's highest vantage points, with impressive views over the City, the location gained notoriety as a suicide bridge, passing over land rather than water. An inspiration for Nick Hornby's 2005 novel, *A Long Way Down*, one man contemplating suicide on the bridge was successfully talked down in 1969, by actor Peter Sellers, who lived nearby.

Ian had worked on 'The Journey' and the "man on a bridge called suicide" theme for a considerable period, and the song was really a milestone in his writing. One critic astutely remarked that 'The Journey' demonstrated that Hunter could become a major contributor to rock music and the track was a personal favourite of Verden, whose Al Kooper-style contribution on Hammond shone. "I remember I switched to an Acoustic amp to get a real rusty sound for *Brain Capers*," says Allen. "There are some nice little bits on 'The Journey'. As the record was done more-or-less live in the studio, you tended to play things automatically. I was proud of that one."

Opening Side Two of the LP, 'Sweet Angeline' was another strong Hunter "rocker", but the band's delivery was sloppy. *Rolling Stone* would later remark that Ian scored heavily with 'Sweet Angeline' – "the first of his great songs about rock and roll women". Originally titled 'Indian City Queen', it remained a favourite in concert sets for Mott and Hunter, but Ian was not happy with the *Brain Capers* recording. Dale even protested to Guy that he should let Mott the Hoople play it again – "properly" – before Stevens enforced his "first-take-is-good-enough" philosophy. Griffin was generally critical of the recording methods employed by Stevens and Johns for the *Brain Capers* sessions.

"It drove me crazy when Andy positioned a *big* microphone low over my drums that made it all but impossible to get from one side of the kit to the other or to lift the sticks up. There are a lot of clicked sticks, missed beats and even a breakdown because we did 'Sweet Angeline' totally pissed. Guy was leaping about, raving over the take that he said was 'the one', but when we listened to it again the next day, sober, it was diabolical. There's one point where it almost collapses because we all make a similar mistake at the same time – and the song all but stops, then re-starts and carries on. We said to Guy, 'We can't use that, that's awful, let's try it again,' but he refused point-blank so that was the take on record that we had to live with."

> **IH:** "*Brain Capers* almost has me in tears. It was done as a rush job. We did all the backing tracks live and then I added all the vocals. You can hear my voice getting progressively croakier. It really upset me, because I obviously wasn't doing the songs justice. 'Angeline', for example, was one of the best numbers I'd ever written, but the way it turned out makes it sound like nothing more than another average rocker."

'Second Love' was the first Verden Allen song recorded by Mott the Hoople and it was an intensely personal debut. Ian's lead vocal was used on *Brain Capers* and the track featured a guest appearance from Texan-born Rolling Stones session man Jim Price, on trumpet – a Stevens suggestion. The intimate nature of 'Second Love' and the original take with Verden's voice showed that the content was painful for the writer.

"My vocal take was terrible," admits Verden. "I couldn't get away with the emotion of that song. It was about religion, nothing to do with physical love. I was going out with this girl called Elaine Pampel and I thought the world of her. She was a Jewish girl and the 'second love' was religion. Her father was an orthodox Jew and he said it's either the family or him – emotional blackmail! She was torn between her love for her family and religion, and her love for me."

IH: "'Second Love' was Verden's first stab at songwriting and what a day we had with that! I couldn't say, 'Phally you're not up to this song. I've got to sing it' – but he was so intense about it, so finally Guy told him. Verden was always trying to get his songs in the band and legitimately so, since we hadn't had any success with our stuff."

Hunter-Ralphs collaborated for *Brain Capers'* most frantic track, 'The Moon Upstairs'. Originally titled 'Who's Cheating Who?', after a stage number that The Buddies played in the Sixties, Mick had written a country song in the vein of The Band's 'The Weight'. The original chorus included Ralphs' lyric, *"Red, red, wine and the moon upstairs, are gonna make a big fool out of me."* The song died but the planetary reference lived on. "Originally the song mentioned the lunar factor and red wine which both have the same effect – they make you go loopy," says Mick. "Rather than analysing it, it was just a way of making words hang together well. The moon upstairs sounds better than the moon in the sky. It meant nothing really."

Mott the Hoople's 'The Moon Upstairs' was a cyclone – a song ahead of its time – a new-wave premonition that would expose later Seventies 'punk' as an anarchic sound but with low-grade lyrical leanings. Hunter's words of defiance referenced a desperate individual and shone a light on a band at the end of their collective rope.

IH: "Something happened when Mott the Hoople played – we were loud, aggressive and desperate – so we started to write to that. 'The Moon Upstairs' made sense to me. I liked the line – *'We ain't bleedin' you, we're feedin' you, but you're too fuckin' slow'* – that still applies to this day. *Brain Capers*, to me, was five days of total chaos. I didn't think anything came out of it, but when I listened to it many years later, you can actually hear The Sex Pistols loud and clear. I'm quite chuffed about that. Guy just wanted manic excitement in the room. He'd start telling stories and they'd escalate until they were absurd. You'd be waiting, desperate to play music. It was like winding up elastic so by the time you eventually got to record, the whole band would be playing with a manic intensity. That's what Guy wanted – and it worked. 'The Moon Upstairs' exemplifies his and our desperation. *Brain Capers* was Mott the Hoople – flat out – with the bailiffs at the door!"

The coffin lid closed on *Brain Capers* with a chaotic two-minute fragment titled 'The Wheel of the Quivering Meat Conception'. On cover versions like 'Your Own Backyard', Mott demonstrated that they could shape other writers' material sensitively and place their own mark on it, but when Guy directed the band, he would invariably twist their music out of recognition. This was exemplified by the coda clipped from the climax of 'The Journey', illustrating how raw and frantic Hunter's composition had become once Stevens applied his influence. The ending sounded like a collective about to implode, Ian howling above the musical mayhem – *"This has been the Mott the Hoople Light Orchestra... we've been playing some goodies, and some newies, and some oldies, and some filthies, and some weirdies and some queeries... just for you..."* – before the album ended ablaze with confusion and a flurry of feedback. 'The Wheel of the Quivering Meat Conception' – essentially 'The Journey (Part Two)' – was listed on the LP as a Hunter-Stevens composition, but like 'Wrath and Wroll', it was another "royalty seam" for Guy. Dale Griffin, often at odds with the group, described Stevens' frenzied edits as "orchestrated lunacies" and felt the "songs" were justly credited to Guy.

Mott's mentor played the role of magpie twice, naming Hunter's song fragment with a line from American writer Jack Kerouac's *Mexico City Blues (242 Choruses)*. A poem comprising 242 stanzas, Guy 'lifted' the opening line – *"the wheel of the quivering meat conception"* – from the 211th Chorus to title Mott's track. Kerouac talked of escaping an endless cycle of suffering and attaining Nirvana where life ceases. His world of meat objects, on the wheel of reincarnation, painted life as a separate ego that is pained all the time. Kerouac had reflected on existence as he tried to shake off alcoholism and the theme struck a chord with Stevens. Ralphs thought Guy came up with titles simply to sound outrageous and to shock, but Griffin felt he was on a troubled road. "Guy was heading in a dangerous direction, breaking and smashing things," said Dale. "Mott was one of the things he was going to smash. He was having mental problems – very sad."

> **IH:** "There were a lot of ideas that were Guy's in the early days. You never knew where the hell they came from. He was *full* of it and was a fabulous guy but a bit of mess and not alright, by any means. We were living quite crazily at the time, especially Guy."

Having dropped *AC/DC* as a working title, *Bizarre Capers* and *Brain Damage* had been floated by Guy as ideas before they were spliced and combined; then, with *Brain Capers* confirmed as the album, Stevens' record cover concept was promptly credited to 'Bizarre Damage'. Guy's inspiration came from the "leather, fetish and fem-dom" photo magazine, *Bizarre Capers* and *Bizarre Sex Underground*, the UK title of Michael Leigh's celebrated novel, *The Velvet Underground*. The cover of Leigh's book depicted paraphilia paraphernalia including a black eye mask and Island Records promoted *Brain Capers* with a full-page music paper advertisement featuring the LP's inner sleeve and superimposed black boots, mask and whip from Leigh's paperback. Combining *Bizarre Capers* and *Velvet Underground* literature with the art movie *Death May Be Your Santa Claus*, Guy's lifestyle was weird and worrying.

As the melancholia of *Wildlife* had given way to searing rock, similarly the gatefold sleeve styling adorning the first three Mott LPs was now abandoned in favour of stark simplicity. *Brain Capers* was presented in a plain scarlet single cover with band name and album title in prominent white font, Diane Stevens remembering that her husband had taken inspiration from supermarket boxes and packaging of the period. Photo sessions for *Brain Capers* in various locations became predictably chaotic, so the band picture on the rear of the album sleeve was taken at Guy's flat by his friend Richard Polak, whose credits included stills for *The Rolling Stones Rock and Roll Circus* and Stanley Kubrick's *A Clockwork Orange*, as well as LP covers for Traffic and Free. "I knew Luther Grosvenor and Jim Capaldi quite well and I saw Guy Stevens at Island Records often," says Richard. "He was either manic or depressed and was a pretty crazy chap."

Initial UK copies of the *Brain Capers* LP included an inner sleeve featuring a photo collage of bomber planes and a free cut-out eye mask (termed the Zorro mask), while Atlantic Records pressings in America featured the jet-black eye-wear as an imprint on the front cover with the band's name repositioned along the top of the sleeve. Stevens dedicated the LP to one of his heroes, James Dean. Released on 19th November 1971 in Britain, the overall feel of *Brain Capers* was barely controlled, backs-to-the-wall chaos but it remains a crucial album, possessing a wonderful surliness and cynicism. Mott had become a live behemoth and taken their power and experience from stage to studio, even if Guy was not the best at recording the transfer.

Mott the Hoople was now a band on the brink and some of the *Brain Capers* tracks screamed with anger and ragged glory. Once described as "the great lost hard rock LP of all time", *Brain Capers* remains an important album that should have gained wider renown. Adored by die-hard fans, the record was also close to the band's heart, Buffin excepted. Dale later described it as "the pissed album" and "a pain in the arse", admitting that he had made so many mistakes during recording. Ralphs sat at the opposite end of the scale. "*Brain Capers* captured it all," enthused Mick. "We'd realised what we lacked when Guy wasn't around. *Brain Capers* is my favourite of all Mott the Hoople albums and the cover is brilliant."

At the end of 1971, the British album chart was spear-headed by John Lennon's *Imagine*, *Led Zeppelin IV* and T. Rex's *Electric*

Warrior. Sadly, the do-it-or-die *Brain Capers* did not register with the record-buying public and became the only Mott the Hoople album not to chart in the UK and America, even though Hunter would claim that it sold more than *Wildlife*.

Despite fluffed notes and clicked sticks, the press noted that *Brain Capers* was an enticing, energy-laden return for Mott, after the "lightness" of *Wildlife* and the "over-produced *Mad Shadows* set." Reviews of the band's latest offering were excellent, one British headline proclaiming, 'MOTT NEAR PERFECTION' and *Sounds* describing *Brain Capers* as a confident return to form. *Rolling Stone* wrote: "Mott the Hoople rocks as hard and raucous as could be, 'backsliding fearlessly' as it were, in their eternal quest for fame, fortune, 'whisky women' and the elusive 'wrath and wroll'. Can't accuse these Brain Caper kids of subtlety or innovation, but they sure do get it on."

A 2003 *Head Heritage* review reflected on Mott's Island swansong, mythologising Guy's bizarre antics and lack of discipline: "Once they're done, the studio piano's not only missing two front legs, but its innards are saturated with a crate of Stevens-directed ale, left whipped and belaboured in the confines of the blackened husk of what was once a studio. Even worse, he left the kettle to boil dry white hot in the studio canteen until the handle melted while he was busy climbing the walls driving everybody crazy with his unique methods of madness that ensured every last bit of rock 'n' roll was truly wrung out of his charges."

Mott had often echoed and fed their fans' personal fury and 'The Moon Upstairs' and 'Death May Be Your Santa Claus' harnessed the angst of a powerful group. The rip-roaring *Brain Capers* was edgy, explosive and possessed a raw strength that became a chapter in the primer for punk rock. Sex Pistol vocalist John Lydon, would form Public Image Ltd in 1978, screaming, *"Anger is an energy"* in his 1986 song, 'Rise'... a lyric expressing feelings about daily existence that was reminiscent of *Brain Capers*. Undoubtedly, Mott's Island farewell remains a neglected but influential classic and Hunter looks back on the album with affection.

IH: "I like *Brain Capers* now more than I did. I think it was an accurate personification of what Mott the Hoople really was. I was very surprised, because I never listened to it for many, many years and then the punks started talking about it. I did the vocals all in one go because Island weren't too flush with the money there. It's not like we were doing well. We were still failing miserably. By the time we reached *Brain Capers*, I hated Island Records. I hated every fucker. Me and Guy really didn't know where the fuck we were. There was real heavy shit going down, but it all seemed to contribute to that, so I guess it's alright."

After the *Brain Capers* sessions Mott played a European concert at La Taverne de l'Olympia in Paris on 29th September. Filmed for France's *Pop Deux (Pop 2)* television show, the band tear through 'Rock and Roll Queen', 'The Moon Upstairs', 'Walkin' with a Mountain' and 'Keep A-Knockin', with Hunter's infamous Maltese Cross guitar captured on celluloid.

IH: "Mott always hated the Olympia in Paris, which gave us an edge. I don't think the people understood us. They didn't have a clue what we were about. It wasn't their fault as French radio banned everything but Johnny Hallyday, who was a really good actor, but a lousy singer. I recall Stan Tippins throwing the DJ out of a first-floor window at Olympia."

As Mott toured Britain in October and November to promote *Brain Capers*, they managed to carve a gap in their schedule on 25th October to re-record three tracks from the album at Maida Vale Studio No.5. This was their fourth BBC session and 'The Journey', 'Darkness, Darkness' and 'The Moon Upstairs' were broadcast on Radio One's *Sounds of the Seventies* on 4th November to showcase the LP. The "live" studio version of 'The Moon Upstairs' featured an interesting treatment with Hunter's expletive in the final verse replaced by a sardonic cough. By the time *Brain Capers* was released, Mott was already two-thirds of the way through fourteen UK concert dates with Paul Rodgers' new band Peace as support. The tour opened in Sheffield on 7th October and ended in Wolverhampton on 29th November taking in the London Rainbow, Glasgow Green's Playhouse and Newcastle City Hall. Island produced an attractive fold-out programme for the shows featuring a Guy Stevens essay.

During the tour, Hunter considered inviting Rodgers into Mott the Hoople as a fully fledged group member in order that he might concentrate on songwriting, leaving Paul to take over as lead singer. Rodgers and Ralphs got to know each other well on the road and seeds were being sown for future collaboration. Hunter also thought of expanding Mott with a brass section and female singers for live work, much to Watts' annoyance.

"I just could not believe it," said Pete. "Ian wanted Paul to be the singer and Hunter would just play piano and do some backing vocals. I remember looking at Ian and thinking, 'What's the matter with you? Are you totally fucking mad or something?' I shouted at him, 'But YOU are the singer in Mott the Hoople. YOU are the singer!' Ian just replied, 'But he's the best singer in the world.' We had to assure him it didn't matter. These were the sort of ridiculous arguments we had in Mott. I never went for the 'best in the world mentality'. That's why Ian liked Leon Russell. All these people who are 'great musicians' – in the end, it doesn't really matter. The Beatles weren't the greatest individual musicians in the world but together they were. It was the sum of the five people in Mott the Hoople that counted."

In December 1971 Mott the Hoople embarked on a series of eleven European gigs as special guests to Grand Funk Railroad. Mott retained mixed views about Grand Funk and as they toured Denmark, Germany, France and Holland, the continent remained a drag for the roadies who watched a group of Cold War East German guards "taking the piss" out of them one day – "doing pop-star impressions using AK47 guns as guitars".

"On that tour we were down in Munich and had to drive north to Berlin, and cross over into East Germany at a place called Hoff," said Richie Anderson. "That was pretty horrific because they took away our passports and did nothing, leaving us freezing in the cold. We eventually sorted the documentation and moved along but it was dark and there were searchlights, machine guns, razor wire and concrete walls – and soldiers in grey coats with dogs. The images were horrible. When we crossed into West Berlin, they opened our truck and spotlight boxes – anything they could open, looking for people. The shock was when we got stopped behind a lorry loaded with Christmas trees and the soldiers were thrusting spikes into the foliage, checking for blood as they pulled the probes out. It was frightening. So much for the Democratic People's Republic!"

> **IH:** "Grand Funk was okay to tour with in the US, but they did a disappearing act on Mott in Europe. We only did a couple of gigs with them then, suddenly, they left. We thought we were going down a little too well, but I'm sure there was a much more mundane explanation for their pulling out."

Mott's fourth and final BBC *In Concert* was recorded on 30th December 1971 at London's Paris Theatre. Six tracks from the show first re-surfaced on a bootleg LP, *Sticky Fingers* and a CD, *Hoopling Furiously (Guy Stevens' Testament of Rock and Roll Part 1)* before the material received an official airing. In 1996, Windsong Records issued *Original Mixed-Up Kids*, the fifty-two-minute CD including Mott's five surviving BBC session tracks plus 'The Moon Upstairs', 'Whisky Women', 'Your Own Backyard', 'Darkness, Darkness', 'The Journey' and 'Death May Be Your Santa Claus' from The Paris Theatre show.

In the opening weeks of 1972, Mott continued to tour heavily but squeezed in more brief recording sessions at Island Studios with Muff Winwood acting as executive producer. Starting with 'Movin' On' on 24th January and ending with 'Black Scorpio' on the 27th, the band taped three tracks for an intended March single release to coincide with more planned live dates. 'Black Scorpio' and 'Ride on the Sun' would soon be re-recorded by Mott under a different title, but Mick's 'Movin' On', cataloguing the strains of touring and hinting at his fear of flying, was intended as the A-side. "I'd had 'Movin' On' for ages," says Ralphs. "It was about being on the road and was written in open tuning which is a good way to write rock songs, because it restricts you to basics and you can't go wandering off on to posh chords. The hardest song to write is a rock song that sounds simple, but different."

In 1971, Mott the Hoople had cut a ferocious album that would prove influential over time and they had built up a solid live following – but by early 1972, the band was burned out – and Island Records was worried. Frustrated by their failure to make a commercially successful recording, the 'Movin' On' single was shelved and Ralphs gifted his song to Island label-mates Hackensack instead. With low album sales, no hit single and the ever-mounting costs associated with touring, Mott was falling heavily into debt. The band felt misunderstood and unwanted by Island, and divisions had developed between the group, the label *and* Guy Stevens.

IH: "*Brain Capers* had been an accurate personification of what Mott actually was – more than *Mad Shadows* and *Wildlife*. The Stones and Dylan were used as the initial yardsticks for the band, but all Guy wanted was for Mott the Hoople to be Mott the Hoople – preferably the crazy version! We achieved that with *Brain Capers*, but we were on our last legs at Island and started to wonder if it was all worth it. Mott was making some money on the records, but we were losing money on tours when everybody thought we were making a fortune, selling out everywhere. I remember a piece of paper once, where we'd sold out The Fairfield Hall Croydon, but wound up owing 248 quid. We couldn't sell another ticket and we'd had a support band and light show – but you storm the place, then find out next day that you've lost money. It became very demoralising. We really

> wanted a good producer, but we couldn't go to Island and say, 'Get us Bill Szymczyk,' when they were losing money on us. The label didn't know what to do with us. I think they figured we were just another group, like Vinegar Joe."

Island supremo Chris Blackwell's roots were in jazz, the label's classy R&B singer Jess Roden describing Chris as a man besotted by the human voice. Against this backdrop, Ian reflected that Mott the Hoople had eagerly joined a signature-hungry Island Records in 1969 without any other label considerations, and that the band had probably been inappropriate for Blackwell's empire all along.

> **IH:** "We learned that Mott was really on the wrong record label. Ralphs had been sold on Island from the start, so we went with them, but we never approached anyone else and there was no queue wanting us. We were really a show-off band, while Island was very organic and had 'talent' like Free and Traffic. We just played rock 'n' roll, played our asses off, didn't know what we were doing – and it was great fun – at first. However, I don't think Mott the Hoople was Chris Blackwell's favourite band by any means. He liked great singers and the label was full of naturally talented people, but Mott wasn't great natural anything. We looked absurd to the rest of the Island bands, especially me. I was up against the cream of British singers, but I was like a cut-price Bob Dylan. Freddie Lee was probably right when he'd told me to forget about singing. While I do have a way with my voice, I was surrounded by people like Paul Rodgers at Island. Was I paranoid? Yeah! Did I think I was going to last? No!"

Ian suspected that Traffic's 1971 song, 'The Low Spark of High-Heeled Boys' and it's *"the percentage you're paying is too high-priced"* theme referenced Mott's situation: Steve Winwood claimed his lyric was directed generally at label executives and the nefarious side of the record business, but Ian felt the statement was closer to home.

> **IH:** "I asked Steve Winwood once at Media Sound Studios in New York if the song was about us and he smiled and was totally non-committal. I remember the day that Island died for me was when Blackwell came back from Nashville and he said he'd been working with Winwood in the studio, 'the way it should be done – 9 'til 5.' I nearly wept when he suggested we adopt that sort of approach. Chris was always very civil to us, but we were really Guy's baby. If it hadn't been for Guy, I'm sure Chris would have dropped us. Blackwell never understood our kind of music. Traffic drummer Jim Capaldi never got his head around Mott the Hoople either. He just didn't get it, but we got on fine and begged to differ."

"We weren't selling records at Island and they were concerned," says Ralphs. "Island thought we were a dead loss and we always felt like the runts of the litter – the outcast band. We were always very nice to people, got on with everybody, never made any money or had any hits and became a bit of a joke. We were always fun while all the other groups were very serious."

Mott had become despondent and although Hunter had some praise for Island, he believed the all-encompassing arrangement that the band had signed for agency, management, recording and publishing was agreed at a time when they were totally inexperienced. Island had various horses, but they seemed to own the track, the paddock – and the bookies too.

> **IH:** "It seemed impossible to make money. The money from records and gigs would go against each other – cross collateralisation – and, in addition, Guy Stevens took half of our royalties. I think we saw three and a half points out of seven, split between the five of us. We were certainly screwed but then again, who isn't in this business? On the

plus side, if Island hadn't taken us on, Mott the Hoople would never have happened. Years later we'd have been kicked out by the business after the first album but somehow Guy helped us to hang on, and Island stuck with us. I had no career plan at all because I thought it would all be over in a couple of years. That's why we signed stupid bits of paper. We thought it was time off and it would delay working back at the factory!

"At that time, I'd never been in a taxi cab, I'd never been in a Chinese restaurant and I'd never been represented by a lawyer. The cabs and the Chinese restaurants we could have done without, but the lawyer situation was quickly remedied. I had this deal where Island gave me fifty per cent of the writer's share and they kept 150 per cent. I always remember a couple of years after that, Lionel Conway at Island said, 'It's not right. We should be giving you more.' And I'm thinking Lionel's a wonderful guy as he gave me seventy-five per cent of my money and kept 125 per cent. At that meeting I said, 'You know Lionel, I'm paying maintenance now on my first wife and my two kids – I need some kind of guaranteed income. Can you give me twenty quid a week for three years and then I'll sign another three-year contract?' And Lionel said, 'Oh I'll get back to you on that.' They never did."

Mott the Hoople never agreed on the status of their finances. Hunter and Ralphs expressed the view that Mott's records lost money while Griffin claimed that their four albums were in profit by 1972. Watts was just permanently exasperated by "the money side of the business", believing the band made nothing from their recordings. Pete did accept though that whilst things tailed off horribly with Island in the end, the label had allowed Mott to carry on.

"After four albums, Island was starting to think, 'How much more are we going to plough into this group?' Our career was always very volatile, and they could see that Mott really could have broken up at any second. There were always rows and threats of people leaving. We weren't a nice diplomatic band like Traffic. We ended up in debt to Island and they called us into a meeting and said we'd have to cut back on our lighting and PA as we owed too much money. We said we wouldn't do it, as the group had always agreed if we didn't keep going upwards, then we'd split. There was no way we were going backwards live as all we'd really got was our following – that was our strength. We couldn't get back on our feet with Island from there on."

In early 1972, Ian Hunter had mentioned to a music journalist that Mott the Hoople was looking for songs and one day a box arrived at Island with a note suggesting that the enclosed tape may be of interest to the band. The package was from David Bowie – an ambitious singer-songwriter who had cut a 1969 hit single with 'Space Oddity' but had yet to have major album success – and the tape within contained a song entitled 'Suffragette City' that David had just recorded. Watts was aware of Bowie as Steve Hyams had turned him on to David's third LP, *The Man Who Sold the World*, but Mott didn't respond, and the spool lay dormant in the box, while the band continued touring.

On 10th February, Mott the Hoople played a concert at Glasgow's Kelvin Hall Arena to mark its re-opening after renovation. The 2,600-seater venue had been the location for a Kinks live LP and the first rock concert there was reputedly a 1964 Jerry Lee Lewis show. 'Hoople Star at New Rock Hall' wrote *Record Mirror* while the Island Agency back in London arranged yet another British tour for Hunter and the band: but this time, it was to be a tour with a difference – Mott the Hoople's Rock and Roll Circus. With the headlines, 'MOTT ROCK CIRCUS' (*NME*), 'Hoople Rock Circus in April' (*Record Mirror*) and 'Vaudeville Hoople' (*Sounds*), it was announced that the band would play fifteen shows in seventeen days supported by Island cohorts Hackensack, knife-throwers and English music hall comedian Max Wall.

Before their Circus tour Mott was booked to play two torturous live dates in Switzerland. From 23rd to 26th March, the band was despatched by the Island Agency to play the Swiss gigs travelling by train and boat for over eighteen hours each way. Mott only earned £250 a night for the shows and Island listed four of their touring party as R. Patterson, T. Allem, M. Ralph and S. Pippin. Island Artists Limited didn't even seem to know their artists!

On 24th March, Mott appeared at The Volkshaus (People's House) in Zurich and on the 25th at a strange venue in Bern called Jugendzentrum Gaskessel, scheduled innocently (or craftily) by the Island Agency as "Youth Centre, Berne." Group spirits were low, and crisis ensued in Bern after the band arrived to find they were expected to play at a surprising venue. Time was they would never have played such a show; they would certainly not have taken boats and trains from London on 23rd March through Dover, Calais and Ostend to perform only two European gigs, before crawling home on 26th March via Basle, Calais and Folkestone. The trip proved to be an exhausting, emotional and exasperating disaster.

Pete Watts recalled that Dale got drunk at the first show in Zurich, could hardly play and stepped forward wanting to sing all the lead vocals. "We were in a posh restaurant after the gig and Buff was still out of his brains," said Watts. "He tried to leave but the taxi driver refused to take him and some fans outside went mad at the driver, which resulted in a big punch up, while Buff was shuffled into the restaurant, where he passed out, semi-naked, in the toilets."

The next night Mott would play in the bastardised Bern Youth Centre, built inside two steel domed hemispheres that had once been the city's gas supply reservoir. Verden recalled the group's arrival with horror and it was inevitable that the strains in Mott would now come to a head, the final fracture occuring when Hunter and Griffin fought on the Gaskessel stage.

"I remember driving down a concrete road to that gig," says Verden. "When the band drew up to two horrible gas tanks we just thought, 'Fuckin' hell – this is the pits.' We played the gig, but the sound was awful, and the crowd was awful. I was wishing they'd put some bloody gas inside the tanks, to finally put us out of our misery."

IH: "Mott's problem was that we were touring all the time, playing to packed venues but then, when we went into the studio, we didn't know what the hell to do. We were too busy doing gigs in fuckin' gas holders! Our time was running out. Guy was off on another of his jaunts and Island, who were fed up with us, sent us off on two pointless gigs that were a woeful waste of time. We were knackered. We played in this Swiss gas tank, we had an argument on stage and we thought, 'Fuck it! We've had enough.' Island had been putting us in places we should never have been, so we split in Switzerland, which is not a very good place to play – I mean, the people are very, very nice but we were right at the bottom of the ladder, playing in a fucking metal gas holder. You can imagine the sound. It was a terrible gig and a truly horrible place to break up. We had a big row and didn't see the point anymore. I thought if this is fame, forget it. We genuinely felt that nobody wanted us, so we quit. I always remember how fucked off we were but what a big relief it was to split up. Coming back on the train the pressure was off. None of us did drugs but I remember somebody gave Buff a block of something in Switzerland, so we had a great time travelling home. Then, when we arrived back in London at Victoria station our wives and girlfriends were crying, which was odd as I thought they were all angling to split us up anyway. The band liked each other and were friends again, which we hadn't been for some time, but we did think that was the end of Mott the Hoople."

Mick Ralphs recalls: "In Switzerland we said, 'Is this really all there is to our lives? This is pretty sad. We don't seem to be getting to where we want to get. Why don't we go home and do something else?' Really, the problem was we didn't know how to write a hit record and we were just fed up with being unsuccessful. As bands always do, they point fingers at each other, but it wasn't really anything to do with us – we just couldn't get a hit for love nor money. We thought it was a shame, but a good idea just to stop. Somebody had the bright idea to split up, which was a relief at the time, but only for about five minutes."

"A number of things contributed to the split," admitted Watts. "I just thought, 'I can't go on like this.' It turned ugly. Everything we'd had turned horrible. So, we came off and I said, 'I've had it. I'm going.' We went back to the hotel and at breakfast next morning Ian said he was jacking it in as well. We all went to see John Wayne in *The Cowboys* at the local cinema in Bern, then decided to come back together and all got pissed on the train. It was an amazing journey because all the tension had gone. We had a laugh and were joking as to what we were going to do next. Ian was always on about digging holes in the road – that was always his dreaded terror. If anything went wrong, he used to say, 'I'll be digging holes in the road next week.' None of us knew what we were going to do but we didn't care."

"The Zurich and Bern dates were absolutely pointless. I don't know why we even bothered to go to Europe to be honest," offered Richie Anderson. "Nobody liked us there. It just seemed like a waste of time and they always seemed to be two years behind the times. In Britain, it was brilliant most nights and the kids just couldn't get enough of Mott. Because so many of those gigs were so good, you tended to notice how bad Europe was. It was a pain to travel there with all the customs and check points. You would have daft situations, like exiting Germany at midnight, but they wouldn't start letting you into Belgium until six next morning. So, you'd sit in the truck for five hours in the middle of winter and it did give you time to think how much you don't like Belgians.

Mott splitting up in Switzerland was no surprise to me. Things were always on a knife-edge with that lot!"

Mott's unrewarding Swiss concerts had been an unpleasant nadir, full of disappointment and disenchantment, but the episode would soon inspire one of Ian Hunter's greatest lyrics – 'Ballad of Mott the Hoople (26th March 1972, Zurich)'. In fact, the group played The Volkshaus in Zurich on 24th March and Bern Gaskessel on the 25th, so there was some poetic license in Hunter's writing. When Mott slunk out of Bern and headed for Basle by late night train on the 26th, all the frustrations seemed expunged and band relations became amiable. There had been Swiss snarling and the yoke had been removed from Mott's shoulders, but Verden remembers driving in London soon afterwards, almost in tears over their demise as the band had quit after so much hard work.

The final ballad of Mott had seemingly been sung and the band had come to a shuddering halt. Strangely, M. C. Escher, the restless genius whose 'Reptiles' artwork had adorned Mott the Hoople's first LP, died the following day, aged seventy-three, in his native Holland.

Following their Swiss nightmare, Mott decided to meet Chris Blackwell at Basing Street to explain their demise. The band thought that they would simply walk out the exit door, but Island had arranged another series of British concerts and suddenly, at the meeting, they were encouraged to play 'Mott the Hoople's Rock and Roll Circus'. Hunter would soon use the line, "the rock 'n' roll circus is in town" as a self-deprecating reflection on Mott the Hoople in a classic song.

"We got back and had to have a meeting with Chris Blackwell and went upstairs to his flat in the Island Records' building," says Verden Allen. "We sat down, and Chris said, 'How is it going boys?' We said, 'Alright.' And he said, 'Somebody said you're thinking of packing up.' 'Yes,' we said, 'we've had enough.' 'Well,' Chris said, 'I've got this tour arranged for you – The Rock and Roll Circus.' And I think Mick said, 'Oh, we don't want to do it. We've decided to pack it in.' 'Oh, I see,' said Chris. 'I've spent two to three thousand pounds on organising this for you. You don't have to do it, but I shall tell you now and I'll only tell you once,' he said. 'If you don't do this tour, I shall personally see to it, that not one of you will ever do anything again, ever, ever, in the music business. That's it!' So, we said, 'Oh well, perhaps we'll do it!' I was bloody happy that Chris said that because I didn't want to split. Why pack up after struggling so hard?"

"The Rock and Roll Circus tour was not of Blackwell's making," claimed Dale Griffin. "It was Hunter's idea I think, borrowed from the Rolling Stones' film. In fact, Ian was upset in front of Blackwell when forced to do it. I think he had thought he was free at last to pursue a solo career after Zurich and now he was being dragged back into Mott the Hoople again. I couldn't understand what all the fuss was about. I could not imagine anything better than being in Mott, 90 per cent of the time anyway. We had great fun together, on stage and off, for most of the time, and there was no group with which I would rather have been involved."

> **IH:** "We mis-read the situation, because I thought Island Records would be glad to get rid of us, but they'd booked another tour – Mott the Hoople's Rock and Roll Circus – with Max Wall and some circus acts. I thought I was finally going back to the factory, but it was also dawning on us that if we're not Mott the Hoople, then what are we? We're nothing! Anyway, Mott all loved Max, so I went to meet the great man. I remember flying out to the island of Jersey, where he lived, to persuade him to join us for the tour and we got on really well, so he agreed."

Whilst Mott would honour their Rock and Roll Circus tour dates for Island, Pete Watts still sensed death throes for the band. However, Bowie's 'Suffragette City' demo tape, sent before the Swiss debacle, was about to become a creative catalyst. Just as it seemed that Mott the Hoople might be referenced in the past tense, it would transpire that David was a secret admirer of the group – and *Brain Capers*.

Hunter would reject Bowie's opening play – but David would persevere.

CHAPTER EIGHT

Dandy at the Circus

Apparently, Brain Capers *had turned David on.*

Despite their fraught gigs and split in Switzerland, back in London Pete Watts listened to the 'Suffragette City' demo that David Bowie had sent to Island Records. "We'd received the tape at Island Studios one day, after the *Brain Capers* sessions," said Pete. "It was a seven-and-a-half-inch spool in a box, and I was knocked out because I'd bought *Hunky Dory* and seen him on stage and thought, 'Bloody hell, he's brilliant.'" Watts decided to let Hunter hear the tape but whilst Ian felt there was good movement and rhythm in Bowie's song, he considered it wasn't strong enough to give Mott the hit that they desperately needed. Ian felt Pete should politely decline David's gesture as he believed radio exposure was shut for the band following three failed Island singles. Hunter knew Mott the Hoople could only survive with a sure-fire hit song. Something special had to happen.

> **IH:** "After the horrors of Switzerland, Pete came around to my flat and played me this tape of 'Suffragette City'. It was very odd because Watts had been the first to quit

in Bern but now, he thought that we might record David's song. We'd read about Bowie in early 1972 and he wasn't a superstar yet. David had sent the tape to us weeks before with a note to the effect, 'A song for you to hear. Hope you'll ring sometime and tell me what you think.' 'Suffragette City' was okay. It was a decent song, but it wasn't a great one in my view, and we needed a *great* song. I'd been looking for a classic number like 'You Really Got Me'. 'Suffragette City' was a good tune and it rocked, but Mott the Hoople had a lot of good tunes and we rocked. 'Rock and Roll Queen', 'Midnight Lady' and 'Downtown' had all missed the charts and once you'd had a couple of shots without a hit, you needed a classic to open the door again. We were writing rockers like 'One of the Boys' and 'Walkin' with a Mountain', and I put 'Suffragette City' in a class with them. They were good songs, but they weren't great ones, so, I told Pete that David's idea wouldn't work for Mott the Hoople."

Watts decided to telephone Bowie to thank him for the tape reel, but he also hoped that he might need a bass player. Pete mentioned Mott's problems to David and with the rejection of 'Suffragette City' and the revelation of the band's break-up, an astounding chain reaction was triggered. Bowie decided to try and heal Mott the Hoople's wounds by offering them another song and one last attempt at singles success. "We got talking for an hour and I was telling him about the group and Island, and all the problems we'd had," said Watts. "Bowie had got our albums and seemed quite into the band. David said, 'You *can't* split up. Look, leave it with me for a while. I've got a great manager – he's the business.'"

Bowie had been searching for a niche since his semi-pro days in the Sixties, flirting with theatre and music. Born David Robert Jones on 8th January 1947 (Elvis Presley's birthday) his dad had been a promotions manager, so David met performers from an early age and, at school, had a go-ahead art teacher, Mr Owen Frampton, the father of future guitar virtuoso, Peter.

Educational reports had described David as an exhibitionist who was incapable of continuous effort, but friends termed him a thinker who was very driven. He moved briefly into a London advertising job as a junior visualiser and learned storyboard techniques, but Bowie loved music – obsessing over actor and singer Anthony Newley, admiring Lionel Bart and exploring the London jazz scene. At a tougher level, David adored The Pretty Things, The Who and the rebellious American rocker Little Richard who had so inspired Ian Hunter – and further influence flowed via Jacques Brel, Syd Barrett and Scott Walker. The boy who became Bowie possessed a creative mind and short-attention span, but he was studiously absorbing what he saw and heard, becoming a collector of personalities as he sought to differentiate himself. Merging music with fragments of drama and literature, David experimented with everything he could think of to achieve acceptance. Hunter would discover that Bowie was full of ideas and ambition, but astutely, Ian would characterise David as possessing huge curiosity.

In 1965, with his band The Lower Third, David was rejected by a BBC audition panel because he was deemed amateur-sounding and devoid of personality. An R&B singer, tenor saxophonist, beatnik, aspirational mod and Donovan-style folkie through the Sixties, to avoid confusion with Monkees vocalist Davy Jones, Brixton Dave took the surname Bowie from a school certificate glued inside a Rudyard Kipling book owned by his manager, Ken Pitt.

After working with mime artist Lindsay Kemp and a fey trio called Feathers, Bowie entered a vaguely Dylan-influenced acoustic period. There had been nine bands on his eight-year musical journey; he had adopted various guises and a theatrical vocal style and was mixed-up creatively, but following several failed groups and flopped single releases, suddenly David scored a Top 5 British hit in 1969 with 'Space Oddity', inspired by Kubrick's mind-bending sci-fi space movie, *2001: A Space Odyssey* and featuring his first fictitious figure, Major Tom. Fearing one-hit-wonder syndrome, Bowie formed The Hype who played The Roundhouse as an early glam band of costumed super-heroes. It was not the right incarnation, but suddenly David realised that he could use rock music as a conduit. He didn't envisage himself as a rock star anyway, rather a theatrical performer who could now employ rock 'n' roll as the vehicle for his material.

In the lead up to 1972 and his encounter with Mott, David had tried to find traction with a bizarre debut LP of quirky songs including the macabre child murderer soliloquy, 'Please, Mr Grave Digger', and the much-mocked 'The Laughing Gnome'. A second album, *David Bowie* (later re-titled *Space Oddity*), followed by *The Man Who Sold the World* and then the literate and abstract *Hunky Dory*, created cult interest but, initially, none of the records charted. David's Sixties trial-and-error period had resulted in several dead ends but, crucially, on *The Man Who Sold the World*, Bowie had started collaborating with guitarist Mick Ronson, an exceptional musician from Hull who became his most renowned sideman. David was smitten when he first heard Mick play, describing him as a guitarist who seemingly wrenched every note from his soul.

Ronson had introduced Bowie to fellow Hullensians, bassist Trevor Bolder and drummer Mick 'Woody' Woodmansey, for the recording of *Hunky Dory* and by early 1972 David had found clarity of mind; everything made sense in 1970 when he met Ronson and by 1971 Bowie became very serious about his writing, without diversification. Harder rock was the transport "medium" – while a hybrid of all the diverse elements and influences that he liked would be "the character".

Notably, as Bowie swooped on Mott the Hoople, his career had not yet left the launch-pad, but lift-off was imminent under the direction of a new mercurial management figure named Tony Defries. Bowie and Defries would *both* impact on Ian Hunter and Mott the Hoople.

Pronounced "de freeze", Tony had followed his brother Nicholas into the legal world, gaining entertainment and copyright experience at Martin Boston & Co, and he also acted as an agent representing photographers and fashion labels which led to his first music business connection. Like Bowie, Defries saw the importance of style, identity and image. He was viewed by many as an interesting and intelligent man, but Tony wasn't *from* the music industry. Defries encountered show business accountant Laurence Myers in 1970, who had been encouraged by Mike Leander to form an entertainment firm, Gem. Named using the initials of Laurence's accountancy practice, Goodman and Myers, Gem provided music services and represented Alan Price, Mike D'Abo and Gary Glitter. Defries worked for Gem and had learned that Bowie was looking for a new manager.

"I first met Tony when I made a legal recommendation to Mickie Most and proposed Martin Boston to help him out," says Laurence Myers. "They sent along Tony Defries, who was a lawyer's clerk. I well remember the first time I met Tony: he was wearing a Dickensian frock coat with checked trousers and I thought he was weird initially, but soon found out that he was *very* bright indeed. It wasn't long before I invited Tony to join Gem as an in-house lawyer and business affairs man. Tony came into my office one day with David Bowie. I'd heard 'Space Oddity' two years before and had met David at the Ivor Novello Awards and congratulated him on his fantastic record. Bowie was a very nice guy and Tony had absolute belief in David."

Defries convinced David that he was star material and imagined a world of stardom with Bowie at its heart. Referring to him as "the product", Tony wanted to turn Bowie into the new Elvis. Fame seemed to be a fascination for both men but, in practice, Defries shunned publicity and never gave a music interview, believing that mystery was a pre-requisite of super-stardom. He admired Presley's manager Colonel Tom Parker and was seemingly influenced by Allen Klein's toughness. "I was involved with Klein at one point," says Myers, "and he taught me so much about the music business. Tony met Allen and thought he was great, and I think that was part of the reason that Defries developed his management style. I remember when I encouraged Tony to do a publishing deal between Bowie and Chrysalis, Defries kept everybody waiting for two hours, arriving late, to exert control."

Tony Defries threw the music management manual aside signing Bowie to Gem and arranging a deal with Elvis's label, RCA Records. Advancing the money for recordings before licensing them to RCA, Defries shifted power away from the label and even bought back *The Man Who Sold the World* and *Space Oddity* from Mercury Records for re-issue on RCA.

Defries predicted that Bowie would be a star by 1972, would peak in music terms by 1975 and that he wanted to see David in feature films. Echoing the monolithically stamped Elvis and Dylan, Tony intended to make David an international success as BOWIE. Record producer Tony Visconti once described Defries' early reassurances to David that he was already a star, as syrup and honey to the singer's ears. A wary Visconti also told Bowie that he would stop working with him if he partnered with Defries, and he did, turning his attentions to Marc Bolan and T. Rex.

Hunky Dory had given Bowie some initial groundswell and the LP grew to become a career landmark, but David still hadn't nailed the blueprint for rock 'n' roll success. He decided to create a surrogate band to test his next project which would feature a fictitious alien rocker, Ziggy Stardust. Two rudimentary-sounding singles of Ziggy songs released as Arnold Corns had flopped, but Bowie believed the idea of a space-rock icon would work.

When David brought Mott the Hoople to Tony in April 1972, Defries was representing Bowie, Iggy Pop and Dana Gillespie but he still worked for Laurence Myers and Gem. David had joined Gem in August 1971 after which he signed with RCA Records in New York, where he encountered a bizarre new world. Bowie met Iggy Pop and Lou Reed, and experienced the city's underground counter-culture, drug world and gay establishments. He was transfixed by Andy Warhol's Factory Studio, Manhattan's hip hang-out for artists, drag queens and speed-freaks, and Andy's belief that people could be stars if they simply said they were. Enraptured by this oddly different canvas, David now loved the idea of blending Little Richard with Jacques Brel, backed by The Velvet Underground.

One of Gem's London employees was Nicky Graham, who had played in Decca band The End. Nicky joined Gem in 1971, and Defries had him booking a Bowie tour, on his first day. "With a phone and a diary, I did it all on pure intuition," recalls Nicky. "Tony was forthright and looked eccentric in his low-slung flared trousers, big belt buckle and fur coat, but he really pulled the best out of people." Then, in 1972, Laurence Myers decided to join forces with David Joseph's management business Toby, forming the Gem-Toby Organization. Myers sensed Tony's overriding belief that David would be the greatest-ever rock star, but he was concerned about Gem's accruing Bowie debt, so Myers and Defries did a deal.

Myers recalls: "I proposed that Tony take his stable away from Gem, including David, and I would take points on earnings and 5 per cent as a return for my investment in Bowie, at a time when management took perhaps twenty per cent. David's 'Gem debt' at this juncture was some £75,000, which was a lot of money then. We met and agreed that Tony would take David under his wing and I would eventually get my money back and payment of half a million pounds within five years. But Defries was smart – he sent me a cheque for half a million within eighteen months, before the money had been earned – and it was a very, very clever thing to do. He'd got rid of me, he had control, he had the rights and he sat as the interface between the world and David the diva. Defries took the kudos for making Bowie a star, but Bowie made Bowie a star while Tony perpetuated the myth. I'd seen David playing acoustically in Aylesbury a few years before and it was terrible, but as soon as he delivered his music as an actor, he was great."

Quitting Gem, Defries launched his own company, MainMan Limited. The term main-man was black American street slang for a drug dealer, but the definitions also included a close and trusted friend, an important person or a boss. Defries' new operation was constituted during June 1972 and in July it would be announced that MainMan, not Gem, represented David Bowie, Iggy Pop, Dana Gillespie and Mott the Hoople.

Defries considered that to be a star, you had to act like a star and MainMan created an image of success, funding the cause with record advances and the referral of bills to RCA. Having signed a Gem agreement in March 1972, Bowie then signed with MainMan. David believed he was a co-owner of the business who shared profits equally with his manager but, in practice, Tony was the main man.

As Mott and Bowie met, David had just completed recording sessions for the album that would bring him worldwide acclaim – *The Rise and Fall of Ziggy Stardust and the Spiders from Mars*. He had finally focused his storytelling with a staggering record centred on an alien who adopted human form, the concept allowing David to mix theatricality with a space fixation and orientation towards the apocalyptic. Shamelessly wielding androgyny, Bowie would find it so enticing to play the part in his mutation as a rock 'n' roll star – and David's rock 'n' roleplay was about to take the music world by storm.

Like Guy Stevens, David Bowie was a magpie who dropped influential resonances into his material and appropriated, even in the engineering of his alter ego. American outsider performer, The Legendary Stardust Cowboy, recorded cacophonous music but David chewed off part of the singer's name and combined it with a *Ziggy's* tailor shop sign, and a splash of Detroit rocker, Iggy Pop to generate Ziggy Stardust. Ziggy and the Spiders' bright lace-up boots and quilted jumpsuits were inspired by the droogs' dress in Stanley Kubrick's controversial dystopian film, *A Clockwork Orange* but Bowie employed "schmutter shop" material to present his "ready-for-action gang" in softer, florid fabrics. David had also been influenced by Robert Heinlein's *Stranger in a Strange Land*, a Sixties novel that told of a man from Mars who came to a post-Third World War earth, was feted as a messiah and was eventually killed by a mob: Heinlein had also written *The Man Who Sold the Moon* and *Starman Jones*. But Bowie's alien rock star, who would try to save planet earth, break up his band and commit rock 'n' roll suicide was largely based around the real C-list Fifties rocker,

Vince Taylor – an "LSD basket-case" whose real-life fall from grace underpinned the Stardust story.

David still considered himself as much a writer as a performer and with a degree of Tin Pan Alley mentality, he believed that placing songs with other acts would bring him exposure. He had composed 'Oh, You Pretty Things' with Leon Russell in mind, but it was recorded by ex-Herman's Hermit frontman Peter Noone; 'Life on Mars?' was offered to Barbra Streisand and David would later re-craft 'The Man Who Sold the World' with Lulu. Bowie wrote songs quickly because he became bored quickly, later admitting that in the early Seventies he tried to get anyone who would open their mouths to record his material. David had scripted the Ziggy drama and cast himself in the leading role but as he sought to re-boot his career with the fall to earth of his alien rocker, Bowie also opted to breathe new life into an extinct Mott the Hoople: *Ziggy Stardust* would bring David into music's mainstream, but the Mott connection would help his cause along the way.

Bowie intended to create his own super-hip clique and whilst he started with Mott, he would soon turn his attention to the resurrection of Lou Reed, who was happy to jump on the pop audience that Ziggy was sky-rocketing on. Ian often termed David a mover, and Bowie was astute, realising that affiliations with other artists of substance could increase his own popularity. David had charisma and artistry but was tapping into rock reality through Mott's commanding frontman. Mott the Hoople, Lou Reed and Iggy Pop also exposed Bowie to energetic wildness and some perceived that David admired Ian's stage presence, and that he was slightly scared of Hunter.

David had absorbed much and later admitted that he'd plundered high art and taken it down the street, creating a brand of rock 'n' roll theatre. He had been a secret admirer of Mott, Verden Allen later admitting that Bowie particularly enjoyed *Brain Capers* for its "edge" and "air of madness". But whilst Bowie was about to provide Mott with new blood, he would also gain knowledge from the band. Having rubbed shoulders with Hunter, a Rolling

Stones fan, David would record 'Let's Spend the Night Together' and write 'Watch that Man' within a few months of his Mott liaison. Hunter first "met" Bowie in 1972, although Ian had seen him play a few years before.

> **IH:** "I saw David Bowie live in the Sixties when he had his perm, did weird mime and played an acoustic guitar with a Revox. I didn't like what he was doing much. He was supposed to be a 'performance artist' then – that's what David was – but we didn't know what to make of him. The striking thing about it was, that he later came off as ultra-fey, but there was a mile-long queue to the dressing room after that acoustic gig – and it was all women. It was obvious he had something. Apparently, *Brain Capers* had turned David on. I never asked Bowie why he took such an interest in us but was told he saw Mott the Hoople as the only true punk band ever in England and I could see those sentiments but always thought the word punk was over-used. David knew Marc Bolan, but when I used to read Bolan saying that he was a street punk, I just laughed. I think Bowie saw real heart in Mott plus, for some obscure reason, he had this impression that we were heavy biker types. Seemingly, he thought I'd been the leader of a biker gang – and that didn't hurt!"

When Watts telephoned Bowie after Hunter rejected 'Suffragette City', David urged that Mott the Hoople should not quit and said that he would introduce the band to Tony Defries, who could mastermind a new record deal and provide fresh direction. Bowie phoned Watts back saying that he had an ideal song for Mott called 'All the Young Dudes' and that he wanted the group to hear it, meet Defries and record the song. Despite David's determination, Pete didn't know how Mott would react to recording again, but he agreed to meet anyway. Bowie and his wife Angie picked Watts up in an old Jaguar and David seemed nervous. Pete learned that Bowie was a fan of Mott's wildness and he "raved" about

Brain Capers. The trio went to an art exhibition in Park Lane that afternoon before meeting Tony for tea at the Inn on the Park. Defries seemed disinterested initially, but Bowie was positive and at Tony's Chelsea flat that evening, David played Pete some of 'All the Young Dudes' on a twelve-string acoustic guitar. Suddenly Defries spoke of extricating Mott from Island Records and pursuing a good contact at Columbia.

One of MainMan's acolytes was David Michael Rock, a journalist-photographer who had recently met Bowie at a Birmingham Town Hall gig. Mick sold photos to *Rolling Stone* and *Club International* and became house photographer for MainMan. He recalled being with David and learning of the song that Bowie said would save Mott. "I remember cabbing through Hyde Park with David one afternoon in the spring of 1972 on our way to Bowie's management office. He was full of that crusading zeal which would be a hallmark of his rush to stardom that summer. The subject was Mott the Hoople. Bowie had a song for Mott and he was very excited. 'You'll be the first to hear it,' said David. We were just passing Marble Arch as David sang the chorus to 'All the Young Dudes'. It's not often one gets to be present at the birth of an anthem."

An arrangement was made for Mott to meet Bowie in Gem's management offices at 252–260 Regent Street. It was here, on the top floor of Regent Arcade House, above Dr Scholl's shoe business, that Bowie had recently given a "coming out" quote to *Melody Maker* journalist Michael Watts – and it was here, at Gem, that an anxious David, in his one-piece blue-green Ziggy jump suit, first played 'All the Young Dudes' on acoustic guitar to Ian and the band.

> **IH:** "When Pete first rang David and mentioned that Mott had split, it turned out that Bowie was a fan of Mott the Hoople and he threw a minor wobbler saying, 'Oh you can't finish. Leave it with me.' We'd rejected 'Suffragette City' but David called Pete back and said he a song called 'All the Young Dudes'. The story goes that Bowie wrote 'Dudes'

especially for Mott the Hoople in two hours, but Mick Ronson told me later that he'd already done it for himself and wasn't happy with it. He'd had the track apparently, tried to record it and had put it to one side. I guess it was resurrected for Mott and I'm glad that Bowie did that. It felt amazing because 'Dudes' was clearly something special. You can do that thing on anything – it doesn't have to have all the bells and whistles that some songs need. There were also two immediate things that struck me – firstly that I could sing it well and secondly that I'd never been behind a hit before. When David finished playing it to us, there was a brief silence and then he said, 'I thought that might do the trick?' I said, 'Yeah, that's fuckin' great. Thanks, we'll do that one.' I knew that British radio would have to play 'All the Young Dudes' because *HIT* was written all over it. I felt a chill and thought, if we don't mess this up, it's a sure-fire cert, so how do we make it a monster? There was no way in hell that I'd have given 'Dudes' to Bowie. I couldn't work out why he was doing this for Mott. It's a fantastic feeling, knowing that your life is about to change."

Verden Allen remembers that all of Mott loved 'All the Young Dudes' instantly and Mick Ralphs recalls how Bowie asked the band to consider recording the song, even if they still insisted on breaking up afterwards. "After hearing David play 'Dudes', we thought, 'Bloody hell! This is what we've been looking for – for years,'" reflected Ralphs. "It was clearly the 'hit' that we hadn't had."

Re-ignited, Mott the Hoople agreed to record Bowie's song, but they had to fulfil Island's Rock and Roll Circus tour. The band's live schedule kicked off at Plymouth's Guildhall on 4th April and as well as Hackensack and Max Wall, their shows were to feature circus acts from Noel Day Agency including Silver Knives of La Vivas, juggling unicyclist Paul Fox and juggler Frank Paula. Barrie and Jackie Winship of La Vivas combined knife-throwing and whip skills with Apache dance in their show.

"We all rehearsed at a cinema before the tour and when Mott first played, we were deafened," says Barry Winship. "I remember we were sitting with the jugglers holding cue sheets, and we couldn't read them as our hands were shaking. Paul Fox and Ann didn't like the din at all, so at the break they said they were going out for a coffee but left, headed straight back to Blackpool and never came back."

Mott's main "circus" support was fall-about funny man, eccentric dancer and music hall mime artist, Max Wall. For years Max's absurd antics and battered appearance with scraggy wig, moth-eaten black tights and outsize boots had made audiences laugh but, pilloried by the media, he became virtually forgotten as variety theatre waned. Suddenly, following a *Guardian* newspaper interview, he was approached with a different proposition and the comic grabbed the strange invitation to tour Britain with "a pop band". Performing to young music fans would present a challenge for Max and at Newcastle, he walked on to booing but finished his set with a standing ovation, while in Glasgow and Liverpool the receptions were hostile. Wall was known to shout, "They told me you'd throw things if you liked me," as beer cans flew towards the stage from enraged audiences. Max once said that he "died like a louse in a tramp's beard" at the bigger venues Mott played, but he stuck it out.

> **IH:** "It was difficult for Max and we had to talk him out of leaving more than once. If our fans had shut up they would have been blown away. He was a comic genius but, to weave his magic, Wall used silence a lot. I told him, 'Tell them to shut the fuck up', but he was an old Vaudevillian and a gentleman. I also told him, 'Hang in there, Max – the further south you go the easier it will get.' Fortunately, the southern shows were quiet, and Max unleashed his unique brand of humour to devastating effect. I actually saw people fall out of their seats at Guildford Civic.
>
> "On the last night of the Circus tour the knife thrower had it all arranged that we'd have Stan Tippins against the board,

so the knives would be thrown at him. Stan, however, had other ideas and I found myself pinned and the knives hurled at me. I survived, but it was terrifying. Max would sit right in front of the speakers at our soundchecks. 'You and The Who,' he used to say, 'You and The Who.' He just loved the power and the energy. We kept in touch after the tour and later saw him in plays as he made his way as a serious actor. He was a brilliant man but, as always, there was a sad side. His eternal regret was that none of his kids would go near him and he was lonely. It happens a lot with gifted people. Max was a sad man, but I like to think we perked him up."

Mott loved Max Wall and he marvelled at the way the band worked, the efforts of their road crew and the sheer volume of equipment. Pete Watts described it as the nicest tour that Mott the Hoople ever played and, subsequently, Max received fresh publicity and returned to the Vaudeville Theatre in London's West End, reviving his fortunes in a revue called *Cockie!* Max wrote charmingly to Mott after their Circus tour: "I am lonely for you all! I miss the SOUND. I wish I could adopt you – can't afford it. I wish you all – collectively and individually – BEST of luck, plus a hit single. I loved the tour and the emotional cacophony. I hope you were not sending me up? LOVE. WALL."

Mott's Rock and Roll Circus set had featured three new songs – 'One of the Boys', 'Ballad of Mott the Hoople' and 'Until I'm Gone'; the group also played 'Mr Bugle Player' (a variation on Bob Dylan's 'Mr Tambourine Man') and The Rolling Stones' 'Honky Tonk Women'. As Tony Defries worked behind the scenes to extricate Mott from Island and place them with CBS, David Bowie attended the band's Circus gig at Guildford Civic Hall in Surrey. Also present that night was an important A&R figure from CBS Records – American Dan Loggins – an "Anglophile" who had seen most Sixties British bands in San Francisco. Dan would spend several years at CBS, was later employed at WEA and RCA Records, and was the older brother of Kenny Loggins who would find fame via the hits 'Your Mama Don't Dance' and 'Footloose'. Posted from CBS New York to CBS London in 1971, Dan described his seven years in the UK as the favourite time of his life because "the industry was still the *music* business."

"When I arrived in England my brief was to find British talent that could be successful for CBS in America, as the label was missing out on interesting UK acts. My first London assignment was to connect with Chris Wright at Chrysalis and, that afternoon, I was played an acetate by Bob Grace, David Bowie's publisher. The disc was *Hunky Dory* and I was blown away. I sent it to my CBS boss Clive Davis, but Columbia's A&R 'Ear' people in New York just couldn't 'get' David's music at that moment in time."

At Guildford, Dan stood with David at the back of the hall marvelling how the band was stronger live than they had been on record. Loggins felt Mott the Hoople had great presence and that they didn't really have a "British Bob Dylan" as some claimed, but a leader and focal point – with *the* look and *the* personality. "I witnessed rock 'n' roll with pacing and dynamics that night at Guildford," said Dan. "I saw Ralphs as a lead guitar hero in the making and the bass and drums were so tight after three years of continuous stage work. Mott played a great show but, for me, at that time British bands needed real front men and there he was – Ian Hunter – with solid star quality and IMAGE!"

Having missed Bowie, Dan was encouraging Clive Davis to call Tony Defries to "get into the Mott the Hoople situation", while David was "wooing" the band on their Circus tour, bombarding dressing rooms with flowers and telegrams. Tony 'Zee' Zanetta of MainMan once described Bowie as a real seducer, noting that David made you feel as if you were the only person who existed in the centre of *his* universe – but, at Mott's Guildford gig, Ian observed that Bowie was nervous.

IH: "I remember being backstage at the Guildford show. Defries was there with David and Angie, and they were at one end of this long dressing room, and we were up at the

other end, with a table in the middle, between us. We were changing stage clothes, which was a bit embarrassing, with nobody knowing quite what to do, so Pete sort of bridged the gap, and went and stood with them. I remember looking at Bowie in glossy red boots with red spiked hair, and he really did look other-worldly – like he *had* come from another planet. After the gig David took me, Trudi and Angie in a limo to a club. I sat in the back of the car, between Angie and David and she whispered to me that it had taken him four hours to get ready to see us and do his make-up. Later I discovered it only took Ronson an hour! Bowie was quite nervous around Mott for a while and was certainly trembling when he came to see us that night. Apparently, he was 'scared' of us. He thought I was the ace butch of all time for some reason and that we were very heavy, but really, we were just ordinary people who would get legitimately upset about things. On tour, David was courting us, sending big bouquets of flowers to our dressing room at every gig we played. That was his way of getting involved with us – and meanwhile the guys from Island were wondering, 'Hmmm, what's going on here?'"

Four days after the Guildford encounter a telegram arrived at Mott's Newcastle City Hall show, which read: "Dear Boys. How's it going? Tony is announcing to the music press sole responsibility for your recording, agency and management. Prepare for showdown with Island. No anxiety please. Defries guv'ner at this kind of thing! Studio booked at end of tour for purpose of recording smash single. Aren't your live reviews fabulous, Love, David and Angie."

Verden Allen recalls Tony Defries attending Mott's 19th April concert at London's Lyceum and by the time their tour concluded at Luton College of Education on 21st April, Defries had taken the band under his wing for David. Tony secured their departure from Island, persuading Chris Blackwell to release Mott from their recording contract in exchange for retention of their publishing.

Before he moved David away from Mercury to RCA Records, Defries had approached Columbia. Now, he reminded CBS that they had missed Bowie but could "have" Mott the Hoople, making an independent production deal for MainMan and Mott with Columbia Records in America, and CBS Records for Britain and Europe.

Tony Defries sold Mott to Columbia's Brooklyn-born label-chief, Clive Davis, who later admitted that he felt Ian and Mott the Hoople had a magnetic presence on stage and in their music. Defries' label choice was good, because by the end of 1972 Columbia would be "top dog" for LP and singles sales in America. CBS Records was the international arm of Columbia Broadcasting System and, like Island's eye-catching pop-pink identity, CBS sported strong orange record labels with their famous black "Walking Eye" logo. Their roster included Bob Dylan, Simon and Garfunkel and Barbra Streisand but Mott's move to CBS and their Island exit pleased Stan Tippins, who had not been a fan of Blackwell's organisation. "I didn't have fond memories of Island Records and didn't feel welcome there," says Stan. "I think they really lacked ambition for Mott the Hoople. Island seemed a bit small-time to me and it felt great when the band went to CBS."

Mott the Hoople was now part of a Columbia-Bowie-MainMan axis. Initially, Tony Defries handled MainMan's affairs with former Gem assistant Nicky Graham, from a duplex in Gunter Hall, near Chelsea's Kings Road, but Defries would move to MainMan Limited in New York. With an ethos of expansiveness, MainMan West in Los Angeles and a Connecticut property were added while limousines and books of gold-headed MainMan matches reflected stardom. Defries was focused most on magnifying Bowie, rationing press access, thereby increasing public interest and enhancing the mystique. Tony was a determined driving force behind the singer's rise but, to some, the slightly intimidating man with the crushed velvet suits, gigantic fur coat and large Havana cigars seemed to be a wannabe star as much as David.

Crucially, the additions to MainMan's stable were all solo artists apart from Mott the Hoople – the only band that MainMan ever tried to sign. The roster didn't matter, as David would always be Tony's key client. Defries believed that Bowie was potentially bigger than Dylan and convinced RCA to continue funding investment in his superstar.

MainMan Artistes in London was fronted by Hugh Attwooll, former drummer from Bill Wyman's Sixties proteges The End, who had been drafted in as "a complete novice" to look after David, Mott and "sundry others" under Defries. Attwooll was later an A&R man at CBS and Warners, and an affable consultant at Sony Music in the Nineties, but in April 1972 he had joined Gem, just before Defries created MainMan. Ian was grateful to David and Defries, but he harboured doubts about MainMan being a workable long-term arrangement for Mott and Attwooll was similarly astute, swiftly perceiving that Mott the Hoople was not right for MainMan – and that Defries was not right for the band.

"Tony was a highly intelligent, charming man," said Hugh Attwooll. "People took him to be a trained lawyer, but he wasn't, so Tony in turn liked people to be untrained individuals who would do something from a different and original perspective or, more cynically, people he could mould to his way of thinking.

"Defries wouldn't have understood remotely what Mott was about musically. He would understand there was something there, although he wouldn't know what it was, but it was probably convenient to add to the roster at the time, which included Dana Gillespie and dabblings with Iggy and the Stooges, and Lou Reed. But, as right as Defries was for Bowie, Mott were the wrong band for him because they didn't conform to something which could be moulded into something else. Mott was Mott and the very individual thing they were. Unfortunately, Defries didn't have any grand plan for the band. Mott was an amusing thing to have along with Bowie, but what wasn't so amusing was when they had to be paid. When Defries went to New York to set up an office, I was left in Fulham – part-tea boy, part-booker, part-Chief European Executive – running the London office when there was essentially no money to pay this huge entourage. I'd be calling Defries and he would magic up money to fund the cause, but *the cause* was to make Bowie a star."

> **IH:** "Defries didn't want to manage Mott the Hoople because he knew how big Bowie was going to be. David didn't know, but Tony did! Bowie persuaded Defries to manage us because David was keen and Defries did what Bowie wanted. David would fall in love with ideas, was interested in Mott and just had to have us. Tony wasn't that keen on Mott, but he was professional. His idol was Tom Parker and Defries did it the old-fashioned way. You had meetings once a week with Tony and he sat you round and was very much a manager. He told me at a meeting one day that he hated me talking on stage, I think because he wanted to give me that 'Bowie mystique'. Tony said to me, 'Every time you open your mouth, it drives me crazy. I wish you would not do this.' I said, 'I'm not David. I'm Ian.' But at the time I was going for it because I thought he was taking so much of an interest. Tony also saved me in America one night and got between me and a guy who was going to stab me, after I freaked out about things backstage and hadn't realised who I was talking to. But, Defries preferred David, who had star appeal."

Mick Ralphs described MainMan as a circle of "nice, interesting, arty-farty, different people" but felt that he never really knew their figurehead. "Defries was the first full-on travelling-with-the-artists type of manager," says Mick. "He was a bit of a blur with Mott because he was very, very much into Bowie and I really didn't get to know him to be truthful. He was a bit too showbiz for me." Whilst there was appreciation and fresh impetus surrounding Mott through the Bowie-MainMan connection, there was always reluctance from Ian to become formally attached to Defries. Mott the Hoople was suddenly described as a MainMan artist, but Hunter was cautious and although Defries circulated contracts amongst the group, Mott never signed any MainMan agreements.

IH: "I wouldn't let the band sign the MainMan contracts we had been given. I remember my wife being 'concerned', so I collected the papers, took them home to the flat and put them in the piano stool. Now and again Tony would say, 'Where's the contracts?' and I'd say somebody forgot. Mott was very grateful to Tony Defries, but we never signed anything with him. When David offered us 'All the Young Dudes' we were with Island and suddenly we're sitting on a song that we *know* is going to be a huge hit. Then, Lionel Conway took me and Trudi out to a French restaurant in Ladbroke Grove one day and offered me quarter of a million dollars to re-sign with Island Records. He could have had it months before for three thousand pounds, so I said, 'Lionel it's not enough'... and it wasn't."

Mott the Hoople's first CBS album, *All the Young Dudes*, was recorded at Trident Studios in Soho mostly through late June, but the 'Dudes' single and its B-side were cut earlier at a different location. The records were 'Produced for MainMan' by Bowie, the songs were 'Arranged' by David and Mott, and the session engineers included Dave Hentschel, who had aided George Harrison, Lindisfarne and Genesis, and Keith Harwood who later worked on Bowie's *Diamond Dogs* and various Stones and Zeppelin albums.

Mott the Hoople recorded 'All the Young Dudes' at Olympic Studio No.2 on 14th May 1972. Bowie provided backing vocals and rhythm guitar, while Gem's Nicky Graham and David's bodyguard Stuey George joined Mott on the studio's rear staircase, where the stone walls helped to create "great-sounding handclaps" that would snake through the choruses. Over two consecutive nights, Mott taped 'Dudes' plus Hunter-Ralphs' 'One of the Boys' that they had first attempted at Island in April 1971. There had been no time to rehearse Bowie's song, so David played it to Mott, and they played it back. 'All the Young Dudes' was a genius composition with a killer chorus that could not fail, but Mott took the track to levels that Bowie had been unable to reach.

IH: "We cut 'Dudes' and 'One of the Boys' in two six-hour sessions and that was going some, because the song was a monster. The first time Mott actually played 'Dudes' together was when we recorded it. Bowie had tried his own version previously but wasn't able to finish it, so once he was in the studio with Mott, he knew exactly what he wanted and worked his ass off for us. I think David became fed up with 'Dudes' but he loved 'One of the Boys'. I remember on the second night Bowie said, 'Maybe this is the single,' but I said, 'You must be fuckin' joking. What are you saying that for?' David said, 'Well, the back end of 'Dudes' goes on and on – it's so boring. It just goes around and around – nothing's happening.' So, the tail-end talk on 'Dudes' was suggested by me to appease Bowie who felt the song was flagging. Just when he was thinking the conclusion was sounding bland, I said, 'Let me try this' and I went out into the studio and did the spoken ending.

"A week before, I'd done this on stage rap to a kid who'd heckled me and the vocal 'jamming' on the end of 'Dudes' referred to the incident at that London show. Our fans could be strident, so we had what we called 'Heckler's ten seconds' at gigs. The odd nut in our crowd would sometimes shout – 'you suck' or 'fuck off' – so we'd get his mates to drag him down to the front and I would empty a bottle of beer over his head. I know it's daft, and you couldn't do it now, but that was then. So, this poor kid came down this night and I poured the beer over him. I remember being in the building – Imperial College as I recall – until four in the morning and he was still outside waiting for us when we came out, but it was all fine. I just did that on stage 'rap' again on the back-end of 'Dudes' at Olympic and the 'chat' and 'rant' made David enthused and happy.

"The 'Dudes' intro came about in the small room at Olympic. Ralphs did a few intros over the years that were instantly recognisable and memorable. David supplied the chord sequence at the beginning and all the harmony lines, and he spent time with Verden on the keyboards. He'd tried 'Dudes' in the lower key of C and we did it in D. We added to David's song in a few respects, but the B-side was more Mott the Hoople really. We'd been selling out every venue we played in Britain and a night at a Mott gig was like an army. We had lieutenants organising the troops and they always had an intense loyalty. It was a sense of all of us together – not just me – not just the band – a whole movement. 'One of the Boys' was Mott – that's what we were – but towards the end of the second day we knew that 'Dudes' would still be the A-side."

There were three notable aspects relating to Mott, David and his amazing song. Firstly, Mott the Hoople were improbable candidates for the Bowie seal-of-approval, his music publisher later suggesting that David made a mistake by giving the song away. Secondly, at the time of the 'Dudes' sessions, Bowie was not yet the starman he was about to become, and the *Ziggy Stardust* LP was not due out until June 1972, just before the release of Mott's single. Thirdly, Bowie's own version of 'All the Young Dudes', resurrected for his 1973 *Aladdin Sane* album, was a pale reflection of Mott's effort. Ralphs' opening guitar lines and Hunter's baiting *"come on"* one-way conversational vocals were crucial contributions that helped turn Bowie's song into an infectious classic. With its beautiful melody set against Allen's descending Hammond chorus chords, 'Dudes' grabbed listeners in a powerful way. Bowie wrote a brilliant song in 'All the Young Dudes' – but time has proven that Mott the Hoople will always own it.

"The recording of 'All the Young Dudes' was a different approach to working with Guy Stevens," says Verden Allen. "Bowie held us back in the studio and got the recording right in a controlled and commercial way. There was a buzz when we were recording it and producer Mickie Most turned up to see what was happening, so we knew something was afoot. At first, when Bowie mixed 'Dudes', the organ was extremely low. There was a guy seated in the corner – a top bloke at CBS. He could see I wasn't very happy and came over and asked David to mix it again with the organ track up."

Dan Loggins recalls visiting Gem's office where David and Angie played a rough mix of 'All the Young Dudes'. Bowie asked for an opinion and Loggins loved the vocal from Ian, who embraced the flavour of David's lyrics. As a single, it was a stunningly assembled recording: a grand opening intro, an attention-grabbing vocal and a hugely melodic sing-along chorus with words locked into the zeitgeist. Dan went straight back to the CBS offices on Theobalds Road and played the disc to his A&R team: people who were rock fans and knew Mott from earlier Island tours. "HIT" was written all over the record and Loggins' team pleaded: "Sign them, please!" Dan recalls that Defries was making his physical move from Gem into MainMan, but Tony sent a personal copy of 'Dudes' to Clive Davis. Columbia had craved British rock success and here was a chance to sign a classic band, with a classic song: 'All the Young Dudes', produced by David Bowie. Davis did not delay. Mott the Hoople was on CBS.

Mott's 'All the Young Dudes' recording was magnificent and magical, and it has often been classified as *the* definitive glam and gay anthem of the Seventies, the tag flowing from the reception to the song in America and a cross-dressing reference in Bowie's lyrics. In 1971, David had met Andy Warhol in Manhattan and was smitten by ex-Velvets star Lou Reed who often wrote of dark urban experiences and fascinating people. Bowie would soon produce Reed's sensational and risqué 'Walk on the Wild Side', a factual, lyrical portrait heralding Candy Darling, Holly Woodlawn and Jackie Curtis – some of Warhol's rag-tag crowd of sexual-changelings, speed-users and glamorous misfits from his New York art studio, The Factory. The blurred gender lines in David's 'All the Young Dudes' also referenced unique characters and some of his flamboyant acquaintances from 'The Sombrero', a predominantly gay disco on Kensington High Street, and a style laboratory for Bowie.

254

The Sombrero patrons included Kings Road fashion designer Freddie Burretti who became "the man who sewed the world", making several Ziggy costumes – but he had also been "the face" in Bowie's dry-run Ziggy band, Arnold Corns. Wendy Kirby was another of David's champagne-drinking entourage who described her posse of Sombrero chums as the young dudes – Freddie, panda-eyed Daniella Parmar and hairdresser Antonello Parqualli. The 'Som' dudes – a collective of outlandish personalities who shaved their eyebrows, changed their hair colour and let Bowie check out their wardrobes – helped to embellish the Ziggy landscape, and 'All the Young Dudes'.

David had encountered the 'Som' crowd and started a space concept in 1971, 'All the Young Dudes' evolving with other shelved songs including 'Only One Paper Left' and 'Blackhole Kids' for projects called *Shadowman*, then *Ziggy Stardust*. Bowie would later admit that his song was not a hymn to youth, as it possessed a darker edge and was linked to his apocalyptic space fantasy. Specifically, the 'All the Young Dudes' narrative echoed the news theme of Bowie's apocalyptic 'Five Years' from *Ziggy Stardust*, where it was announced that the world would end in that time period because of a lack of natural resources. The hopeless message revealed by the newsman in 'Five Years' was the same "news" carried by the "Boogaloo Dudes." Against the backdrop of the Cold War and prior to mid-Seventies detente fashioned by America and Russia, many considered, in 1972, that a five-year life-span for earth was entirely believable.

Generally, 'All the Young Dudes' was considered a Seventies rallying call for a glam generation – a new movement that was, in many respects, a re-cladding of Fifties rock 'n' roll embracing Little Richard's sounds and looks but enhanced with spangled excess. Glam was fronted by a UK powerbase of young teenyboppers who adored Marc Bolan, Sweet and Mud, while older "pretentions-towards-art" teenagers loved Bowie and Roxy Music. Mott the Hoople was more accurately "flash rock" like the Stones, while in the USA, the glam fad was tangential via The New York Dolls' "mock rock" – a term famously coined by British DJ, Bob Harris. 'All the Young Dudes' was brandished as a valiant anthem, while some even regarded the lyrics as a song about the joy of simply being cool.

It didn't matter if listeners perceived 'Dudes' as gay or glam, or if Bowie had imagined Mott as a gang of "droogs", because multiple meanings were fun. The lyrics carved a trench between the Sixties and Seventies; the song spoke of jaded hippies, revolution, The Beatles, the Stones, inner-city alienation, youth suicide, bisexuality, androgyny, T. Rex and even incorporated Cockney rhyming slang with the term "boat race" (face); the track mentioned Bowie's acquaintances Freddie and Wendy from the Sombrero; but it really referenced *Ziggy Stardust*'s sci-fi Armageddon where all the young dudes were the last generation, ecstatic in a finale of crime, clothes and sexual camaraderie. Bowie's writing was seldom about nostalgia in any case, rather the present – or even better, the future.

Like all great songs, the heart of 'All the Young Dudes' was the chorus – where, as Alice Cooper once remarked, every anthem breathes. 'Dudes' crystallised a new pop audience that had missed the Sixties, Bowie later suggesting that generations have to try and kill their elders and develop a new vocabulary by re-structuring the past. David's world was no longer retrospective Sixties hippie-dom. The Beatles had split. John F. Kennedy, Martin Luther King and Marilyn Monroe were gone. Jimi Hendrix, Jim Morrison and Janis Joplin were rock casualties. Bowie's canvas was clockwork orange coloured – a futuristic world.

Mott the Hoople and Ian Hunter had placed their stamp on a David Bowie song that would never be forgotten. Now they would cut an album that would be termed "the ultimate document of an era."

Mott The Hoople

island records ltd
basing street london w11

"Two Miles from Heaven"
Mott the Hoople Island Records promo card, 1969: (back) Buffin and Overend Watts;
(front) Verden Allen, Mick Ralphs and Ian Hunter

"Guy's proteges"
Verden Allen, Buffin, Mick Ralphs, Overend Watts, Ian Hunter, with Guy Stevens in the foreground,
17 September 1970

Carl Bruin/Mirrorpix/Getty Images

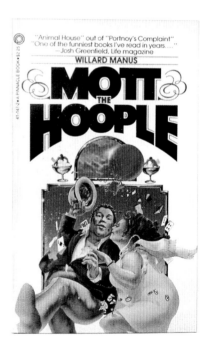

"It'll look good written down"
Mott the Hoople novel by Willard Manus: the original 1966 Secker & Warburg UK hardback
and the 1980 Pinnacle paperback

"The dreaded RMI piano"
Royal Albert Hall, 8 July 1971
Brian Cooke/Redferns/Getty Images

***Wildlife* album photo shoot, Carlton Bank, Cleveland Hills, 1971**
Buffin, Overend Watts (standing), Mick Ralphs (crouching), Ian Hunter and Verden Allen
Brian Cooke/Redferns/Getty Images

"The Maltese Cross"
Ian Hunter with "distinctive" Harvey Thomas guitar,
Rock at the Oval Festival, London, 18 September 1971
Michael Putland/Getty Images

"Mott at Island"
Basing Street session, 1971: Ian Hunter Mick Ralphs, Buffin, Overend Watts and Verden Allen
Alamy

"Mott at the BBC"
Ralphs, Hunter, Allen, Watts and Buffin, 1971
Chris Walter/WireImage/Getty Images

"Hey Dudes!"
Ian Hunter with Guild guitar on Mott's 'All the Young Dudes' American tour,
Auditorium Theater, Chicago, Illinois, 16 December 1972

"There's a star man..."
David and Angie Bowie at Trident Studios during Mott's
All the Young Dudes album sessions, June 1972

"Guiding Light"
Ian's wife, Trudi Liguori

Columbia Records *Dudes* promo card

**1972 Mott the Hoople
Seadivers membership card**

"Hot Mott"
Mott the Hoople Mark II CBS promo card from early 1973: Hunter, Buffin, Watts and Ralphs

CHAPTER NINE

Boogaloo Dudes

'All the Young Dudes' is a truly great
song – a classic – up there with 'Layla'.

By May 1972, Mott the Hoople were working informally through
manager Tony Defries with their recordings licensed to
Columbia USA as MainMan Productions. With their 'All the Young
Dudes' single and a B-side captured at Olympic, David Bowie
accompanied Mott to Trident Studios at St Anne's Court in Soho,
to supervise sessions for an album.

Squeezed into an alleyway off Wardour Street and formed only
four years earlier in a converted printing works, Trident sat on the
lower floors of a narrow six-storey building. It had been the first
eight-track recording facility in Europe and was *the* fashionable
studio at the time having welcomed The Beatles, John Lennon
and Elton John. A non-corporate experimental establishment, the
studio was a useful playground for engineers and producers such
as Ken Scott, Tony Visconti and Gus Dudgeon who helped put
Trident on the map.

Arranged on two storeys with a ground floor control room
overlooking the subterranean basement recording space, Harry

Nilsson termed Trident the most important singular studio in the world. Lou Reed was a confirmed admirer and Bowie regarded it as high-tech and so it was here, tucked away in a Soho alley, that Mott the Hoople would successfully evolve their breakthrough album.

Following the Olympic sessions, Bowie and Mott had celebrated completion of the 'Dudes' single at a party in London, then the band played seven concert dates with Fairport Convention in Sweden and Finland, from 17th to 24th May, before heading to Trident, with only one gig scheduled at Croydon Greyhound during June. Across some twenty sessions, Mott the Hoople re-vamped another two shelved Island tracks – 'Black Scorpio' and 'Ride on the Sun' – taped five more self-composed songs and, at Bowie's prompting, covered Lou Reed's 'Sweet Jane'. David was generous with his time for Mott and whilst Dale Griffin later voiced criticisms, the drummer noted that recording was a breeze for Bowie, who was great to work with.

> **IH:** "When we recorded 'Dudes' at Olympic, David said we should do an album and asked if we had more songs. He was a genuine fan who was writing morning, noon and night. I remember he came down to our rehearsals on the Kings Road one day to hear what we'd written. He had more songs for us, but he listened to what we had, liked what we'd written and thought we had enough material to make the album work. He heard 'Sucker' and said, 'Look, this stuff is great. We'll go with this. I don't see why I should have to write anything. You sound like you're writing great.' That was because when David came in there was a resurgence of energy. He could have given us a couple more of his songs, but he went flat-out with what we'd written."

David originally thought he would have to contribute more material but deemed Mott's songs their best ever, saying the band was riding on a wave of optimism after the apathy of their previous management and record label. In July 1972, Bowie would tell *NME* that Mott the Hoople had broken up for three days but that he caught them just in time and put them together again. He later described Mott as a macho and early laddish band, and lavishly claimed that he wrote 'All the Young Dudes' within an hour or so of reading about their imminent break-up in a music paper. David also "believed" that he got his management to phone Mott's people and offer the song and that when the plan worked, he was "flabbergasted" – vastly different versions of the real events.

People around Mott the Hoople at the time believed that David looked up to Ian with a degree of wonder. Bowie could manipulate image but apparently sought the same control over live audiences and a mastery that Mott's frontman possessed. Hunter described David as "the charming, disarming urchin from Brixton, who never misses a move or a point", but Ian appreciated that Bowie's efforts gave him renewed confidence and convinced Mott to persevere.

The band went along totally with what David wanted to do at Trident Studios and Bowie gave their album a commercial edge and laid-back feel. Mick Ronson would recall how David took a firm interest in Mott the Hoople and what they were doing, and soon the guitarist was visiting the studio during *Dudes* to "hang out" with Ian.

> IH: "It was great between Bowie, Ronson and Mott. We hit it off immediately and it just fell together quite naturally. Mott and the Spiders were in Trident at the same time at one point and I remember David rushing me in to listen to his next single, 'John, I'm Only Dancing'. He loved it, but I wasn't so sure, although I didn't say anything. The first time Ronson surfaced for me was with Bowie. I seemed to get on well with Mick from the start as we had the same background. Bowie could be very warm too but could change his colours. You'd go out to his place at Haddon Hall and David Bailey and Cat Stevens would be there, and he was charming the pants off them. David was analytical and wanted to make it

real bad. In those days he was on the make and was going all the way – no messing! Defries poured cash in all directions to fuel the illusion and make Bowie's stardom happen, but David *was* special. Bowie was one of few people who could walk into a room and there was magic in that room. He had a very inquisitive mind and you felt that he knew more than you, so you put yourself in his hands. That has never happened before or since with me.

"During the *Dudes* sessions David spent a lot of time on the keyboards and really knew what he wanted with us in the studio, but I think Mick knew more about the inner workings of the board. Ronson had been working with Tony Visconti for Bowie and had been watching Tony, so we found out that you could be a little more particular about how you did it than we'd been with Guy Stevens and all his incitement. Up until that point, we had treated recording like a live gig. We never really understood what a studio was about at Island, but we learned a lot from Mick and David. Bowie was generous, and his work rate was extraordinary. At Trident I recall Angie bringing in clothes for David to try on, daily. Angie was a lot of fun but uncontrollable. David and Trudi would compare make-up and it was strewn all over the floor. It was very much a gang affair – totally positive – no egos. I really enjoyed it. We were now hot, and Bowie was becoming meteoric, so, the confidence was high. I noticed that David was a great mover. He knew he had the gay thing sewn up, but Mick came from Hull and was thinking of his mum and dad and the reaction to all of this. There was some story that for an American tour they wanted Mick to announce he was gay, as the girls were paying more attention to him than Bowie. I don't know if that was true, but Ronson, who'd already suffered some embarrassment back in Hull, was supposed to have quit the Spiders briefly, when he was asked to go along with this."

Although Bowie-driven, the *All the Young Dudes* album would retain some of Mott's style and Hunter's influence, exemplified by the Stones-flavoured 'Jerkin' Crocus'. The album was also notable for another Mick Ralphs classic, 'Ready for Love' and Ian's emotional 'Sea Diver' featuring a moving orchestral score arranged by Mick Ronson. When *All the Young Dudes* was released, the consensus amongst press and fans was that Mott's album would not have reached such a high standard without Bowie. He had given the band renewed confidence and injected fresh enthusiasm and recording refinement into their music. At the time Ian praised David's production as *All the Young Dudes* was cleaner and clearer than the "muggy sound" on previous Mott albums. 'The Brain Caper Kids' were now 'The Dudes' and things were different, not least a slightly more sinister Mott appearance and a brighter recorded sound. Bowie's production style was once described as antiseptic and it was certainly based on dry, thin mixes and a studio touch that seemed to sacrifice power. Mott later admitted that David's tampering on 'Sucker' was a case in point and Bowie would subsequently confess that *Ziggy Stardust* was lightweight too.

> **IH:** "Mott listened and learned during the *Dudes* sessions. I remember when we first recorded the tracks that it was a much heavier album than the one that was released, as David's taste ran a little lighter than ours. 'Sucker' was particularly heavy, but David's production was mild and pop-orientated, and it was a weak album mix. There was talk of going back and re-mixing the masters when Sony Music released a box set years later but the multi-track tapes had magically disappeared. The *Dudes* album was also finished very quickly in the end because Bowie had to do other things. We were halfway there – and halfway where we'd been."

With 'All the Young Dudes' in the can during May, it looked as though Mott the Hoople's CBS release might be MainMan's first major single success so, while Bowie and the Spiders played town hall gigs, RCA Records issued 'Starman' from the forthcoming *Ziggy Stardust* album. Carrying melodic echoes of Judy Garland's 'Somewhere Over the Rainbow' and Glen Campbell's 'Wichita Lineman', the single eventually scraped into the UK chart at No.49 towards the end of June. Then, on 5th July, David and the Spiders filmed a TV performance for *Top of the Pops*. Aired the next day, as Bowie draped his arm around Ronson's shoulders during their mimed delivery, the provocative pose frightened parents, startled youth and burned a classic image into British rock history forever. The orange-haired creature with bright blue acoustic guitar and multi-coloured jumpsuit transfixed a nation. Ziggy had landed!

Ian realised that Mott the Hoople was finally on the ladder to commercial success too and though Mott deferred to Bowie in the studio, Hunter would not do so in a live setting. Mott the Hoople was lined up to support David on 8th July at London's Royal Festival Hall, but Ian had already sussed Bowie and declined to play second fiddle. On the night, David was supported by Lou Reed.

'All the Young Dudes' was issued by CBS on 28th July 1972, entering the British singles chart at No.22 on 12th August and riding high for eleven weeks. Bowie's 'Starman', released in April, eventually reached No.10 but Mott the Hoople soared to No.3. Ironically 'All the Young Dudes' was David's highest-charting composition at that point, Mott's single became an international Top Ten and *All the Young Dudes* was the band's biggest-selling album to date.

> **IH:** "Defries had seen Bowie's great potential at an early stage although he'd needed a year to line up 'the big plan.' David was impatient after his 'Space Oddity' hit but Defries went off on other things. Then, as Ziggy started to build, and with 'All the Young Dudes' heading up the charts, Mott the Hoople was briefly the biggest earner in MainMan – but we only had £165 in the bank."

'All the Young Dudes' received rave reviews, *Melody Maker* praising the epic quality of the choral build-up which they felt recalled classics like 'Hey Jude' and 'All You Need Is Love'. John Peel said in *Sounds*, "This is a most important record. It's the first Mott the Hoople has made for CBS and it's a great start." *Fusion* in America soon described 'Dudes' as, "The most exciting piece of white rock 'n' roll released all year"... while Columbia adverts read... "Get ready for the next National Anthem." UK press headlines included 'Mott have a smash 45' (*NME*) *and* 'Bowie gives Hoople a Hit' (*Record Mirror*)... while the 26th August edition of *Melody Maker* featured a full front-page photo of Hunter and a caption that read: "MOTT THE HOOPLE are racing for the chart top, courtesy of their producer David Bowie – and this is their Starman, Ian Hunter." Cockney Rebel frontman Steve Harley later admitted, tongue-in-cheek, that you almost grew to loathe Bowie, because not only was he writing his own fantastic songs, but he was now Pegasus, reviving Mott the Hoople's career from a funeral pyre with a great anthem that would live forever.

Mott produced a promo video for 'All the Young Dudes' directed by Herefordshire friend Richard Weaver, utilising film from a Bristol Top Rank sound check and concert, mixed in with footage of teenagers and football fans. 'Dudes' was the first of three "promos" that Richard would make with Mott the Hoople and the band also recorded two 'Dudes' *Top of the Pops* TV appearances on 3rd and 10th August.

Top of the Pops was the BBC's singles platform and whilst it helped to drive huge record sales, miming to discs or pre-recorded backing tapes was a rigid diktat. There was often "rivalry" between artists over small and large dressing rooms and fights over "Free Bar" vouchers at the BBC studios: Ian would later vocalise Mott's feelings towards the sanitised television show on a 1974 single, but whilst *Top of the Pops* was deemed uncool by serious bands, Hunter knew it was a route to recognition.

However, Mott's excitement surrounding 'Dudes' was suddenly tempered after release when a problem arose with BBC Radio One. Ian had sung Bowie's line referencing the 'Som Dudes' stealing clothes from "*Marks and Sparks*" on the single, but the use of a slang term for a British high-street retailer (Marks and Spencer) was in contravention of BBC product placement policy. Whilst "the Beeb" would soon fail to observe Candy Darling's sexual predilictions in Lou Reed's 'Walk on the Wild Side', The Kinks had recently been censored over Coca-Cola in their hit single 'Lola', and now Mott the Hoople was 'Banned on the Run' as their allusion to a department store was deemed transgressive. When BBC radio threatened to pull Mott's 45, Ian was rushed back to Trident to substitute the offending term with "*unlocked cars*", edited into the original mix by engineer Ken Scott. Despite the drama, Mott's specially adapted single would soon be forgotten, with the BBC often playing the original offering.

> **IH:** "In the good old days, the chaps at CBS were scared of being sued – they still are – so I had to replace the line for the single record. 'Marks and Sparks' has slowly eased its way back into the song over the years. I was more pissed off by some of the American reaction, because we nearly had a major international hit with 'All the Young Dudes' until a lot of radio people in the US wouldn't play the track because of the reported gay connotations attached to it."

Mott the Hoople's *All the Young Dudes* LP was released on 8th September 1972 and featured nine tracks: 'Sweet Jane', 'Momma's Little Jewel', 'All the Young Dudes', 'Sucker', 'Jerkin' Crocus', 'One of the Boys', 'Soft Ground', 'Ready for Love', 'After Lights' and 'Sea Diver'.

Bowie had placed a further direct stamp on Mott at Trident Studios by suggesting they attempt Lou Reed's 'Sweet Jane' from The Velvet Underground's 1970 LP, *Loaded*. David had written 'Queen Bitch' on *Hunky Dory* in direct response to the Velvets and was smitten when he first met Lou in Manhattan in 1971. After Mott the Hoople, Reed would become the next useful side-project for Bowie when he and Mick Ronson produced *Transformer*, Lou's influential second solo album depicting fascinating figures from

Andy Warhol's Factory and vivid lyrical images of urban experiences and encounters from the seedy underbelly of New York. David was astute, and his designer collaborations proved valuable; he admired Lou and Ian, adored *Brain Capers* and *Loaded*, and had been playing The Velvet's 'White Light/White Heat' and 'Waiting for the Man' in his live set. Reflecting on Lou and Mott thirty years later, Bowie would remark that it had been part of his early crusade to present wonderful underground artists to the world and help to get them an audience – adding that he'd found real joy in that type of, "You ain't seen nothin' yet" support. Importantly, Reed later lauded Ronson's playing and arrangements on *Transformer* after 'Walk on the Wild Side', 'Satellite of Love' and 'Perfect Day' made Lou an international star.

According to Griffin, Watts thought the song 'Sweet Jane' was called 'C.J.' until he saw the title printed on the *Dudes* LP sleeve. Dale also claimed that the band had no idea the Velvet's take was so slow and that Lou turned white at Trident when he heard how fast Mott played it. During the sessions, Bowie invited Reed to record a guide vocal for 'Sweet Jane' in order that Hunter could pick up the phrasing and spirit of the lyric. At a Dorchester Hotel press conference, David was soon playing *Dudes* tapes to London journalists with Lou singing 'Sweet Jane' alongside Mott, explaining that he had yet to add Ian's lead vocal. Mott's interpretation of 'Sweet Jane' illustrates Bowie's production touch more than any other *Dudes* track, the original rough and ponderous 'Jane' livened up but softened by placing acoustic guitar prominently in the mix, along with cowbell percussion. Ralphs played beautiful guitar fills and a great solo, but Bowie's production touch limited the power, placing more of an emphasis on the song's irresistible four-chord riff and Reed's street-wise message. Lou became a friend to David and Mick Rock, but Hunter had not "hit it off" with Reed at Trident.

IH: "I couldn't understand what 'Sweet Jane' was about, not being a New York gay, so David stood next to me and I sang line after line exactly how he was telling me. Then David

suggested Lou Reed come in and do a guide vocal and I had less idea of what to do than before. Lou did the rough and I sang it, then I told Lou an awful joke that went wrong and he was not amused. He glared at me and we didn't speak again. Lou and I did not get on. I didn't really know him, and I hadn't got a clue what Lou was about then – but, obviously, I did later on. He simplified and was a minimalist on the music I heard, and that's one of the hardest things to do. I still can't figure out how he came up with the riff for 'Sweet Jane'."

'Sweet Jane' was issued as a Mott single in North America and Europe and was the first recorded cover of the Velvet's song. Lou later admitted that he really liked Mott the Hoople's take and *NME*'s Charles Shaar Murray claimed it was "the best Mott" he'd ever heard. Some listeners considered that Bowie brought poppy, glam magic to the track while Mott performed Reed's great song with energy and irony, in a way that Lou hadn't. Notably, later 1972 live performances of 'Sweet Jane' by Lou Reed and the Tots, were delivered close to Mott's tempo and re-interpretation, rather than the Velvets' original take.

Side One of *All the Young Dudes* contained some darkly sexual themes, sado-masochistic references and inventive vocabulary, such as the tale of 'Momma's Little Jewel', who had just left school and needed *"re-incelibation!"* 'Jewel' was a slower paced re-recording of 'Black Scorpio' that Mott had attempted five months earlier at Island Records, Watts writing the guitar riff to complement Ian's song and flirtatious lyrics. An intriguing musical construction, the syncopated track snapped into shape after a languid introduction while guitars are complemented throughout with chugging piano and Bowie's sax frills. Amidst the new polish, Hunter still can be heard on the instrumental entrée urging Mott to continue a missed take saying, "No, don't stop, carry on."

IH: "Watts wrote 'Momma's Little Jewel' with me while we were still at Island. It was called 'Black Scorpio' when we first recorded it, but it was too fast. This was one of David's best tracks. He really had got the knack of knowing what to do. How 'Black Scorpio' became 'Momma's Little Jewel' I haven't got a clue. Lyrically it sounds like Trudi – *'Momma's little jewel, just left school'*. Nuns – Catholics – Scorpio – there's probably a bit of her in there."

Mott's signature hit single was placed as track three on the LP, 'All the Young Dudes' commencing as soon as 'Momma's Little Jewel' collapsed, with an abrupt jerk and slur on the master tape. The cut still fades out with Ian's novel ad-lib, Griffin claiming that Hunter's spoken line, *"I've wanted to do this for years,"* referenced the band's craving for a hit record and that *"How do you feel, sick?"* was slanted at Island Records and Chris Blackwell. A rehearsal tape with Bowie singing a guide vocal, was finally mixed in with Ian's choruses and released as a "Dudes Audiomorph" on a 1998 Sony Anthology collection. Pete Watts felt strongly that this proved the importance of Ian's original input and delivery.

"I thought Hunter was brilliant on 'All the Young Dudes'," admitted Watts. "If you listen to Bowie's vocal it shows what a fantastic job Ian did on the final recording. Dave's vocal is fantastically 'cosy', like a friendly Uncle, whereas Ian's is 'cool'. Hunter made that song. His vocal was a killer, especially the rap section at the end. Part of Ian's ad-lib was taken from *The Billy Cotton Band Show*, a lunch-time family variety programme on the radio in the Fifties and Sixties, featuring the old band leader Billy Cotton, with horrible singers. One part of the show had an American voice, meant to be an alien in a spaceship, who flew down and said, 'Hey you down there, with the glasses', to Billy Cotton – or Thrilly Bottom as I called him."

IH: "I've never tired of 'All the Young Dudes' because great songs are great songs. It's slow and easy. Years later, Bowie's recorded version was released, and you can make up your own mind how much he had to do with it. David couldn't do 'Dudes' as well as we did. His version was too fey. I wasn't even keen on other later versions. Mott the Hoople gave 'All the Young Dudes' *real* energy."

Dudes fourth track was 'Sucker' – an unusual, funky, mid-tempo song containing role-playing allusions, written principally as a Hunter composition but with input from Ralphs and Watts. Cited by Griffin as the heaviest, hardest-hitting track that Mott ever committed to tape, the final mix was sugar-coated by Bowie courtesy of acoustic guitar, cowbell, more distant sax, handclaps and a blacksmith's anvil. Watts had contributed a chunky guitar riff to the song, but this was altered to a 'Volga boatman' style background vocal. Pete was horrified when he heard the change and didn't like it but later accepted it was an interesting twist. "Bowie was a strange bloke," said Watts, "He was very talented, but he could be difficult and a bit moody."

"When we met Bowie, I realised he was an artist who used music as a vehicle for his painting," says Ralphs. "We had a good relationship with David, and I thought he was a very interesting and intelligent man. He was unconventional, which I liked, and he looked unconventional, which he did for effect. I remember Pete asked David one day why he wore women's clothes and Bowie said if he didn't, nobody would take any notice of him. He had his red Ziggy hair at Trident and was wafer-thin. I recall David used to drink 'Complan'. I never saw him eat a meal once, in all the time we recorded with him.

"Bowie was good at working out arrangements and dynamics and opened our eyes to imaginative recording ideas. I remember when we were trying to get the sound of an anvil on 'Sucker' and he said, 'Why don't we just use an anvil?' And, of course, we never thought of that. So, I said, 'How the hell do we get an anvil in the middle of Soho?' but David said he'd just find one and sure enough, an hour later, a bloke arrives and says, 'Sign here for this anvil, Squire' – and there it was!"

Ian felt that 'Sucker' illustrated the essence of Mick Ralphs' guitar playing perfectly. "If people can't relate to the guitar solo on 'Sucker' then there's something wrong," said Hunter upon release. "It's funny with guitarists, the emphasis often seems to be on speed, but character is important, and I think Mick's guitar playing is very individual. I still think 'Sucker' could have been a lot heavier, but David heard it that way."

'Jerkin' Crocus' was Hunter's ode to a persistent female who Watts knew, and it closed the first side of the *Dudes* LP. 'Momma's Little Jewel', 'Sucker' and 'Jerkin' Crocus' had seen the band lurching into new lyrical territory and sexual imagery, and one reviewer described Hunter playing the "unusually vindictive rock misogynist." 'Jerkin' Crocus' had been written by Ian just before Mott recorded at Trident and, thankfully, Bowie tried to emphasise Ralphs' biting lead guitar and Hunter's rhythm playing. Ian's composition was an underrated track and the Stones' 'Dance Little Sister' and ELO's 'Ma-Ma-Ma Belle' (both cut in 1973) would echo Hunter's 'Crocus' riff. Originally called 'Rock House', Ian's song title was adapted by Watts from the name of an old Ross-on-Wye tramp, called Creepin' Jesus – on this occasion Pete was able to corrupt the vagrant's nickname to Jumping Craparse, then Jerkin' Crocus.

IH: "There was a tramp who lived in Hereford whose name *wasn't* Jerkin' Crocus – but by the time Pete Watts sieved him through his humatic processors, he came out so."

Side Two of *All the Young Dudes* kicked off with Hunter-Ralphs' 'One of the Boys', completely re-vamped from the original demo that Mott had taped at Island in 1971. Some of the band felt that the new *Dudes* version was too long and that the single B-side was the stronger option, minus special additions that Bowie included in the album cut. At Trident, a rotary telephone dialling effect was mixed into the introduction which soon dated the recording, but the twist sounded clever when the song seemed to approach a conclusion before the phone rings and is answered, with the music reappearing and rising back to normal volume via the telephone handset. A great rock song with a melodic introduction from Ralphs prefacing simple power chords, 'One of the Boys' was issued as a single in America. Hunter says that the song began life with a riff that Ralphs had written but as Ian felt he couldn't sing 'Can't Get Enough', they adapted it for 'One of the Boys' with Mick receiving a writing credit.

"Ian wrote most of 'One of the Boys' and I'm not so sure that it did come from 'Can't Get Enough', although it probably has got similar construction," says Ralphs. "But Ian did have some difficulty singing some of my songs at the time, because his voice was more naturally suited to the material that he wrote."

'Soft Ground' was Verden's second composition for Mott the Hoople and although some reviewers and fans found it difficult to fathom, Watts rated Allen's contribution highly. "I thought 'Soft Ground' was brilliant," said Pete. "It's the best song on the album for me. It wasn't very 'Mottish', but it was more futuristic than anything else we'd ever done." Ian recalls that Verden had wrestled with 'Soft Ground' for months. Allen was proud to sing under Bowie's guidance and considered the track might have been discarded without David's involvement; he also admitted the subject matter smacked of "band politics".

"I don't think the boys were happy about that track, as I couldn't sing too well at the time," says Verden. "I ended up talking the song, rather than singing it. I recall that Bowie liked it and he played freakish guitar and added backing vocals. I think he could see where I was at with 'Soft Ground' and he did spend time on it and gave me a chance. The song was a little bit about the Mott guys as something was going on within the band. There was a lot of back-talk and the boys weren't open. Things were happening that I knew nothing about."

Mick Ralphs contributed a superb composition for *All the Young Dudes* in the form of the engaging and dusky 'Ready for Love'. Coupled with an instrumental coda titled 'After Lights',

270

they essentially became one song with two hooks, two choruses and an ending showcasing Mick's musicianship. 'Ready for Love' was cemented into the final *Dudes* running order after almost becoming a Wishbone Ash cover, according to their bassist, Martin Turner.

"I was driving in Shepherd's Bush one day and saw this guy pushing a broken-down car. Suddenly, I realised it was Mick Ralphs, so I stopped and helped him, and we ended up back at Mick's flat for a cup of tea. He let me hear a demo of a song called 'Ready for Love' that day. He said he'd written it but that neither he nor Ian was going to sing it on Mott's next album as they couldn't get the vocal right. I thought it was a brilliant song, so I asked for a cassette copy and took it and played it to Wishbone Ash, but the band said we shouldn't record it. That was the wrong decision for me, but I was delighted when Mick's song was released – it was a great version. I loved the album, adored 'Dudes' and 'Momma's Little Jewel', and have picked 'Ready for Love' on radio shows as one of my all-time favourite tracks."

Ralphs always remained pleased with his composition: "'Ready for Love' is one of the best songs I've ever written, but I had to sing most of it in my squeaky little voice. 'After Lights' was the coda – a kind of drifting off into dreamland type thing. I used the Echoplex for the effect on the guitar. I like that sort of drifty stuff. It's like an after-sex cigarette really; you've said what you want to say and you're just musing."

> **IH:** "'Ready for Love' was bluesy and Mick was a Neil Young-type singer with quite a high voice. The song needed a particular vocal and Ralpher wanted me to sing it, but I couldn't. It was difficult for us in Mott sometimes because of my voice. At the time of *Dudes*, 'Ready for Love' didn't seem strong enough to me so I added and sang an extra bit because I thought I could handle that. Ralpher went along with it but I don't think he liked it – he said he did, but I felt he was being diplomatic."

271

All the Young Dudes closed with 'Sea Diver', one of Hunter's most tender and bittersweet ballads. Previously attempted at Island Records as 'Ride on the Sun', for this version Mick Ronson scored and conducted striking strings and beautiful brass, Mott concluding the LP with a tearful exclamation mark. Hunter laid bare his reflections on the realities of the rock world in 'Sea Diver': the highs and lows; the dramas and dashed hopes; the struggles and strains. The subject matter centred on the trauma and *"sweet savage grace"* of songwriting, Ian conveying a degree of desperation at the apparent emptiness of success, as he strived to compose for the band while remaining hooked and driven by rock 'n' roll. The song would soon turn out to be a wonderful bridge to the theme that would run through Mott's next album. Ronson's arrangement on 'Sea Diver' was doubly valuable as it turned out to be the entrée to a life-long partnership with Hunter.

> **IH:** "Writing songs is almost a perversion. Most writers can go six months and not get a song. They panic and then suddenly they start again. That's what this song was about. I remember 'Sea Diver' being very intense and it was hard not to cry during that one, for some reason. I think I could see myself, twenty or thirty years ahead and knowing this would be all I did and hoping not to be pathetic – not to be one of those guys falling about the stage, fucked up! Ronson didn't do much on *Dudes*, but I got him in to help on 'Sea Diver'. I asked Mick what it would cost for a string arrangement on the song and he told me twenty quid. He wrote the score on a Player's cigarette packet and fortunately the guy who ran the orchestra understood and was as daft as he was. I don't think Mick ever got paid for his contribution. I knew what I wanted on 'Sea Diver' strings-wise. I'd heard the *Randy Newman* album, which was sensational. He was a beautiful writer and a beautiful character singer, and I wanted Mick's 'Sea Diver' arrangement to echo the strings and sadness on 'I Think It's Going to Rain Today'."

"Mick Ronson was such a lovely guy and a truly excellent musician," says Verden Allen. "He arranged the fantastic orchestral section on 'Sea Diver' for Ian and we were all very pleased indeed with the final results of his work. Mick's talents were invaluable for Bowie's 'project' with Mott. You could tell he was going to be a huge star. David was at the start of his fame when he worked with us and the collaboration created a buzz in the business."

A Mott buzz in the music business was echoed by the Mott buzz at CBS Records when Dan Loggins and his team heard the band's labours via some early album mixes. "I remember Ian came by the CBS office one day and played the first mixes of *All the Young Dudes*," says Dan. "I was stunned as it was much more than I could have hoped for. There were several possible singles to follow 'Dudes' including 'Sweet Jane', 'One of the Boys', 'Ready for Love' and possibly 'Sucker', although we weren't sure about the lyrics on that one! Radio was always ready for the next exciting British trend – in this case Mott the Hoople – with the buzz of a hit British single – and the Bowie connection."

All the Young Dudes entered the UK charts on 23rd September 1972 climbing for four weeks to No.21 while it reached No.89 on America's *Billboard*. Columbia promo LPs declared: "Just when their sudden loss of direction was to become a problem who should come upon Mott in this hour of need but Ziggy Stardust himself – David Bowie. Bowie really did a hunky-dory job of producing this, their fifth album, *All the Young Dudes*. The title track was written for the group by Bowie before he had even met them. It's already a classic. Mott the Hoople's back, stronger than ever."

The critics acknowledged that *All the Young Dudes* conveyed a much cleaner sounding Mott and noted a Rolling Stones atmosphere on some tracks. One British feature proclaimed, 'Bowie gives Hoople new lease of life', while a five-star *DISC* review enthused, 'AT LAST MOTT GET IT ALL ON WAX!' – describing 'Sucker' as "a real beauty", 'One of the Boys' as "one of the band's most certain show-stoppers" and concluding, "As they say in the trade papers, expect massive sales!" *Record Mirror*'s review was titled 'Subtlety Pays Off for Mott' but there wasn't univeral praise. Chris Charlesworth headed his *Melody Maker* feature, 'A Mott of fuss about nothing', highlighting the "nifty production – numbers sliding into each other, telephone calls and winding-up clocks included to keep the interest from waivering" – but adding, "some of the spontaneous quality which I detected in their last album *Brain Capers* is missing." It seemed that Mott could never win, although Charlesworth felt that two tracks, in addition to 'All the Young Dudes', stood out – 'Sweet Jane' and 'Sucker'. *NME* was kinder, describing the record as a 'Mott-Bowie compromise'.

In America, *Billboard* expressed relief that the band's new producer had chosen not to tamper with the endearing qualities of Mott, saying: "Bowie's immaculate production has been conducive in transforming Mott the Hoople into a modestly avant-garde mini-supergroup." Describing Mott's fresh material as "powerful", *Village Voice* termed the band's cover of 'Sweet Jane' as "definitive" and 'Sea Diver' "a triumph". *Rolling Stone* praised the album but astutely commented on the hopes for Mott's future, saying: "There's an extravagant amount of power-driven, hook-laden rock 'n' roll on *All the Young Dudes*. Hunter off-handedly strolls his way through 'Sweet Jane' and Ralphs' lead vocal on his own 'Ready for Love' is the best he's ever done. For this album producer Bowie has taken thinning shears to Mott's wild, thick sound and given it a smoother, more streamlined shape. Bowie deserves plenty of credit for cleaning and refining, but he had plenty to work with. The new element of sexual ambiguity may be in deference to the producer or in quest of attention. Now they've got everything, and they're bound to make it on the strength of this record. I just hope they can take what Bowie's given them and move off in their own direction, rather than staying in his shadow."

As *All the Young Dudes* hit British record racks in September, Bowie was heading skyward. A new music figure named Freddie Mercury asked David to produce his band's debut album, *Queen*, to be released by EMI Records but Bowie declined in the light of Ziggy's meteoric rise. CBS and Dan Loggins meanwhile were delighted with Mott's new single and album. "*All the Young Dudes* was Mott's transition album and a huge record in their changing to a more original rock 'n' roll definition," says Dan. "It was the jump from the anarchy of *Brain Capers* to a 'real' long player with grooves and looseness, whilst retaining some 'Stonesy' texture. It was a bit too mid-frequency because Mott had much more dynamics as a live band, but Ian gained self-confidence via Bowie and *Dudes*, finding his place in a very democratic band where he often had to defer."

The sleeve concept and art direction for *All the Young Dudes* was led by Mick Rock, the man who shot the golden age of Seventies rock. Now renowned for many iconic LP covers including Lou Reed's *Transformer*, *Queen II* and Iggy Pop's *Raw Power*, the original cover concept for *Dudes* comprised a black-and-white shot of a youngster brandishing a cardboard cut-out guitar, photographed by Rock on an adventure playground on London's Regent Park Estate. 'Dude 72', as the picture became known could have become another seminal sleeve that reflected the generational aspect of Bowie's song, but it was shelved and eventually adopted as a 2003 cover by Third Eye Blind.

IH: "Mick Rock's photo of that kid as a young dude was a great shot. I remember wanting to use it, the second I saw it."

Mott's eventual *All the Young Dudes* album cover incorporated an archaic US tailoring advertisement of three finely attired and dapper dudes. Dale was dismayed by the sleeve which he termed "dull", "boring" and "a typical Seventies browny sort of colour," but it was a cool and classy concept that Ian also rated. The rear album jacket and inner bag for the UK release featured black-and-white photos of each 'Mott' taken by Rock, while the back of the US cover comprised individual colour live shots of the band members. The British photographs conveyed a slightly sinister image and Verden was not enthused. "I remember Mick Rock taking those photos in a London West End studio," says Allen. "They were far too glamorous for me. I never liked that. Personally, I'd have taken the denim route and gone back to 'square one' rather than follow Bowie's glam."

The slang term "dude" derived from "duds" – a noun for clothes, dragged from obscurity by a Robert Sale Hill poem and originally employed to describe figures who possessed fastidious dress and speech. Dudes now included Bowie's futuristic Armageddon kids, the 'Som' crowd, and glam music lovers of the early Seventies, as well as the stylish trio of early 1900s dandies on Mott's sleeve. Though dismissed and dissed by Dale, the *Dudes* album artwork cleverly presented classic gentlemen's tailoring echoing House of Kuppenheimer clothing ads and imagist J.C. Leyendecker's Twenties signature style that had featured in America's *Saturday Evening Post*. The *Dudes* front cover image was a straight "lift" from a 1917 black-and-white ad for 'Society Brand Clothes' – suits by Chicago's Alfred Decker & Cohn, described as tailoring for "Young Men and Men Who Stay Young". Mott's new sleeve was ambiguous, suggesting dudes in terms of dandyism and male bonhomie, and even the advertisement's Old English font was echoed on the LP cover.

"The front image for the album was a nick from an old *Saturday Evening Post* ad," says Mick Rock. "I remember I shot lots of other pictures of young guys hanging around outside clubs for *All the Young Dudes*. The band would probably never have seen the 'brown' cover before it was agreed. Things were moving very, very fast indeed that summer. 'Starman' was just out and Mott's 'Dudes' single was the big set-up for *Ziggy*. As I recall, nobody objected to the playground photo; we just went for the artwork from *The Saturday Post*. They were crazy days back then. I got on well with Hunter. Pete was the most glam, but Ian was Mott really; he had the look, the hair and the voice. He is charismatic."

Colour retouching of the black-and-white ad for Mott's LP cover was credited to Bowie's school friend, George Underwood of Main Artery, who had been an illustrator for Pye Records and worked on

David's *Hunky Dory*. "Mick Rock just handed me a monotone print of the front cover image for Mott's album and asked me to hand-tint it," says George. "I presumed it was a royalty-free picture that he had found. I didn't know at the time that it may have been by Leyendecker or was lifted from an ad. I simply colourised the print, so Mick takes most of the credit for employing a picture which I thought worked perfectly for *All the Young Dudes*."

Dan Loggins says: "I recall literally bumping into Tony Defries at the CBS office entrance on Theobalds Road one day. He was bringing in several men's fashion magazines from the Twenties and showed me interesting artist renderings of clothing advertisements. He was particularly fond of one and it turned out to be the eventual cover of *All the Young Dudes*. It showed that with Bowie's input and Tony's vision, Mott was embarking on a different journey. CBS Marketing loved the new direction and image for our first Mott the Hoople album. It was a pity Dale didn't 'get' the imaging, at least at the beginning – he certainly got more dapper as touring began!"

While Griffin originally praised Bowie's production for Mott, the drummer was later "miffed" with the banning of the band from David's mixing sessions. Dale felt the finished product was "rendered puny," that Bowie did little in terms of arrangement because of budget constraints and that his only contributions were the addition of telephone and anvil effects, saxophones and acoustic guitar. Dale described 'Sucker' as the heaviest track that Mott had ever cut when it was first played back at Trident but felt that the final mix was weak. He puzzled over Ralphs' soaring guitar on 'Sea Diver' that had become "almost lost" after David's "tampering" and the "thin sound" that removed the power and size of Mott's playing. Griffin said it later emerged that Bowie's penchant at the time required that bass guitar and bass drum should feature very little in his mixes. In 1996, during tape research for a Sony box set, Dale was keen to work on some *All the Young Dudes* tracks, targeting 'Sucker' and 'Jerkin' Crocus' for "more gutsy" treatment but it was reported by Sony that the multi-track tapes had been destroyed in error, in February 1992 and so Griffin's excellent re-mixing plan was thwarted. Annoyingly, the master tapes later re-appeared and were discreetly sold at auction.

> **IH:** "The *Dudes* album still sounds good to me which is amazing because it was done very quickly. I think we improved 'All the Young Dudes' because Mott took it up one tone for more impact and we wrote our harmonies and guitar hooks. David was great but if he had a problem it was that I think he was a bit fey in the mixing. We did want to remix *Dudes* years later, but the tapes had magically disappeared. It's annoying that we couldn't find the album masters because there was a lot of balls on that record that never saw the light of day."

During the Trident sessions Mott attempted two other Hunter songs: 'It's Alright' and 'Henry and the H-Bomb', the latter eventually released as a demo version on a 1993 Columbia retrospective. Neither of these tracks featured Verden Allen and neither were completed. Other rehearsed songs from the *Dudes* period included Ian's Beatles-inspired 'I Don't Dig It', Allen's 'The Black Staff', 'Beside the B-Side' and 'Electric Robot'. Three other numbers were "jammed" and recorded at Trident Studios on 5th July 1972, all featuring Stan Tippins on lead vocals. These were taped in one evening when Bowie failed to attend Trident following a "huff" over a *Top of the Pops* appearance so the band asked Stan to sing with them again. Although he was Mott's tour manager, Stanley's vocal talents would soon be utilised secretly when they played 'Dudes' live. "We asked Stan what he'd like to do that evening at Trident," says Ralphs, "and we did some of the numbers that he loved. He sang very well too, but they were done for fun, and for Stan."

"When Ian left the studio that night the boys said, 'Why don't you do a couple of songs?'" says Tippins. "They came up with 'So Sad', which I'd never heard of, but they just talked me through it, and I sang it. 'Please Don't Touch' and 'Shakin' All Over' I loved, although these versions annoyed me. Half the chords are wrong

278

because they didn't really know them. When we did the *Dudes* album I helped vocally, and Bowie turned to the band one day and said they should make an album with Stan. David saying that was incredible, but he couldn't even finish off Mott's album because he was into so many things. Sometimes he would be missing and sometimes he would dash back from something else, so near the end of *All the Young Dudes* it got harder. Nobody could do high harmony parts on 'Dudes' when Mott played it in concert, so I was backstage, counting money and talking to promoters, then suddenly I'd have to be at the side of the stage. I had my own microphone, amp and monitor behind the curtains, singing, while everyone thought it was the band. I still sang 'Please Don't Touch' and 'All the Young Dudes' years later, at soundchecks when I was road manager with Simple Minds to test the PA. It seemed to amuse a lot of people every day!"

As *All the Young Dudes* marked a fresh beginning for Mott the Hoople, Dale suggested to Mott's management that he should adopt a new stage name. "I never liked being called Buffin," said Griffin in 1998. "It wasn't my idea. It was all down to Watts. Watts – the bane of my life! By 1972, I desperately wanted to dump the name and I thought the new era with CBS and Defries was the time to relaunch myself as somebody who was not Buffin. I wanted something that was dynamic and tough-sounding, like a comic book character, so the name I came up with was Johnny Smack, which was quite punky in hindsight. I had no idea that smack was heroin. I put the idea to Tony Defries thinking he'd go for it. He didn't – the bastard."

Mott the Hoople was now ready to promote the *Dudes* album, and they commenced a twenty-one date British tour running from 16th September to 15th October, supported at most shows by Home, a fellow CBS band featuring guitarist Laurie Wisefield who would soon find fame with Wishbone Ash. Ian was now prowling the stage in black leather suits tailored by the creator of Iggy Pop's silver *Raw Power* clothing – Watts was seven-feet tall having graduated to outrageous winged leopard skin platform boots and a platinum-coloured hair-do – while Allen continued to display glam-reluctance in a burgundy velvet jacket. Tippins recalled that clothes-wise, Mott had always wanted to do something different, especially Watts who had gladiator-style waistcoats made and boots with platforms and heels so high that he could barely walk around on stage.

"After the release of 'Dudes', I'd taken Ian to sales and promo meetings at CBS and he was greeted warmly and was becoming 'the face' of Mott the Hoople," says Dan Loggins. "Hunter had an identifiable image, but he always insisted that the band's publicity be equal. I got to see Mott the Hoople as serious working people but also a fun-loving rock group. Pete gave me a nickname and I enjoyed their inside-humour and banter, especially the Hereford accents which the great Stan Tippins helped to translate and clarify for my American ears. At a rehearsal for that tour I sat with Miller Anderson and observed as the band's new live act evolved and 'All the Young Dudes' became a true Mott the Hoople tune. At the end of the rehearsal, Ian shouted to Miller, 'Hey, remember this?' – and segued from 'One of the Boys' into 'Honky Tonk Women'. Ralphs provided great riffs and shattering lead and, underlying it all, Verden's keyboards gave a solid sonic foundation. This was, to me, a real revelation at that moment – the pure joy of rock 'n' roll that took you to emotional places you didn't know existed. That was the special thing Mott the Hoople had. They were in and of their time but were more than that. They were great musicians and were becoming rock 'n' roll stars, but they never seemed above their loyal, growing audience."

Mott the Hoople's British shows were well received, but they were not the whirlwind that had been anticipated. Supported by Home, Mott was excited by the prospect of their appearance at the tour's "big gig", in North London's famous 3,000-seater venue, The Rainbow. Recently refurbished, the first attractions to play at the reborn theatre included Jethro Tull, Procol Harum and David Bowie. Mott's show was the climax of their British tour and although MainMan wanted it to be an event, it was a disappointing gig. Guy

Stevens was present to see his boys, but Mott's original mentor was red-eyed and inebriated, and seemed somewhat contemptuous of the band's new-found fame via Bowie.

> **IH:** "When 'All the Young Dudes' was a hit, Guy was mixed up in all kinds of problems of his own. The Island days were gone, and he was just trying to survive at that time. I don't think Guy cared about 'Dudes' either way, but he'd probably have said 'justifiable sell-out' – if pressed."

Dale Griffin recalled how Mott considered introducing some theatrics to their Rainbow concert – a *Past, Present and Future* concept where the band intended to invite three legendary pop singers (Billy Fury, Adam Faith and John Leyton) to perform a couple of numbers each, then Mott would play, and the finale would be a song played by a younger group. The past would be the famous stars of the Sixties, Mott the Hoople was the contemporary and the future of rock was to be kids in punk vein. The young band would include future Clash guitarist Mick Jones, but in the event Billy Fury was unavailable, and Adam Faith would not hear of the proposition. Instead, Mott re-planned alternative 'theatrics' utilising The Rainbow's special interior and a window located above the stage that opened out into the top of the hall. The band decided to have a figure chased off stage and up to the window, where "the figure" would be thrown out after a fight, causing a reaction in the crowd below. On the night, one of the road crew, clothed as a scruffy tramp was pursued upstairs and a dummy, dressed like the roadie was jettisoned – over a totally impassive audience.

Always a man of eclectic musical tastes and with a love for Gloucestershire-born classical composer Ralph Vaughan Williams, Pete Watts devised a new walk-on tape for Mott's live shows when he adopted a central portion of Gustav Holst's 'Jupiter', from *The Planets*, and added a heavy guitar chord to create a dramatic electric ending at an appropriate break in the orchestral music. It was a spectacular introduction, but Mott the

Hoople's Rainbow appearance was hampered by equipment problems after only two numbers – 'Jerkin' Crocus' and 'Sucker'. The band got back on track and finished their set with two encores but attacked some stage gear while Dale demolished his cherished drum kit. Mott were upset and said that they directed their rage at a cynical music press, but the frenzy did not trouble Dan Loggins or CBS personnel in the audience.

"Home had played a dynamic opening set and the gauntlet was thrown down," recalls Dan. "The theatre buzz was palpable, and Mott electrified the anticipation by utilising their pre-concert Holst tape. This served to build the tension as the band appeared in smoky darkness, plugging in and creating folds of feedback overlapping with the 'Jupiter' theme. They took to the stage with a swagger and confidence that was thrilling and the roar that greeted Mott the Hoople that night was incredible. It was clear they had a dynamic new sound, and despite some sound glitches, the set flowed. With Mick's lead guitar intro on 'Dudes', the audience stood up as one and began to sing along with the new anthem of the time. The crowd stomped for five minutes before the band obliged with two encores including 'You Really Got Me'. The gig should have been a triumph for the group, but something was wrong, and Buff smashed his kit at the end. Mott were not satisfied, but all the CBS promo people were happy. I couldn't care less about some press guys who supposedly held grudges from 'the Island days.' I could only deal with the band as they were – 'hot' and 'now' at The Rainbow, with a hint of Dylan, the glow of Bowie, the mystery of Lou Reed, the funk of the Stones, the swing of Chuck Berry and the madness of Little Richard. In 1972, Mott the Hoople was defining rock 'n' roll."

Hunter claimed after The Rainbow gig that Mott "deliberately blew it," turning up the sound and letting journalists like Allan Jones and Chris Charlesworth "have it". The press let the band have it in return, Charlesworth heading his *Melody Maker* review, 'Mott Are Shown the Way Home' while Ray Fox-Cumming felt that fans forgave any shortcomings including Mott's "sinister visual transformation, dodgy equipment and poor sound, which caused 'Sea Diver' to be ruined."

> **IH: "I can remember being opposite The Rainbow in a pub and I got the strangest feeling, because behind the bar was this huge mirror. There was a ton of press people there. All I had to do was put a bottle through that mirror and I was front-page famous. But we weren't the types to do that. We probably did the gig at The Rainbow and it just passed into insignificance. We weren't movers. David Bowie was a mover – he was brilliant at it. We weren't."**

All the Young Dudes was well-received by critics and hit the British Top Thirty, but the LP was not the huge success that the band had hoped for. The letters pages of the music papers even carried opinions from some die-hard Hooplers who were seemingly not wild about their heroes' new direction. Hunter and the group reluctantly accepted that the UK *Dudes* tour had created a new conundrum, as it became evident that some of their traditional fan-base had drifted because they considered Mott to be "an albums band" and had sniffed a smidgeon of "sell-out."

This was 1972 – the era when lifting a single from an album was viewed as a low move for "real rock bands." The Beatles, The Stones and The Who were singles acts in the Sixties and had changed the landscape with *Sgt. Pepper*, *Let It Bleed* and *Tommy*, but Led Zeppelin ditched the single concept completely. The long player provided groups with peerless legacies, so it was ironic that Mott the Hoople had embraced the albums medium alongside label-mates King Crimson and Free, but changed horses to capture singles success. Suddenly Mott found that audience gains via the chart success of 'All the Young Dudes' were low because many considered the single to be a first release. It would be a temporary hitch because the Bowie experience had been a signpost in the sky for Hunter, highlighting a realisation that the conception and design of a song could vary. Ian would pen successful follow-up records that generated substantial new support, but Mott found the 'Dudes' versus live audience situation worrying at the time.

Dale later suggested that 'All the Young Dudes' "ruined" Mott the Hoople. "We had a massive fan base and as soon as those people heard 'Dudes', all those fans went away," said Griffin. "It completely buggered us for a while. People had to get over the shock of Mott the Hoople, the losers, having a hit. It was the sin of sins to be successful. 'Dudes' affected Ian too. He was doing slightly cod Bob Dylan things that we'd been getting away with for some time, and one of Bowie's suggestions was that he didn't do that anymore."

The entrenched attitude of some rock fans often surfaced in conjunction with commercial success, exemplified by the nonsensical thesis that "when the hits start coming, the band's gone off the boil." It had seemed to a few Hoople followers that the Bowie-Mott liaison was a curious relationship and the loyal coterie of fans that flocked to see "their group" in the early days, worried that things had changed. Mott the Hoople had a special solidarity with their supporters and Ian sometimes wrote songs to them and for them. In their quest to become superstars Mott didn't look down on fans, as they came from the same background and harboured similar frustrations. Their audience had an affinity with Mott the Hoople and a similar kinship would continue with Ian Hunter as a solo artist for over forty years. Mick Jones felt sad in 1972, as change seemed inevitable after 'All the Young Dudes'.

"Island was our period where we followed the band seriously," said Jones. "Mott came out to the bar and met you and spoke with you as a fan. They were personable people. They made you feel welcome, but they were stars in our eyes. After the first four albums, when Bowie bailed them out and they did 'Dudes', 'The Mott Lot,' as we were called, felt a little left behind. You can't stop progress and it was good for them, but we lost *our* band. When I first heard 'All the Young Dudes' on the radio one night, I knew it was going to be massive. After that, we didn't have the same access that we'd had before. All the singles were great tracks, but the earlier stuff was more organic."

> **IH:** "'All the Young Dudes' didn't do us any good in the way of live gigs and of course there was that nagging thing that we hadn't written it ourselves. I can't understand why David didn't do his own version, like the version that he did with us. I remember I was really brought down when David decided not to release 'All the Young Dudes' on *Aladdin Sane* – *Aladdin's Vein* it was called at the time – because then people would have seen just how much of a Mott the Hoople song it really was. He wrote it and produced it, but that was our song, for our audience. All of a sudden, we were 'gay' after 'Dudes', not that there's anything wrong with that, but a lot of the old crowd went off us. We finally had a hit and gained new fans, but they were *Top of the Pops* come-and-go-type fans. It was a tense time. Some people said we were 'living off Bowie' and we'd also upset some of our regulars – and that was serious. We also thought maybe we've lost something here – that's what the song 'Ballad of Mott the Hoople' was about."

While the band reflected on their UK tour, Pete Watts considered that Tony Defries was effective for Mott the Hoople during this period as he managed to increase the live earnings of the group. With a successful single and album in their locker all seemed well between Mott, Bowie and MainMan Management. Ian remembers it was decided that Bowie would record when Mott toured, and Mott would record when David toured, the artists sharing virtually the same road crew including MainMan's Leee Childers and Tony Zanetta.

However, Mick Ralphs now sensed that the ethos of the original Mott would have to change. The band was a different, commercial animal and a 'Mott the Hoople Sea Divers' fan club was formed. The secretary was Aylesbury-based Bowie fan and

Mott follower Kris Needs, who had produced membership cards for David's Appreciation Society. The Sea Divers membership would include Mick Jones, soon-to-be 'Smith' Steven Morrissey and a young Oxford University student named Benazir Bhutto (fan club member #248) who later became a politician and the eleventh Prime Minister of Pakistan, before her assassination in 2007.

"Mott survived on struggle, adversity and disappointment," says Ralphs. "We'd always said sod convention – sod the system – but there comes a point where you can't be famous and be like that. We were always the underdogs and that was part of the reason we were so spirited and so exciting. And then we got into this thing with Bowie, which was a great success and helped everyone but, in a way, we'd become part of the system we were dead against."

In October 1972 Mott the Hoople featured on Bob Harris's *Sounds of the Seventies* programme, however the aired versions of 'Ready for Love', 'Jerkin' Crocus', 'Sweet Jane' and 'One of the Boys' were adjusted album tracks and not a bona-fide radio session. The BBC would often use studio rhythm tracks and add alternate live vocals for *Top of the Pops* appearances, but some radio session songs often sounded like album cuts. Dan Loggins believes the 'Whispering Bob' session tracks might have been from the Trident sessions with David Hentschel or Keith Harwood "tweaks" – but it sounded doubtful!

In the same month Mott's former label attempted to cash in on their new-found commercial success by releasing a collection of Island recordings. Compiled by Muff Winwood and planned as *Mott's Greatest Misses*, but issued as *Rock and Roll Queen*, the LP contained examples of the band's more aggressive up-tempo songs and avoided their softer side. Tracks such as 'Waterlow', 'Angel of Eighth Avenue' and 'I Can Feel' were omitted but the disc marked the debut of 'Midnight Lady' on an album pressing. Island's publicity for the *Rock and Roll Queen* LP proclaimed: "Now that Mott the Hoople have had a massive hit single with our friends at CBS, we thought we would re-introduce them on a new album that contains all that was best of the four albums that they recorded with us over three years. Rip off? Certainly... but unavoidable considering the material on this album..."

Rock and Roll Queen's interesting "Marilyn Monroe look-a-like" cover was produced by British airbrush artist Philip Castle who had crafted images for movies, advertising and *Playboy* and *Mayfair* magazine stories. Prior to *Rock and Roll Queen*, Philip had devised art designs for Stanley Kubrick's film, *A Clockwork Orange*. Castle's subjects were usually a juxtaposition of scantily clad women and shiny machinery including aircraft, but he also created celebrity pictures of Elvis Presley, James Dean and John Lennon.

"I never met Mott the Hoople for the *Rock and Roll Queen* record sleeve and I had no connection with the group," said Philip. "I was an illustrator and it was really an image factory in those days. *Rock and Roll Queen* was a nice design, although I wish 'the girls' had been prettier. I was sent a sketch of an idea, with line lettering and I developed chromed 3D letters, added the grille effect and produced the female images from photographs of a fashion model. I have no idea who she was, but the poses were good. I was a Marilyn Monroe fan and incorporated some Marilyn effects. I didn't know that Island Records was going to include a single blow-up of a girl's head on the back of the cover and I was bothered by that when I saw the eventual record. My diary tells me that the Mott cover was done in August 1972 – sandwiched between an Air Show illustration for *The Times* and the 1973 Pirelli calendar!"

With no rare or previously unreleased material, *Rock and Roll Queen* seemed a rushed and thoughtless affair – Island's 26-second cut-down version of 'The Wheel of the Quivering Meat Conception' being a pointless edit and inclusion. Some reviewers felt that only four of the eight tracks were truly representative of early Mott the Hoople, "the claustrophobic hard-rockers", whilst their sensitive material had been ignored. As Island's LP hit British record racks in October 1972, Hunter expressed concern that their former label's cash-in might outsell *All the Young Dudes*. "They've got all the favourites on there," said Ian, "and they've made such a good job of the packaging. I don't know – it could happen, but we are not going back to doing all that stuff again." *Record Mirror* pathetically proclaimed the LP as 'Rock 'n' Roll Raunchy Mott' and the compilation failed to chart, but Island would soon have one more shameless shot, releasing a 1973 Dutch single version of 'Lay Down'. Atlantic Records in America elected not to issue *Rock and Roll Queen* in 1972 – but they would in 1974.

"Island never treated us with much respect – even after we'd gone," said Pete Watts. "I remember one of the greatest feelings I ever had was when 'All the Young Dudes' was a hit and I went to The Greyhound in Fulham Palace Road one night to see a group. Johnny Glover and Alec Leslie of Island were there, and I went to the bar dressed in a leather suit. I had money and we had a hit. Now they'd always said, 'Oh, you'll never get anywhere' – but now, Alec Leslie was saying to me, 'Well done mate. You've done well. I knew you'd do it' – and I thought, 'No you fuckin' didn't.' They never had any faith in us at all."

Turning to preparations for their next LP, on 18th October Mott spent a day at CBS Studios, a newly conceived sixteen-track facility on London's Whitfield Street. Termed prestigious by some engineers, the band's rhythm section was scathing of their label's new recording set-up, Watts describing the day as "miserable" and Griffin calling the session "a nightmare that I would rather forget." Mott recorded three demos at CBS – a new Hunter song with the working title, 'Honaloochie Boogie', 'Hymn for the Dudes' that they had performed on stage, plus Allen's autobiographical 'Nightmare' with lyrics that painted a picture of Verden's increasing band paranoia.

Dan Loggins recalls, "I was asked to get Mott to 'try' CBS Studios, but they were not happy there. Studios are always a matter of comfort, sound specifics and costs: the key is the engineer who makes it all happen, as Mott would soon find out. Dale was unhappy at CBS, but we would soon use Studio 3 successfully for *The Clash*. We'd wanted Mott the Hoople to attract new British albums bands to CBS. We got The Clash, Judas Priest and The Only Ones so, our immediate success with Mott and Hunter paved the way for signings and gave credibility to the label after all."

On 28th October 1972, Ian married Trudi Liguori at Brent Registry Office in Wembley, with Colin York from Hunter's Northampton days acting as his best man. Angie Bowie threw a celebratory party afterwards at Gunter Grove attended by The Stooges; David Bowie sent a belly-dancer along as a wedding gift and Angie's present to the happy couple was a Spode tea service.

In the following month, Mott the Hoople only played one show before a five-week American tour to promote *All the Young Dudes*. Originally set to commence on 22nd October in Atlanta, the band's departure was put back to 24th November with the first live date played in Hollywood, followed by an uncertain and patchy MainMan gig schedule running through to 22nd December in Memphis. Seventeen American dates had been planned when the band left London for Los Angeles, as 'All the Young Dudes' climbed to No.31 in Canada and No.37 in the US singles chart.

The 1972 tour was Mott's third US visit, but their first under the aegis of Columbia and MainMan, and the sojourn became frustrating for some of the group. With Bowie, MainMan had already shown a propensity for booking American live schedules including large gaps and downtime, one of the Spiders' road trips between gigs being 1,600 miles from Kansas to Santa Monica. In the end, only eleven of Mott's US concerts were played, with appearances in Los Angeles, Florida and Texas cancelled. Dale Griffin was unhappy with what he termed "the MainMan Disorganisation" and recalled distress because some Mott gigs "were not what they should have been" – concerts were pulled hours before the band was due to perform, and the entourage sometimes flew from city to city but played no show. Newly married to Trudi, a happier Ian decided to write a diary as he toured America. While Griffin found Mott's US trip "low-key" and "disappointing," Ian's scripted account, jotted down in planes, hotels and concert venues would cleverly capture all the highs, lows and honesty of rock on the road.

One of Mott's highlights was their first headline US performance at "Philly's Fillmore": The Tower Theater in Pennsylvania. Appearing at the refurbished 3,000-seat cinema in Upper Darby, west of Philadelphia, the band was introduced and accompanied on two encores by Bowie. Tony Defries got the promoters, Midnight Sun Concerts, to advertise the 29th November gig as "David Bowie Presents Mott the Hoople" but, on the day, David missed his train from Pittsburgh and inflated MainMan's costs for Mott's show with a seven-hour, $200 cab fare.

"I went to Philly to see Mott the Hoople and renew my relationship with Tony," says Dan Loggins. "I still remember seeing him wandering through the Tower Theater in ninety-degree heat, wearing his full-length fur coat and smoking a long Cuban cigar – he was becoming a version of Colonel Tom Parker, before our eyes! Mott's US tour was a hit-and-miss affair though. Some dates went well in Philly, New York and Memphis but several gigs were cancelled, which was depressing, however, America's door was opened for the band and the 'Dudes' single continued to gain radio play."

> IH: "I remember that US tour pretty well, because of 'the diary' perhaps. I recall our Ford Auditorium gig in Detroit when I threw my guitar, an upside-down Firebird, thirty feet at Buff and it split on his cymbals as I walked off in disgust. God knows what that was about – sound I think, and me being silly. Some of the PAs and the people who ran them were dire, and they really could ruin a gig. Here we were in Detroit in 1972 – here the crowd was – but in between that, a horrible sound, that we were paying good money for. Detroit was one of our favourite cities too. I remember the band stayed on that night, Ralpher took over on vocals and they got a resounding ovation. I came back on and was soundly booed for my tantrum – and I probably deserved it."

290

Mott's Providence, Rhode Island, gig was also notable for three reasons: Ian's Hoople-Mahavishnu Orchestra comparisons, a bottle assault on guitarist Mick Ralphs and Mott refusing to deliver 'Sea Diver' until some jeering, wasted punters halted their heckling. The interruptions had been muted by Hunter before he asserted that Mott's music was more valid than the headliners, The Mahavishnu Orchestra. During the band's next number, the crowd reacted but under the headline 'HUNTER HITS BACK', reviewer Lou Papineau noted how Ian commanded the stage with his domineering presence:

"Halfway into 'Sweet Angeline' an empty wine bottle struck Ralphs' guitar. Hunter left the stage, walking to the edge of the crowd to accost the attacker. Asking 'Whodunnit?' he reached out and slapped the kid who was more surprised at the violent return than anyone. The band then went back to finish the number. They didn't come back for an encore despite loud applause, but a finish like that couldn't have been topped. Mott's self-image is a product of bad press and rude audiences, as their rock is almost second to none."

> **IH:** "I leapt offstage on to an organ in the pit that night, and from there into the audience. The crowd pointed to the chap who'd thrown the bottle and I hit him. I then leapt back on to the organ and the stage. The place was going nuts – but so were my trousers – which split at the seams down to the back of my knees. I camouflaged by crouching down and pointing at the guy, thereby concealing the problem. The song ended, but when I tried to assume a normal standing position, I found I couldn't, so I sidled off – crab-like – into the wings."

Mott's live set was now focused almost entirely on their new album although they included 'Midnight Lady' and 'Sweet Angeline' from their Island catalogue, a nine-minute encore of The Rolling Stones' 'Honky Tonk Women' and 'Hymn for the Dudes', which would appear on their next studio LP. Mott's Tower Theater performance was aired on FM radio and pirated. A bootleg LP, *Mott the Hoople Live with David Bowie*, soon appeared and the tape was later coupled with their February 1971 Swedish radio show as a double CD set entitled *All the Way from Stockholm to Philadelphia*. Sadly, tracks from this collection continually surfaced for years, re-ordered and re-packaged on more confused compilation CDs than could ever be listed.

After the Philadelphia gig, Hunter met Bowie again in Manhattan on 10th December, the day after he and the Spiders had recorded 'Drive-In Saturday' at RCA's New York Studios. David played Ian a tape of the song – which Hunter described as "beautiful with a hell of a chord run-down" – and it was soon earmarked as Mott's next single. Bowie also let Ian hear his new take of 'All the Young Dudes', but Hunter preferred Mott's version, as he felt David's was lacklustre and delivered at a pedestrian tempo that didn't work in a lower key, or with added saxophones. Bowie was slating 'All the Young Dudes' for his next album, to be titled *A Lad in Vein* and possibly a new musical, *Tragic Moments*, and Ian thought David was holding up well under the strains of his new-found stratospheric success.

Mott witnessed "weird scenes inside the goldmine" during their US tour, Verden Allen recalling that the gay society of Los Angeles suddenly smothered the band with bouquets of flowers and gifts. In the early Seventies, as post-Manson Family paranoia and unease reigned on the boulevards, musicians colonised Laurel Canyon in the Hollywood Hills while Sunset Strip below was studded with billboards advertising numerous rock albums. The music industry and groupie circle boomed, and personal and performance identities could be malleable. Watts recalled that Mott's Bowie-association was immediately misconstrued in the States with "gay hangers-on" appearing in abundance including Les Petites Bonbons, who courted music celebrities they admired, sending out glittered items and ornate cards. The Bonbons aimed to be "a walking exhibition" and drag-rock sensation, and their manipulative style worked: Columbia Records soon enlisted Les Petites Bonbons as hosts for a 1973 Iggy Pop party, but Mott the Hoople didn't want to know.

"As soon as certain Americans knew we'd had something to do with David, they thought we were gay," said Watts. "We had people following us round, like Les Petites Bonbons, but they realised very quickly that they were on to a loser. At one gig the hall had signs which said, 'Those costumed cuties – Mott the Hoople'. The link with Bowie also got us banned on some radio stations that wouldn't have anything to do with 'gay music'. I even had blokes crying outside my bedroom door – 'I'm in love with you Overend. Let me in. I've loved you for two years.' I had to leave the girl I was with and open the door and pat some guy on the shoulder and say, 'Sorry mate – there's no chance – ever!' It was pathetic really. We had girls too of course, like The Hot Motts, although I had little to do with them. I also had a bloke in Boston who took a shine to me and insisted on taking me to see a cheap Les Paul in a pawn shop. The guy became a nuisance. The night of the gig, Stan came for me and took me down to the lobby and the bloke was sitting there. He leapt up saying, 'Oh, Overend,' and Tippins pushed him back into the chair by his throat and said, 'Not you. You fuckin' stay there!' This had the desired effect. Hunter had it too with a guy called Wayne – a photographer in New York. We weren't nice to him and he got pissed off in the end and went after Badfinger. There were people who could be a pain in the neck."

> IH: "People who came on as intelligent, within five minutes could often be freaks – then you try to get rid of them but it's too late, as you've spoken to them. I couldn't believe that after 'Dudes' we were considered instant 'fags' in the States. We soon found out that the single had made us tranny magnets when we hit the US again. It was comical. A lot of gays followed us around in America and we were scared at first because we all happened to be straight, but

then we started talking to people and there wasn't anybody pushing you. I met some incredible people. I never saw anything all that sexual about 'All the Young Dudes' as a lyric. To me, it was just a great song. We had a No.3 hit in the UK with 'Dudes' and it was Top Forty in America when we went there on the 1972 tour, but it stalled when the 'Bible Belt' wouldn't play it on the radio."

Some of the band was glad to reach the end of their American tour not least because it was becoming increasingly apparent that Mick Ralphs was suffering with his extreme fear of flying. To reach their final gig in Memphis, Mott flew on a commuter plane, landing periodically to deposit and collect passengers, much to Ralphs' increasing distress. At one location Mick refused to go on and travelled the rest of the journey by road, taking Verden for company. Mott continued with the flight and although Phally asked the group to take care of a guitar he'd bought, the airline lost it, the promoter hustling Mott into Memphis with a police escort minus Allen's beloved "axe". The band's road crew, equipment, Mick and Phally were lost in transit and, in Memphis, despite the marvellous Joe Walsh and Barnstorm as support billing, ticket sales were reportedly poor. The atmosphere was grim, but the missing personnel finally arrived, and, at Ellis Auditorium, the hall was full and the air electric. Mott decided to enter the arena from the rear that night, walking through the crowd to an ecstatic reception. After a stunning show, where Joe returned to the stage to jam with Mott, Walsh joined Hunter and Allen in an attempted assault on Elvis Presley's Graceland mansion.

IH: "At our hotel in Memphis we had a floor for Mott, Joe Walsh and our entourage. Some of the people that turned up after the gig included a bunch of Elvis's relatives and they said they could get us into Graceland. Apparently, it involved them chatting up some people at the gate while we slipped round the back. It's a stupid idea when you're sober, but not so daft when you're pissed. So, we went in a limo and Joe stayed in the car, and they caught Verden at the front gate while I got to the back of Graceland. Then, there I was, inside Elvis's house and all of a sudden I sobered up and thought, 'Christ, this is trespassing.' I was walking along this corridor with shag carpet on the floors, walls and ceiling, and I remember a gymnasium on the right; then this door opened in front of me and Elvis's maid Alberta was there. She said that she didn't think I should see Mr Presley as he'd just seen a movie and didn't like it. Apparently, Elvis hired a cinema when he wanted to see a film and it had been a bad film, so I could have been done over by his henchmen. Fortunately, they knew that we weren't breaking and entering because they had Dobermans, and they were barking, but they didn't let the dogs go. Alberta told me to get back out – in a nice way – so, I left. They wanted to take me to the gate in a security vehicle, but I was now sober enough not to get in and maybe get bounced off the walls of the van by the Memphis Mafia. I was being an idiot and they knew that, so I walked down the driveway with the van behind me, with all its headlights on, and a Christmas nativity scene on the right-hand side of the drive. It was amazing. There I was silhouetted in all these lights at Graceland – and nobody took a fuckin' photo!"

"I remember the front gates at Graceland being opened and I saw Ian going one way and I went the other way," says Verden. "I got to the front door and a Land Rover picked me up because they'd seen me on the cameras. They could have shot me, but took me down to the gate, then Ian came and got in the car and said, 'Here you are,' and put a load of leaves in my hand and said, 'We've got a memory – me and you were there.' They gave us a card – 'Merry Christmas from The Colonel' – so I wrote on it and posted it, because we were coming home the next day. When I got home, I'm in a pub the next night in Hereford, and I said to this friend – 'Incredible last night.

I nearly got shot at Elvis Presley's house' – and they thought I was round the bend."

The celebrations at Mott's Memphis hotel with Joe Walsh were also bizarre. "I remember in the middle of this wild party," said Watts, "there were policemen rolling joints, half-naked girls on the floor and wild music going on, and me and Joe, playing chess – on the bed!" After all the in-transit trauma and Memphis madness, Mott had wrenched a triumphant night from the jaws of potential disaster. Ian would soon immortalise the episode in one of his finest songs – 'All the Way from Memphis' – dedicated to two of MainMan's entourage who helped the group on the road – Leee Childers and Tony Zanetta.

It had a been a sensational year for Ian and the band, and *Fave Raves* in the USA placed *All the Young Dudes* at No.4 and Mott's 'Dudes' single at No.2 in their 1972 best-records listings. The press intimated that Mott the Hoople planned to record another album with David Bowie but mis-reported that the group would first release a single, recently re-cut in New York during their tour. Rumours of collaboration with Kim Fowley was also mentioned but Dan Loggins knew that it was Kim's style to "plant" press releases involving himself. In fact, in early December, Hugh Attwooll at MainMan London had booked Trident Studios for the recording of Mott's next album and single, to be produced by Bowie in the New Year. In practice however, David was now working at a gruelling pace and was struggling to write for himself, let alone gift another song and produce it.

Mott were now troubled as the next Hoople single was overdue and in December even loyal journalist Ray Fox-Cumming astutely questioned whether Defries' path for the band was leading to stardom or destruction, speculating that Mott the Hoople must be worried.

With their American trek concluded, Mott returned to London on 24th December and Ian and Trudi went to spend Christmas with Colin York in Northampton but, on Boxing Day, Hunter received a call from Bowie saying he had important business to discuss at his Beckenham apartment. Ian and Trudi had last seen David and Angie when the Spiders and Mott collided in New York and relations had been good. Ian duly drove down to the neo-Gothic gloom of Haddon Hall where Bowie's fashion guru, Freddie Burretti sat in attendance... but the "big meeting" proved to be an aggravating non-event.

> IH: "That was a very annoying incident. I was shattered after the US tour and jet-lagged, but David asked me to go down to discuss 'Mott ideas' which he said were 'important'. I duly ruined our Noël by plodding off down to Haddon Hall with Trudi. We turned up waiting to hear 'The Idea' but Bowie kept sloping off to the bathroom – going in one person and coming out another – and playing peek-a-boo at Freddie with some sofa cushions. I had no fuckin' idea what was happening. I just sat there totally bloody clueless and he never got around to telling me about the world's greatest idea!"

An enraged Ian could either ignore David or react, but he respectfully opted for the former in the presence of Trudi and Angie. He did realise however that Bowie had probably acquired all he could from the group. The Bowie-Mott association had reached the end of the road.

> IH: "Looking back, Bowie was a good bloke and we enjoyed our collaboration. He gave me the knowledge of what Mott was. I watched the confidence he had, and my confidence grew with it. David was a great performer, but we never formed any kind of social bond. I was much closer to Mick Ronson. I admired David and he certainly arrived during a crucial phase of my life, but we didn't have any real contact after *All the Young Dudes*."

"I don't think Ian knew just what to do at that time," says Verden Allen. "I remember him talking about Bowie doing the next single, and I said, 'You can forget about that. He's taken off. He's too busy. David won't write a single, we've got to do it ourselves.' It had to come from the group. It was obvious, because don't forget, David hadn't made it when he gave us 'Dudes', so helping Mott helped him as well."

Dale also perceived that the novelty of Mott had worn off as far as David was concerned. "He'd lost interest," Griffin would say. "I think one of the things that bored Bowie was there wasn't anything to suck from Mott. We were desperately boring for him. Once David had sussed that, it all became rather tedious for him."

> **IH:** "I remember when David took me, Trudi and Angie out to The Stage Deli that December evening in New York. Bowie advised me to take over the band that night because Defries was getting really pissed off with us and had told David he couldn't deal with us, as a band. Mott was always a democracy and that was the problem. Not only was it a diplomatic group – it wasn't 3-2 – it had to be 5-Nil – so obviously one guy was going to say 'No', just for fun. That's the way Mott the Hoople always was. I understood what David was saying because management could never get a 'Yes' out of us – or a 'No'. So, I went back to the hotel and told the band that David thought things were slow because we didn't make decisions about anything. When I said that Bowie had recommended I take over in that regard, Mick Ralphs said, 'Fuck you,' and that was the end of that. I never ran Mott. I think certain people will have you believe it, but if I was running Mott the Hoople it sure didn't feel like it to me."

Mott had started as an equal five-man billing set up in a straight line across the front of the stage for live performance, but the formation changed when Ian stood stage-centre and switched to rhythm guitar. Griffin accepted that most observers associated Hunter's face and image with Mott the Hoople. He also felt that with his shades off, Ian was mortal, but, with shades on, he was someone to be feared. "Who would you remember most?" said Dale. "Me, Ralphs or a shaded Hunter? It was David's idea that rather than push the group's image we should push Ian's image. Ian's leadership was discussed and met with the explicit approval of the band. It was the right and sensible thing to do."

In January 1973, 'One of the Boys' reached No.96 in the US singles chart but the first fracture in the group's original line-up emerged. Verden had grown tired of touring and disliked the "glam tag" that had been pinned on Mott via their Bowie involvement. There had also been increasing tensions between Allen and the band, particularly from Verden towards Ian. Now, emotions reached boiling point again, during two concert performances. The first drama occurred in Wales, when Mott played an indifferent show at Llanelli's Glen Ballroom and vented their anger on and off-stage. One journalist described the band's gig to a half-empty hall as lacklustre and wrote that the warm Welsh welcome soon died, whereupon a mike stand was thrown, and a beer bottle was used to douse some fans before it was smashed on the stage.

"It wasn't a good gig," says Stan Tippins. "The band got frustrated and Ian knocked a mike stand off the stage in a fury, and it went into the audience. Then in the dressing room afterwards, bottles were smashed, and windows were broken."

Unhappy that his songs would not be used by Mott and the damping-down of the band's original rough edge courtesy of Bowie's cleaned-up sound, Allen became restless. The following evening during Mott's gig at Sheffield University, with Nazareth as support, Verden refused to play on stage and heckled Ian. A parting of the ways had become inevitable and Allen quit.

"I left Mott because I honestly don't think anybody knew what to do at that time," says Verden. "We were sent down to play in South Wales too soon after our third American tour. We shouldn't have done that gig. Buffin slung a cymbal out into the crowd and it just missed this girl. It frightened everybody. I could also see there was

299

no way I could do any more with the band. I'd left Jimmy Cliff to get a chance to record. Now I had to leave Mott to record my own songs. I told the boys, 'I think you've got to carry on, on your own now, because I can't do any more with the group. I'm going. I'm off. That's it.' I'd said it a few times before and didn't really mean it. I think we'd all got a bit confused because we assumed David was going to help us out again with another song, but I felt Bowie wasn't coming back."

Ian admits that Verden often threatened to depart but he also felt that Allen had engaged in increasing outbursts and moods aimed at him, culminating in the flashpoint at Sheffield.

> **IH:** "Verden was not my biggest fan and would always be threatening to leave Mott, but nobody would ever take him up on it. Mick would say, 'Don't be so stupid. Everything will be alright.' Then, at the Sheffield gig, he pulled the usual. I was on stage saying, 'I'm going to do this slow number. The band doesn't really want me to do it, but I forced it on them' – and from behind I heard Phally saying, 'You're fuckin' right you forced it on us!' Afterwards, in the dressing room, he said, 'I'm leaving' – so, Mick turned around and said, 'When do you want to go?' That was it! Mick had finally decided enough was enough."

"We were very sad to lose Phally," said Watts. "He played the fool a lot, but he was great, and we all loved him. Then, suddenly, it all changed; he started writing and wanted to be taken deadly seriously. It was very hard for us all to change our attitudes towards him. I think he was worse when he'd gone home and seen his folks. He'd come back to London demanding his songs were recorded by the band."

"Phally had become increasingly intense and I remember he actually had Ian by the throat after a gig at Portsmouth once. Even worse, he jumped the queue to get him," said Dale. "Verden and I still shared adjoining flats at Stonor Road which became difficult as I was exposed to Phally's wanting to be allowed back into the band. It was a time of sadness because Verden had been a pillar of the group and was a good-humoured and kind-hearted man."

> **IH:** "Verden started getting very heavy and pushing for his songs to be used, to the extent that he wanted the whole Mott sound changing completely. What he was into was a combination of Black Sabbath and Lou Reed, which sounds weird, but there's no other way to describe it really. His songs were morbid at a time when Ralphs and I thought we should be up. Anyway, it just wasn't Mott the Hoople."

Unhappy with the lack of space afforded his songs and secretly discontent with Mott's new glamorous ethic, Allen was out! *Sounds'* 10th February 1973 front page headline proclaimed... 'MOTT SHOCK ALLEN QUITS – Hoople to continue as four-piece'... the official explanation given to the press by MainMan's Hugh Attwooll being, "a difference in musical policy with Verden wanting to develop as a songwriter and vocalist, and to work in a group that was more organ-based." The announcement stated that Allen would form a band for recording more than live work and that Mott would continue as a quartet, all the players remaining friends.

Verden signed a four-year deal with Polydor Records, releasing a 1973 single, 'Wine Ridden Talks', but the label credited the disc to Mooni – Peter 'Moon' Gosling, the father of producer Jake Gosling and songwriting partner of Bill Wyman. 'Wine Ridden Talks' failed to chart so the next project was The Cheeks, formed with future Pretenders drummer Martin Chambers and guitarist James Honeyman-Scott. Despite some good support slots with The Arrows, Hot Chocolate and Trapeze, and an appearance at London's Marquee in 1974, cheered on by Hunter and Watts, The Cheeks folded. A string of abortive projects followed including Violent Luck (a Stevens choice and initiative), High Mileage and Verden Allen's Seven Inches – then a single, 'On the Rebound', recorded with Luther Grosvenor, for Don Arden's Jet label. In the

Eighties Allen released several singles on Spinit Records including two tracks recorded with Watts and Griffin. Verden issued his first album in 1994 – *Long Time No See* – as Verden Allen and Thunderbuck Ram, containing 'Son of the Wise Ones', originally written in Mott the Hoople as 'Black Staff' and utilising adapted aborted artwork from Mott's *Sticky Fingers*. Verden later produced three solo albums: *For Each Other* (2000), *20 Year Holiday* (2002) and *My Masochistic Side* (2009).

> **IH:** "Phal's written some good songs, but he's been in the studio re-mixing them twenty times. There are people that were interested but he's ruined that by his intenseness. One day in Mott we told him he was fat and at the time he weighed 179 pounds. Within a month he was 155 and then he went down to 130. We'd get in the car with Phal and I'd say to him, 'What's the matter with you? You don't look too good.' He'd sit and think for 300 miles and you'd be talking about something completely different, almost to the gig, and he'd turn around and say, 'Well, you don't look so good either.'"

"Verden was a first-rate musician who could play the sensitive and subtle, the brutal and bellicose and all musical steps in between," said Dale Griffin. "When he left, it was the end of the 'Mott the Hoople wall of sound' that bands like Slade used to hear and then argue about what made that sound. Much of it was Verden Allen Esq."

> **IH:** "Phally's contribution to Mott the Hoople was underrated, although not by the band. He was the best musician in Mott but Phally likes to do things his way and sometimes that can go against the grain. In a way, when Verden left, Ralpher kind of left mentally too as he was left a bit stuck. The Bowie association had altered Mott radically as far as they were concerned, and neither of them really liked the glam tag."

302

"'All the Young Dudes' changed everything," says Ralphs. "As much as we wanted success, we became more like a pop group and lost our underground subversive thing. Mott changed after Bowie. The band was different."

David had helped make Mott the Hoople the stars they wanted to be, and they were now on a new flight-path, heading towards the fame that Ian sought. Bowie's glam aesthetic would be unjustly associated with Mott for decades, but Ian felt there were mitigiating circumstances behind the compartmentalisation, not least the band's survival. Mott had to change courtesy of David and 'Dudes', but Hunter always remained grateful for the intervention.

> **IH:** "With Bowie it was like we were at school together, for a while. David gave us the single that we needed badly, but it's still a mystery why he did what he did. I can't honestly say I'd have done that if I'd written 'All the Young Dudes'. We learned a lot about production and realised that we had to go up a level. Had we not done the 'Dudes' single and album I think Mott's legacy and mine would have been much smaller. I know some people preferred us as we were, but I think what we did was right for the time. I'm happy we did it – not because of the glam thing – but because 'All the Young Dudes' is a great song."

A 2002 retro-review by *Rolling Stone* described *All the Young Dudes* as "a central document of the glam era, a time when English rock wore its reckless heart on its sleeve in a truly endearing fashion." In 2003, *Zagat's 1,000 Top Albums of All Time* described *All the Young Dudes* as "sexy, rocking fun" and Mott's take of 'Sweet Jane' as the definitive version of The Velvet Underground's classic song.

All the Young Dudes would be ranked among *Rolling Stone*'s '500 Greatest Albums', and the single 'All the Young Dudes' among their '500 Greatest Songs' – moreover, it was chosen as one of the Rock & Roll Hall of Fame's 500 songs that shaped rock music.

In 2010, *David Bowie News* wrote: "It is intriguing to think that if Mott had not recorded 'All the Young Dudes', Bowie would at that time have included it in *Ziggy Stardust*. David did record the song for himself during the 1973 *Aladdin Sane* sessions, but deliberately made his version entirely different in style from Mott. He had left himself few options and his slower, more ponderous version was not suitable. In the Nineties, Bowie took to performing it live again, this time roughly in the Mott style."

Mott's 'Dudes' recording has appeared on numerous compilation albums and movie soundtracks including *Clueless*, *Juno*, *Wackness* and *Cemetery Junction*. It has also been covered by artists as diverse as The Skids, Jimmy Barnes, Bruce Dickinson, Travis, Def Leppard, Aerosmith, Ozzy Osbourne, The F-Ups, The Form and The Rebelles. The Clash even paid loose homage to the song with 'All the Young Punks (New Boots and Contracts)' on *Give 'Em Enough Rope*.

> **IH:** "It's always great to sing 'All the Young Dudes' and it doesn't get tedious. They say everybody gets 'lumbered' with a song and I'm just happy I got that one because it's interesting no matter how you play it. I helped Ozzy Osbourne on his recording of 'Dudes' in 2005 and the guy from Alice in Chains took a U-turn halfway through; the song went somewhere else and that was fascinating. For Ozzy's session I had to get our original single and find out what I did, as it's evolved so much. I had it written down as I hadn't done it that way in years.
>
> "When you've got bugger all, you know that if you don't get a hit, you'll be back in the fucking factory. Stan used to say, 'We'll be in Wiggins' on Monday' – and we all used to go white when he said it. Without 'Dudes', I wouldn't have written the songs I wrote later. Some people say they wish Mott hadn't gone the route they did, but the truth is *we had to*. There was no alternative. We were damned if we did and damned if we didn't. We were also desperate and running

out of options. It's all very well talking about it in hindsight but, at the time, everybody in the band went for the Bowie thing hook, line and sinker. We just listened to David playing 'All the Young Dudes' and knew it was a hit the minute we heard it."

Pulled out of the waves by Bowie, 'All the Young Dudes' offered Mott salvation but it would also provide everlasting stature by virtue of Hunter's and the group's special musical and vocal stamp. In 2018, *Uncut* issued *GLAM* as part of its 'Ultimate Genre Guide' publications series. Whilst Ian laughed at the labelling again, 'The 40 Best Glam Singles' section was topped by Mott the Hoople's, 'All the Young Dudes'... its No.1 caption describing the record as... "an eternal hymn."

But as Ian Hunter has always acknowledged... "'All the Young Dudes' is a truly great song – a classic – up there with 'Layla'."

CHAPTER TEN

Hot Mott

*Mott was produced by us purely
because Roxy Music wanted us to.*

After Verden Allen's departure in January 1973, Mott the Hoople encountered musical turbulence and although they would take time to fill the vacuum, the band made a conscious attempt to stabilise swiftly as a four-piece by scheduling a short British tour.

Mott was back on the road during February playing some provincial concerts supported by The Sensational Alex Harvey Band, a new and intriguingly unique Scottish outfit fronted by another magnetic leader. Harvey's group served up manically bizarre and unsettling live shows and their sensational prefix cockily challenged audiences. Some punters did not "get" Alex's defiant approach, while others loved SAHB's rock 'n' roll burlesque theatricality, but there was no middle ground.

Ian and Alex had much in common, their early musical aspirations often thwarted by spells in demoralising employment. Harvey, a carpenter by trade, claimed he'd had thirty-six different jobs including plumber's assistant, apprentice tombstone saw-cutter and lumberjack. Like Hunter, Alex had also oscillated between

Britain and Germany in the Sixties when the Hamburg clubs were thronged with rock 'n' roll stars and wannabees. The pair had pursued musical recognition for years and, finally, it was imminent for Harvey, SAHB promoting their debut album *Framed* on Mott's tour. Several acclaimed records followed, including *Next*, *Tomorrow Belongs to Me* and 'The Faith Healer', and Ian would soon describe SAHB's fifth single release, 'Sergeant Fury', as "incredible".

Glaswegian Harvey was a pithy commentator, feisty in his views, famously telling Charles Shaar Murray once: "Politicians don't know a light. When I see these poor men, Wilson and Heath, walking about and blustering and saying, 'We'll do this, and we'll do that,' with their silly suits on, they're a hundred years out of date. They've got nothing to do with what's going on. I'd rather see Ian Hunter in charge of the lifeboat, 'cuz at least I can trust his motives."

With the Caledonian connection, Harvey and Hunter got on well and Ian fondly remembers Alex introducing him to members of his Glasgow family before their 1973 Green's Playhouse gig.

IH: "Alex was for real and extremely passionate. People didn't choose him as a friend – he chose them. He was a ranter too. Alex's political comment about me was one out of left field. I guess we must have been talking politics that day as he was pretty vicious that way. Alex liked what he liked and didn't like what he didn't like. He usually decided in the first minute he met you whether he wanted to continue the conversation or not and he didn't suffer fools gladly. I'm half Scottish, so that was noted, and we got on well. The last time I saw him was at The Mayflower Hotel in New York years later and he was wandering round the world looking for pipe music. 'The pipes – the pipes,' he lectured me – and I nodded appreciatively, as I didn't want to be smacked!"

"The mini-tour with Mott was very amiable," said SAHB drummer Ted McKenna. "Alex and Ian already knew each other fairly well from their Sixties days in Germany I think, so they spoke a lot and had empathy. I remember Pete Watts with his long platform boots and Buffin bringing huge Ludwig drum sticks out at the end of each set. I also recall Buffin being upset on that tour. After one show he was getting very frustrated with things. Buffin was certainly pissed off, perhaps because SAHB was on the rise by then and I think we gave a really good account of ourselves on those dates."

"Mott was quite scared of Alex as he was somewhat older than most of them and a powerful presence on stage," says Mott roadie, Phil John. "His act was also very aggressive, though he was fine off stage. I would say it was a very close-run thing as to who went down best, Mott or Alex. I personally thought SAHB's show was brilliant. A 'Glasgow tale' of Ian jumping into the orchestra pit is wrong – well, it was an exceptionally high stage and I certainly don't remember Ian jumping into the pit – and as for taking his keyboard with him, no way. Buff also didn't hit an Apollo bouncer in the crowd with a drum stick that night either. He regularly skimmed sticks off his cymbals into the crowd, until a girl was hit in the eye one night and he stopped after that."

During their British concerts Mott played three new songs – 'Drivin' Sister (Rock 'n' Roll)', 'Rose' and 'Ballad of Mott the Hoople' – that were scheduled to feature on their next studio album. Appearing for the first time as a foursome, the band seemed somewhat at odds to diehard fans and although the new material sounded good, it seemed that Mott's sun might set once more. *Sounds* headed their review of Mott's Birmingham Town Hall gig – 'Hoople... Brash and Stomping' – but *New Musical Express* described the band's Glasgow show as shaky and sluggish saying: "They need a kick. Could be they're missing their keyboard player."

Seven months had elapsed since 'All the Young Dudes' hit the British charts and Mott the Hoople needed a new single release. Bowie had seemed prepared to donate another of his compositions as Mott's follow-up to 'Dudes' – a song entitled 'Drive-In Saturday', that appealed to Ian. David's soon-to-be-released recording was a Fifties-pop pastiche referencing Mick Jagger and Twiggy, but it was another futuristic piece that visualised post-atomic sex. Conceived as Bowie observed reflections on a series of steel domes during a US train journey, the song described a strange 2033 fantasy world following a nucleur holocaust, where a radiation-affected populace who have forgotten how to make love, seek reminders and guidance at local drive-ins, by watching erotic films. Apparently, the desert domes offered David a vision of America, Britain and China after a catastrophe. The subject matter was *not* Mott material and the band never attempted the song.

"The best thing David did was offer us 'Drive-In Saturday' and then not give it to us," said Dale Griffin. "That made Ian very keen to write a hit single, which he did. In a way, dangling that carrot and taking it away, made us all more determined, particularly Ian. Let's face it, 'Drive-In Saturday' isn't the greatest song in the world, so Bowie's instinct to withdraw it was good for all concerned."

> **IH:** "After 'Dudes' I wanted 'Drive-In Saturday', although now I don't know exactly why. Verden and I discussed how we'd handle the chord run-down and I re-worked it in a way that I was rather excited about. Memories can play tricks and a whole lot of shaking was indeed going on in 1973, but I did try to get the song for Mott. I rang up Tony Defries and said I wanted to do it, then back came the answer from Tony telling us that David didn't want us to do it. I should have spoken to Bowie direct. Then, years later, David said he wanted us to do the song and that we said no."

In 1999, Bowie told an American audience of Mott's rejection, saying he was so annoyed that one night in Florida he got drunk and shaved his eyebrows off, because the band didn't do the song, but Bowie had removed his eyebrows before he played Hunter 'Drive-In Saturday'!

> **IH:** "I'm not sure what eyebrows had got to do with us and 'Drive-In Saturday'. Bowie was always fond of saying he

309

offered the song to us and we rejected it. To my recollection, that wasn't the case at all. We never turned it down. The only thing I can think of is that Tony Defries told David one story and us another. When we were advised that Bowie wouldn't budge, I thought he might have been slightly miffed he'd given us 'Dudes'. Anyway, we now had to write our own singles. At Island, Mott always went from a pretty heavy live situation, into a studio and pounded them out the same way. With Guy Stevens we weren't very good at making records, but after we saw Bowie and Ronson at work we really had a good idea of what to do."

Hunter was lyrically and musically active at this point and had returned from the band's 1972 US tour with several new song ideas; he had drafted 'Rose', 'Ballad of Mott', 'Drivin' Sister', 'Hymn for the Dudes' and 'Honaloochie Boogie', and Mott was rehearsing 'Did You See Them Run' and 'Silver Needles', tracks that were shelved by Ian before reappearing later in more developed form. Griffin claimed that Watts had also composed a number entitled 'Symphony in O Minor'.

Says Dan Loggins, "By early 1973 I had got to know Ian Hunter as an individual, as opposed to a rock star. Still, it was rare for Ian to phone and say that he wanted to come into my office and play some new demos. He had tons of song fragments and unfinished lyrics and I asked Ian where this amazing array had come from. I remember his uniquely funny laughter as he said, 'After all these years, I think I am finally 'getting' songwriting – even singles. The ideas come in bunches now.'"

In early February, Mott the Hoople commenced recording of their second CBS album, but the group would part company with MainMan. Hunter had worked amicably with Defries, but Mott the Hoople's laddish image clashed with Tony's lavish management strategy. Mott's personnel practised absolute democracy which often resulted in disagreements and Ian admitted that the group was a cooperative that could not make a final decision without complete conferral. Defries soon became irritated with such a conflicted unit for when it came to Mott, Tony faced multiple phone calls and had to wait for multiple replies. Tempestuous relationships were seldom a rock rarity and bands are usually not a perfect democracy, but the foundation in Mott the Hoople – unanimous agreement or not at all – was an unreachable goal.

Hunter praised Defries in early 1973, conscious that during their nine-month MainMan association, Mott had sold over half a million singles and a quarter of a million albums. Describing Defries as a great manager, Ian felt Tony was the first hustler Mott had, but his comment was the public face of the Mott-MainMan association. Hunter now realised that there was an urgent need for undivided management attention if the band was to make its big break.

In 1975 Hunter would claim that initially Defries paid a lot of attention to Mott, but when David became enormous in America and then Japan, Defries was gone and they had no effective management at all. Ian knew Mott the Hoople had got to get back to America as the time was right for them – and Mott would get back to America under different management and the timing would be right – but, Defries was trying to bring Bowie and Mott in and out of the States at different times, while Hunter was becoming increasingly impatient.

IH: "Defries would only have one baby and we weren't the first. I got very upset about it because the *Dudes* album was in the American charts for over twenty weeks and we had a No.3 single in Britain. It was a shame because I liked Tony and he was excellent in the early days when it mattered."

MainMan associate Tony Zanetta could see that Mott the Hoople was a frustration to his boss. Their "street-corner" image was at odds with Defries who wanted a Bowie-style Mott mystique. "MainMan had two capital M's," says Zanetta. "Who can say why, other than it was Mr Defries who was undoubtedly the Main

311

Man. MainMan never managed bands. We fancied ourselves as 'Starmakers' in the tradition of MGM: Bowie, Iggy, Dana Gillespie, Amanda Lear and, later, John Mellencamp. We did not even have management contracts with the Spiders or The Stooges – they were 'mere sidemen'. We were much more conceptual and idea-driven in our approach. Mott the Hoople required a day-to-day, on-the-ground-running kind of management, which was *NOT* MainMan. I did make this point during one of our marathon staff meetings after a few too many brandies."

MainMan had control of the *All the Young Dudes* album release as they licensed it to Columbia Records under a production deal, but no MainMan-Mott the Hoople contracts were ever signed. Given the Haddon Hall and 'Drive-In Saturday' episodes, and MainMan's prioritisation of Bowie, Ian felt that it was time to fly. As relationships withered, Dale Griffin would claim that management involvement became increasingly remote, wages erratic and contact problematic. The band cancelled a proposed five-week American tour; main roadie Richie Anderson opted to take time-out with Black Sabbath, helping on their sound system while Phil John worked for Bowie, moving gear and working as a spotlight operator on one of the most exciting tours he ever experienced.

Mott the Hoople had to find someone else to produce their next album or do it themselves. Trident was ditched, AIR Studios nearby was booked, and Mott commenced recording.

> **IH:** "We went into AIR to start the next album even though we'd reached the stage where we considered Tony's strategy for us would no longer work, so I got Stan Tippins to call Defries and he came to AIR Studios one day. We explained why we felt it wasn't working and Tony agreed that we call it a day. Then we were told we had seven days before MainMan's income to the group would cease. We had a guy called Robert Hirschman in the wings as a lawyer and he was having kittens, so I went to CBS Records and told them where we were at with management, and that the band

needed some wages. When the label said they wouldn't pay wages I said, 'Fine, but if you don't, there won't be any Mott the Hoople – the band will fold.' They paid."

As Mott had pushed for undivided management attention, Bowie had descended on the USA for a loss-making tour. The Spiders' bassist Trevor Bolder later claimed the heat was on to crack America and re-pay RCA, but the atmosphere was turning sour. David had donned a mask, played the part of a star and had become a superstar; he was heading through the ozone but, just as Vincent Furnier became lost in the character of Alice Cooper, so Bowie was consumed by his alter ego. After nearly 200 live shows, he couldn't wait for Ziggy to end and, always with one eye on publicity, he would discard the adopted persona on the Hammersmith Odeon stage in July 1973: it was a cruel blow for Bolder and Woodmansey, a reported wages dispute with MainMan being re-paid by David's "retirement".

Under intense pressure and frightened by the speed of success, Bowie's narcotic of choice became cocaine and his resultant weight-loss and gruelling stress was depicted in *Aladdin Sane*, reflecting David's psyche at the time. Bowie later expounded that Aladdin wasn't as well defined as Ziggy as he was more of a situation than an individual, but *Aladdin Sane* reached great musical heights, with Ronson's astonishing guitar work and Mike Garson's eccentric and exotic piano playing helping Bowie secure his first No.1 album.

David's last record with Mick Ronson would be a treading-water covers project, *Pin Ups*, before he moved on to his 'Thin White Duke' character and a 'Berlin trilogy' that included *Heroes*. RCA sought to keep the past alive by releasing Bowie's 'Rock 'n' Roll Suicide' as a sales-grabbing 1974 single, but it only reached No.22 on the British chart. Symbolically, Ziggy really was dead – glam rock was breathing its last – and the Spiders were gone too, with Mick Ronson encouraged by Tony Defries to go solo. In early 1975, Ian would reflect on Bowie's success.

IH: "Dave really disappeared in the midst of his own creation. What he figured was going to happen, he suddenly found himself right in the middle of, and it's sad, because in his own way he created, initially, the same impact as Dylan. By the time David delivered *Hunky Dory* and *Ziggy*, he was pretty exhausted, and everybody was having a great time slagging him because he was the new phenomena, but I didn't think he was a phenomenon – I thought he was for real. Bowie was very Jekyll and Hyde. A lot of David's genius was an almost Dracula-like quality of draining what he wanted, before moving on to the next victim and then he had this great quality of converting it into what he believed the public wanted – and he was often exactly right."

Hugh Attwooll believes Defries' genius was that he possessed incredible insight and had formidable faith in Bowie, believing he could make David a star where others had failed, using clever and unconventional means. "Defries took Bowie away from previous labels and managers and stirred up a lot of trouble in the process, because he operated in a way that hadn't been seen from an artist's manager in the UK before," said Hugh. "By hiring me and lots of others who really knew nothing, Defries could also totally control the way things were done. Bowie arrived at a point in the mid-Seventies where he was fantastically famous, but didn't have much money, because Tony had ploughed all previous earnings from Bowie into running MainMan. Defries told David he would make him a star – and he did – but I don't think David would have made it as far as he did without Defries."

Over the years David's collaborations would involve Peter Noone, Mott the Hoople, Lou Reed, Iggy Pop, Lulu, David Sanborn, Brian Eno, Robert Fripp, Earl Slick, Adrian Belew and Nile Rodgers – but he would drop assets as swiftly as he embraced and mined them. Crucially, Hunter summed Bowie up in 2016 as "having curiosity in many things", and throughout his life that inquisitiveness included relationships, culture, art and religion. David Robert Jones had become Davie Bowie, Bowie became Ziggy Stardust and Ziggy would become immortal. David's complete story would be special, but his "five years" with Mick Ronson remain his super-fertile period and the era that created the greatest storm.

Dan Loggins says, "It seemed with MainMain by early 1973 that Mott the Hoople had been relegated to a less significant role so, as the band had faced a similar situation at Island, they were determined not to let that happen again. It was time to sort out management and define who they were and where they were going."

As Mott worked in AIR Studios, the exit of MainMan from Mott's orbit created a managerial void, but an American lawyer named Robert Hirschman already represented the band in Britain. Californian-born Hirschman had played bass and trombone professionally and toured in the States with various jazz ensembles. He also appeared in two early Sixties American movies, *Elmer Gantry* featuring Burt Lancaster, and *Tender Is the Night* starring Jason Robards. Deciding that road-life was not for him, Hirschman attended the University of California and with business administration and legal degrees, moved into entertainment law and business consultancy, negotiating publishing and recording agreements. Described by Loggins as "soft spoken, easy-going and the definition of California mellow", Hirschman came to London in early 1972 to set up a UK-European publishing wing for a Los Angeles legal firm who represented artists, including chart-toppers Bread. Bob handled a contract for progressive rock band Genesis then ran International Entertainment Associates (IEA), operating from Davies Street in London's West End.

"I arrived in the UK to 'set up shop' in January 1972 and acted for Genesis and later became the band's manager," recalls Bob. "I heard about Mott the Hoople in the winter of 1972 and started representing Mott in early '73. I was first contacted to negotiate a contract with CBS Records, so I guess I was starting to become known as a music lawyer."

"I'd run into Bob at a London music biz gathering," says Dan Loggins. "We had not met previously in the US but, as two 'Yanks' in London, we had a personal affinity. He had a very good reputation as a legal mind and artists' advocate, and he possessed a completely different persona to Tony Defries – no mink coats and Cuban cigars! So, when Mott's production deal with Defries was ending, I asked Bob if he could look at the situation. We set up a meeting with the band and Bob renegotiated a new arrangement for Mott as a 'Direct Artist' signing to Columbia Records. Once Mott was free of the MainMan production deal, Bob Hirschman remained as an advisor to the group.

"I had tried to pick a second 'stop-gap' single from the *Dudes* album and felt 'One of the Boys' was another hit, but the track had been the B-side to 'All the Young Dudes', so I wasn't sure where to go from there. Ian then said we should hold off as he was very excited about his new material. At the 'Honaloochie Sessions' in AIR, I watched Hunter's song being created, step by step, with Andy Mackay of Roxy Music adding sax. Ian planned out all the parts, structured the vocals and arranged the instruments, as Dale Griffin alertly wrote notes in his ever-present 'journal', so as not to miss anything. Dale was one of those quiet types who didn't say a lot, but when he did, you listened. I called him 'The Silent Assassin'. He didn't miss a thing! At this time, Dick Asher asked me to become CBS's UK A&R Manager, so I had more autonomy to sign British acts. Clive wanted to build on the success of *All the Young Dudes*, so Mott's next LP would be hugely important as we hoped the band would attract more new blood to the label. Our wish would soon be realised with the signing of David Essex, a Cockney lad and Mott the Hoople fan, who went on to great success in Britain and America."

Hunter appreciated that Hirschman was keen to act as Mott's new manager based in Britain, but he believed strongly that the band's future lay in America. Watts recalled that Columbia chief Clive Davis flew over to London after Mott's split from Defries and became instrumental in a new management arrangement.

An alumnus of New York University, record producer and music executive, Davis was President of the Columbia label. He rated Ian Hunter and would sign him more than once. Clive's Hoople management propositions included Bud Prager who looked after Mountain, the physically imposing former wrestler who led Zeppelin, Peter Grant, and Fred Heller who represented Blood Sweat & Tears. Mott wanted strong representation and met Bud Prager but rejected him. Watts recalled that Prager was very upset and believed he never forgave Mott the Hoople. Ian recollects that the band didn't like Bud's hair and a paranoid Watts was worried there was "mafia involvement" in the air. In the end, Bob Hirschman was retained to oversee the group's legal affairs and manage them in Europe, but Mott accepted a dual structure when Fred Heller was appointed as their manager for North America.

New York-born Frederick Heller had studied finance and business affairs, and then acted for the successful jazz-rock collective, Blood Sweat & Tears. Fred managed the band for eleven years and innovatively set up a corporation that owned the group with the partners buying buildings in a pension and profit plan. Heller would also represent Lou Reed, The Brecker Brothers and Jaco Pastorius who signed to PVT, a label that Fred partnered with BST's drummer Bobby Colomby. During his career, Fred also managed Jess Roden, Stan Getz, Garland Jeffreys and Columbia bands Private Lighting and The Dudes.

"In 1973 Clive Davis of CBS Records flew me to the UK to meet Mott the Hoople," says Heller. "Clive and Dick Asher, who was running Columbia, both wanted me to manage the band. Al Teller was also a powerful executive at Columbia Records. He was Vice President and a big supporter for Mott the Hoople, and he and I were responsible for the promotion of Mott's albums. None of this would have been possible without Clive Davis who recommended me to the band."

IH: "Fred and Bob were on ten per cent each, but Heller had kittens when we told him. Fred was managing Blood Sweat

& Tears and he also managed Lou Reed. Mott liked Fred and I liked him too. He was a whizz kid, but I think his tastes were more jazz than rock 'n' roll. Fred was young, he was fresh, and he was a nice guy."

Watts recalled that Robert Hirschman had offered to act as British and American manager for Mott and whilst Ralphs liked Bob's drive and positive thinking, Tippins was not convinced that Heller and Hirschman harboured real imagination for the group. "Hunter liked Heller because he was young and very enthusiastic, but I wasn't so sure," admits Stan. "I could suss these people out a lot quicker and easier than the band."

"I remember Bob at a meeting saying, 'Look, why don't I become your manager over here too? I know the ins and outs of the group'," said Watts. "'I've been running it for two or three months.' And Ralphs said, 'I think it'd be better you do what you're doing Bob – it'd be good – we should keep it like that.' We didn't in the end, and he became the other half because it seemed sensible to have one manager here and one over there."

H&H Enterprises was launched in 1973 by Fred and Robert for the exclusive management of Mott the Hoople, with Heller looking after their US affairs, and Hirschman handling European matters and acting as the band's legal adviser. By 1974 however, the duo would be acting as Robert Hirschman Business Management from London and Fred Heller Enterprises Limited based at Dobbs Ferry in upstate New York. Fred would help structure plans for Mott's "assault" on the American market. Dan Loggins described Heller as a good man who was very positive for Mott the Hoople at the time.

"I don't know who," said Hirschman, "but someone suggested that Mott the Hoople should have a dual management structure, Fred for North America and me 'elsewhere' – and that was it. In practice, Fred Heller and I maybe had six conversations during our time together with Mott the Hoople. There was no enmity between us at all, it was just that we had two distinct provinces and on the few occasions it was necessary, we spoke business and decided jointly. To be fair, I didn't have the management experience that Fred did in the USA. I'd never managed in America. I was a music lawyer."

Away from the mad shadow of MainMan, Mott the Hoople's next move would be crucial. They needed a follow-up single and album release to trump 'Dudes'. *All the Young Dudes* had been a success but the demands for stronger and better Mott songs was rising. The pressure fell largely on Ian but devising fresh material on a continual basis was difficult. Tippins admitted that it was tough for Hunter to originate a new album each year and, that whilst he wrote great songs, Stan felt Ian deserved greater band support.

Mott the Hoople recorded their new album from early February through to April 1973 at AIR with some overdubbing at EMI Abbey Road in St John's Wood. The two London locations had strong connections to Beatles' producer, Sir George Martin who had founded AIR in 1965 as a freelance production business. In 1969, Associated Independent Recording (London) Limited leased a fourth-floor former banqueting hall above 214 Oxford Street and constructed 'sprung' studios to eliminate rumbles from the London Underground train system and traffic noise around Oxford Circus below. AIR Studios had two recording areas – Studio 1 "for orchestras" and the smaller Studio 2 "for bands" – and their client list embraced Elton John, Wings, Roxy Music, King Crimson, T. Rex and Rod Stewart. Described as a studio "built by producers for producers," AIR's team included Chris Thomas, Geoff Emerick and John Punter.

Another special engineer, Bill Price, had been part of George Martin's studio launch, helping to make AIR London one of the world's best recording facilities. Purloined from Decca, Price worked on film scores for Martin when the business branched into movies and AIR No.1 was equipped with the best in film technology. Price also collaborated with Richard Perry, Muff Winwood and Alan Harris, mixing recordings by Badfinger, Nilsson and Sparks. The understated and dedicated Bill Price became a crucial recording and mixing figure for Mott and Ian Hunter.

Mott the Hoople's second CBS LP would be titled *Mott*, but the name was chosen after recording work was complete. Watts explained that the band opted for the scant title because they wanted to consolidate the group's status and further establish their name. "We'd had all these wild Guy Stevens titles during our early period," said Pete. "*Mott* was simple and direct for a change!"

Mott would be a true test of Mott's mettle, but Dale later suggested that CBS and Hunter had panicked, Ian deciding at AIR that he'd "gone solo", inviting Ralphs, Watts and Griffin to play on his first single. Griffin said he was furious but, having taped 'Honaloochie Boogie' and 'Ballad of Mott the Hoople' so well, the drummer claimed Hunter's intended solo career was forgotten. Why Ian would cut a Mott the Hoople ballad as a solo track remains unclear and Hunter always rejected the drummer's solo aspirations claim.

> **IH:** "The way I remember it during the *Mott* sessions, Buff came up to me and asked if this was my solo album. I was astonished, but Ralpher was already thinking about his future so I can see why they may have thought that way. If I'd have had any fucking brains I would have answered, 'Yes', but it never dawned on me. In retrospect, it wouldn't have been a bad move though. I guess I was in a position of power and I didn't know it. I was doing all the writing for them and was too busy to think about it. It was obviously a Mott album, but if I had been out for myself and not the band, as Buff imagined, that would have been the move."

'Honaloochie Boogie' was one of the first takes committed to tape at AIR and it was unlike any previous Mott song. The oddly undecipherable lyrics, tricky rhythms and funky sax surprised Dan Loggins but he loved the modern radio sound, narrator-style verses, and memorable chorus. Faster than the original Whitfield Street demo, it felt like a hit. Loggins recalled that Lionel Conway who ran Island Music's publishing wing was very excited about Hunter's new songs and whilst Lionel may have seen Ian as a potential solo act, Dan saw that Ian was still "a band guy" and felt he didn't want to appear to be on a "star-trip".

In addition to 'Honaloochie Boogie', the other early songs that Mott laid down at AIR were, 'Ballad of Mott the Hoople', 'Hymn for the Dudes', 'Drivin' Sister' and 'Rose'. Ian wanted Roy Wood of Move, ELO and Wizzard fame to produce the *Mott* sessions and, at one point, the British press announced, 'Roy Wood Producing Mott'. The feature claimed that Wizzard's leader would be overseeing Mott the Hoople's new tracks, but this was soon followed by a denial stating that Wood would not be involved. Roy's personal recollection is that he was too busy to help Mott at the time, but he particularly remembered that Hunter liked the horn section in his band, which Wood had used to stunning effect on their 1972 hit 'Ball Park Incident' and Wizzard's next single, the No.1 chart-topper 'See My Baby Jive'.

"Ian idolised Roy after 'See My Baby Jive' and we had a few arguments about Mott adopting that style," said Watts. "Ian often went on about Roy Wood and the Stones, asking Buff and I to play like Charlie Watts and Bill Wyman. I never liked Wizzard's records much, simply because everything was automatic double-tracked. I thought they sounded messy. Stan Tippins, encouraged by Hunter, phoned Roy's manager who got quite nasty saying, 'What do you want? What's your game mate?' All we wanted was to see if Roy would produce one album."

IH: "I think Roy was having an awful time management-wise with Don Arden, so we never got the chance and the link-up never materialised. Roy passed on the *Mott* album and I think he chose the wrong one to turn down. I always liked Roy Wood's voice and songs. I'd seen the original Move in a Birmingham club in the Sixties and they were great. I liked Roy's early stuff like 'Blackberry Way' and 'Fire Brigade' – all great singles – but the track that would keep me alive in 1973 and save my life was 'See My Baby Jive' – great production, great song, great everything! That charted for weeks when there was not much good music about. I was getting totally disenchanted, then suddenly that single appeared. It was brilliant."

Mott also considered asking John Lennon to assist them and although it was only discussed amongst the band, Pete felt it proved that Mott the Hoople was thinking big-league. "Lennon was the only guy that all of us respected," said Watts. "Everybody in the group wanted that because we just loved him. He would have been good for us and I'd loved to have met him."

Ian also asked Mike Leander to produce *Mott*, a songwriter who had stamped his distinctive arrangements and production style on Sixties pop music with Billy Fury and The Small Faces. Mike was now the driving force behind Gary Glitter and The Glitter Band, and Ian admired Leander's work.

> **IH:** "I liked Gary Glitter's sound and I thought Leander was great. I figured it would be different for Mott the Hoople, but it would be good, because he was an intelligent producer."

"We discussed several possible producers for *Mott* including Gus Dudgeon, Glyn Johns, and Ken Scott," admits Dan Loggins. "Trident Studios was also nurturing several new engineer-producer types like Roy Thomas Baker. At that time, Ian *was* certainly enthralled by Roy Wood and *was* 'a fan' of Mike Leander. Bob Hirschman, Dick Asher and I went back and forth on possible producers. With Mott's 'new' CBS contract we didn't have room for expensive 'A-Listers' who usually looked for up front money – and a royalty too!"

Mott had invited saxophonist Andy Mackay to guest on 'Honaloochie Boogie' as Roxy Music was camped in AIR No.2 during February, recording their stunning second album, *For Your Pleasure*. Roxy had just taken Britain by storm at a rate of knots

322

with their inventive eponymous album and debut single, 'Virginia Plain'. Hunter rated Roxy Music highly and their frontman, Bryan Ferry, had fond memories of AIR describing it as one of the great London recording studios. "I remember the sessions alongside Mott," recalled Ferry. "AIR was a great studio. We used to work and look out of the window and you'd see London's rush hour running around. You felt you were in the centre of the universe." Suddenly Roxy Music made a comment that influenced Mott the Hoople – and *Mott*.

> **IH:** "We'd started the *Mott* album with Bill Price as engineer and were still looking for a producer. I remember Andy and Eno popped in to AIR No.1 to listen to 'Honaloochie Boogie' and said, 'This is good. You don't need a producer. Just do it yourself. It sounds fine.' We never did get a producer, so Andy and Eno saved us a few quid! They made us realise that maybe we didn't need outside help. Really *Mott* was produced by us purely because Roxy Music wanted us to!"

"We thought, 'If they think we can, we'll do it,'" said Watts. "Andy Mackay used to come and sit with us at AIR a lot because he didn't like being in the studio with the rest of his group. Andy was really nice. I got quite friendly with him and we were going to go to greyhound racing at White City, but it never quite happened. He asked if he could join Mott but, sadly, there was no way because we only needed sax on two songs."

Watts claim was not the case according to Mackay, although Andy accepts that 1973 was not a joyous period in Roxy Music's history. The band relationship between Bryan Ferry and Brian Eno had become strained and Mackay was concerned about what might happen if Eno quit, which he did, before the recording of their third album, *Stranded*.

"I do remember the *Mott* recordings at AIR," says Andy. "It was a great place to work at that time and bands did tend to pop in and out of each other's sessions. As for joining Mott the Hoople, although I enjoyed playing with them, I had no intention of leaving Roxy Music. It was not a particularly happy time working on *For Your Pleasure* and when it looked as if Eno was going to leave, I considered options if Roxy broke up. I think I had one meeting with Mott's manager, but I certainly didn't try and join Mott the Hoople as Pete Watts claimed. When Eno did leave, he strongly persuaded me and Phil Manzanera to carry on with Roxy."

And so, bolstered by Mackay and Eno, the *Mott* album would be 'Produced by Mott the Hoople' and 'Arranged by Ian Hunter'. Hearing sax and cello on 'Honaloochie Boogie' and inspired by Roy Wood – who had also used AIR Studios to record 'See My Baby Jive' – Hunter grabbed the engineer that Wizzard employed for that "life-saving" single – Bill Price. Bill would become a virtual Mott mainstay helping to graft Wood's Phil Spector-styled "British Wall of Sound" onto two future Hoople hits. Price acted as main engineer throughout on *Mott* aided by Alan Harris at AIR and John Leckie at Abbey Road: the tape operators were offspring of former *Goons Show* stars – Peter's son, Mike Sellers and Spike's eldest, Sean 'Pinball' Milligan.

Bill Price possessed great stamina and was an engineer who was brilliant at "getting a sound". He would often work for sixteen hours a day with Mott, always unruffled but sustained by his 100-a-day chain-smoking habit. Dan Loggins felt Bill had special people skills and that he was crucial in the production of *Mott*, helping to make the album work successfully on many levels.

> **IH:** "Bill Price was fantastic as an engineer, but he really became our 'semi-producer' with us filling in the other holes. He was a great unsung British recording hero and was on countless hits and people don't even realise it. Hits were coming off Bill morning, noon and night and he never got much credit. I remember when he called us in one day at AIR and said, 'Listen to what I was working on last night.' Then he played us Paul McCartney's 'Live and Let Die' and we nearly died. He'd played us a few of his tapes over the period but

I said to him that day, 'Bill, you've got to stop playing us this stuff – it's fantastic, but demoralising – we'll all want to pack it in and go home.' After all the studio dramas and frustrations like *Brain Capers*, when we recorded at AIR with Bill, that was the first time we had a decent shot at a good drum sound. He became well known later, with The Sex Pistols, Clash and The Pretenders but Bill was a real asset on the *Mott* album. I think we managed to 'produce' ourselves because of him. Frankly, it was always a disaster when we couldn't use Bill."

Mott the Hoople knew that with *Mott* they had to utilise the lessons learned on *All the Young Dudes* but surpass rather than simply maintain those standards. George Martin observed some AIR overdubs and then, with the bulk of the recording completed, the band moved to Abbey Road, where Pink Floyd had recently completed *The Dark Side of the Moon*. Dale claimed that nominal *Mott* recording work was done at Abbey Road, but the band were pleased to be there as they thought the studio name would look good on their album sleeve. John Leckie was one of the Abbey Road recording team who worked as desk balance engineer on *Mott*, Pink Floyd's *Meddle* and Paul McCartney and Wings' *Red Rose Speedway*.

"I remember us doing 'All the Way from Memphis' with Ian trying out piano in Studio 3 at Abbey Road," says John. "They worked out the song and it was basically done in an hour or two. I also recall adding the car sound effects to 'Drivin' Sister' and doing some work on 'Violence'. Bill Price was a great engineer – who always smoked lots of St Moritz Menthol cigarettes – and wore good shirts with cuff links!"

Mott finally arrived as a sensational album, containing nine sparkling tracks: 'All the Way from Memphis', 'Whizz Kid', 'Hymn for the Dudes', 'Honaloochie Boogie', 'Violence', 'Drivin' Sister', 'Ballad of Mott the Hoople (March 26, 1972, Zurich)', 'I'm A Cadillac/ El Camino Dolo Roso' and 'I Wish I Was Your Mother'.

On 19th April, the band listened to a complete playback at AIR and were blown away, Ian describing the record as "bleedin' amazing". On 5th May the headline on *Sounds'* front page read, 'MOTT: AFTER SIX MONTHS' SILENCE: ALBUM, SINGLE,' and announced the release later that month of 'Honaloochie Boogie' to be followed by an LP (untitled at that time) in July. On 23rd May 1973, Bob Hirschman confirmed to Tony Defries and MainMan that Mott the Hoople had delivered finished master tapes of their second album directly to CBS, constituting fulfilment of obligations under the MainMan Columbia contract of 1st June 1972. All subsequent recordings would be between the band and their label directly.

CBS issued 'Honaloochie Boogie' on 25th May, the single being rush-released minus the picture sleeve originally planned. It had been ten months since 'All the Young Dudes' but now, Mott the Hoople was back. In a swathe of blistering reviews *Record Mirror* described 'Honaloochie Boogie' as 'Instant Commercialization by Mott'. Chris Welch wrote in *Melody Maker*: "Mott have struck hard and deep with this echoing, menacing boogie: it's a winner" – while Steve Peacock of *Sounds* said: "This is much closer to what I've always thought of as the spirit of Mott the Hoople and it's an excellent single." *Beat Instrumental* proclaimed 'MOTT THE HOOPLE BOOGIE MINUS BOWIE' while *DISC* trumpeted 'HOT MOTT'. After almost a year, 'All the Young Dudes' had seemed like an unbeatable hit single and Bowie's song was in danger of becoming a cross for Mott the Hoople – but Hunter had delivered, conscious that the band's first 45 after 'Dudes' was a crucial record.

IH: "I knew that 'Honaloochie Boogie' was a very important track and that if it stiffed, we had a big problem. At the time, some people looked incorrectly on 'All the Young Dudes' as David's single and said we couldn't do it on our own, so I set out to show them. We didn't want to become a Bowie satellite and I realised we couldn't live off David for the rest of our lives. We knew we had to follow up with one of our own, so after 'Dudes' there was nine months of panic stations, with Mick and I frantically trying to 'write a hit'. Luckily, we managed it – well, finally I did – which pissed Mick off. It would have pissed me off."

'Honaloochie Boogie' entered the UK charts on 16th June where it stayed for nine weeks, rising to No.12. Mott promoted the single with a *Top of the Pops* television appearance on 8th June and made a seldom-seen promotional video of 'Honaloochie Boogie', directed by Hereford acquaintance Richard Weaver. For the princely sum of £150, the film was shot in a basement near the Hard Rock Café close to the junction of Park Lane and Piccadilly in London's West End. "We featured a jukebox in the video with Ian and the band," recalled Weaver, "and I found a real Teddy Boy and brought him over from the East End. I remember that the filming took all day as the camera broke down and the whole event had to be watched over by a union crew – who sat and read the daily newspapers. Watts was not happy as I filmed him side-on and he considered it was not exactly flattering in the nose-department."

"It's about being on the streets of Northampton,' Ian would say of 'Honaloochie Boogie', "with no money, and then a kid turns you on to rock 'n' roll. It's the story of the guy who turned me on. But the title was just word invention. 'Honaloochie' is just a word that looks alright written down."

The B-side of Mott's blistering new single was Hunter's 'Rose', a sorry and intimate tale of a doomed *"Rock 'n' roll slag"* drowning in drugs. 'Rose' was a sublimely moving song with Ian mourning a girl losing her youth in a dead-end street of dope, creating a uniquely paternal eyewitness account of the tragedy. Hunter would only ever say that the song was based on someone, but that he has long forgotten who it was. 'Rose' was originally placed as the closing track on the first running order for *Mott* but was employed as the B-side of 'Honaloochie Boogie' instead.

Vancouver band The Payola$ would include a song called 'Rose' on their Mick Ronson-produced 1982 album, *No Stranger to Danger*, relating the tale of a girl with the cocaine stare and rock 'n' roll

327

mind, crying in London's Wardour Street. Payola$ singer Paul Hyde loved lyrics and marvelled at Hunter's compositional skill. "Ian's 'Rose', for me, is a lovely little song, full of empathy and quite sad really," says Paul. "I think it's one of the top ten rock and roll songs ever written. My 'Rose' was loosely based on a brief encounter with a prostitute in London and is largely a work of fiction, but I gave her the name in the song out of respect for Ian's 'Rose'."

With Ralphs using volume swell to create a violin-effect for his guitar solo and featuring Thunderthighs on backing vocals and organ passages reminiscent of Verden's style, the removal of 'Rose' from *Mott* was a strange decision. The song would be one of several excellent single B-sides by Mott the Hoople and the first that Ian generously credited jointly to the group. Watts stated that these were handed to the band partly because other members were sometimes contributing arrangement ideas towards Hunter's numbers, without declared credit.

> **IH:** "Writing is where the money is, and many great musicians don't write and get fed up about it – understandably. It all depends on the value you place on a guy. Maybe you work out something where you give him a piece of one song as his contribution. The first time I did that was with Mott when I gave them the writing and publishing on the B-sides that I wrote – which collect the same amount in royalties as A-sides!"

On 20th July 1973, CBS released *Mott,* and the record-buying public discovered that Hunter and the band had delivered big-time. The album retained shades of the group's early wildness but embraced a fresh sonic clarity, while Ian exhibited a growing sensitivity and unique skill in relating the snakes-and-ladders life of a rock musician. Mott the Hoople had found their feet, their voice and their survival instinct with *Mott* and the album remains a classic chronicle of the trials, tribulations, inspirations and desperation of rock 'n' roll. 'Ballad of Mott the Hoople' immortalised their

March 1972 split in Switzerland, 'Hymn for the Dudes' exposed the absurdity of music-related fame and 'I Wish I Was Your Mother' remains one of Hunter's finest personal songs. The proto-punk 'Violence' conveyed tongue-in-cheek angst and Ian had penned two cracking tracks that nestled in the album grooves as hit singles – 'Honaloochie Boogie' and 'All the Way from Memphis'. There was sheen, sass and sensibility in Hunter's writing now, and his burgeoning creativity was predominant on *Mott*.

"The *Mott* album" as it was instantly known, became a Seventies milestone and has received much acclaim over the decades. Featuring fine songs, crystal production and exceptional musicianship (notably Mick Ralphs' guitar work), *Mott* was the band's most complete musical statement. Ian's autobiographical tales addressed the travails of stardom, the highs and lows of touring and the battle for and pitfalls of success. This was exemplified by the exciting élan of the album's opening track 'All the Way from Memphis', where Ian chronicled the fraught but fantastic events surrounding Mott's recent Ellis Auditorium gig. Referencing Verden's *"six-string razor"* that was lost in transit and laced with shards of sarcasm and wit, Hunter's inspired song possessed a piano-pounding introduction that bouyantly echoed his admiration for Jerry Lee Lewis and Leon Russell – the latter being another important inspiration on Ian, who enjoyed the American's piano abandon and rock-country-gospel mix.

> **IH:** "I was a huge fan of piano players like Richard Tee and Leon Russell. I first heard Leon on the Delaney and Bonnie album in the late Sixties and I had never heard piano playing like it. It was magnificent. I loved 'In the Ghetto' and Dylan's 'Watching the River Flow', and Leon was a big influence on me. His piano playing was incredible, he had a southern gospel feel and his singing was amazing. I loved the *Leon Russell* record and *The Band* album. I wish I'd been born south of Memphis as I adore that stuff from the Deep South, going back to Jerry Lee Lewis and Little Richard."

'All the Way from Memphis' described the troughs and peaks of rock's dusty trail, Ian colourfully portraying a tongue-in-cheek vision of a roadworn rock 'n' roller who was *"still on the dole"* despite Mott's new-found stardom. One of Hunter's finest songs, he dedicated it to Memphis, Tennessee, Leee Black Childers and Tony Zanetta. Kentucky-born Childers had photographed "happenings" at Warhol's Factory studio, assisted on Andy's controversial play *Pork* and, being MainMan Vice President, had acted as an advance PR figure for Bowie. Wardrobe man for Mott, Childers rated the band's fans "number one" for sheer enthusiasm and he was a rock for Mott on the road, always helping, always smiling and taking photos everywhere. Zanetta also acted in underground theatre, had a central role in *Pork* and was MainMan manager for various Ziggy tours.

> **IH:** "It was a magical one-off night in Memphis. We were headlining, the place was packed, and the people were fantastic. Some of the lyric is true and some lines about the Liverpool docks and the Oreoles were poetic license. The evolution of the song was a pain; I wrote the music on piano, but I'd worn out all the white notes and had to go on to the black notes, which I didn't know anything about – but that's when it's best, because nothing is relevant. After doing the music, I had a cassette recorder by the side of the bed for weeks, but I couldn't get the words. Following the Memphis gig, I wrote the lyric so eventually the track got finished, but I always hated the mix. I remember after the band left AIR one day I tried to get Bill Price to do something with the bass because it sounded like a mole burying through the ground. Then Pete came back to the studio, as he'd forgotten to take a bag with him, and caught me at it, so there was a rumpus."

Mott's working title for 'Memphis' had been 'Rocker in Sea Sharp (And Bristol Fashion)'. Written in C-sharp, which is not a sax-friendly key, the song climaxed with a blazing tenor part from Andy Mackay, battling alongside Ralphs' soaring guitar lines in a sensational duel. Watts felt 'Memphis' turned out "insipid" and he "wasn't too keen" on Andy's playing. Whilst some thought Mackay may not have been as slick as session players like David Sanborn, he was more interesting and distinctive for it, and was chosen by Mott ahead of Bobby Keys, famous for his work with the Stones.

> **IH:** "Bobby Keys came into a session for 'All the Way from Memphis', totally out of it. When he couldn't make the cut, the band left me with him to try and salvage something. In the end, he said, 'If you don't use it, don't pay me.' We didn't use it, but he was paid. Bobby Keys did great stuff. We just caught him on an off-day."

Watts complained about the 'All the Way from Memphis' recording but Dan Loggins of CBS viewed it as a major Seventies story-song that echoed classic early rock 'n' roll, with contemporary observations of touring-grind thrown in. Loggins loved Ian's pounding Jerry Lee piano tribute, Andy Mackay's sax and Ralphs' lead-guitar responses. Fun, rhythm, mystery and an unmistakable catchy chorus – 'All the Way from Memphis' had it all in Dan's eyes and director Martin Scorsese was also impressed enough to use it as an "overture" to his acclaimed 1974 film, *Alice Doesn't Live Here Anymore*, where a teenage boy insists on playing "Mott the Hoople" vinyl at maximum volume.

'Whizz Kid', perhaps the most underrated track on *Mott*, was Hunter's tale of a mystifying New York City beat – a girl from Brooklyn Heights with a battered background who still possessed stardust and an engaging smile. The American story in the verses contrasted nicely with Ian's nod to Britain's 'send you victorious' National Anthem and the arresting melody was enhanced with Ralphs' guitar, synthesizer and child-like background vocals. Dale Griffin was upset that the song was spelt incorrectly on the album sleeve with one 'D' and recalled that 'Whizz Kidd' was originally given the working title 'Catch a Cold' because Mick thought the song was reminiscent of Free's 'Catch a Train'. Cohort Miller Anderson had helped Ian with a few chords on 'Whizz Kid' and was duly aknowledged on Mott's LP credits. Musically, 'Whizz Kid' was complex and Hunter had to encourage the rest of the band to accept and develop the track.

> **IH:** "Mott's 'writing strategy' was that you played something in a rehearsal room and if they picked up on it, it was 'in'. If they ignored it, it was back to the drawing board. 'Whizz Kid' was very troublesome because we didn't know what to play on top of the backtrack which was involved and sounded weird on its own. The band was worried, but I could see the finished article. That was the only time I ever pushed a song. Mick Ralphs contributed a beautiful guitar part."

Mott's third cut – 'Hymn for the Dudes' – credited to Hunter-Allen, had been played live by the band for some months and was first demoed at CBS Studios with Verden in October 1972. Now, it too had evolved majestically and during the final playback session for *Mott* at AIR Studios, 'Hymn for the Dudes' was cheered and applauded by all present. Ian teasingly sang of musical transformation – *"a new song rising"* – highlighting come-and-go idols and demolishing the pedestal accorded rock artists whose star status is invariably temporary. The Nazz referenced David's 'Ziggy Stardust' lyric and a Fifties jive-talking salute by American comic-poet, Lord Buckley. Ian said at the time of *Mott's* release that he had directed his message at the band's young and enthusiastic audience. 'Hymn for the Dudes' showcased Hunter's voice, acoustic guitar and stately piano alongside soaring Ralphs' guitar and organ. It also featured backing vocals from Thunderthighs, a female trio of Dari Lalou, Casey Synge and Karen Friedman who had worked with Dana Gillespie and

Lou Reed. 'Hymn for the Dudes' remains Dan Loggins' all-time favourite Mott the Hoople cut.

"When Mott was putting 'Hymn for the Dudes' together, I remember thinking that the band was so 'on point' and precise," says Loggins. "The intro presented an air of majesty with Hunter's bold Rachmaninoff piano and Ralphs' explosive and searing guitar solo remains one of the most moving lead breaks ever. It was thrilling. Glancing around the control room I looked at Ian, eyes closed, but grinning. I turned to Dale, who had put his notebook down and had a look of absolute awe. I made eye contact with Bill Price – he just shook his head and his eyes widened as our expressions met. I will never forget that session. The song was the highlight of *Mott*, but nobody could have foreseen its arrival – even a serious early Mott the Hoople fan, who had loved 'Walkin' with a Mountain'. Ian had written an *anthem* for the day, if not for a generation."

> **IH:** "I often see the glass as half empty and that comes out lyrically with me. 'Hymn for the Dudes' was 'the goldfish bowl'. The song was also a way of saying to our fans that it's going to be alright. The Thunderthighs were our excellent session trio who just seemed to understand what we were doing. It's always easier if walk-ons 'get it'. Thunderthighs had done the backing vocals for Lou Reed's 'Walk on the Wild Side' and were connected to Lynsey de Paul. They were totally into it. After the 'Nazz' line, I remember we slowly lowered the dB level so that we could get full impact for Ralpher's great solo. It worked."

Clocking in at a mere 2 minutes and 35 seconds, 'Honaloochie Boogie' was the first Mott single written by Hunter, post-Bowie. Ian felt he had contrived too much, but he worked hard to get the song right and it duly reached No.12 in the UK singles chart. Descriptions of "*steel-toed shoes*" and a friend who had converted Ian to rock and roll referenced Freddie 'Fingers' Lee in Sixties Northampton.

There was humour in Hunter's words too with a clever Chuck Berry reference and a treated, 'robotic' chorus vocal that was more than cute.

> **IH:** "Honaloochie didn't mean anything and was simply the word I used when I played the song to Mott as it fitted the chord run-down – an early misdemeanour! When you write songs, sometimes before you get the lyric you just sing rubbish and hope for the best. Then, when we did it, the band immediately talked about 'Honaloochie Boogie' quite naturally. I was very dubious, but Buff and Pete convinced me it didn't matter, and they were right. In the end we just left it, but it was all a bit too 'poppy' for me. I don't think Ralphs was very impressed. The verses mean something so I suppose that's okay. I wasn't completely mad about 'Honaloochie Boogie' but I did not labour in vain – it was a hit."

Alongside Andy Mackay's tenor sax, 'Honaloochie Boogie' featured electric cello played by Paul Buckmaster, a Royal Academy of Music graduate who arranged rich horns, brooding woodwind and lush strings for recordings by Bowie, Nilsson and Elton John. Hunter had written a fantastic single but in 1998 Pete Watts carried a jaded view, saying, "I'm sick of 'Honaloochie Boogie.'" In 2018 *GLAM Uncut* would include the song in their 'Top 40 Greatest Tracks' and Joe Elliott of Def Leppard has described 'Honaloochie Boogie' as "the perfect pop record."

Side One of *Mott* closed with the frantic and relentless 'Violence', a Hunter-Ralphs composition with a cute guitar figure that was reminiscent of Cat Stevens' Sixties hit, 'Matthew and Son'. The track featured nerve-jangling, screeching violin each time "*Vi-o-lence*" was sung on the choruses, before a "mock punch-up" and blazing musical fade. The song was not entirely sinister as Hunter dramatised, with wit, the youthful disaffection and street corner blues of the missing-link character in his lyric. The police siren effect, played by Ralphs on organ between the first chorus and second verse, was another clever touch. 'Violence' was later covered by Duran Duran guitarist Andy Taylor, but Watts griped that the song's original menace was never captured on tape. Mott also engaged violinist Graham Preskett for the 'Violence' session, a multi-instrumentalist, writer and arranger who found fame via film and TV soundtracks.

"I had a rehearsal tape where the idea for the song took shape," said Watts. "Hunter remarks that it sounds 'really violent'. It's menacing, heavy and unrelenting – not like the record. I still like it, but it could have been much, much greater! Graham Preskett looked like Keith Moon – always unshaven – and we didn't know who the hell he was. We'd come into the studio and he'd be sitting on a couch. Normally I'd have asked Stan to sling him out, but when we got talking, it turned out he was doing a session in another studio and he had a fag packet and was writing. We said, 'What are you doing?' He said, 'Writing a string arrangement. I haven't done it yet.' 'What do you mean?' 'Well I'm writing the orchestra arrangement.' 'How many players are in the orchestra?' 'Fifty-two.' 'And you're doing it on a fag packet?' 'Yeah, I forgot to do it at home'... and we thought, GREAT! We liked him straightaway – then we wondered what he was really like, so he worked with us and wasn't wooden like most classical musicians."

'Violence' was the last track recorded for *Mott* on 11th April 1973. It would also be the last time that Hunter and Ralphs wrote together. The song was meant to be a parody of the group's anger and frustrations, but it exposed their instability when genuine fury erupted between Ian and Mick during its conception, following a tiring twelve-hour session. Alan Harris, Mott's assistant engineer, stepped in to break up a fight, but the damage was done and a cooling in the pairs' relationship followed.

IH: "The words *'Violence, violence, it's the only thing that'll make you see sense'* were written through the eyes of an eighteen year old – a deprived reject who hated everything he hadn't got – including love. It was supposed to be a maddening song and it was the crunch between Mick and me. It would be the crunch between lots of people. Try listening to that for three days – it's fuckin' murder! I'd sat with the whole album like a baby, Mick called me a name, I went for him and he went for me. I rang him the next day and apologised, but I could tell things were different between us. He really steered clear of me. We were never close – you couldn't get close to Mick – but it severed things musically. It was never the same after that."

The second side of *Mott* opened with another fine Hunter-Ralphs' collaboration, 'Drivin' Sister', but Dale Griffin was unhappy with the recording because he considered the cut to be lacklustre and small when it was intended to be hard, raunchy and big. Inspired by a car journey that Ian had taken with Guy Stevens and partly influenced by a Rolling Stones *Let It Bleed* outtake, 'Jiving Sister Fanny', Hunter never forgot the wild trip taken with Mott's former mentor in his yellow Beetle.

IH: "I remembered Guy Stevens racing his Volkswagen through Hampstead Heath, but he was driving it to the beat of a song from our first LP, 'Half Moon Bay'. The track had at least ten time-changes and Guy raced the car to seventy miles per hour, then abruptly dropped down to two miles per hour and back up again, in time with the music."

'Drivin' Sister' was structured in a similar way to 'One of the Boys', with sound effects woven into the start, central section and end of the song. In this case, Mott employed a BBC archive recording of a car starting, accelerating, screaming at speed with horn blazing across the right to left stereo channels, then stopping with the driver walking out on to the street. It was smart studio trickery, soon to be echoed by Roxy Music in their 1975 hit 'Love is the Drug'.

'Ballad of Mott the Hoople (March 26, 1972, Zurich)' re-lived the band's pre-Bowie split in Switzerland and was "dedicated to The Sea Divers", Mott's fan club. If any prospective musician sought a précis of the sacrificial requirements for rock success, then this was the primer. Musically the song was light and melodic, but Hunter's narrative was soul-bearing and sentimental as he depicted realisation and an almost untenable position amid the whole *"rock and roll circus"*. Ian's lyrics recalled the saga of Mott's downward spiral to their fateful day in Bern and their Swiss tour, confessing that music is like a drug with the lines... *"The grease paint still sticks to my face, but what the hell I can't erase, the rock 'n' roll feeling, from my mind"*... and acknowledging each member of Mott... *"Buffin lost his child-like dreams and Mick lost his guitar, and Verden grew a line or two and Overend's just a rock 'n' roll star"*. Brilliantly cataloguing the band's ups and downs and Ian's fight for, but mistrust of success, the track always remained one of the group's favourite songs as it ended up almost exactly as they intended. Watts felt that Hunter succeeded in putting into words what they all felt and described the song as "a lovely piece of writing – sad and pessimistic."

> **IH:** "In the *Mott* lyrics I tried to get it across that rock isn't superstars and God in the sky. There are losers and winners, and varying degrees of losers and winners. It's honesty really. Mott was a very honest band. Bowie was very dishonest, but I still think he was incredible. I was just saying, 'Wait a minute – this is how it really is.'"

Ian was relating the joys and pitfalls of being a rock 'n' roll star, inviting his audiences to identify with his and the band's experiences. He could celebrate music ('All the Way from Memphis') and yet paint rock as a circus and a loser's game ('Ballad of Mott the Hoople') his frayed reflections in the latter adding up to the most poignant song ever written about the lure of the stage. There were many clever, incisive observations in Hunter's writing, but Allan Jones of *Melody Maker* started to criticise Mott, complaining of Ian's propensity to self-mythologise the band.

IH: "All I saw during my time in Mott was halls, hotels, studios, limos and planes. We were also a troublesome and event-laden group. It was never easy to achieve things and we were never managed properly. I just wrote about Mott the Hoople and our 'us against the world' situation. At least I was honest. Mott and music were my life – so you write about life – so it is autobiographical. Isn't being auto-biographical being honest?"

Mick Ralphs was awarded the penultimate spot for the second Hoople album in a row with 'I'm a Cadillac/El Camino Dolo Roso', a bouncy pop-rock track that was potential single material – followed by another reflective instrumental coda, echoing 'After Lights' on *All the Young Dudes*. Ralphs and Watts were interested in American cars and Mick's song referenced the iconic Cadillac and Chevrolet El Camino coupé, and likened the girl *"cruising round my heart"* to a Ford Thunderbird. 'Ready for Love' was a hard act to follow but 'I'm a Cadillac' was a fine song, ending with an understated acoustic passage titled with a Spanish phrase meaning, the painful path or painful way.

The working title for 'I'm a Cadillac' had been 'Nice One Stan' and 'El Camino Dolo Roso' originated as 'Elephant's Gerald' and 'No Jive'. Early hand-written studio drafts of *Mott* tracks by the band also listed Ralphs' song as one piece, 'I'm a Cadillac (No Jive)'. The closing instrumental comprising drums, bass and acoustic guitar evolved before Mick over-dubbed a second acoustic, but Dale claimed that the track was really a Ralphs-Watts-Griffin composition. "I just came up with these little titles, so it was almost like a different piece," says Mick, "but it was really just the tail end of a song."

'I Wish I Was Your Mother', written by Ian Hunter, was the final track on *Mott*, recorded after the album sessions had been completed to replace the original closing cut, 'Rose'. Dale said it was because the band wanted a more up-beat song for Side Two, but 'I Wish I Was Your Mother' was the fastest they got, its inclusion emanating by accident from a Hunter studio try-out.

"The *Mott* album was completed," says Dan Loggins, "but as Bill Price and his assistants were sequencing and preparing to send master copies for test pressing, someone stopped me in the studio one day and said, 'Have you heard the new song that Ian's practising in the rehearsal room?' We were focused on *Mott*'s deadline, but I went to the room where Ian was doodling on keyboard and said, 'What's the new song?' – and he played 'I Wish I Was Your Mother' – just his vocal and piano. I couldn't believe it. We had wrapped the album and yet here was another classic. I asked Ian if he would write out the words, and then I knew. This was a personal, almost Dylanish ballad – an incredible moment – from 'At the Crossroads' to 'I Wish I Was Your Mother' – a perfect circle. Booking more studio time, I got my 'Stop the Presses' movie moment."

At the 'Mother' session Mott utilised a mandolin and bells that were lying around the studio, just as AIR's timpani had been employed on 'Hymn for the Dudes'. Mooted as a single, 'I Wish I Was Your Mother' was a clever concept, the song addressing the personal trauma of jealousy, Ian highlighting possessiveness towards his wife and yearning for the close-knit family upbringing that he felt he had been denied as a youngster.

> **IH:** "I don't think the song could have been a single because it's a bit psychological and not quite simple enough. 'I Wish I Was Your Mother' was truthful though. It is a strange song and it is about heavy jealousy. Trudi and I had just got married and I was envious of people who'd had really nice childhoods. You never lose that, and you wind up manipulated with people saying, 'Don't go near him'. It's not much fun and of course you didn't ask for it – it just came your way and you suffer for it. When your own young life is a mess and you're a mess, you tend to look at the other happier less-complicated people and envy them. Trudi's

> parents heard the song. Her dad said nothing. Her mum said, 'Get rid of him!'"

The *Mott* album was pivotal for Mott the Hoople and the band knew they had cracked it. There was an openness and quality in Hunter's songs and voice now that was supreme. Ian was highly optimistic about the LP at the time of release and the British press praised it universally. Under the headline 'MOTT TAKE A GIANT STEP', *DISC* called *Mott* a majestic and triumphant set, and referenced the record's special effects, Ralphs' stunning guitar breaks and Hunter's beautifully controlled vocals. Describing 'Violence' as the best track and a fabulously insidious piece of musical schizophrenia, Ray Fox-Cumming added: "This album marks a giant step forward for Mott. The band's writing hits the high-spots more consistently, the playing is surer and more inventive and the production, which they've done themselves, is amazing." *Sounds* proclaimed, "Mott: A Most Improved Band... Ian Hunter, every inch a dude in his spiffy white suit... the lights shining through that absurdly curly auburn mane framing the X-ray eyes: the same old Ian from years back, but oh my, what a different band now."

Record Mirror wrote of *Mott*, "The combination is explosive... each track a gem. With the foundations firm, Mott's music soars." Other UK reviews said: "Truly great albums aren't released every week – in fact I can only name six this year that fall into that category. Now here's the seventh and I assure you it is the finest Mott the Hoople have done"... "Unreservedly I'd say this was a superb album, from the heart of the songs, through the excellence of the band's playing to the bright imaginative production"... "John Peel thinks it might easily be one of his albums of the year"... "*Mott* is an exceedingly impressive album."

The American press was also fulsome in its unanimous acclaim of the LP as "a damn-near irresistible textbook of killer riffs 'n' hooks." *Let It Rock* described *Mott* as the record *All the Young Dudes* should have been, branding the album arrogant and defensive, with the band burned, but still insane and making their best music ever. *Rock* said, "*Mott* is a brilliant album... a lyrical masterpiece and one of the greatest rhythm conquests of the 70s"... while *The Village Voice* wrote, "*Mott* is their best yet and a work every bit as brilliant as those of the Stones at their best." Under the headline 'Triumph of the Dudes', *Creem* described the LP as, "Not only the best thing they've ever done, but an unqualified rock 'n' roll masterpiece. *Mott* is an impressive accomplishment. It's one of the first new-age classics and without it your record collection is lacking indeed." *Crawdaddy* audaciously announced, "It seems fair to call this LP one of, if not *the* best rock release of the year."

Rolling Stone described *Mott* as, "The best album from the best band of the early Seventies" and their feature, 'Mott: No Success like Failure' became a notable review, Bud Scoppa writing: "What an array of weapons this band has: awesome firepower, an ever-increasing depth of expression, timely themes and an artistic way of mixing these qualities on record. In terms of my own bias, Mott the Hoople has been the most productive band of the last three years, with only The Rolling Stones – a significant source of inspiration for Mott – in the same category. In six attempts, Mott has made four excellent albums and the latest may be the best. This album is so well done and so absorbing on every level."

Within three weeks of release, on 11th August 1973, *Mott* entered the British album chart where it remained for fifteen weeks. The upper reaches were monopolised by The Rolling Stones (*Goats Head Soup*), Status Quo (*Hello*), David Bowie (*Pin Ups*) and Roxy Music (*For Your Pleasure*), and *Mott* had a strong run, peaking at No.7 – Mott the Hoople's first Top Ten LP. In the USA, *Mott* hit No.35 and the record was soon voted 1973 'Album of the Year' by *Rolling Stone* while *Creem* named Mott the Hoople 'Band of the Year'.

The UK album presentation for the LP was also praised, but only after a false start. CBS in London had asked designers Hipgnosis to submit proposals for the *Mott* sleeve, but their most creative concept was a girl's face with no mouth and a tear trickling down one cheek. The label turned to their in-house Art Director, Roslav

Szaybo who provided stylistic direction, logo designs and cover concepts for *Mott* and later albums from the Hoople-Hunter stable. Roslav had graduated from the Warsaw Academy of Fine Arts and moved to London as a non-English-speaking Pole in the Sixties, joining an advertising agency, then CBS Records. Roslav won many awards and conceived notable record sleeves for Judas Priest, Home, Soft Machine and Argent. For a man who once noted that covers do not sell records and that it would be a crime to devise a sleeve so lavish that production problems could slow down distribution, Szaybo embarked on a lavish design for the *Mott* LP. The front of the glamorous gatefold package was centred on the head of Michelangelo's biblical hero David, printed on acetate sheet with colour pictures inside the gatefold appearing through the plastic and a die-cut outline. The background ran from dayglo pink into white with MOTT in bold customised computer style font. The image was stately and historic, while the labelling was sci-fi futuristic.

"I saw Mott the Hoople live several times and I greatly admired Ian on stage and his writing," says Roslav. "I thought he looked like a real rock star and the cover image gave Ian and Mott justice. The sculpture was a symbol of masculine strength. The MOTT logo was specially customised and the exclusive die-cut cover came about because Ian and Mott had good relations with Dick Asher at CBS. My sleeve concept got the go-ahead because the label thought, 'If The Rolling Stones can have a zipper on their album, why can we not have a cut-out on Mott's cover?' The clear printed acetate was my inventive side and was a first. The pink fading into white meant nothing but the dayglo drew attention and hadn't been done on an LP before. The *Mott* cover was just meant to be eye-catching and powerful, but simple. For the collage inside the gatefold, I got a hold of every picture and Mott photograph I could lay my hands on."

A young designer, Simon Cantwell, who had been employed alongside Roslav at Young & Rubicam agency, followed Szaybo to CBS and worked straightaway on the *Mott* cover. "I pasted up some type on the rear of the album sleeve," said Simon, "I believe the MOTT logo design was inspired by a Letraset typeface transfer sheet. Roslav liked to customise things. His name was actually spelt Roslaw, but he adapted it with a 'v' when he came to the UK – so that people pronounced it correctly!"

Sadly, the costly British *Mott* gatefold was soon changed to a simple single sleeve with no die-cut and, for the first time ever, a Mott the Hoople album cover was entirely different in America. Columbia had refused point-blank to utilise the UK artwork and employed a colour shot of the band taken from an aborted "Do Not Use" photo session that had been held at a studio in Bayswater, West London. The group was unimpressed, and Dale Griffin "hated" the American gatefold. In 1990 a fourth cover variation materialised when CBS Italy licensed *Mott*, with a different running order, to Di Agostini, the producers of *Il Rock* series. The original UK *Mott* packaging remains classic and classy, and it is still Ian's favourite of all the band's record sleeves.

> **IH:** "The British cover for *Mott* by Roslav Szaybo was great. The difference over in America was that Columbia wouldn't go for the extra two cents manufacturing or whatever it was – some minuscule amount – saying it would create a precedent. I stood in a room in New York with label people when they showed us the 'brown' US version. I was horrified and said, 'Who the fuck is responsible for this crap?' The bloke right next to me smiled and said, 'Me.' He wound up running Columbia Records! Mott the Hoople thought the American *Mott* album cover was total crap – and I still do!"

Mott the Hoople's music was angry but intelligent, verging on anarchy but just for the fun of it. The back of the *Mott* cover contained verses from 'A Sane Revolution', by D.H. Lawrence, the poem epitomising the band's character and echoing their rallying cry, claiming that a revolution should not be done in ghastly seriousness or deadly earnest, for equality, money or hate – but strictly for fun. "Upsetting the apple cart" was Mott the Hoople's *modus operandi* long before the *Mott* album and Hunter has always remained proud of the record.

> **IH:** "*Brain Capers* was the nearest you ever got to hearing the original Mott the Hoople live. The *Mott* album was when we figured out what to do in the studio. They both stand up. *Mott* was pressured because Bowie had helped out a lot on *Dudes*, producing and giving us a huge hit. Then all the critics said we couldn't do it without him. We made bloody sure we could, but it was the hardest I've *ever* worked."

Says Dan Loggins: "*Mott* finally defined Mott the Hoople as a premier rock 'n' roll band. It was all there in the grooves so it was down to the record company, fans and the unpredictable rock critics to embrace a brilliant album that so many had waited for. I think John Peel might have said, 'Many people felt David Bowie saved Mott, but, in the end, *Mott* saved Mott.'"

During June, Mott the Hoople made two separate appearances on *Top of the Pops* to promote 'Honaloochie Boogie' and flew to Germany to perform their new single plus 'Drivin' Sister', for the Swiss-German TV show, *Hits a Go-Go*. Hunter sang live to backing tracks in the Seeheim television studio and former Man guitarist Deke Leonard appeared in the background during the filming of 'Honaloochie Boogie'. Lynsey de Paul also featured on the show and an event surrounding the sessions would soon be inextricably linked to Mott's history. The *Top of the Pops* 'Honaloochie Boogie' performances were wiped but the *Hits a Go-Go* film of both *Mott* songs survived.

Following Verden's departure, Ian and Mick had played piano and organ parts during the *Mott* sessions, but the band had to fill Allen's space for future live work. Hidden behind the scenes however, more change was blowing in the wind, according to Dan Loggins.

"After *Mott*, Ian came by CBS and said that he wanted to record two more new songs, especially a number titled 'Roll Away the Stone' – the other number was called, 'Foxy, Foxy'. Ian had really found 'the knack' for crafting three-minute singles. The two songs were gems and with Bill Price alongside they would soon be great productions with a Spector-Wood wall of sound template. We booked studio time before the next US tour to record 'Roll Away the Stone' but, suddenly, Mick Ralphs wanted to talk with me too. His attendance would be a rare visit and I sensed something might be in the air."

Addressing the keyboard vacancy, in the 12th May edition of *Melody Maker*, Mott the Hoople advertised anonymously for two players: "BIG NAME BAND requires SUSTAIN ORGANIST and ROCK PIANIST for approx. three-month period. Two-thirds of the engagement will be in America. Please: no swingers, fiddlers or bluffers." From auditions, Mott recruited Morgan Fisher and Mick Bolton to augment their line-up for concert performance, but they were not taken on as full band members.

Born on January 1st 1950 in London, Morgan Fisher had received classical piano tuition, and his previous groups included The Soul Survivors, Love Affair, Morgan and Third Ear Band. At Olympic Studios in August 1973, Hunter and Griffin were engaged to produce ex-Love Affair singer Steve Ellis on a cover of 'I Wish I Was Your Mother', as his band Ellis was signed to CBS's sister label, Epic, but Dale found the set-up disorganised and they aborted the session.

Fisher's Hoople try-out was in a Chelsea basement rehearsal room under an off-licence and he strolled in sauvely to meet the group with a glass of white wine. This seemed to impress Mott and after running through four songs, Stan Tippins called that evening to offer Morgan the job. The band had been encouraged by his history and felt he knew what the music business entailed. Soon after recruitment, Fisher remembers that he went to a café for a cup of tea with Andy Mackay one day. The cool, Roxy Music saxophonist looked impeccable and it blew Morgan's mind that people of Andy's quality wanted to hang out with Mott the Hoople.

"Before I joined Mott, I had spent five years as a professional musician, but only in two bands," says Morgan. "With Love Affair instant stardom was thrust upon us, almost like Beatlemania, so the musical element got over-run. Then I went in the opposite direction forming the progressively inclined Morgan with singer Tim Staffell, who joined Smile – the nucleus of Queen. By the age of 23, I'd become jaded and looked at doing something else. Then I saw the ad and found Mott the Hoople. The band Morgan had played complex material so joining Mott was a fantastic breath of fresh air for me and an opportunity to get with a real band. Within a few weeks I had my first glimpse of America and it was an eye-opener. I'd seen Mott once at Cooks Ferry Inn and thought they were a good rock band with a really great image. I guess I joined for the travel and a chance to play new music but then I realised what good guys and monsters of rock Mott really were. They had two brilliant songwriters, a decent amount of fame and a real communication with audiences. I witnessed what it meant to play to crowds who respond. The USA was an amazing continent, the fans were great and the people who loved Bowie now loved Mott the Hoople too."

Mick Bolton also joined Mott as organist for live work, having played previously with White Myth, Blind Eye and London band, Clockwork Orange. Bolton thought Fisher was a much better pianist and that he was lucky to be given the job of organist simply because Mott perceived some potential. Morgan describes Mick as a quiet, charming guy who read his bible in hotel rooms while he got up to on-tour mischief.

Before Mott's next US trip, Fisher recorded some keyboard synth overdubs for 'Roll Away the Stone'. Clearly single material, the track had been cut just after the *Mott* sessions at AIR No.2 with engineer Bill Price, Howie Casey on sax and Thunderthighs on backing vocals. It woud be Mick Ralphs last recording with the group.

IH: "I wrote 'Roll Away the Stone' during the recording of *Mott* but it was decided to hold it for the next album as CBS

knew it was a hit. I think the song came at rehearsals which were held near the Kings Road. I was a huge fan of Leon Russell and he had a song with the 'Roll Away the Stone' title, but I certainly didn't nick it – not consciously."

Mott the Hoople aimed to focus on the US market in 1973 and Ian wanted to leave Britain for a period, because he felt the scene seemed swamped with what he considered to be "below-standard rock and roll." Mott's management had planned a two-part American tour for the summer and autumn of 1973, comprising fifteen dates on the East Coast in July and August, followed by thirty-six concerts from September to early November. T. Rex pulled out as support act, as Mott were making commercial inroads in America – rare for UK bands. Then, in the week that *Mott* hit British record racks and the band got ready for their US trek, on 21st July, *NME* announced, 'MOTT ON THE BRINK... A Smash Album and maybe a Line-Up Change?'

Mott the Hoople flew to New York on 22nd July for two days of final rehearsal at the Capitol Theatre in Passaic, New Jersey. Their tour opened in Chicago on 27th July, included an ABC *In Concert* television appearance in New York and finished on 19th August in Washington. The New York Dolls and Blue Oyster Cult supported Mott at several gigs but their first show at Chicago's Aragon Ballroom featured the brilliant Joe Walsh and Barnstorm; Mott the Hoople loved Walsh's music and soon warmed to the sensational guitarist.

"Joe was a real nice guy," says Morgan Fisher. "We did several gigs with him and before he went on that night, he came to the dressing room and said, 'Hi, I'm Joe. I'm staying in the same hotel as you guys. That might be kinda dangerous!' Ian happened to remark, 'Joe, you can't go on stage like that, you look like a scruff.' Hunter had just bought this really flash new leather jacket and it was all different coloured patches – a really nice piece of work. He just gave it to Joe – took it out of his bag and with great generosity handed it to him and said, 'Joe, it's yours. Wear it, for Christ's sake.' The combination of Walsh and Mott was great because he warmed audiences up with his organic, gutsy rock and then we came on with our attitude and smashed them to the back of the wall. I remember on 'Ready for Love', Ralphs' playing his solo in this vast antique Chicago ballroom under a huge mirror ball, with the spots of light whirling round gracefully and Mick's notes echoing out over the crowd. It was one of the most moving moments in my whole career and the perfect example of how delicate a rock guitarist can be."

"I knew Ian Hunter since the early Seventies when Mott the Hoople toured with Barnstorm." says Joe Walsh. "We became good friends and have crossed paths several times through the years and traded stories about 'the good ol' days'. Ian has always been a commanding presence on stage and is a fine musician and songwriter."

The New York Dolls – voted 'Worst New Group' AND 'Best New Group' of 1973 in Creem – were an interesting support act. Frontman David Johansen would make off-hand remarks about Mott the Hoople and became a public rival of Ian, though they admired the band. The Dolls' bass player Arthur Kane adored Mott's style and adopted a Gibson Thunderbird bass and thigh-length platform boots a la Watts, extending it into cross-dressing.

"We had quite a lot to do with The New York Dolls and they were good guys," said Watts. "Johansen was so quick-witted and such a lovely bloke. He was super-intelligent and used to give Ian a lot of verbal. I think David loved Mott the Hoople, but he pretended otherwise. They treated us like establishment and claimed they were now the rebels. Arthur Kane had to have three or four of his fans holding him up most of the time at airports. He used to like the platform boots I had made so, when I'd finished with a pair and had new ones on order, I'd sell a pair to him. Max, their roadie would carry equipment, wearing in my leopard skin boots for Arthur, letting them trail along the floor four feet behind him because he hadn't got them done up properly. He could have broken his neck."

348

IH: "I remember before we met The New York Dolls our management showed us a picture of this band that was to support us on tour. I thought, 'Fuck, if they can play like they look then we've had it.' The Dolls opened for us on a few gigs and were great chaps, but America was perplexed and wasn't ready for these 'trannies from hell'. The New York Dolls stuck together like glue. In the Midwest they would literally be clinging to each other for support – terrified! When we played The Felt Forum – a 4,000-capacity theatre in the grounds of Madison Square Garden – they left the stage after forty minutes in total silence – no encores, no applause – and this is forty blocks from The Bowery, their heartland. We went down a storm that night, but the *Village Voice* did this review, comprising columns on the Dolls and two lines at the end saying, 'Mott the Hoople closed.' Talk about looking after your own. Arthur Kane absolutely adored Watts and covered Pete's moves. Everything Pete did, Arthur copied. We got on great with the Dolls but, in truth, they weren't that great as musicians. They had good songs – the songs were better than they were – but I thought they were pushed too soon. If somebody could have dried the Dolls out, they would have stood more of a chance. I still have a chat with David Johansen when our paths cross – another clever chap."

At The Felt Forum every freeloader hit Mott's "after-show bash" – Iggy Pop fell through a glass door and Mott was furious when they were refused entry to their own party, but Ian did introduce Dale to Todd Rundgren that night as Griffin was a fan. One Mott-admirer was Black Sabbath singer Ozzy Osbourne who often attempted to get backstage. "I didn't know much about Ozzy and had never met him," said Watts, "because he was never allowed into the dressing room, unfortunately. He turned up at a few gigs and the first I knew of it was when somebody said, 'Oh, Ozzy Osbourne's been to the gig', and I asked where he was, and they said, 'Stan wouldn't let him in – he's too noisy.' That happened three of four times with Ozzy."

Whilst attracting much admiration from fellow rock acts, Mott received some criticism from America's middle-of-the-road darlings, The Carpenters, who opined to the press that Mott the Hoople was the most outrageous and unprofessional-looking group they had seen.

> **IH:** "The Carpenters came to England and in their excitement at being feted all over the place, they let slip they'd seen this awful inhuman band called Mott the Hoople. I think they'd just got off the plane and Karen Carpenter was asked about us and I'm not convinced she'd even seen us. Karen said she didn't like the guy with the shades and the boots, but Pete had the boots and I had the shades. She was silly, but we got massive publicity out of it – Mott and Carpenters fans arguing – the best thing that could have happened for us at that time."

"I could feel the interest in us rising after that press," said Watts. "I noticed it when we went to Disneyworld in Florida – a horrible place. People were looking at us and stopping us everywhere and asking for our autographs. The Carpenters really helped us. Mott the Hoople couldn't have wished for better publicity!"

Having navigated Verden Allen's departure and delivered *Mott*, and as commercial success started to come Mott the Hoople's way, stories started to filter back to Britain that a second band member may depart. Ian soon confirmed if that were the case, no replacement would be made, leaving Mott the Hoople as a trio.

"Mick Ralphs had asked to see me at CBS after *Mott*," recalls Dan Loggins. "I'd noticed he hadn't been staying late during the final mixing sessions and I'd heard a rumbling that he was perhaps less 'in sync' with Ian over the band's new direction. Always mild-mannered, Mick came in and said he was conflicted. He was thrilled by the band's breakthrough success, but he felt, in his heart, that

Mott was now Ian's. Hunter was on a roll, Ralphs' rockier songs were not meshing with the new direction and he wasn't comfortable with the 'pop' sensibility. Mick felt it was time for him to split. I was very distressed as I was a Ralphs fan and felt he was valuable to the balance of the group, with Hunter as a counterpoint and focus. Mick told me he had talked it over with each group member and Bob Hirschman, ironically, just as Fred Heller was coming onboard. 'Welcome Fred – your lead guitarist is leaving!' Heller was a young dynamic manager with proven success, and he had a very positive working relationship with Columbia Records. Mick promised he'd do whatever was necessary to promote the *Mott* album – and he did."

By the time Mott the Hoople performed an early September promotional slot on *Top of the Pops* for their second single release from *Mott*, 'All the Way from Memphis', the band had a new guitarist. British music press headlines included: 'Ralphs quits Mott to join Free', and 'RALPHS QUITS HOOPLE!' Mott's management explained that Mick had left to join Free's singer Paul Rodgers and drummer Simon Kirke because he felt, after a long time, that he wanted to do something else, adding that it had taken from February for him to make the decision. Ralphs' farewell Mott performance was the band's 19th August concert in Washington, DC.

Mick felt that Mott the Hoople's original recklessness had waned but the seeds for departure were sown in 1971 and had grown alongside the dramas of former Island stable-mates Free, another band with an unmistakeable aura, but who were often combustible. Personnel differences had caused them to split too and Ralphs became acquainted with Rodgers when Paul's post-Free trio, Peace, supported Mott in 1971. Free then reformed in 1972 but folded again in early 1973, enabling Paul and Mick to build on their earlier connection, stockpiling new songs with a view to recording a Rodgers-Ralphs album. Ian regarded the tour with Peace as the catalyst for Ralphs' departure, but the recording of 'Violence' played its part too.

IH: "After Bowie, when I started writing hits, I think it put Mick's nose out of joint, and I can understand that. He was free-form bluesy and I was going stiff-quasi-European style. Ralphs was writing great songs, but I couldn't sing them that well and neither could he, and we reached the stage where we were not matching musically. I remember I asked Tippins if Mick was leaving and Stan said, 'No, he'll never leave this band as long as he lives' – and five minutes later Ralphs left. During *Mott*, I'd said to Ralpher, 'Tell me what's going on with Paul – do you want to join his band?' He said, 'Well, he ain't got a band.' So, I said, 'If he asked you to join a group, would you go?' Mick replied, 'I'd have to think about it.' Then I knew. Eventually, I spent three hours with Ralphs in Fred Heller's house trying to talk him out of leaving and offered half my royalties because Mick used to be perfect for my songs, but he wasn't keen on doing it anymore. He'd played great on *Mott* considering his heart wasn't really in it. I always thought if they'd waited quarter of an hour at the 'Violence' session they could have had the real thing."

Ralphs felt that 'All the Young Dudes' had created a schism and the real Mott the Hoople had reached a logical conclusion. He also thought Ian wanted to create hit recipes, while the guitarist favoured a more grounded approach. The Bowie "break" had given Mott a Top Three single but for Ralphs, Mott had lost its subversive feel and drifted away from its original DNA. All of the band would have given anything for single success before 'Dudes' but, having hit the target Mott was not the same. The new glamorous angle did not sit easily with Mick who loved the band's original style: he sensed that Mott the Hoople's out-and-out "full-tilt rock" had been compromised.

"After writing the intro for 'All the Young Dudes' I came up with a few opening hooks for Mott, but it all became a bit manufactured for me. Following the success with David, suddenly Ian concluded that we had to do songs like 'Dudes'. So, Ian set about a mission of writing songs that built up to a big chorus – and they were great songs, but then there was no room for the simplistic stuff I'd been writing. Mott had broken into the mainstream, but they changed from an underground band with a cult following, to a pop group, and it wasn't my cup of tea. Mott had survived on struggle, adversity and disappointment and that gave us the spirit to carry on. We'd always said, 'sod convention – sod the system,' but there comes a point where you can't be famous and be like that. We were always the underdog and that was part of the reason we were so spirited and exciting. After the Bowie connection, in a way, we'd become part of the system we were always dead against. I didn't have the same commitment and interest. Mott was like my adolescence and I decided it was time to go off and do my own thing. I just wanted to play some different music. It was like leaving your parents. It's not that you don't love them – you just want to go and do something else.

"When Paul Rodgers' Peace toured with Mott, I couldn't believe that someone of his calibre was supporting us. I said to Paul I thought it was ridiculous him opening for us, so we got friendly and used to sit together noodling on guitars in the dressing rooms. I played him 'Ready for Love', 'Can't Get Enough' and 'Movin' On', and he liked them and said he wanted to sing them. Initially, I was just going to record a few tracks with Paul, but it became obvious I was more interested in that. We were doing the *Mott* album and Paul wanted to record and put a band together, but I told him Mott the Hoople had a US tour coming up and I had to do that. I just couldn't leave – I wouldn't do that – it wouldn't be fair. Because I did the tour, they probably thought I wasn't going to leave but I told Paul I'd be back in a few months if he would like to do something. Once I got working with Paul, I was on a roll. We were just knocking some songs together as a side project, then Simon Kirke asked if he could sit in on drums, and then I suggested that we might as well get a bass player and form a band. It grew by accident. We were just lucky."

The Rodgers-Ralphs-Kirke bass player recruitment list included sixteen candidates and Mick scrawled the reasons for rejection in a notebook – "Looks like Clapton", "Bald at the station" and "Foaming at the mouth" – before they finally engaged former King Crimson bassist Raymond 'Boz' Burrell. Laid-back and amiable, Boz was deeply into music, tone and space, and played in a melodic manner with an exacting but understated technique.

The new quartet threw around some band names including Fury but, inspired by a gritty 1972 Western, they opted for Paul's suggestion, Bad Company; Island Records hated it. It was rumoured that Rodgers and Ralphs might join Raw Glory, a new band managed by Guy Stevens and Mick also declined an invitation to join Wishbone Ash, as Bad Company was already evolving under the management services of the formidable Peter Grant.

Ralphs revelled that Bad Company had been put together purely for the music and their no-frills, blues-rock alloy secured swift acceptance. The debut album, *Bad Company*, won five platinum awards and the Mott compositions, 'Can't Get Enough', 'Movin' On' and 'Ready for Love' became iconic cuts and proved perfect for American radio. Further success followed with *Straight Shooter*, the songs exhibiting continued compatibility between Ralphs and Rodgers.

"I was originally a soul and R&B fan, and Mott the Hoople had a roughness that we'd captured on *Brain Capers*," says Mick. "I wanted to go back to more simplistic songs. Bad Company gave me freedom to stretch my playing and I unleashed a lot of songs because I had the greatest singer in the world and the best drummer."

Run with the Pack would be the band's third Top Five LP in Britain and America, and third million-selling album. Peter Grant seemed to be fashioning a super-group to rival Led Zeppelin, however Ralphs felt Bad Company soon started to run out of ideas; "The dreaded second album, *Straight Shooter*, went well because we had written a lot of songs and we were full of ideas at the start, but we cobbled together a fourth LP, *Burnin' Sky* and after that we were struggling. Paul wanted to come off the road and I didn't blame him for that, as the fizz had gone out of it all."

Bad Company re-grouped several times over the years and Ralphs released three solo albums – *Take This!* (1984), *It's All Good* (2001) and *That's Life* (2003). He also guested on projects by Jon Lord, Jim Capaldi and The Who, produced Maggie Bell and Gun, toured with David Gilmour and collaborated with George Harrison on a song titled, 'The Flying Hour'. In 2011, he formed The Mick Ralphs Blues Band, playing music at a grass-roots level again which he described as good for the soul, but bad for the bank balance. Mick also appeared on the British leg of Bad Company's 'Swan Song Tour' in 2016. With subtle touches that coloured but never dominated the music, Ralphs accented rock songs beautifully and in the late Nineties, Pete Watts reflected on Mick's playing in Mott, believing that the guitarist didn't really receive the recognition he deserved.

"When I heard Mick on Mott's 1970 Croydon live tapes during an Anthology project in 1998, some of his playing that night was just so blistering. He was a natural in the studio and very adaptable, but Mick always liked to have his guitar playing quite refined. On reflection, hearing his live work, it was so much better than anything I ever heard him do on record. It was nastier and had more of a rough edge. Mick said, years later, that he would never have left Mott the Hoople in 1973 if he'd known they would become so influential and that is typical Ralpher. He always opted for safety and Bad Company was a very safe band. They couldn't fail. They were run to a formula."

"Mott the Hoople was a special period in my life," says Ralphs, "the step from a local band to professionalism. We were magic live – a special band. We always stuck to our principles and we always went against convention although, without the help of Guy, I don't think we'd have got any further than the village hall. I always felt Mott the Hoople was ahead of its time and were never quite accepted as a musical band – quite an enigma really. We were a financial disaster until David came along and presented us with

'All the Young Dudes', then Ian got into writing in a structured way and we lost something in the transition. I was also uncomfortable with the Bowie glam rock association. It was illogical for me to go but I'd just lost the feel for it. We were all very pleased with *Mott*, and David had helped turn it all around for us, but ironically 'All the Young Dudes' was half the reason I left!

"I've always regarded Ian Hunter as a strong character, and I respect him enormously. He's an excellent songwriter and has a great handle on the business. He's also very good at dealing with the press – much better than I am – because Ian has the art of always saying something interesting. He's a very good wordsmith and a great chap to have in a band as he's so assured although, like all of us, a bit insecure underneath. Pete Watts was an easy-going guy who could be stubborn and always had lots of great ideas, while Buffin often underestimated his strength in the band because he was always a driving force and believed so much in Mott the Hoople. Verden Allen was a good, passionate man and was extremely musical; he wasn't afraid to try something different for effect and would often play a wild style rather than adopt a conventional approach, which all contributed heavily to the sound. Mott the Hoople was special."

> **IH:** "With hindsight, the seeds of Mick Ralphs' departure from Mott were really sown with 'Dudes'. We started writing hit songs and it got a little strenuous. We did 'Ready for Love' and it sounded alright, but not like it should have for me, then the *Mott* album became bittersweet, because at the end of the sessions it was clear that Mick's nose was out of joint. Ralpher leaving was a turning point on so many fronts. I'd wanted to keep the band as it was. I guess 'All the Young Dudes' had been both a blessing and a curse. The blessing was that we had a hit that enabled us to continue – the curse was that we were a different band – so Phally and Ralpher quit. Looking back, to me, it was the end of Mott the Hoople when Mick left.

356

"Ralphs is one of the most beautiful, inventive and melodic guitar players I ever heard. He's also a great songwriter and his approach comes from enhancing the whole of the song – that's why he's so good. You can say Mick is underrated but David Gilmour of Pink Floyd invited him out to play shows, so he is really rated by people that matter. What people didn't realise when Ralpher left Mott, was that he was really into the blues, and I wasn't. Years later there was an interview where Ralphs said the best career move he ever made was to leave Mott the Hoople. That wasn't harsh, it was true. When Mick left, I secretly knew our credibility was gone."

Mott the Hoople had reached a startling zenith on *Mott*. Ian had depicted struggle, grandeur and melancholy and there was a wonderful vibe that ran rampant through the whole album via several classic compositions: 'All the Way from Memphis,' 'Hymn for the Dudes,' 'I Wish I Was Your Mother' and 'Ballad of Mott the Hoople'. However, true to their dramatic and destructive form, as soon as *Mott* was completed, Mick joined Bad Company leaving a void that would never be filled. Ironically, CBS's best-selling albums in the latter part of 1973 were Paul Simon's *There Goes Rhymin' Simon*, the Carlos Santana-John McLaughlin LP *Love Devotion Surrender...* and *Mott*!

IH: "Guy Stevens had a wind 'em up and let 'em go approach in the studio. He held Mott back when we were meant to be recording, then he'd let us go and it was like a wild stampede – but then I noted David and Mick Ronson's production style was different, so suddenly, with *All the Young Dudes*, the studio was a whole different art form. Then, with hit records we were playing to the masses who weren't as well informed as the fans we'd had before, but we found ourselves on *Mott* – it was a complete album."

1973 was a vintage year for rock's long player, the roll-call including David Bowie's *Aladdin Sane*, The Faces' *Ooh La La*, Genesis's *Selling England By the Pound*, Elton John's *Goodbye Yellow Brick Road*, King Crimson's *Larks Tongues in Aspic,* Led Zeppelin's *Houses of the Holy*, Pink Floyd's *The Dark Side of the Moon*, The Rolling Stones' *Goat's Head Soup*, Roxy Music's *For Your Pleasure* and *Stranded*, The Sensational Alex Harvey Band's *Next*, Joe Walsh's *The Smoker You Drink the Player You Get*, The Who's *Quadrophenia*... and the award-winning *Mott*.

Still widely regarded as Mott the Hoople's finest work, *Mott* is often cited as a seminal Seventies album: A *Music Hound Rock* five-star classic in its *Essential Album Guide*, among *Rolling Stone*'s '500 Greatest Albums of All Time' and hailed as one of the *1001 Albums You Must Hear before You Die. Classic Rock* published 'The Real 100 Greatest Albums of the 70s' in 2016 and placed *Mott* at No.36 describing it as the band's definitive recording because of its rollicking classics, jubilant hits and introspective autobiographical ballads that proved Ian Hunter's top-form credentials. Def Leppard singer Joe Elliott pinpoints *Mott* as the band's best, describing it as "all killer, no filler" and his greatest album of all time. It remains Ian Hunter's favourite Hoople record too.

Mott is the jewel in Mott's crown for critics and fans alike. Ian had crafted songs that trumped *All the Young Dudes* and Mott the Hoople had proven they were their own men, weathering outside scepticism with determination. They had fallen down several holes and now they were climbing up the mountains, but the double-edged sword of success fell swiftly on the band. Hunter admitted that with Ralphs' departure, Guy Stevens' Mott the Hoople had been irreparably wounded. They had raised the bar, their game *and* their commercial profile brilliantly, but despite personnel changes and fatigue, Ian was about to deliver more creative and influential songs.

Guy's Brain Caper Kids and David's Dudes were about to be usurped... by Hunter's blood and thunder Crash Street Kidds.

CHAPTER ELEVEN

Fragments of Madness

'Marionette' was a nervous breakdown on record.

Mott the Hoople had become emergent stars on *All the Young Dudes* and reached virtual perfection with *Mott*, but personnel changes were taking their toll. If the band was to counter *Rolling Stone*'s observation that "the *Mott* album" sounded like a terminal statement, then the next Hoople chapter would have to be based on Ian Hunter's invention, writing and delivery. Mick Ralphs' shock departure had placed Mott the Hoople under increased pressure, as the group had to fulfil the second part of a US tour, promoting their greatest-ever album, but with no lead guitarist.

> **IH:** "We toured America with *Mott* before it came out in the USA and it was decided there would be a two-week break, the record would be released and then we'd go back and tour again. Ralphs played the first tour then left. This gave us two weeks to find another guitar player, so everybody sat down and said, 'Well, who are we going to get?' And it really wasn't a question of who are we going to get? It was a question of who can learn the songs, in the next fourteen

days, because we're playing The Hollywood Palladium two weeks on Saturday!"

Guitar candidates for Mott included Deke Leonard formerly of Man, Zal Cleminson from The Sensational Alex Harvey Band and Ray Smith of Hackensack. Watts and Griffin favoured Smith but the band was negotiating a new record deal with CBS and the guitarist stayed, subsequently claiming that telegrams sent by Mott to Hackensack had not reached him. Stan Tippins recalled Hunter being "flabbergasted" that Ray wouldn't leave the group to join Mott the Hoople. SAHB guitarist Zal Cleminson, an astounding talent, later said that he was never approached or invited to join Mott the Hoople – but, if he had been asked, he would have joined!

Hushed up behind the scenes was Mott's interest in Mick Ronson. Dan Loggins remembers that Hunter tried to invite Ronson into the band, but Mick was recording his first solo album and differences between MainMan and H&H Management prevented this. Ian also considered Miller Anderson and Mott discussed American candidates like Ronnie Montrose, Joe Walsh and Leslie West. Loggins approached Montrose who he described as a killer on stage, but Ronnie was already much in demand and wanted by Edgar Winter, and Dan recalls that Fred Heller suggested Tommy Bolin of The James Gang. Joe Walsh was not disputed because Mott loved him, but Watts did not want any Americans in Mott the Hoople as he felt strongly that they were "British", while Griffin opined that Mott was *not* "some kind of hybrid".

IH: "Leslie West had been discussed as was Joe Walsh, Ronnie Montrose and Tommy Bolin. Zal Cleminson was considered for Mott and I can't remember what happened, but I remember his name coming up. Joe Walsh was a great character. We'd played with Barnstorm and they were a fantastic band. I can remember Joe joining us on stage for different encores and he was a brilliant guitarist, but far too good a musician for Mott the Hoople. We simply had to decide who was reasonably good and could do our gigs – and it turned out to be Luther Grosvenor who we knew from Island days and Spooky Tooth."

Born on 23rd December 1946 in Evesham, Worcesterhire, Luther James Grosvenor began playing music at eleven years of age on a £5 guitar. His musical influences included Jeff Beck, The Rolling Stones and, ironically Joe Walsh, but all Luther ever wanted to be was a professional guitarist. Grosvenor had played in Deep Feeling, The V.I.P.s and Art, who morphed into Spooky Tooth, appearing with them in the rock documentary *Groupies* – a film that nearly cost Luther his Hoople post. When he left Spooky Tooth, he stayed with Island Records and issued *Under Open Skies*, a solo album that embraced several musical styles. Grosvenor then joined Stealers Wheel to replace original member Gerry Rafferty, but whilst he promoted their hit single 'Stuck in the Middle with You', he moved on when Rafferty returned.

"I was lying in bed one morning and shall never forget the phone ringing at Hampstead, and it was Ian Hunter," says Luther. "He said, 'Look, we know you, we're from the same stable – Island Records – you know Mick, he's leaving the band – we're in the middle of a tour, we've all spoken and narrowed everything down – do you want to join Mott?' I said, 'Of course!' Mott the Hoople felt they had to have somebody who was British and perhaps a little bit flash. Guitarists like Joe Walsh and Ronnie Montrose were fabulous, and they were probably better guitarists than me, but it's like the Stones having an American guitarist – it doesn't really work – they're English – they're ours. Mott kept it British, which was important."

Miller Anderson, Hunter's friend and fellow musician from the late Sixties recalls, "At the time Ariel Bender, or Luther Grosvenor, joined Mott, Ian thought about inviting me but there was already friction in the band. It was starting to look more and more like Hunter's group after Ralphs left and I think they felt if

361

Ian got his friend in, it would strengthen that position. I could certainly play well enough – better than bloody Ariel Bender anyway."

Grosvenor was thrilled that Mott the Hoople had opted to retain their British DNA, but a revealing portion in the *Groupies* film had tilted the band towards the concept of their new recruit adopting an alter ego – and it would be one of rock's greatest, incomparable stage names.

> **IH:** "We knew Luther and really liked him, but the problem was that movie, in which two groupies were discussing the length of Luther's extremity – in not too glowing terms. So, the feeling within Mott was, 'What are we gonna do – maybe we shouldn't have Luther in the band' – because it was a big movie at the time. We had recently done a dismal TV show in Seeheim and Ralphs had been a little bit out of it. I heard Lynsey de Paul say, 'Ariel Bender' as she watched Mick run down a street, bending aerials on some parked cars, before he dunked his head into a horse trough, of all things.
>
> "I kept the name Ariel Bender in mind and when we decided to engage Luther, we used Lynsey's pseudonym to cover Luther up and make it sound like a guitar player out of nowhere. I felt so embarrassed about it that I carted him out to a Hampstead pub to break it gently to him over a quiet drink. I said, 'Luther Grosvenor's a great name.' He said, 'I know, I *love* that name. I wouldn't change it for the world.' I had to say, 'Well, that's the problem. We don't want to call you Luther Grosvenor. We want to call you Ariel Bender.' He said, 'Ariel Bender. I *love* that name. I wouldn't change it for the world. *Call* me Ariel, not Luther – *call* me Ariel.' So, he joined and within eight days this maniac had learned our songs and got the whole act off. We went back to America and played The Hollywood Palladium, and went down great. Bender settled in quickly and people loved him. He was crazy and colourful."

362

"Mott was a job I couldn't refuse," says Luther. "They could have fuckin' called me Joe Bloggs as far as I was concerned. Ariel Bender was a great name for a guitarist who happened to be Luther Grosvenor, but Ariel really was created that night, in a pub, in North London."

On 31st August, a second track was released from the *Mott* album as a single. The band had recorded 'Roll Away the Stone' as the follow up to 'Honaloochie Boogie', but the song was held in reserve to make way for an edited version of 'All the Way from Memphis' – CBS Records' preference. Issued with 'Ballad of Mott' as the B-side, the rock press termed 'All the Way from Memphis' "magnifico" – describing the song as "genuine rock 'n' roll" and a number that demonstrated "vitality and wonderful writing." *NME* headlined with 'A Whole Lotta Hoople' and several publications selected 'All the Way from Memphis' as their 'Record of the Week'. The single entered the UK chart on 8th September and stayed for eight weeks reaching No.10, battling against The Rolling Stones, David Essex and Wizzard.

CBS in-house producer Paul Phillips had been involved in editing 'Memphis' for single release, but after Mott had left for their second slew of American live dates. At 2 minutes, 35 seconds 'Honaloochie Boogie' had been a perfect '45'. Side One, Track One on *Mott* seemed to be a sure-fire hit too, but the five-minute track screamed out for single surgery. Embarking on his first edit experience, Phillips cut the song down, tweaking bass and "roughing the edges" for radio. Like some observers, Phillips found Mott quite intimidating, and after their US tour, Dick Asher threw a London party where the band approached the producer, knowing that he had been messing with their music. After toying with him and creating some degree of discomfort, Hunter simply smiled and complimented the A&R rookie on a job well done.

IH: "'All the Way from Memphis' was an album track to me. I always hated the mix and never wanted it released as a

single because I didn't think it was good enough. I remember saying to Dick Asher, Head of CBS, 'Do not put this out as a single.' He promised he wouldn't and the minute our backs were turned, on our next US tour, they edited it and released it anyway. 'All the Way from Memphis' went Top Ten and became a bigger hit than 'Honaloochie Boogie'. Sometimes I can be a pretty bad judge of my own work."

Once again, *Top of the Pops* was placed on the band's agenda and, resplendent in green Roxy suit with baritone sax, Andy Mackay appeared with Mott for the promotion of 'All the Way from Memphis' at the BBC on 3rd September. Filmed on Wednesdays and transmitted every Thursday evening, the BBC programme was becoming a regular slot for Mott, but Pete Watts despaired of the programme.

"*Top of the Pops* was hell – absolute hell! It was always a day of grind and misery. You *had* to get there for ten in the morning, but they didn't need you – then, at about one o'clock, you'd go up for a camera-angle rehearsal – then at four o'clock you came down for a dress rehearsal and ran through the song, miming – then you came back down again and did the filming at seven or eight o'clock. After every show, you would want to go to the BBC bar on the top floor but the old blokes with the caps wouldn't let you in. Stan would wrangle, argue and eventually fight with them, and after an hour you got in. You'd end up talking to other artists and be legless by the end of the night. It was always a horrible day at the BBC."

IH: "BBC rules demanded that tracks had to be partly re-recorded before they could be mimed on TV. The BBC bloke who checked this would get bored, so Stan would take him to the pub. When they came back, the track would be magically 'done'. I hated the entire charade. *Ready Steady Go* was the right way to do it, while *Top of the Pops* was a phoney pop show, but it was powerful and sold records. I never liked most of the DJs there either. I remember

Emperor Rosko liked us, the idiot Tony Blackburn being the only dissenter. One of our fans flattened Blackburn at one TV session after he'd said something about us on the radio. I remember Pete and me one day, driving into London on the Westway, listening to Rosko's *Round Table* programme. It was the first time we heard 'All the Way from Memphis' on the radio. Rosko played the single and then asked Tony Blackburn for an opinion on it. 'What can I say,' proclaimed the bard of stupidity – 'If I had a party and I wanted to clear the room, I'd put this on.' And Blackburn wondered why people didn't like him. He was a waste of skin – an insipid piece of work."

Pete Watts recalled: "Blackburn used to say mildly offensive stuff about us and our material on his breakfast radio show and our supporters didn't like it. We had one fan that used to come to all our London gigs and during this tele-cast he jumped on Blackburn, pulled him to the ground and punched him. Blackburn came up to me afterwards and asked what it was all about, so I said, 'You want to be careful what you say on the radio. Some people won't like it.' He replied, 'I can say what I like,' and I said, 'Yeah, and you can expect to get what you get as well.' He looked at me – and walked off."

Mott prepared for the second leg of their US tour with rehearsals in Shepherd's Bush and at Manticore, an abandoned Fulham cinema that had been converted into a production and rehearsal facility by prog-rockers Emerson Lake & Palmer. ELP's working area was upstairs in the former balcony while the hollowed-out downstairs was rented as a hall for bands to practice stage productions. Mott's tour preparations did not please Dale Griffin as he felt the sound and feel with Bender at rehearsals was not right, even allowing for his short acquaintance with the band. There were, however, mitigating circumstances.

"We rehearsed the two-hour set very quickly, which really wasn't fair," says Luther. "We all knew the time wasn't enough, but that's the way it had to be. We did what we could – it could have been worse – it could have been better – and any guitar player could have done with a week or two more. Then we had a few days in a US auditorium with the lights to do the final run-through of what we'd under-rehearsed in London."

Mott flew out to Los Angeles and featured on America's rock show *The Midnight Special*, filmed in front of a live audience at NBC TV studios in Burbank. For three days the band also rehearsed at LA's Aquarius Theater on Sunset Boulevard then appeared on *Don Kirshner's Rock Concert* performing 'Drivin' Sister', 'All the Young Dudes', 'All the Way from Memphis' and 'Sweet Angeline'. The mini-set was memorable for Hunter's audience greeting: "It's nice to be back in Los Angeles. We really mean that – actually, we don't mean it. It's always a drag to be back in Los Angeles, but one must go to these places in the course of one's business!"

Mott the Hoople's US tour opened on 14th September at the Hollywood Palladium and ended on 3rd November in St Louis, Missouri. Such was the speed of change that people at the Palladium were shouting for Ralphs during Mott's set. "I shall never forget the first night in Hollywood," says Luther. "It was fucking chock-a-block. Everybody was sympathetic, but I was absolutely petrified. You had the first number in your head and then you've got to remember all the others in this new set. It wasn't quite polished, but we had a blinding first night and it was wonderful. I looked the part and we played the part. After that first gig, I could settle down as a member of Mott the Hoople, but it wasn't easy."

Mott's tour included two nights at San Francisco's Winterland supported by Joe Walsh and Bachman Turner Overdrive; Fisher was already learning "Wattisms" and re-christened 'BTO' – "Bachman Turner Overweight". Mott also played a prestige gig at New York's 'Art Deco' Radio City Music Hall on 26th October. In the course of rehearsals, the band had decided to utilise an elevating section of the stage to create a dramatic opening to their set. During the introduction tape, the front section of the stage would rise up from thirty feet below, gradually revealing Mott as they launched into their first song. Denied an afternoon try-out by a stage manager, confident in the mechanism, hubris struck on the night as the intro tape ended – with Griffin and Fisher stranded for an eternity, waiting for the front half of the stage to rise out of the pit.

Mott the Hoople had aimed high for their 1973 American tour, not only in terms of stage performance but also equipment and PA. Mott's stalwart Richie Anderson would discover however, contrary to his recommendations, that a new, small sound company was engaged by Mott's management for the tour and one side of the PA died at the Radio City gig. Despite a *DISC* feature headed 'Mott Rip into Radio City', Ian retained bad memories of the New York show.

> **IH:** "Radio City was an unmitigated howl of a monster disaster, just when we didn't need it. We played with one side of the PA out and the other side distorting. It was one of the cruellest things that ever happened to us, and it wasn't our fault. We played great even though we knew it was a nightmare. I remember Pete finding an old wheelbarrow and wheeling me back on for an encore. It was bloody awful, but we laughed it off afterwards."

Loud and larger than life, Luther (or rather Ariel) was greeted favourably by press and fans alike. Fisher had adored Spooky Tooth and Grosvenor was a personal hero, so the pair got on famously. The new guitarist also had a generous nature and would swap clothes backstage to anyone who admired an item, turning dressing rooms into a flea market. As Ariel Bender, the daredevil guitarist brought chaos and carnival to the band, with a flashy exhibitionist persona that was as mad as his stage name. Playing manic solos and making demented dashes across the stage, 'Walkin' with a Mountain' became Grosvenor's grizzled guitar showcase as he tried to steal the centre spot from Hunter every night. Ian would remain relatively impassive until his patience snapped and in a wild act of showmanship, would grab and wrestle Bender around the stage before hurling him, still playing, to the floor. The pair also devised a series of arguments for the press to feast on, creating more attention for Mott.

"The part that I played with Ian on stage was very powerful," says Luther. "Ariel tormented Ian and started to steal a bit of the limelight and take away some of Hunter's glory. It became dynamic with me out front playing up to Ian who would pull and push me, and then throw me on the floor and drag me across the stage by my hair – literally. Before I joined, I think it had started to become a bit angry and jealous with Ian's writing. When Ariel joined the band, they woke up again. The comments Ian and I made about each other were meant to be taken lightly, but it fired everyone up and was made to sound malicious. The press thought there was a problem, but it was just good fun. I knew Ian too well. We were great friends. We went to Bermuda on holiday together for three weeks with our wives, we shared hotel rooms together and we genuinely liked each other as people and artists. The jibes were just a publicity stunt – and it worked."

> IH: "Luther and I used to 'mock-battle' for the middle mike. Sometimes we'd deliberately kick lockers in dressing rooms and the press thought we were fighting. We were young and daft – what can I say?"

"Luther was incredible," said Watts. "I remember Stan getting Bender to a plane one day. Luther had his glitter cap on, left-over make-up from the night before running all down his face and Stan had him by the scruff of the neck with one hand and the arse of his trousers with the other, dragging him across the tarmac to the plane. It was all in fun. Hungover, Luther was saying to me as we got onboard, 'Oh Pete, never again mate. I'm not drinking again today. That's it. I'm tee-total from now on. Excuse me Miss, can I have a whisky and coke please?'"

During Mott's tour there was almost a third change in original personnel when Peter Grant tried to lure Pete into Bad Company.

Watts worriedly telephoned their "intimidating" manager, having received several telegrams at various hotels: "I telephoned Peter and he said, 'It's like this – Bad Company want you – the boys want you in the group.' I thought, God, how can you say no, to Peter Grant? He'll have your bloody knee caps off. So, I had to be real tactful and said, 'Well, I'm really happy doing what I'm doing to be honest Peter, but I'll think about it.' I think he could tell eventually from my tone of voice that I was going to stick it out in Mott the Hoople."

Mott played a demanding schedule across the US and, inevitably, adrenalin was released from time to time. There were no Rolls-Royces in swimming polls or TV sets dropped from multi-storey hotels, but one room-trashing event exposed the inventive style and fiscal skills of Stan Tippins. A separate episode in a Holiday Inn did provide some press coverage for Ian, who endured a night in an Indianapolis jail cell, even though Stan Tippins tried to rescue the situation again.

IH: "Mott the Hoople was never into room-wrecking but I remember that the aftermath following one show was bad. We were eighteen gigs into the tour, and we were absolutely shot, because in those days fans were banging on your door all the time. We discovered it cost 1,800 dollars to fix a hotel bedroom but after that event, Stan paid, then took the messed-up TV and sold it at a garage for 100 dollars – so it worked out at 1,700 dollars for room repair. I recall that Aerosmith watched that wrecking from the door. You couldn't wish for a nicer bunch of guys, but they just wanted to be famous and bad, so much. When Mott blotted their copybook with that rather unfortunate episode, later, in a *Creem* interview, Aerosmith were the perpetrators. It was nothing to be proud of – but they seemed to be.

"I well remember when we were in Indianapolis with a promoter called Charlie Fain, who also managed Sha Na Na. We were sitting in this Holiday Inn and Charlie had our gig money, and then he found this ten grand had disappeared from the bar area, so I demanded loudly that they lock the doors of the hotel. Being English, I was outraged and got mouthy when they wouldn't shut the place and check the people in the bar – but I was suddenly handcuffed by a guy, who turned out to be an off-duty sergeant and was dumped straight into the jail. I was bailed for thirty-eight bucks the following morning, but the band could have bailed me at 2.00am for four hundred bucks, so that's the esteem I was held in. Stan could barely restrain himself from laughing and Charlie never got his ten-grand back – but I got a song out of it later!"

"Hunter decided to handle the situation," said Stan, "and addressed the cop saying, 'Right. I'm telling you. You can't do that. We've got rights. My dad's a policeman in England' – and, as he pointed, the cop grabbed his arm, threw him through the front doors of the hotel and Ian was gone – at speed – off to a cell for the night."

Watts considered that "tales from the road" were to be expected amongst rock groups who faced extreme highs, lows, tiresome travel and periods of boredom during demanding tours. "Every night was wild with Mott, because every night we had a party," Pete recalled. "When you're older it seems totally stupid, but when you're young and exuberant and things are going your way, it's like letting off steam – especially after doing a brilliant gig, or even if you had a lousy gig. We weren't prone to doing damage, but we did it more in anger if something went wrong – like Buff, kicking in a dressing room door that wouldn't open after a bad show."

Morgan Fisher found US touring disorientating, being in a different city every day, but in endless guest rooms that looked the same. The road was exhausting but the adrenalin-filled band would take turns most nights at hosting a room party, with a crew member going into the audience to organise guests. "We'd make a few requests like, 'That one in the fifth row!' It went on with

370

American girls," says Morgan. "Pete used to keep a score and was always asking the next day, 'Right. How many did you have last night?' I pissed him off one month, when I finally beat him. Of course, we were taking a risk, but nothing like the risks that there were later. We'd visit the doctor in Harley Street, and you'd see all sorts of music people there."

"Any room wrecking generally took place in the States," said Richie Anderson. "In England and Europe, they would get nasty about damage but in America, assuming you paid, they didn't care too much. I remember a Holiday Inn room that was systematically destroyed and almost reduced to four walls."

The members of Mott had great respect for their crew. Morgan Fisher described Richie Anderson, Phil John and Mick Hince as an utterly dedicated "A1 team" who put in long hours and always delivered – and Pete Watts regarded each of the road crew as great characters.

"Richie Anderson was so slow we used to call him Snail Shit. He was like a vile Clint Eastwood and used to wear 'The Riverbed Shirt' – brown and grey, it looked like something that had been buried underground for a thousand years and he'd wear it all the time. Richie always had a cigarette hanging out of his mouth, but he was a very clever bloke. He knew about electronics, so you always felt safe with Richie and knew if you picked up a guitar you were going to be okay. Phil John (Phil Carruthers Pilkington Neasby Smythe, The Earl of Leicester), dealt mainly with the drums and our roadie Mick Hince was nicknamed Booster; he was rough and ready, and loud, and was fired in the end because he kept shouting at Ian and insulting him in front of fans while he was signing autographs."

The treadmill was now spinning faster and faster for Mott the Hoople and having successfully completed the second leg of their American tour, they returned to Britain on 5th November, four days before their new single 'Roll Away the Stone' was released. *Sounds* sensed a smash hit when John Peel wrote on his 'Singles' page: "Proud stuff. It's great. Mott the Hoople just gets better all the time." *Record Mirror* proclaimed, "Just a Motter of Time". Other encouraging verdicts included: "A hit if ever I heard one" and "This single is another sharp and laconic gem", while Columbia advertised the record with Mott in ultra-flash pose under the corny banner – 'Roll Away the Stone... The Motter you are, the hotter you get.'

> **IH:** "'Roll Away the Stone' just happened quickly. I remember the lyric being secondary. I was playing in the key of C and it was the first time I realised you could bung an E major in. I thought great – it made it melodic and that is what gave me the verse. The title I held out on for a while because it sounded like The Rolling Stones. Eventually I couldn't find anything better so 'Roll Away the Stone' it was. That was a deliberate single and it sold over three times as many copies as 'All the Young Dudes'. It seems that I sang 'Roll Away the Stone' quite high, but, in those days, we would slow the tape a tad and I'd sing over it, and then we'd put it back to normal on the singles. I knew 'Roll Away the Stone' was special and so did The Hollies, who really wanted the song – badly! We went to America and their guitar player went into the publishing company and said The Hollies wanted 'Roll Away the Stone'. The publishers explained it was a Mott the Hoople song and they couldn't do it but apparently the band said, 'Oh yeah, they've given us permission.' That's the story as it was told to me."

The spoken boy-girl section in the middle of 'Roll Away the Stone' was a nod from Hunter to the 1957 American single 'Rockabilly Party' by Hugo and Luigi, a writing team from New York's Brill Building. Engineered by Bill Price and reminiscent of The Ronettes and Phil Spector, 'Roll Away the Stone' entered the UK chart on 24th November and stayed for twelve weeks reaching No.8, earning a silver disc for the group. Although Bender was now in tow, both sides of the 'Roll Away the Stone' single featured Mick Ralphs' original guitar parts. On 14th November Mott re-appeared on *Top of the Pops* and Ralphs and Thunderthighs accompanied the band on the broadcast. "Elton John came into our dressing room at that *Top of the Pops* session," recalls Ian. "He loved 'Roll Away the Stone'."

"The Thunderthighs were a real joy to work with," says Morgan Fisher. "I found out much later how many great artists they sang with. They rehearsed with Mott prior to the 1973 US tour but, unfortunately, due to budget problems we couldn't take them with us. They claimed they got their name from a man who visited a clothes' shop in San Francisco where Dari Lalou worked. He asked for jeans for 'thunderthighs'. The gent in question was an American footballer."

Ian's songwriting had now furnished three consecutive hit singles and a Top Ten album for Mott the Hoople and finally the band felt free from the desperation they had experienced at Island Records. Publicist Tony Brainsby recalled how Ian discovered the thrill of writing hit songs and said that it was great to witness Hunter's exhilaration.

> **IH:** "I made a huge mistake. I went into Tony Brainsby's office one day thinking I'd cracked it and it was a great feeling. I said to Tony, 'I've got the formula. I now know the secret. I know the formula for writing a hit song' – and that was the end of the formula. I opened my big mouth and paid for it dearly. By this point it was a huge pressure and hard work writing singles. A few years later, I stopped thinking about hits and simply got into music."

The B-side of 'Roll Away the Stone', 'Where Do You All Come From', employed the title of a shelved Island-era instrumental and was composed by Hunter, but was credited band-wide again, so that publishing proceeds could be shared. The bluesy track was recorded totally live and loose, in one take in AIR No.2 with Bill Price. Ian recalls that the song was simply an observational nod to Mott's fans, but the lyric also possessed a *"thank you for reason"* acknowledgement to Ralph J. Gleason, the deputy editor of *Rolling Stone.*

> **IH:** "When I wrote 'Where Do You All Come From' it was about our audience, I think. I was just looking at people."

On 11th November, thirty US radio stations broadcast *The Pioneer Concert* featuring Mott the Hoople, "recorded at San Francisco Winterland" – but the music was not live. *Pioneer* had collated studio versions of Mott songs sandwiched between a live recording of band introductions and audience reactions, with added crowd noise on top! *Rolling Stone* reported on the debacle with the headline, 'The Hoople Live Show That Wasn't', noting that rock 'n' roll and the White House had something in common – an embarrassing tape recording. The President of Pioneer pleaded that his organisation had been ripped off by hiring an independent producer who assembled the offending tape after discovering a piano mike was unplugged, panicked and used studio material. Mott manager Fred Heller insisted on Pioneer distributing a statement to radio stations after the event, clearing Mott of responsibility. "I was furious at Pioneer as we were supposed to hear the Winterland live recording before it went out," says Fred. "Our contract called for 'creative input'. If we'd known about the mike we could have gone back and dubbed in piano with an explanation before broadcast. The cover-up was discovered, but the engineer could have been a hero. It got bad press initially, until the truth came out. The sad part is that it was a fabulous concert with a great audience reaction. Mott was at their best that night. After the event, the original tapes were never found."

With Mott riding high, it was Britain's turn for in-concert assault when the band played twenty-two British dates opening on 12th November at Leeds Town Hall and ending on 14th December with two performances at the Hammersmith Odeon. The London concerts were recorded by Bill Price using the Island Mobile Studio for a planned live album release. Under a *Record Mirror* headline

'Mott Bigger than Bowie', promoter Mel Bush announced, "The amount of public interest in this tour has been sensational. I believe that Mott will be as big if not bigger than Slade or Bowie in this country within six months."

Mott the Hoople's support act for their British tour was Queen, a relatively unknown band at that juncture, promoting their eponymous EMI debut album. A&R man Jack Nelson of Queen's management company had approached Bob Hirschman to ask if they could support and, whilst Hirschman had initial reservations about the pairing, Queen joined the billing for Mott's British concert dates. A payment was made by Queen, in practical terms 'a buy-on fee', but the two groups became good friends.

"Queen had great respect for Ian and Mott, and Hunter could recognise that they were going to be a big band," said Tony Brainsby. "The joint publicity situation helped that little initial tie-up and friendship between the two groups, but it was quite normal at that time for a support band to pay to go on the bill with a headlining act."

Guitarist Brian May reflected that Queen learned a great deal from Mott the Hoople in terms of outfits, organisation and fun – he felt that Mott looked lived-in, exuded attitude, humour and confidence because they were good and a great cameraderie grew between the two bands. Stan Tippins remembered Queen walking confidently into Mott's rehearsal cinema as though they were stars and Watts felt that Mott and Queen got on fantastically well right from the start. Travelling on the tour bus helped to cement relationships and the two teams of roadies worked well together. Drummer Roger Taylor later described Mott as "a great live, visceral, rock 'n' roll act" and remarked that Queen did "lift" ideas for staging and dynamics from Ian and the band.

"When we first went to a soundcheck with Queen we thought, 'Fuckin' hell, these guys are good,' but we got on great," says Luther. "Freddie would wipe the floor with everybody at table tennis backstage every night. I think Queen did learn a lot from

Mott because on many nights they'd be watching us from the side of the stage – taking it all in."

> **IH:** "I used to arrive towards the end of Queen's set each night and watch the last two numbers – 'Liar' and 'Keep Yourself Alive'. Fred would ask me, 'What do you think? What do you think?' And I said, 'You'll be fine because you've got the songs.' We knew Queen would be okay. I don't think I thought they'd be as big as they became. Fred did though – and that's all that mattered!"

Mott mimed to 'Roll Away the Stone' at BBC TV's *Top of the Pops* on 14th November between live dates in Blackburn and Worcester and during filming the band had fun, Ian fluffing his lines and Griffin playing with his hideous over-sized drumsticks.

On 23rd November, Mott the Hoople played the infamous Glasgow Apollo, a 4,000-seat venue that had been Europe's biggest cinema and was now Britain's best rock arena, famous for its enthusiastic and emotional audience – "The Glasgow Choir". Many resonant and rabid recordings were captured at The Apollo by Wishbone Ash, Roxy Music, King Crimson, AC/DC, Rush and Status Quo and bands that filled any gig there would receive an Apollo statuette trophy. The awards became so sought after that if an act was just short of selling out, their road crew would acquire the remaining seats to secure the prize, complete with inscribed golden plaque and the letters S.R.O. – Sold Right Out!

> **IH:** "The Glasgow Apollo was great. The guy that ran the theatre used to give you these long statuettes if you sold out so, on the '73 tour, he came to our dressing room with a bandage round his head and blood seeping through it, down the side of his face. I asked him what had happened, and he said quite matter-of-factly that they hadn't opened the front doors on time, so they'd used him as a battering

ram. I have fond memories of sitting in the stalls of the Apollo, or The Greens Playhouse as it was, at a soundcheck and being introduced to the entire Harvey family by Alex. It was always a great gig there. The stage was a little high, but that wasn't a bad idea. One bloke punched me on the way out of the Apollo once and shouted 'Brullyint!' God knows what would have happened if they didn't like us. I think the people make the gig and Glasgow never had a problem in that respect. The gigs there were blood and thunder, and they made you play better. Mott's show with Queen at the Apollo was great. Apparently, I caused trouble by telling everybody to stand on their seats, much to the horror of the staff. Things got a little hectic, so they put the lights on and asked the audience to behave. We stopped playing and I told them to switch the lights off again. They did, and we all had a great night. It was all a bit daft, but I was mad – I was crazy – the Rik Mayall of rock!"

"I remember talk of a bouncer being thrown off a balcony in Glasgow," says Phil John. "That was one of Mott's favourite gigs along with Friars Aylesbury and Fairfield Hall Croydon. After the Apollo show we picked up a dour Scottish kid who we named 'Fast Eddie' Richardson. He helped with 'the humping', then ran away with us to London and worked quite a few shows with Mott. A number of our humpers became road crew after working with us, including Peter Hince, who joined Queen's team."

Mott's British tour was a huge success and the exciting performances received high praise from the press. "These are the REAL Dudes" said *Sounds* while *Melody Maker* described Mott live as... 'VERY FLASH – VERY RUDE – VERY MUCH '74 ROCK 'N' ROLL.' *DISC* reviewed Mott's Oxford New Theatre show, where the band was presented with a Silver Disc, for British sales of *Mott*, under the headline 'Goin' On A Bender!' At Mott's Southend gig, Freddie, Brian and Roger of Queen joined the band on backing vocals during 'All the Young Dudes'.

'Sucker' was a favourite track of Morgan's, for whilst Bowie's original thin production was fine in Fisher's view, Mott took the song to a new level on stage and made it "a monster". The live set also included the band's colossal encore of 'Walkin' with a Mountain' complete with manic Bender guitar solo and a fifteen-minute closing 'Medley' incorporating 'Jerkin' Crocus', 'One of the Boys', 'Rock and Roll Queen' and 'Violence', bridged with short influential fragments of 'You Really Got Me', 'Get Back', 'Peter Gunn Theme', 'The Jean Genie' and 'Whole Lotta Shakin'.

The climax to Mott's British tour was two packed performances held in one evening at London's Hammersmith Odeon and events would grab front-page headlines and echo their 1971 Royal Albert Hall appearance. During the second show, as Mott approached the climax of their act, road crew and fans suddenly grappled with stewards to prevent the Odeon management lowering the safety curtain before the band had finished its swashbuckling set. The strategic repositioning of Morgan Fisher's piano under the part-lowered curtain enabled Hunter and Bender to advance down one of the theatre's plinths amongst the melée, as the band ripped through their 'Walkin' with a Mountain' finale. Mott's 'lieutenants' swarmed the stage and Luther was finally left out front, his guitar stuttering to a halt as he was overcome by fans. The episode was a dramatic illustration of the band's dynamism at its absolute zenith, the show concluding with genuine pandemonium. Bender felt like a king after "The Battle of Hammersmith", for whilst Ralphs had been a humble and tasteful guitarist for Mott, Luther exuded mania and a larger-than-life stage presence. His metamorphosis from blues wizard to glam demon and his alter ego Ariel Bender, seemed ideal for the schizophrenia that had become associated with Mott the Hoople. Grosvenor was a fun-loving spirited figure offstage while, "on the boards", he was frantic.

"I believe somebody broke their leg," says Luther "and the management were screaming at us to get off, but the adrenalin was flowing, and it was indicative of the power of Mott the Hoople at that time. Joining Mott gave me the chance to let rip in a way

378

that I hadn't been able to do before, and it gave me license to be myself. The solo on 'Walkin' with a Mountain' was over the top but structured, so as out of control as it was, I was totally in control. On that 1973 tour a guy came up to me and said, 'Jesus Christ! You're a dead ringer for Luther Grosvenor of Spooky Tooth.' I said, 'So they tell me.'"

> IH: "Mott specialised in riots which was to our detriment. We were banned from lots of places in England after The Royal Albert Hall went down in 1971. When the Odeon staff tried to lower the fire safety curtain at Hammersmith, Morgan Fisher did a very clever thing because they had a huge Borsendorfer grand piano there, which was their property, and he pushed it under the curtain. They weren't going to destroy their piano so, sensing the drama, we carried on. I remember Luther was way out front, howling away on guitar. I heard the London show again on tape, years later, and Bender was playing his bottom off!"

The British press raved over the band's Hammersmith gigs, *Melody Maker*'s front page proclaiming, 'Mott Riot – Rock 'n' roll is here to stay!' *Sounds* summed up the blistering performance admirably: "Mott's heavy menacing act is led by Ian who has joined the ranks of the controllers – the select few who can put an audience exactly where they want. During the quiet 'Rose', Ariel Bender fiddles with the stone in the bracelet he's wearing (flash bastard). It looked as though he was looking at his watch. Fuller of themselves than they've ever been, the band plays on and on... the safety curtain comes down... Morgan Fisher shoves his piano under it to prevent its descent... Hunter and Bender advance over the catwalk into the very audience... V-signs are flashed, and punches thrown... the bouncers put up a fierce last-ditch stand, but the front-row kids swarm on to the stage... chaos. Rock 'n' roll madness rampant. It will surely go down as one of the historical gigs when the annals of rock and roll are finally compiled."

Mott's two London shows were recorded, and it was announced before Christmas that the band would release their first live album early in 1974. Another event at Hammersmith had been the surprise announcement of Dale Griffin's marriage to Paula Greaves, a topless model and former "date" of Verden Allen. No one except Ian, who was "Buff's Best Man", knew of the previous day's registry office wedding until it was announced on stage. The celebrations after the London gigs involved Queen, Andy Mackay and Eddie Jobson of Roxy Music, Guy Stevens, Paul Rodgers and Mick Ralphs of Bad Company, and Andy Williams. Mick Jagger and David Bowie also appeared, dancing in the wings behind Morgan Fisher with their arms around each other's shoulders, but the pair departed before Mott's encore. Mick Bolton left the group at the end of the British tour whilst Morgan Fisher became a full band member.

By December 1973 the *Mott* album had sold 65,000 copies and was still selling 3,000 units a week, while 'Roll Away the Stone' had shifted 175,000 singles, putting it only 8,000 behind 'All the Young Dudes'. During their British tour Ian talked about Mott the Hoople's plans for their next studio LP, to be recorded at Advision Studios in January, and he had ambitious ideas. However, the departure of Allen and Ralphs had altered the character of the band, even if Mott had not yet appreciated the impact in studio terms. A Hammersmith live album was initially planned as the follow-up to *Mott*, but a studio project would be the next release.

Grosvenor was not a musical collaborator like Ralphs, so Hunter had become Mott's lone creative force, but he had composed songs that would mark a solid progression and cast the band's highest-ever charting album in the USA. In advance of the recording sessions, Ian had ideas for six songs and wanted Mott's new record to be more aggressive than the last. Griffin claimed that Hunter's original idea was a loose concept album titled *Weekend*, about a group of British kids and their experiences and lifestyle.

By the end of December, Mott's new record was to be titled *The Bash Street Kids* after the long-running cartoon strip from *The Beano,* one of Britain's famous comics that contained stories with an anti-authority theme. The Bash Street Kids strip featured a gormless gang who would cheerfully plot to blow up their school or drive their teachers to the brink of madness. The originator, Leo Baxendale, said the gang were reluctant products of a bizarre alternative to secondary and grammar schools. Hunter had written the title track and the album concept was to be based loosely around a gang of youngsters, following the *Weekend* theme.

Luther recalled that Ian had several possible titles, but he was "very strong" on *The Bash Street Kids* which the guitarist considered a great idea. There were then worries that the publishers of *The Beano* might refuse permission and whilst Bob Hirschman remembers *The Bash Street Kids* album title "being bandied around", he doesn't remember any refusal or intervention from the publishers. Sadly, Hunter's intended title song was changed to 'Crash Street Kidds', the album concept was shelved and *The Hoople* was born. "*Mott* had been effective as an album title," said Watts, "so *The Hoople* was a natural progression. We should have done a trilogy though: *Mott, The* and *Hoople!*"

A chaotic 1974 schedule was mapped out for Mott, requiring the band to record their new album for February release, prior to an extensive European tour but they encountered problems. Mott wanted to utilise AIR Studios and engineer Bill Price again for recording during January, but neither was available. They taped a demo of a new Hunter song, 'The Golden Age of Rock 'n' Roll' in December, with *Dudes* engineer Keith Harwood at Olympic No.2, but Dale Griffin was wholly unimpressed with the ageing studio and the band passed.

Dan Loggins says: "I went to Olympic Studios one day, and after bumping into Mick Ralphs and Bad Company, I got to the right room. Mott was rocking along, playing a new Hunter song called 'The Golden Age of Rock 'n' Roll'. It was a barn-burner with humorous lyrics and Luther was playing screaming lead. Hunter's homage to rock's roots would feature Jerry Lee Lewis pounding piano again, and Ian vocalising in as much Little Richard style as his throat could handle. He excitedly planned symphonic voices on the intro and choruses, with females doing call-and-response vocals mirroring Ray Charles' 1950s girl backing-group, The Raelettes. The new song was all planned out by Ian. Mott truly was Hunter's band now – there could be no doubt."

Advision Studios in Gosfield Street, close to AIR in London's West End, was finally chosen for Mott's sessions and *The Hoople* would be produced by Hunter, Griffin and Watts, and arranged by Ian. Dan Loggins was credited as Production Supervisor and Ariel Bender appeared courtesy of Island Records.

At the beginning of 1974, Britain had moved into turbulent times and events impinged on *The Hoople*. This was an era when Bowie's colourful Aladdin Sane pouted over monochrome Prime Minister Edward Heath and striking workers. Even the mean-spirited British TV comedy figure Alf Garnett was infuriated with his beloved Conservative Party and "ranted" over The Three-Day Week, energy consumption restrictions, a miner's strike, and power cuts. Bizarrely the government's SOS was to instruct the British public to "switch off something" while Slade topped the charts with 'Merry Christmas Everybody'. It was a bleak time for Britain and Hunter was vocal about the country's plight to the press at the time.

> **IH:** "I'm amazed by it all. We've gone back to the Middle-Ages in a week. One minute it's 1973 – now it's 1073. If I ran my group the way Ted Heath runs his Government, we'd be out of work in a week."

Britain's social undercurrent and grim economic pedicament was to surface in some of Hunter's new songs and during Mott's recording sessions. "It was a ghastly experience," said Dale Griffin. "Wrong studio, wrong engineer, country in crisis, strikes, electricity cutoffs, petrol shortage, Bender oddly disconnected and not enough songs." Pete Watts' memories of Advision were not good either – from day one.

"I arrived the first evening for a recording session in my '58 Cadillac Eldorado and asked the uniformed doorman where I could park. He proceeded to go mental at me for owning a huge flash car which used an obscene amount of petrol and ruined things for the poor people. Were they paying for my petrol without me knowing? I told him to 'Fuck off' and there was almost a punch-up – a nice start for *The Hoople* album and things went downhill from there."

The early part of the album sessions yielded a live recording christened *The Advision Jam* where Mott recorded an impromptu take of Jerry Lee Lewis, Hank Williams and Ray Charles standards. Featuring Loggins on lead vocal and Hunter on drums, Griffin described the session as "crap", but Grosvenor held a different view saying the time was great and it was only a jam. "During the sessions we managed to drink too much Watney's Red Ale," admits Dan, "before attempting a version of 'What'd I Say'. It was not for any 'artistic' reasons – it was just letting off steam."

Having recorded most of *The Hoople* album through January, Bill Price commenced mixing of Mott's new material at AIR Studios during February, with some additional guitars and vocals overdubbed at Advision. Price helped to rescue the recordings however, when Mott discovered that the sounds on tape were not encouraging during playbacks at AIR. Frantic calls took place between the two studios and tests were run on machines, but things still sounded worrying. Dale felt that any other group would have scrapped the "dismal" Advision tapes and re-recorded the album at AIR with Bill Price; Griffin complained that Mott was forced to mix the record as it was.

Echoing *Mott*, Andy Mackay helped out on tenor and baritone saxophones and tenor sax player Howie Casey contributed too. Dale claimed that Howie was not keen on Andy's playing and wanted to be left off the album credits as people might think Mackay's input was Casey, so Roxy's star sax man was listed as

'Rockin' Jock McPherson'. Mick Ralphs also attended some *Hoople* sessions and appeared on two tracks.

"I remember Ralpher came in one day with a picture of Bad Company from the States," said Watts. "It said, 'Nick Phelps' under Mick's photo and Paul Rodgers was labelled 'Jock McPherson', nothing to do with his name at all. We laughed and thought it was a great name, so we used it with Andy Mackay. Andy was unconventional, almost avant-garde in his playing and Howie Casey was a 'pro' session player – one of the old-brigade."

"I recall Ian was going for a kind of Roy Wood sound, although my style was a little more experimental," says Andy Mackay. "The Rockin' Jock McPherson name was a bit of Seventies rock and roll humour as magazines were always getting pictures and captions mixed up."

During the *Hoople* sessions, Mott employed backing vocalists Barry St John, Sue Glover and Sunny Leslie, replacing The Thunderthighs. Sue and Sunny were wedded to Johnny Glover and Alec Leslie of Island Records. Watts recalled that the girls were very professional, easy to work with and that some of the band envied their marital status. "We'd be driving back from Manchester at five in the morning," said Pete, "in the freezing cold and would say, 'Look at Johnny Glover and Alec Leslie – look at 'em, lying in bed now with Sue and Sunny and colour TVs – and look at us' – We only had black-and-white televisions!"

The Hoople was the first Mott studio album to feature Morgan and Luther; Grosvenor opted for power chords and riffs quite different from Ralphs' guitar style, but Luther felt the sessions went well, he played what was right for the songs and he deemed the album stronger than previous Mott releases. In January 1974, Hunter was describing Grosvenor as a great guitarist and praising *Spooky Two* as one of British rock's finest albums, but *The Hoople* evolved as a keyboard-dominated record.

IH: "Luther was fine at first, live, because he copied Ralphs' parts, but when we did the album, we found out he had a lot of trouble with creativity. That's why *The Hoople* is geared so much towards keyboards – he wasn't sure what to do. He put a solo on 'Trudi's Song' that was like Jimi Hendrix. It didn't make it at all – it was only a simple little song."

"Bender couldn't relax in the studio," says Fisher. "On stage he was speedy too. Doing *The Hoople* was quite tricky; we had to encourage him a lot as he was trying to adapt himself too much to the feel of the band – to 'replacing' Ralphs. It didn't happen as it should have done. I just steamed in with plenty of ideas and I think keyboards added colour to Mott, as Verden's special style had done."

The group spoke privately about Bender's lack of creativity, but he was a popular guitarist with fans and critics in America, projected record sales were high and with their biggest-ever US tour planned, Mott accepted the situation at the time. Publicly, everything seemed fine as Ariel Bender was pushed forward and handled some press interviews.

Before CBS released Mott's new single and album however, in February 1974, Atlantic Records in America finally decided to issue the *Rock and Roll Queen* compilation LP that Island had conceived fourteen months earlier in Britain. This shameless opportunism was stimulated by the success of *Mott* and the forthcoming *Bad Company* LP on the Swan Song label, affiliated to Atlantic. *Billboard* was complimentary about *Rock and Roll Queen*, though saying: "Mott have always been one of the finest pure rock bands around and they never received the recognition in their early days they surely deserved. Mott show themselves for what they always will be – a superb rock congregation." *Circus* described Atlantic's attempted cash-in as, 'Rock and Roll Queen: Skeletons from Mott's Closet' and whilst the LP had not charted in Britain in 1972, it reached No.112 in America in 1974. Ian was still scathing of the album at the time of US release.

IH: "I don't think we were good enough at the time. We just weren't ready as a band. It embarrasses me – the songs don't

– it's the way they were done – the mixing. 'Thunderbuck Ram' is characterised by its terrible, awful, disgusting mix – it's the worst of them all. It infuriates me when I hear *Brain Capers* for example. I can hear it a million times better. It was a mess, but it was how we were feeling. We thought the whole damn world was against us and it was our way of spitting and saying, 'The hell with you.' We thought we were going out, so we figured we'd go down blasting."

On 15th March 1974, CBS released *The Hoople*'s opening track as Mott's new single. Hunter's 'The Golden Age of Rock 'n' Roll' was a joyous musical rave-up, crammed with Jerry Lee piano and blistering sax, but it also carried a serious comment. The lyrics part-referenced Ian's annoyance at a *"ninety-six-decibel freaks"* lobby that was trying to reduce noise levels at British rock concerts; this followed the actions of Leeds City Council who had applied a 96dB volume restriction for all live and disco music played in the city, based on the sound level that required ear protection for industrial workers; theoretically this even outlawed most classical music and audience applause. The Council would abandon the limit in 1975 but in 1973 Hunter had received a letter from Helen Akitt, the Entertainments Secretary at Leeds Technical College, asking him to try and do something about the restriction at gigs. "I wrote to a number of rock people and was delighted with Ian's response in the song," said Helen, "but not so Mott's concert dates, which were held in Bradford rather than Leeds that year. So much for solidarity!"

At the time of release, Hunter explained that his lyric wasn't meant to be completely nostalgic as the title suggested, but rather a celebration of the glamorous music scene that was thriving in the early Seventies.

> **IH:** "If anything 'the golden age of rock 'n' roll' has been in recent years where they tell me the industry has picked up phenomenally, even without people like The Beatles – so 'The Golden Age of Rock 'n' Roll' is meant to be, what

would it be like if these ninety-six-decibel idiots got their own way? To me, it's ridiculous, the whole thing, because 'now' is The Golden Age."

Mott's blistering single employed a piano introduction and Alan Freed American-style DJ voice-over, before the band crashed in, igniting the song, while the middle-eight featured crazed guitar from Bender. The "loony solo" quivered with tortured tremolo and belligerent bends and Ian described the guitarist's instrumentation as madness.

> **IH:** "On the beginning of 'Golden Age', Dan Loggins did the spoken bit. We loved his silken tones, plus, it always helps if you get your A&R guy on your side. The ninety-six-decibel claim was stupid to me in 1974. Now? I would agree with them!"

According to Dan Loggins: "One day in the studio, Ian said, 'You know, on the intro, we want an American DJ type to announce the song.' So, I said that I knew a few American guys including Paul Gambacinni and Larry Belling, but Mott said, 'No, we want YOU to be the voice and, in fact, we want you to record it NOW!' So, into the booth I went, Ian having written out ten words that I couldn't possibly screw up! Take One. 'Ladies and Gentlemen, The Golden Age of Rock 'n' Roll.' I looked out and could see them smiling and gesturing, and applauding. 'Take.' I thought they were kidding but that was a neat moment for me. I felt that I'd been accepted by the band. It was no prank."

"Those were exciting times in AIR studios," says Fisher. "We met heroes like Robert Fripp, Bryan Ferry and Marc Bolan casually strolling down the corridors. At first, I'd started to add some small musical things live for Mott, but it was really when we got in the studio with *The Hoople* that there was an opportunity for me to contribute. Any ideas were not shot down, so I brought synths into the band. There was so much acceptance and openness and my 'prog' ideas were not laughed at. Ian was keen to play piano on 'Golden Age', but I really wanted to try keyboards. I asked Ian for a shot, played it, and Hunter said, 'Great.' Dan wandered in unsuspectingly while we were recording, and we pushed him in front of a microphone and coerced him into adding a spoken intro in his smooth executive voice. Some fans thought that *The Hoople* was too complicated, but I just got tremendously enthusiastic in AIR Studios and was encouraged by Ian and the band. The making of *The Hoople* was a creative joy. We were on a roll, we just went from one song to the next and we made a great album."

'The Golden Age of Rock 'n' Roll' entered the UK singles chart on 30th March and stayed for seven weeks reaching No.16, while the single hit No.96 on *Billboard* and the Top Ten in Switzerland. The record attracted favourable press headlines including 'MOTT'S ROCK AND SLEAZE', one review describing the song as "raw-edged, with a bounding pounding beat, carefully enunciated vocal excitement and all the required clichés." No.16 was a slightly less favourable British chart placing than Mott's recent run of hits and Watts considered the recording and musical feel were below par, and that the song was really an album track. Even one of rock's most avant-garde practitioners, Frank Zappa, seemed to have an opinion: "Recently I've been listening to *The Hoople*. I enjoy every cut except 'The Golden Age of Rock 'n' Roll'."

Mott appeared on *Top of the Pops* in March and April to promote their single, but these appearances were prefaced by a 2nd March performance of 'Roll Away the Stone' for Germany's TV show, *Disco*. Mott also engaged Richard Weaver again, to produce a video for 'The Golden Age of Rock 'n' Roll', filmed in Wembley. "We made 'The Golden' promo video at Lee International Film Studios," says Richard. "We brought in crates of beer and I got a wind machine to try and create some movement in the band's hair. I remember Pete Watts was worried about that and what it might do to his tresses!"

The B-side of 'The Golden Age of Rock 'n' Roll' was 'Rest in Peace', written by Ian, but co-credited to Hunter-Watts-Griffin.

The track was not included on Mott's forthcoming LP, having been recorded live without any overdubbing by Bill Price at AIR No.2 during mixing of *The Hoople*. With single releases, Mott was always bold enough to place a non-album track as the B-side and it was usually a jewel. 'Rest in Peace' maintained the high standards set by 'Rose' and 'Where Do You All Come From', and the band featured 'Rest in Peace' in their live set. For once, Watts was almost happy, describing the track as, "too churchy – good for a breather on stage though – and a few swigs of booze!" There were no other usable outtakes from *The Hoople* sessions.

> **IH:** "In 1973 and 1974 we were right on the clock in the studio. Reels cost real money and the label and management were tight. They would record over reels if necessary, to save cash. I wrote 'Rest in Peace' after seeing someone very dear to me play Madison Square Garden in New York. They survived the gig and the song. I remember years later, when I was playing in London, a guy came up to me before the show, holding photographs of a gravestone inscribed with my lyrics. This was because I'd written 'Rest in Peace' apparently, but I remember thinking, 'Hang on a minute. I've got to go on stage. Couldn't you have given me these afterwards?'"

The Hoople LP was issued on 22nd March 1974 and was certified Gold in Britain and America before release. The album featured nine tracks: 'The Golden Age of Rock 'n' Roll', 'Marionette', 'Alice', 'Crash Street Kidds', 'Born Late '58', 'Trudi's Song', 'Pearl 'n' Roy (England)', 'Through the Looking Glass' and 'Roll Away the Stone' – all composed by Ian, apart from 'Born Late '58' where Overend Watts made his writing debut.

'The Golden Age of Rock 'n' Roll' opened the LP in rousing style but on the second track, the band went straight for the jugular, as Mott delivered the cornerstone of the album – the smart and sardonic 'Marionette'. A dramatic mini-opera of five minutes duration, Hunter's song was a relentless tour-de-force – relating nightmarish images of puppets, coffins, and insanity, 'Marionette' had it all. With its quasi-classical musical structure, Ian had created a production masterpiece and, unconsciously, a prototype for Queen's 'Bohemian Rhapsody', released some eighteen months later.

'Marionette' presented a star's reflections on the corporate side of rock 'n' roll and its impact on a musician who felt pressurised by record companies, manipulated by management and constricted by commerciality. At the time of release, Ian praised Dale Griffin's production input believing that 'Marionette' was the most important song on the album and possibly the best track that Mott had ever done.

> **IH:** "It's something I've wanted to do personally as a songwriter for a long time and that is to do a five-minute opera, as opposed to an opera that goes on for forty minutes, which I feel might be a bit trying. I mean *Tommy* wasn't trying at all, neither was *Arthur*, but when I listen to music, I like to hear a hook all the time, and I think we got it with 'Marionette'. I think perhaps this is the first track where we've really got it all the way through – one thing hits you, another thing hits you, another thing hits you – and you don't get room to sit back."

As Ian questions his sanity, crazed violin, frantic saxophones, staccato cellos, 'Quasimodo' vocal choruses and manic laughter surround his visions of a rock star driven to submission, making the track a breathtaking experience. Andy Mackay, Howie Casey, Graham Preskett and Mike Hurwitz provide exciting orchestral backing while Hunter, Grosvenor and Watts contribute 'Voix grotesques a la Quasimodo' backing vocals. Luther was also responsible for the cackling laughter in the central portion of the track, while Watts was instructed to hit Grosvenor over the head using a tin tray to create crashing chorus sounds. A young Hugh Padgham, future producer of Genesis and XTC, and a fresh 'tape op' recruit at Advision in 1974, was asked to "mike" Luther during Pete's percussive assault.

Pete Watts remembered: "Advision went potty when the old tea lady reported angrily that her metal tray had been rendered useless, like tin foil. I'd smashed it over Bender's head at least 500 times during the recording of 'Marionette' to get the crashing noises on each chorus. He begged me to hit him – 'Harder Pete, harder' – so I did."

The incessant dramatic madness oozing from 'Marionette' mirrored the insane expectations of the rock business and privately Ian was experiencing stress via demands for new songs, singles, an album a year, interviews and endless touring. Hunter reflected on the strains of Mott's new-found success in 1974.

IH: "It is heavy these days. You've got to be pretty insane to keep your sanity. The pressures are intangible, but it's a twenty-four-hour rush of arguments and people expecting so much of you, not understanding when you can't quite deliver – right from the kids, up to the top brass of Columbia Records."

With 'Marionette' Hunter crystallised rock's claustrophobic circus, pre-figuring themes in Pink Floyd's 1975 release, *Wish You Were Here*. Inspired by similar feelings of alienation, Floyd's 'Have a Cigar' described disillusionment with the demands of the music business and the power of record companies, songwriter Roger Waters noting that the artist is no longer his own man as he becomes "a cipher".

Hunter's title and lyrical theme was soon echoed on celluloid too, in the movie *Stardust*, where Ines des Longchamps, playing girlfiend Danielle remarks, "I thought you were not like the others. You are not a marionette"... Jim MacLaine (Essex's character) replying, "Well, everyone seems to be using me – it's as if you're on a roller coaster and you can't get off." *Stardust* even portrayed Essex recording and performing a mini 'rock opera', *Dei Sancta*.

Queen, Floyd and Essex had surely warmed to Hunter's concept, but years later Ian reflected on *Stardust* and the structure of 'Marionette', with modesty.

IH: "*Stardust*, the movie, is pretty much how it is when you get near the top and I was saying that in 'Marionette'. In fact, in the film, his girlfriend says he has become a marionette, which might be a total fluke, but I got a little chill when I was watching the movie, because that was right where I was at. Once you've got something successful going, you've got to keep it going, because a lot of people are getting paid, so a lot has got to be planned ahead and that's when I started to get a bit funny about it. If somebody asked me at the end of a tour whether I wanted to do another one, I'd be perfectly happy but, there's something about it all lined up in front of you. It looked like too much to me.

"I felt 'Marionette' was something that hadn't been done before – a nervous breakdown on record – that was the idea. I was beginning to realise that rock 'n' roll wasn't all fun – it was a business too and I was beginning to feel a little squeezed and a little used, and a little knackered. I was also messing with musical influences – a European staccato verse and an American groove on the chorus – very dramatic. Crossing Little Richard with the Berlin Philharmonic seemed interesting – sax lines against severe cellos and violins – and 'Marionette' gave us that opportunity. I think Jeff Lynne of ELO was thinking along the same lines – or if he wasn't, then he soon was. The guy doing the strings for us, Graham Preskett was great, Howie Casey was terrific on tenors and the lyric was good and truthful. Bender had manic energy and was in his element on that track – the wicked laugh was Luther!

"Some people have compared Queen's 'Bohemian Rhapsody' to 'Marionette' but I think the only thing they might have considered was doing something in that operetta vein. There are no similarities between the two songs to me. I was at the mixing of 'Bohemian Rhapsody' – well, the third day that it was being mixed! It came blaring out of four huge speakers, a monster cacophony of 'bits' that Fred had assembled. He said it meant nothing, but it was overwhelming after you'd walked in off Wardour Street on a rainy day."

The third track on *The Hoople* was 'Alice', a Manhattan tale of *"the seedy and the snaz"* and a piece that resonated with 'Whizz Kid'. *Rolling Stone* regarded 'Alice' as a standout track, "for its masterful vocal and its account of fellatio on 42nd Street." Featuring Lynsey de Paul as 'the whistling moog mouse' and Watts on Leslie bass, 'Alice' was a busy and ambitious piece with an excessive lyrical outpouring from Ian that demanded careful listening. Mott attempted the song in concert once, but the panoply of words caused the group to abandon it. Hunter said he must have been thinking of somebody when he wrote it, but that the song was just a Mott experience from touring the States. Ian felt that Morgan had fitted Mott like a glove and his excellent keyboard skills were amply demonstrated on 'Alice'. Fisher enjoyed the recording and acknowledged that his playing style was influenced by Al Kooper of Bob Dylan fame, and The Band's Garth Hudson.

Watts' bass line in 'Alice' was inspired by his affection for guitarist Nils Lofgren and his recently disbanded outfit, Grin. Pete was a huge admirer of the group and "forced" Tippins to go out and find Lofgren when Mott played in Washington once. The bassist had been hopeful he might meet his hero, but Stan returned triumphant holding Nils "by the shoulder." Photographs were duly taken, Pete gave Nils various stage rings and the American was mesmerised by the event; years later, Lofgren helped Watts on a Portobello Road market stall that Pete ran.

Side One of *The Hoople* closed with Hunter's sinister jeremiad, 'Crash Street Kidds', a brutal rocker lamenting urban unrest that echoed 'Violence' from *Mott*. Ian explained that he had a preoccupation with British New Towns which didn't seem to have any heart or centre and seemed quite frightening. The lyric told the tale of a street gang in such a town, so disaffected and disenchanted with the way that things were run by local and national government, that they decided to form their own "army" and take over Britain. In the end, youth fails with Hunter adopting a Dalek voice and a machine gun heralding the gang leader's demise in a bizarre finale. Ian remembers that the band had a problem with 'Crash Street Kidds' and he was not convinced that Mott ever "nailed" the song. Dale was unhappy, again, as the track's conclusion was meant to end in a cacophony of guns and explosions to denote the coming insurrection. "Sadly," said Griffin, "the effects available to use were woefully inadequate and it ended up a tad Mickey Mouse."

In a *Sounds* feature titled 'Rock and Roll Rogues', Martin Hayman wrote that 'Crash Street Kidds' appeared to confirm *The Beano* publisher's worst fears about the musical subversion of their homeless ruffians. Another writer glamorously remarked that, "'Crash Street Kidds' is a number which has The Hells Angels and The Monattoes, (people who removed corpses during the time of the Great Plague) alongside the James Dean legend and the romantic myth of *A Clockwork Orange*." Hunter had now crafted 'The Moon Upstairs', 'Violence', and 'Crash Street Kidds' – an aggressive triptych, hammering home frustrating experiences and visions of disillusionment which resonated with the soon-to-emerge punk movement. Ian is slightly sceptical about visionary claims and considers that 'the new-wave' and subsequent British street riots were predictable, but Griffin praised Hunter.

"Ian was capable of astonishing flashes of percipience," said Dale, "and with 'Violence' and 'Crash Street Kidds', he brilliantly foretold the coming and the mood of the punk era in the UK, not to mention the civil unrest of the early Eighties. In many ways Hunter was a punk, in that he had within him great feelings of anger and frustration."

The Hoople Side Two opened with the ode to jailbait, 'Born Late '58' – Watts' songwriting, arranging and lead vocal debut for Mott the Hoople. It was the only number other than 'I'm a Cadillac' that the band recorded without Ian, in a week where he had gone to America for interviews after telling the group to, "Get Bender fucking sorted out!" Hunter thought 'Born Late '58' was a highly creditable effort from Watts and a potential single. The track featured Pete on twelve-string, rhythm guitar and "Manfred Mann's bass", with Luther on slide guitar. Watts used a single pick-up Gibson SG for the riff but was forced to sell the guitar for £80 to pay a gas bill three months later. Although Mott was at its peak, he also had to dispense with the Rickenbacker twelve-string for £120. Pete's writing was simply constructed compared to Ian's, with more emphasis on 'beat' which offered a nice break in the proceedings, although Watts was less than convinced.

"What inspired 'Born Late '58' was, I was told, 'There aren't enough tracks for the album – you've got to write something – Ian's going to America to do interviews – we need another track – it's got to be a rock number – and you've got to write it.' That was it, plain and simple. For my first recorded song, it's almost half-okay, but it lacks a decent hook. I remember trying to finish off the lyrics upstairs at Advision in the middle of a party. There were about ten people there including Wookie, my girlfriend, and Ralpher in gleeful mood. The 'Listen feller' line changed to 'Listen Heller' and we got on a stupid roll with 'Hirschman – log's in a dan.' On the lyric sheet, the words were perceived as 'Hush man, doves in a tan,' which I liked a lot. The poor devil at the publishers must have played it again and again to decipher the undecipherable. He did well in the end! Later that night a posh glass table was broken, the culprit never owned up and Advision went potty the next day."

Dan Loggins reflects, "The band was probably exhausted and starting to run on fumes, I think, and Pete decided to have a bit of lyrical fun at Bob's and my expense, as he was in his cups. I was a bit put off, but, somehow Ralpher showed up, and was to sooth any potential hurt feelings that Hirschman or I might have had at that moment – so, in the long run, no harm – no foul."

'Trudi's Song', a beautiful ballad for Ian's wife, provided a gentle contrast to much of The Hoople's toughness and hard edge. Hunter was inspired vocally by Bob Dylan and he enthused about Fisher's excellent playing again, saying that it felt as though Morgan had been with Mott since their inception. Fisher's piano, played through a Leslie cabinet, added a surreal beauty to the track. Every Mott album featured one ballad, and this was a charming gift from Ian to his partner, but Dale Griffin described 'Trudi's Song' as "Ian Hunter solo material" and considered it had no place on a Mott the Hoople record. More positively, Rolling Stone in America described 'Trudi's Song' as "heartfelt" and "a simple, guileless and lovely tribute".

Ian unleashed a further stinging observation on Britain's social plight in 'Pearl 'n' Roy (England)'. An early Hunter political "rant", Ian humorously described economic strife, the chasm between rich and poor, and spoofed the polarisation of UK Prime Minister Edward Heath and Labour Party leader Harold Wilson. Originally titled 'J.C.'s Alright' the song was one of Hunter's first references to English decline and class war, to be revisited later in his career.

> **IH:** "There was no real difference between people in the street and me. 'Pearl 'n' Roy' was a great backtrack, really up, and was finished, but I hadn't written the lyric. I took it home and these words came pouring out. I couldn't alter them because the lyric was good, but it was a down lyric. At the time we were surrounded by the three-day week and I just couldn't avoid writing in that way. I was being honest – again."

'Pearl 'n' Roy' featured Blue Weaver (of Amen Corner and Strawbs fame) on the choruses and an opening "saloon bar scene". Blue would soon replace Mick Bolton as organ player on Mott's 1974 tours and this was his only studio appearance with the group. Ralphs also sang on the track.

"Mick used to hang around the studio to see how things were going," says Grosvenor. "I think he genuinely came along just to see how things were developing for the love of his old band. You know, you don't play for fuckin' Liverpool for twenty years and move on and have no love anymore. You'll always go back and sit, and watch. It's the same with music. Mick loved Mott the Hoople and liked me – and it was nice."

The Hoople's penultimate cut was Ian's 'Through the Looking Glass'. First titled, 'Why My Love Slipped Away', the song was a unique composition in the Mott canon, with stunning, sweeping orchestration rising and falling dramatically behind Hunter's expressive vocals. The track was constructed in 'Hymn for the Dudes' mode and featured a powerful arrangement written and conducted by Graham Preskett. "Graham had a really good sense of what the band needed," says Fisher. "He was a first-class arranger, but he sensed what fitted over a rock group like us."

During recording sessions, for fun, Mott prepared an alternative version of 'Through the Looking Glass' featuring a torrent of abusive language on the end of the track. The stream of swearing was concocted purely as a personal prank, aimed at Dan Loggins and the "profanity cut" was played to CBS staff. Several sweating, grey-faced label personnel were solemnly told that the obscenities were necessary to dramatise the inner conflict and alter ego of the writer, and some of the CBS personnel even acknowledged that they could understand the need for the outpouring! The band had to pacify a frantic label soon afterwards and admit that the tape was a wind-up – and the "private version" was canned.

With 'Roll Away the Stone' placed as the closing track on *The Hoople*, the album was framed with two hit singles in 'overture' and 'finale' vein. The LP cut featured some subtle changes though, as Mott used the original single version, added a new guitar track played by Luther and invited Lynsey de Paul to re-voice the spoken "rockabilly party" section in the middle of the song.

IH: "We didn't really know what *The Hoople* album was going to do after *Mott*, but we had 'Roll Away the Stone' in the can, so we put it on the LP and sort of knew that we'd be okay then. 'Roll Away the Stone' was our biggest-selling single – over half a million copies – and our last Top Ten. My, 'I know how to write hit songs' claim, to our publicist Tony Brainsby, were fatal last words. You shouldn't say things like that. It was tempting fate and a stupid thing to say."

For *Mott's* new album artwork, Roslav Szaybo of CBS, who had designed *Mott*, chose a complementary *Hoople* image, replacing the Roman male head with a stylised female portrait based on Greek mythology. Roslav continued *Mott's* colour fading and poem theme as *The Hoople* exhibited blue shading with a simple Dylan quote, "*It's life and life only…*" on the rear of the sleeve. The model chosen for the cover image was Kari-Ann Muller, who had graced the first *Roxy Music* LP. Kari-Ann's permed hair housed facial images of Hunter and the band in a pastiche of Medusa, the Gorgon from Greek mythology whose hair transformed into living venomous snakes.

"Where the *Mott* cover had been Roman, *The Hoople* adopted a Greek theme," says Szaybo. "My idea for the Medusa was based on mythology but was really inspired by Ian's hair. For *Mott* and *The Hoople*, I wanted to show Mott the Hoople as something really different to other rock groups. I felt like that after listening to *All the Young Dudes*."

The Hoople secured a silver disc for advance sales before release and became Mott's first gold album. At the time, Ian talked about the record with great enthusiasm.

IH: "This album is about ten times better than the last one. I can't believe it – it's great. I'm knocked out with it – really, honestly knocked out. This time we concentrated even more than we did on the *Mott* album – and that got five awards – so we'll be able to get half a dozen with this!"

398

The Hoople received excellent reviews with dramatic headlines including 'FRAGMENTS OF MADNESS' (*DISC*), 'Street Punk Drama goes over the Top' (*Sounds*) and 'Hoople's Blood and Thunder' (*Melody Maker*). "It's jagged, fragmented, punctuated with bursts of maniac laughter, arrogant and eerie," said one critic... "The whole band sounds as if they find the studio acutely claustrophobic and are fighting desperately to get out. Ariel's playing is as uncomfortable as a high-speed dental drill while Hunter's voice seems all out to provoke a row with the listener," Another writer noted: "The album adds up to Mott at their biggest and best, their most ambitious production yet. It has denser colour than before, each number sprung in Hunter's new punk-poet imagery. With this album Mott absolutely establish themselves as Britain's major new band."

American reviews were equally strong. *Performance* wrote: "Mott may well be the best of the British bands. The strength is in the music – gutsy, loud, brash and exciting"... while *The Los Angeles Times* felt that Mott possessed "spirit, style and intelligence". However, *Rolling Stone* was less happy with the new album and questioned whether stardom was spoiling Ian Hunter – Ken Emerson claiming that instead of the self-awareness, insight and irony found on *Mott*, *The Hoople* purveyed self-pity and dispiriting, less perceptive songs. Emerson criticised the band's heavy-handed sound effects that "cluttered" many of the tracks, the strain towards "melodrama", and the "pretentious" 'Marionette' and 'Through the Looking Glass.' Conversely, he praised 'Trudi's Song' as the LP's most arresting track, 'Alice' as the best lyric and 'Pearl 'n' Roy' as "vivid". *Rolling Stone* added: "Mott has established itself as one of the very few thinking rock bands. Their last two albums succeeded because of the power of Hunter's autobiographical statements and the incisiveness of his observations on music and the sociocultural scene. *The Hoople* cannot compare to its predecessors, *Mott* and *All the Young Dudes*. Let's hope that Mott snaps back quickly."

Columbia advertised *The Hoople* as a brand-new album with all the "mad musical finesse" and "hard-rock punch" that had become Mott's trademarks. Ian's compositions were pointing the group in a new and exciting direction and, given the lyrical content of 'Marionette', it was little wonder that Hunter was soon talking about a photograph of a straight-jacket as the image for the next album cover. *The Hoople* though, was a remarkable record, and a worthy successor to *Brain Capers*, *All the Young Dudes* and the unsurpassable *Mott*.

> **IH:** "I enjoyed every minute of *The Hoople*, apart from Advision Studios, which was a nightmare. *The Hoople* was not *Mott Part Two*. *The Hoople* was a different album – more keyboard-based and string-inclined with less emphasis on guitar to give Luther time to adjust, but that was not Luther's fault. Morgan Fisher was subconsciously steering me towards keyboards and most of *The Hoople* was written that way. I was experimenting, and I liked the idea of cellos fighting it out with saxes. We were doing this before anyone else. Luther was fine with everything and it all just seemed like the next step at that time. Perhaps it was a little over-ambitious, but it's better to be over than under. *The Hoople* was busier and more involved than the *Mott* record, but I still think of *Mott* as the quintessential Mott the Hoople album."

Luther Grosvenor considers that *The Hoople* was probably the best record that Mott made and recalls he had written some material but didn't contribute compositions for his first studio outing with the group. "Mott was geared around Ian Hunter," he acknowledges, "and to some extent Buff and Pete, and should have been. If I'd been there another year, I would have been writing material for Mott. In the meantime, we knocked around with 'Here Comes the Queen' from my solo album and they felt I should come forward in the stage show and do that live."

"Hunter on the case"
Mott rehearsals downtime, Shepherd's Bush, London, 30 August 1973

"The Weapon"
Ian Hunter with the customised 'H' guitar,
North America, 1973

"Take the mick out of *Top of the Pops*, we play better than they do..."
Above: 'Honaloochie Boogie' performance, May 1973
Below: 'All the Way from Memphis', September 1973, with Andy Mackay of Roxy Music (right)
David Warner Ellis/Redferns/Getty Images

"Very flash... very much 1973 rock 'n' roll"
CBS promo photo for the 1973 British tour:
Ian Hunter, Dale Griffin (seated) Ariel Bender (standing) and Overend Watts

AIR Studios
Ian Dickson/Redferns/Getty Images

"The greatest music book ever written"
Hunter's critically acclaimed "on-the-road, warts 'n' all" *Diary of a Rock 'n' Roll Star*, published by Panther Books UK in May 1974

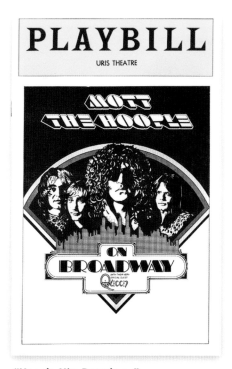

"Hoopla Hits Broadway"
Uris Theater playbill, May 1974

"The Golden Age of Rock 'n' Roll"
CBS promo photo for Mott the Hoople Mark III, March 1974:
Ian Hunter, Ariel Bender, Dale Griffin, Morgan Fisher and Overend Watts

"The Wedding of the Year"
Mott the Hoople Mark IV's press conference "to unveil Ronno", Grosvenor House Hotel, London,
18 September 1974: Ian Hunter, Morgan Fisher, Mick Ronson, Dale Griffin and Overend Watts

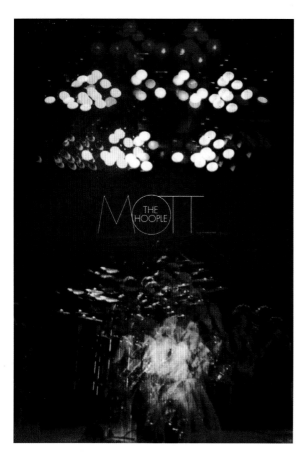

"The tour that never was"
Unreleased UK concert programme,
November 1974

**1974 Mott the Hoople
Seadivers membership card**

"Do you Remember the Saturday Gigs"
European CBS promo postcard, October 1974:
Watts, Hunter, Ronson, Griffin and Fisher

"Last Tango in Copenhagen"
Hunter and Ronson ablaze at Falkoner
Teatret, Denmark on Mott the Hoople's
European tour, 14 October 1974
Jorgen Angel/Redferns/Getty

Mott, however, had become privately frustrated with the lack of imagination they felt Grosvenor had displayed on *The Hoople* and the group was further alarmed upon hearing live tapes of Bender's playing style. On reflection, years later, Dale Griffin felt that Luther was not entirely at fault, as the band really wasn't ready to record *The Hoople.*

"Ariel had to be told what to play," said Dale. "To be fair to Luther, he was a very, very big name in Spooky Tooth. He was classed in the top ten guitarists in Britain. Certainly, he didn't have it once he joined us. Something seemed to stifle his creativity. It's a great shame because you could not wish to encounter a more easy-going, generous, likeable character than Luther, but the record was just forced on us. 'You've got to do a new album. You've got to go on tour' – all the usual record company-management stuff. Then with the three-day week, we would be in the studio halfway through a take and the power would go out. It was a dreadful, dismal, awful period. It just didn't happen."

> **IH:** "*The Hoople* was the beginning of the end. A lot of stupid things were going on. I was real upset with Bender and the trouble was that I liked him a lot. We were working hard, we were successful, but I didn't like it. I knew I had to find another guitar player, but we were touring constantly so there was no room to stop, get Bender out and put another guy in. I think we knew we were cheating ourselves and that we could only get away with it for so long. Mott had always been a big guitar group, but on *The Hoople* album I deliberately wrote away from guitar which was difficult. Everything was leaning towards me. I was writing more lyrics to fill the album while the singing became too stylised. I guess I was subconsciously working my way towards the end of the band."

"Generally, *The Hoople* sessions were okay but there was undue tension as, unfortunately, Luther seemed unable to improvise in

401

a studio situation," says Dan Loggins. "It was rough to watch on 'Born Late '58'. I would never knock Luther, as he was a good guy with positive energy, but I felt Mott had been so spoiled by having Ralpher. Also, I think Ian was now pushing himself too hard at this point, and I believe he felt extra pressure as the nominal new front man and un-official leader."

Despite private frustrations within the band, *The Hoople* entered the UK album charts on 13th April where it stayed for five weeks reaching No.11. It also peaked at No.28 in the USA, became the band's greatest American album success and was pressed by Columbia as a Quadrophonic gold label LP.

Immediately following release, Mott geared up for another US tour when they played six provincial English live dates. During the "mini-tour", they added the opening section from Don McLean's 1971 hit 'American Pie' as a preface to 'The Golden Age of Rock 'n' Roll.'

"We decided to change the key from E to F as it would suit Ian's voice better," says Morgan Fisher. "The first night we tried it live, I completely forgot about the new key. I was the only one accompanying Ian before the band came in, so there was no way that he could know we were in the old key. Halfway through it, I realised my mistake and had no choice but to simply switch into the new key, before the band charged in. The expression on Ian's face, I will never forget."

Once again Mott the Hoople's British concerts received glowing reviews and upbeat headlines including 'SOLID GOLD MOTT' (*Melody Maker*). The gigs retained the band's expected "flash and crash", but Mott's upcoming American tour was about to feature a unique event that was truly golden.

CHAPTER TWELVE

Green Lights on Broadway

Led Zeppelin came to Broadway to see THE greatest rock 'n' roll band in the world at that time – MOTT THE HOOPLE!

It is inevitable that two sources of original material render a rock group richer in terms of creative breadth and recorded output. In August 1973, Mick Ralphs quit Mott the Hoople at the height of their powers, but Ian Hunter had taken up the torch and almost single-handedly composed *The Hoople*. Featuring several lyrical and musically powerful pieces including 'Crash Street Kidds' and 'Marionette', the album was a robust follow-up to the award-winning *Mott*.

Having played six British live shows in April 1974, Mott the Hoople embarked on another lengthy American tour where they became the first rock group to sell out a week of concerts on Broadway, at New York's Uris Theatre. *The Hoople* charted high on both sides of the Atlantic and Ian Hunter's 1972 tour diary was published as a paperback book in Britain. It was a peak period for the group.

Flying to Los Angeles to begin a seven-week tour, Queen supported Mott the Hoople for a second time. Drummer Roger Taylor termed the link logical and perfect for Queen and guitarist

Brian May admitted that being on the road with Mott was when they learned to be rock stars. "Just as you thought that the day was over," said Brian, "one of Mott would burst into your room, loaded with bottles and whatever else, and off you'd go again. It was very full-on and very, very exciting."

Ian Hunter's *Diary of a Rock 'n' Roll Star* was issued by Panther Books in the UK during May, delayed from its original March publication date courtesy of Britain's frustrating three-day working week. Panther specialised in Fifties and Sixties fiction including Kerouac and sci-fi paperbacks, and Ian's touring notebooks from Mott's 1972 US tour were published thanks to writer and radio presenter, Charlie Gillett. Charlie had a deal with Panther but a gap in his delivery schedule coincided with his reading Ian's draft diary: finding it a fascinating account of life on the road, he volunteered to help with publication. Gillett welcomed the chance to work on the book, claiming that he earned more for editing than he did in author royalties for his own publications.

> **IH:** "I was round at Charlie Gillett's one day and people were nipping in and out of his house, borrowing his records. I recall Ian Dury being there. Charlie told me that Panther Books were on his tail as he needed two books to reach his yearly quota and I happened to mention that I'd written this tour diary and he could have it. Panther just took it and printed it, but Charlie told me off years later for not saying that he 'edited' it. I don't remember that he did that. It was just printed from my notes, as I recall."

Originally titled *Diary of a Rock 'n' Roll Star: Ian Hunter lead singer for Mott the Hoople*, the 50p paperback documented Mott's 'Dudes' promotional tour of America. For once sex and drugs took a back seat while music, people, insight and humour thrived, Ian penning a definitive account of the Seventies rock lifestyle whilst deftly demystifying the business in the process. Capturing Mott's first headlining US concert appearances, the opening scene depicts

Ian mopping up cat droppings in his Wembley flat as he worries whether he should travel transatlantic wearing an afghan coat or black leather suit. The story really starts with Mott's departure from London's Heathrow Airport to Los Angeles International on 21st November 1972 and concludes with their return to Britain on Christmas Eve.

Nearly fifty years later, the diary is still a delight as Ian genuinely savours his outbound trip – describing the joys of flying including "free meals, drinks, reclining seats, earphones and windows with pull-down shades" – a common experience nowadays, but something that was foreign to most readers at that time. The book was the ultimate rock travel brochure as Ian placed his finger on the pulse, relaying his experiences with rare candour for fans who didn't know what the disorganised music world was really like. Much of the book's charm rests in its conversational structure, Hunter's humorous frankness about his relationships, his band, the industry and other musicians, and now, retrospectively, transportation – in a quaint time that has been largely forgotten. Ian related in early 1974 that his diary was designed for fans who were not worldly-wise and that his original title had been more modest.

> **IH:** "Charlie Gillett came back from the publishers and said my original title was not good enough and that it had to be something that would sell, so they ended up calling it *Diary of a Rock 'n' Roll Star*. I really regret that. I wanted to call the book *Rock 'n' Roll Sweepstakes* because that's what it was about and that's what it meant. They decided that to put it in airports they would have to call it something more 'Elton John-ish' but star is a funny term; to me somebody like Barbra Streisand's a star. The back cover was even more embarrassing with a reference to 'his personal friends like Keith Moon'. I met Frank Zappa and Keith Moon one night in my entire life – hardly personal friends. The *Diary of a Rock 'n' Roll Star* title made me feel like an idiot. I never was a rock star and I was embarrassed to see that caked over my

> book, but I was told that their title was going to sell copies –
> and they were right – it was a music bestseller for two years.
> I think the book worked though, as I was an enthusiastic
> chap then and America really was new."

Once described as rock 'n' roll at its most hilariously hum-drum, it was Ian's eye for the mundane that made his book slightly *Spinal Tap*, fretting about his weight, grumbling about the price of drinks or grumpily lambasting a belligerent, bossy air hostess. *Diary of a Rock 'n' Roll Star* catalogues the stresses and strains of life on the road and reveals the down-to-earth man that Ian is. Never intended to be a work of literary merit, rather an eyewitness account of the rock business from the inside, Hunter took time to explain recording processes, American cities and his impressions of the stars he met along the way. He was never frightened to air criticisms, maintaining his views were simply personal opinions: guitarist John McLaughlin and his elongated Mahavishnu Orchestra guitar workouts certainly incurred Ian's wrath in one chapter.

Hunter also discussed Mott the Hoople's personnel, describing Buffin as unsure, quick-tempered, polite and paranoid about his nose, and Ralphs as the ultimate loner, perplexed and uncertain but loyal, as he had supported Ian and Verden when Guy Stevens sought to axe them from the band during their Island years. Pictured with great humour, as hypochondriac, fanatic and self-dramatist, Ian felt that Verden Allen had great difficulty in living because he always sought perfection; unpredictable but generous, Hunter claimed that Phally maintained stability with the help of God, his girlfriend Elaine and his beloved Hammond C3. Pete Watts was considered unreliable, eccentric and selfish but portrayed as the backbone of the group, always good-humoured in the face of a crisis and forever trying to bolster band morale.

Thankfully, Ian commented on the man he considered the central core of Mott – their former singer and road manager Stan Tippins, whose actions and falsely credited names became legendary. Chiffon, Tilkins, Timkins, Rippoff, Ticktock, Pippins and Chickens were some of the aliases recorded by the numerous hotels that Mott visited, much to Tippins' annoyance. It was also noted that group morale could vary depending on Hereford United Football Club's results, which Stan followed with a passion. Described as the ultimate eccentric Englishman, Hunter also highlighted Tippins' love of "arguments, panic, rows, chaos and bullshitting" and his propensity to instigate inventive rumours thereby swelling concert attendances for the group.

Further funny tales in *Diary of a Rock 'n' Roll Star* included meeting Frank Zappa after a madcap drive with Keith Moon of The Who and leaping off stage mid-song to sort out a Rhode Island heckler who had thrown a bottle at Mick Ralphs. There were dramatic episodes too, not least Ian's drunken attempt to get into Elvis Presley's Memphis mansion by sneaking through the back door of Graceland only to be advised by his housekeeper that the star had just seen a film he hadn't liked, and that Mr Presley, i.e. his henchmen, would be unwilling to accommodate uninvited guests.

Mott's personal adventures charmingly contrasted the minutiae of rock road-life and the carousel of highs, with the roller coaster of lows, airport lounges, planes, soundchecks, hellish hotels, poor promoters, unwanted groupies and mood swings. Also fascinating were the trials and tribulations surrounding Mott's fanaticism over guitars, the band frantically seeking out bargain-buys in each American city that they played. Mott didn't tour museums and art galleries; they hit the pawn shop quarter, buying Gibsons for as little as 50 dollars and selling them back home in London, at a profit, to supplement their meagre incomes. Acquiring guitars on the cheap from US thrift shops was another of-its-time moments in the book, as instruments were subsequently scooped up by dealers, making Mott's "shawn pops" pastime out-moded. Mott the Hoople also acquired some unusual, photogenic, customised instruments, most notably Ian's white Thomas Maltese Cross, unearthed in a Californian store.

"Shawn pops were good fun but very dangerous, because we always had to go to the nastiest areas in each town to get the best stuff," said Pete Watts. "I was buying a Mosrite twelve-string guitar in St Louis one day. We'd got this old black cab driver to take us down to this run-down area with wrecked Fifties Cadillacs with no wheels and people living in them. I was standing in this shop with glitter in my hair and make-up on, and a black guy along the counter was staring at me, as he was buying a gun. The shopkeeper asked him, 'This is the gun you want?' And he says, 'Yeah.' So, the owner says, 'Well, I'll just wrap it up for you,' and the black bloke, still looking at me says, 'No, don't wrap it up, I'm gonna use it.' I left the money on the counter, took the guitar, ran and barely made it to the cab."

Watts netted the "most important" bass guitar of his life in St Louis for ninety dollars. The 1963 Gibson Thunderbird was originally white, but Pete painted it pink and black in the Eighties when it became "tatty", having used it on hundreds of gigs and sessions. He recalled that he was late for Mott's flight after haggling over the bass, and how the waiting plane passengers were not happy when Pete strolled into the cabin cradling the naked instrument and strapped it into the vacant seat next to him.

IH: "Our roadies always used to be upset when we went to America because we'd go with six guitars and come back with about forty-five. Richie would get very upset. Guitars are beautiful things to look at. Mick and Pete turned me on to it. It was just a thrill and a craze, but you really could pick up Gibsons in the US for fifty or sixty dollars, while in England you'd be paying £150 for them. Some American pawn shops were in dodgy areas. They'd kill hairy people, but they liked the English for some reason, so we talked loudly. Old red-neck pawn shops were the cheapest and sometimes the nastiest. They all had guns under the counter. A guy pulled one on Ralpher once!

"The white 'Maltese Cross' guitar that I had, that used to get photographed more than I did, was a totally useless instrument but it looked great. I bought it in a San Francisco pawn shop with Ralpher for seventy-five dollars. The guy who ran the shop was having an argument on the phone when we went in and he said there was no way he was pulling it down from the wall unless we wanted to buy it. So, we asked how much it was, and he said seventy-five bucks. We agreed, and he said, 'Well, bring it down then.' It just looked so incredibly strange but playing-wise, it was an awful guitar. I'm not even sure there was a truss rod inside. The Cross was made by Harvey Thomas of Midway, Washington, a firm that built organs, but made some guitars too. I later sold the Maltese Cross for £165 to a bloke in Folkestone, because I was skint at the time and he told me at a gig years later, that he took the pick-guard off once and there was a five dollar note inside, with the name and address of the guy that put it together. He tried to sell it back to me, but I didn't want it back! I also remember Mott going into an antique shop in Scranton once and this guy came in with a guitar in a case that was in the shape of a little coffin. The Martin guitar inside had 1870-1890 on the block and the case had No.3 on it, and we still don't know if that was the third Martin ever made. He only wanted 300 bucks for that guitar – and we didn't have the cash between us!"

Mott also commissioned custom-built instruments – a brass-finished 'H' shaped guitar for Ian, known as 'The Weapon' – and a silver bird-shaped 'Swallow' bass for Watts, christened 'The Beast' and based on black felt theatrical face masks that Pete had sometimes worn onstage in Mott's early days. These guitars were specially constructed by Bruce Evans, bassist with Nimbo, a power-pop group that was signed to Pye Records. Watts felt that the Swallow played well enough, but the neck was huge, and the instrument was far too heavy. Consequently, like the 'H', the Swallow became an encore guitar and Pete would pick up stage spots on the silver body to divert light and blind people in the audience. Lemmy of Motörhead wanted to buy the Swallow, but Watts never sold it. Ian eventually wrecked the 'H' on stage in Richmond, Virginia, because whilst the guitar looked incredible, the strings splayed out on the headstock and it was prone to tuning problems. Having suffered enough, Hunter swung the instrument around on stage one night and broke it. Grosvenor, not to be outdone, took an original Gibson Les Paul and smashed it – the 1957 model was irreplaceable.

> **IH:** "The original 'H' called 'The Weapon' was home-made and was fuckin' awful. Watts remembered me smashing that 'H' guitar to pieces on stage in a fit of rage – the stupidity of youth – but I have no memory of that. A second 'H' guitar was specially made for me by Tokai and I loaned it to the Hall of Fame in Cleveland. I used Guilds a lot in Mott. I threw them around on stage and sometimes they broke. We would return them, and Guild was great about replacing the guitars until they sussed out what we'd been doing. I also had some Mosrites which we considered cool because The Ventures had used them."

Hunter's snapshot of stardom differs from the usual rock stories as his 'Diary' reveals the fire and energy expended on the road, trying to turn Mott's flickerings to a flame, in a music world where few made it, and many burned out in their quest for fame. Written as it happened, Ian's exposé managed to strip away music's glittering façade and successfully captured the real flavour of touring including the endless travel, hassles and downtime. Free of fake glamour and ego and peppered with cancelled gigs, Hunter's digestion problems and his hangovers, magic moments always shine through. The book's "warts-and-all" conversational feel still conveys the band's high aspirations amidst the awkward steps Mott took trying to pierce America's massive market. Unpretentious, devoid of self-congratulation and capturing the atmosphere of the early Seventies beautifully, the realities, rigours and rewards are all here. Within, Ian provided this shrewd rock 'n' roll warning: "It may look flashy, but it's over and you are finished before you know it – if you aren't already broken by one thing it will be another – the rock business is a dirty business full stop." Hunter had a shot at music journalists too: "The real problem is the press. These fuckers can ruin a beautiful day."

> **IH:** "Before the diary, Mott got some bad and personal press quite often, but after the book I felt I could tell journalists they were awful. I always used to tell Chris Charlesworth of *Melody Maker* what a wanker he was, and Chris would say, 'Well of course that's because I called you Grand Funk Railroad.' And I'd say, 'Well probably it was, because that was totally inaccurate. You've got it all wrong and you just write shit.'"

Diary of a Rock 'n' Roll Star received excellent press reviews, secured advance orders of over 50,000 copies when it was published in May 1974 and subsequently ran into several reprints.

> **IH:** "The diary was like a little textbook and I considered it more like reportage. I think I was working myself up to writing the *Mott* album and used the diary as a form of self-control. We did that tour in 1972 and I'd just got married again. There was no extra-curricular activity, so when everyone else was partying, I was upstairs writing on my A4 pad. It was all about the boredom of touring basically – and tours are boring, they really are, if you're not going to put your little pecker around. The diary was also a way to remember the tour because my memory was like my mum's – terrible. I thought if I wrote a diary at least I'd remember the tour. Then, it just sort of developed. I had my picture in *The New Statesman* because of the *Diary* and my father, who was never too mad about my rock 'n' roll career, saw that and a review in *The Sunday Times*, and it was his crowning glory. He thought it was incredible. My dad was real chuffed as he always tried to get a book published but never did.

"The *Diary* ended with the end of that tour – our great final gig in Memphis – and that was a natural climax. On every tour you do the last gig and then you go home, but Memphis was special. Normally a tour's a tour, nothing happens much, it finishes, and you make a few quid – but that one finished with the Elvis episode. Where do you go from there? I tried another diary a couple of times but writing any follow-up book is a problem as it can't have the Elvis break-in ending. The diary was written out of boredom on that tour and I was just being myself because that was all I'd got. I've looked back at it a couple of times and within a few minutes of reading bits I remember the whole thing. It's an innocent book. We've all grown up since then and things have really changed like airplanes and technology, so it's like a little piece of history rather than the going thing that it was way back then. We even smoked on planes in those days. It took a long time to do the diary, then they gave me twenty bucks and it put me off it for life. Writing the bloody diary also cost me a lot in terms of lyrics as I'd use a turn of phrase or euphemism that I would probably have been better off using in a song. In the end, Mott was just the same as any other band. It was on planes and in hotel rooms and it played gigs. Most rock books are all the same – 'I was a junkie. I got better.' Yeah – shut up, it's boring!"

Hunter's diary would be republished in America in 1976 as *Reflections of a Rock Star* and having achieved cult status, twenty years later *Diary of a Rock 'n' Roll Star* was re-printed in the UK by Independent Music Press. Promoted with a cover quote from *Q* magazine – "This is the greatest music book ever written" – a new introduction described the diary as, "quite simply, the finest and funniest insight into this life we call 'rock' ever committed to the back of a boarding pass." *Vox* magazine featured the diary at the time as their 'Book of the Month'. A French edition arrived in 2013, titled, *IAN HUNTER USA 1972: A Travers l'Amerique avec Mott the*

Hoople, and an updated and expanded UK version was pubished by Omnibus Press in 2018. Hunter's work is rightly regarded as a classic of the rock writing genre, *The Guardian* noting, "Its mixture of insight, comedy and breathless prose makes it an enduring crystallisation of the rock musician's lot, and a quietly glorious period piece."

Ian's book also became a revelatory read for aspiring musicians like Mick Jones of The Clash, The Cult's Billy Duffy and Duran Duran bassist John Taylor who wanted to be 'one of the boys'. "As a kid, I re-read it over and over," said Taylor. "It wasn't glamourised or sanitised, but it took me there – the romance of America, its highways and cities, the venues and the fans. I was already a keen live music fan going to shows in my hometown of Birmingham, but this book really turned me on to what was different about the road in America."

Billy Duffy says: "Read as a schoolboy in a South Manchester council estate, no doubt like thousands of others across Britain, *Diary of a Rock 'n' Roll Star* to me, was a blueprint to escape to the promised land... America... the cradle of rock 'n' roll... home of the blues. Ian's *Diary* really opened up that world for me in a pragmatic yet exciting way. I loved Mott the Hoople... they represented what I wanted to become... the gang I wanted to be in. My dream, as envisaged through the portal of Ian's book, came true and I am for ever indebted to him for his honest, open and brilliant account of the life of a rock 'n' roll star on the road. Ian Hunter... he wrote my bible."

Jim Kerr, lead singer with Simple Minds, said of Ian's diary: "Those pages more than merely influenced me in somehow wanting to get involved with music, even if Hunter is clearly warning the reader against that very notion. I dearly loved Mott the Hoople in those days and I still listen to their albums, full of songs that both hit you in the heart and are full of swagger and full on fantasy – the entire band made a noise that was way more sublime than most others around at that time."

With the passage of time, Hunter has revealed that parts of the diary *were* sanitised, as there were sometimes outsiders around who shouldn't have been there. The book didn't declare for example that Keith Moon was accompanied by a rather famous girl when he and Ian went out and visited Frank Zappa in Los Angeles. Watts also felt Hunter's proclamation in the diary, that certain band members remained entirely faithful to their partners back home, was stretching the truth somewhat.

> IH: "Moon was relieved when I met him again in London's Speakeasy after that tour. I said, 'You're in the book Keith, but I've left her out,' to which Keith replied, 'Stout fellow Ian, stout fellow.' Moonie was an absolute gentleman. He'd been to see us at The Hollywood Palladium the night before and rang up the next day to invite me out. Keith took me to Frank Zappa's house that night and Frank was extremely nice as was his wife, Gail. Somehow, I wound up in his basement and Frank played me endless two-inch tape reels of endless musical jams by all these famous people I'd never heard of. Well, I'd heard of Jack Bruce and that was about it. I'm not much of a jam man – I'm more of a song man – but I was too polite to say anything. While this was going on Moon was okay of course as he was upstairs playing with Frank's cats. Keith eventually fished me out and we went to the Whisky a Go Go. Years later I was sitting with Jakob Dylan and somehow this story came up and suddenly Jakob says, 'You're not going to believe this, but Dweezil Zappa did the same thing to me, in the same house, in the same basement.' Are we all in some kind of circle, that we don't know about?"

"There was very little about girls in Ian's diary for marriages' and relationships' sakes," said Pete Watts. "It was always hinted at that Buff, and by implication nobody else, was involved, with lines like, 'Buffin was dutifully chatting up the ladies.' When he subsequently got married, Paula went berserk when she heard about the book. We had to ban our girlfriends from tours in the end because they really could cause a lot of trouble, especially when they got talking when we were on stage. I would come off and my girlfriend wouldn't be speaking to me. It was rumoured at one time that they were going to employ a private detective to follow us to see what we did on the road. But I never made any secret of it to Pam. I used to tell her I was going to do what I wanted to do and that I couldn't be celibate, so she should do what she wanted to do. It's a horrible, cruel thing to say but I knew it was going to be true."

The success of Hunter's publication created the chance of a Mott movie for Paramount Pictures, Ian seeing an excellent pitch followed by a thirty-page screenplay draft, but the plans were never realised. 1975 would see the release of *Slade in Flame* to mixed reaction, the Wolverhampton rockers later opining that their time out of the public eye making the movie, and its gritty content, contributed to their subsequent commercial decline.

Mott the Hoople's 1974 North American tour spanned almost two months and the band visited several cities that they hadn't played previously. Booked with "special routing" and successive gigs less than 500 miles apart because of a US petrol shortage, Mott's tour stood a chance of grossing 450,000 dollars according to manager Fred Heller, with 125,000 dollars attached to a week-long slot on Broadway.

> **IH:** "Mott was now doing great in the US. I guess we were always looking towards America. Mick loved Stephen Stills, we were influenced by Bob Dylan and we all loved Joe Walsh and Barnstorm, Nils Lofgren, Grin, The Band and Love, so I guess our music would be more accepted in America."

For their 1974 US dates, organist Blue Weaver was added to Mott's line-up as replacement for Mick Bolton. Fisher knew Blue from his "teeny pop" days and Mott knew he had the ability to do what was necessary for them. Derek Weaver hailed from Cardiff and was given the nickname 'Blue' by the grandfather of Welsh singer, Charlotte Church, as Derek supposedly looked like Bluebottle from *The Goon Show*. Blue had been a member of Amen Corner, Fairweather and The Strawbs, and played on Lou Reed's *Berlin* album before joining Mott.

"After my time in The Strawbs I was skint," says Blue. "I was washing dishes and mini-cabbing, and I didn't even have any keyboards or equipment, but I began hanging around studios to see if there was any work going. One day I wandered into AIR and bumped straight into Morgan Fisher. He told me that Mott had just decided to get a second keyboard player for their American tour, and, within minutes, I was in the band."

At the outset of their US trek Mott was dogged with ill health: Ian contracted laryngitis, Luther tonsilitis, and Overend and Morgan viral flu, but eighty-five per cent of their gigs were sold out with average attendances of around 9,000. Mott played matinee and evening concerts at Santa Monica Civic Auditorium on 12th April and the second show was broadcast by KMET-FM Los Angeles, subsequently appearing on the bootlegs *Behind Enemy Lines*, *Rest in Peace* and *Flash and Crash*. The first "pirate" LP, *Behind Enemy Lines (The Whizz Kidz Meet the Concrete): The 1974 American Tour*, was released in California on The Amazing Kornyfone Record Label. With a printed front inlay sheet mirroring the *All the Young Dudes* album artwork style, and initial discs featuring a slightly disturbing drawing of a semi-clothed female on the reverse, the TAKRL bootleggers noted that the back cover was "drawn whilst on L.S.D." Despite Ian's laryngitis, some fans called the recording a milestone. Mott's concert at The Exposition Hall in Portland on 28th April also featured on bootleg vinyl as *The Golden Age of Mott the Hoople*.

A *Washington Post* review of Mott's Constitution Hall gig was headed 'An Uneclipsed, Outrageous Sound' and *The Oakland Tribune* described the band's music as 'Rock to Grit Your Teeth To!' Returning to San Francisco Winterland, Mott the Hoople was supported by Aerosmith and although five years their junior, one journalist wrote that Mott's set had much more of a Seventies aura. During 'Hymn for the Dudes', as Hunter sang of a greying superstar, he pointed at a Grateful Dead logo, mocking the San Francisco legends – but the audience loved it. The incorporation of Don McLean's 'American Pie' as a prelude to 'The Golden Age of Rock 'n' Roll' also sent US crowds into raptures and Morgan Fisher prefaced 'Rest in Peace' with a beautiful piano introduction from Bach's 'Prelude No.1 in C Major'.

A Mott the Hoople concert now featured Watts parading the stage in glitzy gladiatorial costumes including thigh-high hooved boots and cropped tunics. Coping with the boots was a "pain" according to Phil John as it took two of Mott's road crew to pull the monstrosities on, followed by a further frustrating military-style operation each night to get "Lord Watts" onstage. The crew was overjoyed when Pete finally ditched the platforms. Mott's bassist also drew attention with his special silver hair-do, bizarrely extended to include additional adornment in the form of a cross, spray-painted on his exposed chest hair. The "Watts Treatment" was fraught with problems.

"I started off using Ford silver car paint and went on to Rolls-Royce Silver," said Pete. "Then I used Nestles Streaks 'N' Tips, which is actually designed for it, but, in the end, I'd buggered my hair up completely. The paint wouldn't come out when you washed it, so you'd just re-spray it. I had pinks and blues mixed in with it sometimes. My scalp went horrible and my hair was coming out in clumps and was badly damaged for months. It was so bloody stupid really. Crazy. I should have had it dyed blonde and tinted all the colours I wanted – but image is everything!"

Morgan Fisher, meanwhile, appeared suave and debonair with twirled moustache, tailored jackets finished with Liberace piano-key lapels and berets or trilby hats – a candelabra gracing his grand piano. Out front, Hunter and Bender taunted each other every night before a white-satin-suited Ian sent Ariel sprawling across the floor at the climax of each set, beneath raking blood-red spotlights used to dramatic effect on 'Violence'. Hunter was still the ringmaster though, embroidering his vocal delivery with sneers and accents, whilst mockingly gesticulating. Bender's on-the-road antics still inspired a *Record Mirror* feature back in the UK, titled: 'Look Out! There's a Loony About'.

At the Palace Theatre in Waterbury, Connecticut on 4th May, Mott played 'Alice' for the first and only time in concert. Morgan felt the track was really a studio piece and should have been re-arranged and toughened up for stage performance, but the song's lengthy lyrical outpouring was troublesome for Hunter in a live setting. Grosvenor remembered that Ian often had a nervous disposition before going onstage and Watts also felt 'Alice' was just too difficult to re-create live. "There were so many lyrics and Hunter's memory wasn't the greatest," said Pete. "He came across stage to me on more than one instance to seek prompts on the next line after the middle eight. We also used to finish near the end of our set with a small section from Dylan's 'Blowing in the Wind', and Ian would sometimes get the venue wrong... *'the answer is blowing in the – Goodnight St Louis – you've been great'*... and we were playing in Atlanta."

Following Waterbury, the band headed towards New York and The Capitol Theatre in Passaic to prepare for a triumphant moment when Mott the Hoople broke new ground in rock music history. From 7th to 11th May 1974, the band played at the recently opened Uris Theatre located on West 51st Street, between Broadway and Eighth Avenue in midtown Manhattan. The 2,000-seater Art-Nouveau Uris was situated under a towering skyscraper with escalators rising to the auditorium. Opened on 28th November 1972, the Uris was the first new theatre built on Broadway since the Twenties – it was subsequently re-christened The Gershwin Theatre in 1983 – and it was here that Mott the Hoople became the first-ever rock band to enjoy an extended stay on Broadway.

Mott had truly earned their moment of glory after five years of dedicated touring and creative recording. The Uris extravaganza comprised seven shows over five days with two performances on 10th and 11th May. The second and third nights, played on 8th and 9th May were recorded using the Record Plant Mobile Studio after Columbia Records did a deal with the King Biscuit Flower Hour

418

radio network to pay for live audio whilst the label retained the rights to the masters. The Broadway recordings would be heavily edited and merged with Mott's 1973 Hammersmith Odeon tapes to create a truncated live LP.

Channel 2 in the USA aired a television report on Mott's Broadway premiere, but Columbia did not see fit to film the unique event, a major faux pas as the group introduced dramatic theatrical elements during their performances. Dale Griffin would complain about "the stupidity of Mott's management and record company" and the lack of planning in recording just two nights of a seven-day run with no film or video of the shows or even a dress rehearsal. Fisher would regard Broadway as the pinnacle of the band's career in terms of showmanship and fun.

> **IH:** "We were the first rock band to play on Broadway – and I think we were the last too! We went on the week after Sammy Davis Jr. and it was Ron Delsener, a brilliant New York promoter, who suggested The Uris Theatre and helped to set up the concerts. Fred Heller was great then too. I went along to look at the theatre with Ron and liked it. It was very similar to The Fairfield Hall in Croydon, so we thought we could easily do it. The Broadway run was great. We hired huge white cars from Caesar's Limos in New Jersey that they used for weddings so each evening they played 'The Wedding March' from the top of the limousines all the way from the Gramercy Hotel to The Uris Theatre. With the music and the vehicles creating such a scene, the queues got bigger every evening to see us get out of the limos. We also had circus acts in the foyer – somebody perching a small dog on their finger, flaming knives being thrown at a board, conjurors and magicians – and it was a lot of fun. I remember one night they brought the people from the foyer into the dressing room and the acts performed for us before we went on. It was great, because we hadn't seen that.

"All the major companies were there – ABC, NBC and CBS – and we didn't know who they were at the time. The first night was weird. I looked out and freaked because there was not a person in the audience under fifty-five – it was all heavy-duty business and industry people. I think they thought it was a stage play called *Mott the Hoople*. I went back into the dressing room and said, 'These people have got this all wrong. I don't know what they think they're gonna get. They've come for a show – a Broadway show. They don't even understand what we're doing here!' They got stunned about halfway through though because we had speakers at the back of the theatre and on 'Marionette' the speakers at the rear came in for the screaming and laughter in the middle of the song. That woke them up and was fabulous to watch. I remember I wanted floating holograms in the shows during 'Rose'. I had an idea for this female image to appear in the middle of the theatre hovering over the audience. It would have been ground-breaking for its time, but it needed three bits of equipment anchored on large concrete blocks in the hall to create the effect and they didn't go for that. The first night on Broadway was the business end, the second night was a normal gig and the rest of the week was great. Queen was on fire too, but I had to explain to Freddie Mercury that it took more than a fortnight to conquer America!"

Ian's mini-opera 'Marionette' had been the highlight of *The Hoople* album so instead of Hunter's floating hologram concept, Mott engaged New York's Pickwick Puppet Theater and introduced theatrical figures to the Uris performances. Five life-sized marionettes descended and hung over the set, and smaller figures were worked around the stage by darkly dressed operators to interact with the group. One of the Uris puppeteers was Teddy Shepard from the *Howdy Doody* TV show who manipulated a Sancho Panza figure for

'Marionette', the faithful squire whose common sense contrasted with the visionary idealism of his master. While Hunter delivered the song's closing lyrics, he really did appear constricted on stage as he became dominated by puppets pushing him into a crouch, one of the smaller marionettes even thumbing its nose.

"Hunter is the professional outsider," said Dale Griffin in the Nineties, "and what gets him through life is the idea that he's fighting off these terrible people who want to keep him out. Ian felt he was being manipulated by everybody, which was Ian's paranoia, because Ian was as much a manipulator as anybody on the business side of things. He wrote 'Marionette' as a result of those feelings of being twisted and turned by record company executives and the music business in general. On Broadway we had marionettes and the Cookie Monster which was probably a bit a cheeky because I don't think they had permission from Frank Oz or Jim Henson to use that character. Also, there was a pink ostrich ballerina that came on and danced with Ian during the introduction to 'Rest in Peace' – a little bit twee, but quite sweet. The gooey side of nasty rockers Mott the Hoople!"

With assistance from ex-Bonzo Dog Doo-Dah man Roger Ruskin Spear, the Mott stage set also included two humanoid electronic creations flanking Griffin's drum riser. A French policeman and clown dummies would spring into life and break up the show with frenzied bursts of laughter. The fun also included the figures periodically blowing feathers and confetti out of their hats while eyes flashed and bow ties spun round, but they ended up driving Mott's road crew nuts as they were poorly designed, untested and unstable.

> IH: "After the floating hologram was nixed, we did some 'dramatic theatre' with puppets in the end, mainly for 'Marionette'. I remember they were large, and you did have to be careful around them and the people who were manoeuvring them. There was a small bird that floated and used to fly down and sit on my front monitor. It was

a nice little part of the show. The figures created by Roger Ruskin Spear of the Bonzos were vacuum cleaners in reverse with exploding heads. All that and a spot of Quad as well. Not too shabby for its time!"

"The Uris shows felt magnificent," says Morgan Fisher. "Without wanting to seem flippant, it was like a week-long party on Broadway. The first day we did all the setting up and soundchecking so from then on it was easy going – just drive every day from the legendary Gramercy Park Hotel to the theatre in the white stretch limo with a Union Jack on the front, drinking cocktails in the back seats – do our gig in a nice, cozy theatre, wondering which luminaries were in the audience that night – then meeting them backstage and heading off for a party somewhere. I've never wanted to say much about Mott's management – I guess they pulled off some great strokes like the Broadway show, which was quite a scoop – but the failure to film it was bad management. Fred Heller's attitude generally was that Ian was the man and he considered the rest of the band to be completely dispensable."

Hunter and the group were ecstatic at the Uris, but they found it hard to forgive Led Zeppelin when they gatecrashed and "spoiled" Mott the Hoople's opening night on Broadway. Fresh from an extravagant party to launch their Swan Song record label, Zep arrived backstage and a fracas ensued. Drummer John Bonham was insistent that he should play on 'All the Young Dudes' but Griffin objected and scuffles broke out. Led Zeppelin was a big band, but this was Mott the Hoople's moment.

Stan Tippins remembers: "Zeppelin came in and stood by the side of the stage and interfered with some of the marionettes that were coming down. I wasn't there just at that time, but a little bloke who was working the puppets got upset and explained that somebody called Jimmy Page had tried to halt the marionettes. Then Page appeared and tried to force his way into our dressing room, so I went crazy, stopped him coming in and threw a bottle which smashed above his head."

422

"I was in awe of John Bonham and hid in the toilet because he kept following me around," Dale Griffin would say. "Then there was a scuffle, and somebody booted me in the knee, and it went up like a balloon. It was our first night and we wanted it for ourselves. It was horrible playing with Bonham standing in the wings. I was painfully aware of his prowess as a drummer and quite froze, feeling more · and more inadequate."

> IH: "Led Zeppelin arrived backstage from a press conference and had been imbibing and were well sauced, so it was all hell let loose. John Bonham was a huge fan of 'All the Young Dudes'. He said he knew 'Dudes' and insisted he was going to play on it with us. Bonham playing would have been a great move if Led Zeppelin had walked out and done 'Dudes' with us, but we were 'prepared', and knew what we wanted to do. So, we said, 'No' and an argument ensued. Stan Tippins went berserk and leapt in to help. He tried to get hold of Jimmy Page and two of the biggest blokes you've ever seen in your life suddenly appeared. It got pretty ugly. That was all we needed – our first night on Broadway and there were pitched battles going on. It was silly, so Robert Plant and I did the sensible thing and just slid off and headed for the dressing room – either that or we were the two cowards. I said to Stan, 'I'm going to the dressing room – sod this!' We did 'Dudes' of course but wouldn't let Zep on. It would have been a good move to let them on stage – they were the hugest band in the world – but it was our gig. Bonham was a lovely man, but they were out of order. I remember I was walking out on the stage after the show and Zep's manager Peter Grant came up to me as he was leaving and whispered in my ear, 'Sorry about that Ian.' I think it's the only time Grant apologised for anything in his life!"

"Stan was a human dynamo," said Watts. "You needed someone like that around. He could handle just about anybody – in a nice way at first and, if they refused to leave or problems persisted, he got them by the scruff of the arse – and they were out!"

NME described the unfortunate Uris incident as 'Mott – Zep Bad Vibes on Broadway' and the pushiness of Led Zeppelin was criticised by one journalist who wrote: "Who needs that aggravation. There's a time and a place for games and Zep should have known better." In retrospect however, Luther Grosvenor was wonderfully philosophical and laid back saying: "It's quite simple. Led Zeppelin came to Broadway to see *THE* greatest rock 'n' roll band in the world at that time – MOTT THE HOOPLE!"

The arrival of a telegram at The Uris Theatre was a happier moment for the band, the greeting from author Willard Manus reading: "Thanks for taking the name Mott the Hoople to Broadway." The group was stunned but subsequently distraught to learn that it was a hoax, sent by someone at Columbia Records. Several stars did attend the Uris performances however, including Mike Love of The Beach Boys. Ian has positive memories of Mott's Broadway shows but also regrets that Columbia did not see fit to capture the record-breaking event for posterity.

> **IH:** "There are bits and pieces of Mott on film but really there was no justification for not filming at the Uris. It was a massive error. Mott was royally screwed, not by design but by stupidity. Being a successful band is only part of it, because there must be guidance and vision on a managerial level. Mott sadly lacked this, therefore nothing was capitalised on."

In later years, Hunter admitted that he had been envious of EG, the organisation operated by David Enthoven and John Gaydon who managed King Crimson, Roxy Music, Bryan Ferry, Brian Eno and Robert Fripp. EG sought to represent musical talent and license completed recordings to labels retaining creative and commercial control, an arrangement that echoed Tony Defries' game-plan. EG flourished alongside Island Records at a time when album sleeve artwork was the main promotional tool for music. Rock was music – but it carried visual potency too.

> **IH:** "When I look back at Roxy Music on film, we should have been on that level. Roxy were all lovely people and they had great management, and I'm sure if Mott had got Roxy Music's management then we would have done so much better. It was the same later with Def Leppard. Great managers can help a lot and, I confess, I was jealous as hell of Roxy Music and their management, but nobody cared about Mott. They only looked at things for the short term. We picked the wrong people at the right time. I've seen some idiotic bands on VH1 who should never have seen the light of day in the first place, sitting like elder statesmen, looking at their 'extensive historical footage'. Give me a fuckin' break!"

Whilst no official film exists of Mott's Broadway performances the shows live in the memories of those who witnessed them. Dee Snider of Eighties rockers, Twisted Sister, said in 2014 that Mott the Hoople and Queen at the Uris remains the best concert he has ever seen and *Creem* journalist Ben Edmonds summed up Mott's Broadway appearance with panache: "May 7, 1974. All the way from nowhere to the Uris Theatre in New York, where the ghost of Broadway tradition exchanged its top hat and tails for a pair of shades and a week-long electric seizure. To my thinking there could've been no better rock and roll band to open-up Broadway's belly than Mott the Hoople. They earned the right to that much frosting on the cake with five years of diligently rendered service."

Mott the Hoople's rocking residency created spectacular headlines including: 'HOOPLA HITS BROADWAY' (*Record World*), 'Rock Invades the Great White Way' (*Performance*) and 'What Rock 'n' Roll is all About' (*Scene*). *Circus* said of the band's Uris debut: "Hoople Whoop De Do on Broadway – Mott the Hoople splashed down on their US tour with a spectacular opening night on Broadway at the Uris Theater. The first really-hard-rock act to crack the Great White Way, Mott deserves accolades for more than their top-notch performance. And, according to many blazed critics in the crowd, the overall effect of the act was Clockwork Orange-ville."

The *New York Times* wrote: "Mott the Hoople arrived on Broadway Tuesday night for the first of six shows, the first hard rock group ever to appear there, and the Uris Theatre will probably never be the same again. Apart from the cigarette burns in the rugs and spilled drinks stains on the floor, the overwhelming volume of the music must somehow stick in the theater's walls, deafening mere unamplified speech and song forever. Yet despite the extravagant costuming (particularly Pete Watts, the bass player) and a few theatrical effects (marionettes, dry ice), this was basically an old-fashioned rock concert, and as such it gave a good deal of pleasure."

"Mott On Broadway was definitely 'A First'," says Dan Loggins. "The show was not the best I'd seen, but they ran through it with good pace and Mott style. The band's Broadway after-show reception was held at The 21 Club and Al Teller and his team really put on a special bash, signifying Mott the Hoople's arrival as a first-tier British band in New York City. It was a big event attended by CBS International Chairman Walter Yetnikoff, senior CBS people and members of Blood Sweat & Tears, Blue Oyster Cult and The New York Dolls. Queen supporting Mott was harmonious, but Freddie and the band experienced a hard time in America."

> **IH:** "I remember Queen was treated like crap in the US and they were rather upset. Freddie paced up and down in my suite after a gig in Denver saying. 'Why don't these buggers get it?' Fred was extremely impatient and thought the world should be given to him immediately – and quite rightly so."

Queen guitarist Brian May had been feeling increasingly unwell since the sixth date of Mott's tour in Louisiana and after the Uris

426

concerts, on 15th May, he collapsed in Washington with hepatitis. Brian was flown home secretly to the UK, forcing Queen to pull out of the US tour. Back in England, the guitarist wrote material for the group's forthcoming breakthrough LP, *Sheer Heart Attack*. One song reflected on Queen's experiences in America and was described by Roger Taylor as the band's "nod to Mott". May's 'Now I'm Here' referenced Mott the Hoople directly and became Queen's second British Top Twenty hit single.

> **IH:** "All of Mott and Queen had to get hepatitis jabs at 7 o'clock one morning and, as they're really painful shots, Ariel Bender would not have the injection and locked himself in his room. So, Stan rang him up, disguised his voice and said there was a present in reception – Luther *loved* presents. Stan said, 'Will I bring it up for you, sir?' and Luther said, 'Yeah!' Stan went to the bedroom, Luther opened the door and Stan bodily pulled him out, put him over his shoulder and carried him off to get the jab with Luther shouting. The added joke was that in the surgery Stan explains to Luther that he must have this jab saying, 'I know it's painful, but if you don't have this, *you're all going to die.*' I remember nearly fainting in Washington with that injection. Years later I was re-telling this story about the hepatitis shots to several people and when the room emptied, and Stan and I were the only two left, he turned to me and said, 'I never had them'... the legendary Stan Tippins!"

After the Broadway shows a new American band called Kansas was drafted in as Mott's replacement support act, but fans still arrived at US concerts expecting Queen. Kansas had released one album on Columbia and sensed things were going awry, their lead singer remarking early on that he would have worn sequined underwear if he'd known they were replacing Queen. Another American outfit named Styx also played with Mott on some dates.

> **IH:** "I remember we opened for Styx in South Bend, Illinois, and it was hell. A student came up to me when they were on, glared at me, pointed at Styx and shouted, '*That's* rock 'n' roll.' You can see what we had to put up with. I remember on that tour telling an entire audience I was having a party and gave them the hotel and the room number. The only thing was it wasn't my party, wasn't my hotel and wasn't my room number."

"Bender injected a large amount of new energy and fun into the band and I personally felt I had become a fully fledged Mott on that tour," says Morgan Fisher. "It was a peak time in terms of showmanship, record sales, tension, fun, groupies – all of it – but no drugs, just lots of drink. I never ever saw any drugs going down with Mott the Hoople. Now I may have been naive, but I didn't want any and I don't think the rest of the band did either. Of course, the Americans believed we couldn't do anything or create the energy we did without chemical assistance."

Mott the Hoople returned to the UK on 3rd June and their New York to London flight is fabled for an invitation extended by Ian to a rather famous guitarist, Griffin claiming that Hunter decided to check out whether Eric Clapton would like to join the group or not; whilst the answer must have been in the negative, at least Eric was fun.

> **IH:** "I do recall the flight and the Clapton discussion. Eric said to me, ''Ere, I half like your book.' I said, 'What do you mean half like?' and Clapton said, 'Well, I've only half read it!'"

In June 1974, Mott was one of Britain's top bands. With 'The Golden Age of Rock 'n' Roll' and *The Hoople*, Ian felt that Europe had been cracked while in America the group was rapidly growing in popularity. He maintained that the art was to delay the peak as long as possible and admitted that he possessed a liking for the New York way of life; Hunter was being drawn to America, like

John Lennon, but he stated Mott would always be a British band that would live in England. After years of pitfalls, wrong turns and missed opportunities, the band had finally "arrived" with *Mott, The Hoople*, five hit singles and their Broadway "first" – but it wasn't all glory, nor was it easy for Hunter.

> **IH:** "We ended up doing 10,000 and 20,000 seaters but it wasn't sex and drugs and rock 'n' roll at all – I had to write songs – and it was bloody hard work. The live shows were great, but I could see I was going to get fully lumbered with all the writing for the next album and I was not a bottomless pit of songs."

Mott's sixth CBS single, 'Foxy, Foxy', was released in the UK on 7th June 1974 backed with 'Trudi's Song'. Written by Ian, the A-side was another Hunter-Watts-Griffin production, recorded by Alan Harris at Advision during *The Hoople* sessions and mixed by Bill Price at AIR No.2 Studio. Once again press reviews were strong: 'Foxy Mottsies' Hotsy Newie Whoo-ee!' *(NME)*; 'Mott Get-Round to Spector Sound' *(Melody Maker)*; and 'FOXY MOTT; BEST-EVER' *(DISC)*. With the headline 'Chart Cert', *Record and Radio Mirror* described 'Foxy, Foxy' as "cunning pop", but the single received limited radio airplay and the group was acutely disappointed with the eventual sales figures. Entering the British charts on 22nd June, 'Foxy, Foxy' only stayed for five weeks and peaked at No.33. A higher-pitched Ian lead vocal, Ronettes-style 'Be My Baby' drum pattern and Phil Spector-inspired production were notable aspects of the recording but most of Mott were not over-enthused. Watts thought 'Foxy, Foxy' was a good song but maintained the band "half did it" as a demo for Ronnie Spector; he also felt it was nice to attempt a different project but believed the track was not really Mott material.

> **IH:** "I wrote 'Foxy, Foxy' because I loved The Ronettes. Ronnie Spector's voice was amazing, and I wanted to experiment

a bit with the Phil Spector sound. It was something that everybody in the band was happy to do at the time. Maybe it was wrong in hindsight, but it was great making that noise. I'm not sure if we had a single in mind, but I never offered it to Ronnie Spector. I've never offered anybody a song in my life. I'd say three quarters of the song is okay, but I blew it in the last quarter. Sadly 'Foxy, Foxy' was further decline for Mott the Hoople. It was so different to anything else, you couldn't dance to it and it sounded a real mess on a cheap radio. The band lost momentum after that."

At the time of release Grosvenor commented on 'Foxy, Foxy' and the imminent recording of two new Hunter songs as potential Mott singles that were more in the style of 'All the Way from Memphis'. "I never shared Ian's enthusiasm for 'Foxy, Foxy'," said Luther, "because to me it wasn't really Mott – it didn't make it. It was a good song but too much of a Spector kind of number. Phil could have written the same thing himself anyway." After the single's relative failure, the band discussed taking a break. Griffin complained that Mott the Hoople was a touring and albums band but suddenly they were expected to produce a hit single "every two months", adding that "there was a panic after 'Foxy, Foxy' wasn't a hit". Notably, the single was not released in America.

Ian was interviewed about *Diary of a Rock 'n' Roll Star* by Bob Harris for an eleven-minute *Old Grey Whistle Test* film that was broadcast on BBC television on 25th June. Harris described Hunter's diary as, "one of the most interesting and enjoyable rock books I've read for ages", while Ian explained his motivation for the project and revealed more musical insights. Hunter had written the diary notes "morning, noon and night" but admitted that there was always time on the road, sitting on planes, waiting for Stan Tippins to assemble the luggage each morning or waiting backstage for soundchecks.

"Looking back on it," Hunter said to Harris, "I think I did the book because the group had just left the Defries stable and were rather angry, and I was beginning to realise that a measure of concentration and self-control was going to be required on the following album, if we were to stay in the business at all – so the book was me getting myself a bit organised, instead of ambling aimlessly. I hold very dear, the people that I play to, especially the younger ones, so that's who I wrote it for. When I was fifteen and sixteen, America was this amazing place and I still think it is to fifteen and sixteen year olds, especially the working class who're never going to get the chance to get there. That's where I came from. I never thought I'd get there. I wasn't a star at the time, but Panther in their wisdom said if somebody's going to look at it on a news-stand, unless we put something dramatic on the outside, they're not going to bother to buy it. Hence the title and the stuff on the back about Zappa and Moon, which was a laugh. Panther came back with some questions and asked things like, 'Who's Chris Blackwell?' – everybody in the business knows who Chris is, but everybody north of Barnet probably doesn't, so I had to add descriptive bits – things like, 'Chris Blackwell, the head of Island Records'."

Ian also spoke with Bob about American and European touring. Mott's three US treks since the diary was written had been headlining tours and things had changed; the group was now given their place according to Hunter, and they were receiving proper sound checks and stronger audience reactions. Band personnel and pawn shops inevitably entered the discussion, with Ian's tongue planted firmly in one cheek.

"I can remember in the Sixties in Northampton," said Hunter, "with Freddie Lee, at St Michael's Village Hall, where the top group got six quid and the second-on-the-bill group got eight quid – but the top band on the night got featured in the *Chronicle & Echo* – and it's been like that ever since. In America, you must be top of the bill. *The Hoople* album and the singles that came off it, broke us a bit in Europe – we got a lot of 'Top Tens' there – but they're very peculiar people in Europe. If you go in third on the bill, you get treated like cattle and we'd sampled that in the early days so, now, we've got hits we'll go back. In the States, Watts still visits pawn shops all over the place. It was a laugh in Pennsylvania once. Overend was running around all the pawn shops and this guy walked up and 'gave' me a guitar – so Watts took the guy out for a drink that night, hoping he'd get one the next day. Hilarious! Bender's alright. He's got this nasty habit of coming into the middle of the stage, but the middle of the stage belongs to me. I don't know if he wants to be a star or whatever it is, but I've started hitting him of late and he's covered in bruises. It's still not doing much good."

H&H Management was now actively planning future activities for Mott and the pace was quickening. Part of August was set aside to cut another new single at AIR London. Further US concerts would commence in March or April 1975 through to June, including a date at New York's Madison Square Garden, which meant the next studio LP would have to be rehearsed over Christmas and the recordings completed at AIR by early February. July and August 1975 were investigated for touring Australia and Japan, September was pencilled in for European concerts and October was set aside for a four-week US tour. A London concert during September at Wembley Stadium with Judy Collins, The Band and Crosby, Stills, Nash & Young was also mooted. The Japanese dates were lined up as an "expenses-only" trek with no fees for the band, so those touring plans soon evaporated, but the Mott machine was moving faster and faster.

On 5th July, Mott the Hoople headlined at the Buxton Festival in Derbyshire and on the following day they stormed The Douglas Palace Lido on the Isle of Man where Morgan Fisher ended up pushing his white grand piano off the six-foot high stage. Mott was scheduled to play the London Music Festival at Alexandra Palace on 31st July, but the event was cancelled. The Buxton and Douglas gigs were to be Grosvenor's last performances with the group. Supported by Man and Lindisfarne, the programme from a cold and muddy Buxton Festival spoke of Mott's rock 'n' roll journey and top of the bill status on the 'Rock and Roll Circus' – "right where they were always meant to be."

IH: "At Buxton I remember standing by the stage in torrential rain telling Stan we were *not* going on because of the electrical situation. The stage was covered, but the wind was blowing the rain onto the mikes. It's not nice when you get 240 volts through your lips. I've experienced it a couple of times. Just at that moment the journalist Charles Shaar Murray sauntered up to me and said, 'That's what I like about you lot. You don't care about mere elements!' Needless to say, we donned our finery and survived it."

At their Isle of Man gig Mott exhibited some tension on stage that detracted from their usual spirit and spontaneity and when Hunter delivered his portion of 'American Pie' on the intro to 'The Golden Age of Rock 'n' Roll', Ian seemed to place a stronger-than-usual emphasis on, *"the day the music died."* Were things going awry in the Hoople camp again?

Having mixed the Broadway and Hammersmith concert tapes at AIR Studios during June and July, Dale Griffin flew to Los Angeles to master and cut Mott's long-awaited live album. The record was to be an American-only release, but the plan was changed when it was decided to feature highlights from the UK and US shows on either side of one LP. Although a side of vinyl typically contained around eighteen to twenty minutes of music to preserve sound quality, the initial idea for Mott's project was to incorporate almost thirty minutes of material from each venue on *each side* of the record, using a special disc-cutting lab in LA. Dale remembered "piecing" the album together and having to "slash" Bender's lengthy solo on 'Walkin' with a Mountain', claiming that for the edit, "the engineer rolled the tape, closed his eyes, made chalk marks, cut it and pulled out 200 feet of tape."

In the end, Griffin questioned the American lab's claims and he returned to Trident's mastering suite in London. Mott's vinyl was pressed at Columbia Records' Terre Haute plant in Indiana with music crammed on to two sides, but the failure to release a double live album was inexplicable. Roxy Music would make the same mistake with *Viva! Roxy Music* but these were two rare exceptions. Live LPs were usually double album sets that shone, like Wishbone Ash's stunning *Live Dates*. The single *Mott the Hoople Live* LP was a travesty, but the blunder would be rectified thirty years later with a 2CD set.

During August, the music press caught wind of a rumoured feud between Hunter and Grosvenor. Ariel, not to be outdone by Ian's recent *Whistle Test* comments, referred to Hunter's age and suggested he should have retired from music years before – and the scam, devised to wind up the press, worked. According to Grosvenor, "When we were in the States, Ian and I spent a lot of time together and for a bit of fun decided to cook up a bit of trouble between us – ah, publicity!"

In August, Mott appeared on the Dutch TV programme *Avro's Top Pop Show* to promote a flagging 'Foxy, Foxy' but in early September there was news of Mott's next single and future touring plans. *Record Mirror* ran a front-page headline, 'Mott Bounce Back' featuring Morgan Fisher who explained that the group had spent its summer break from live performance working on musical ideas for a new single that was much removed from 'Foxy, Foxy'. The band had been in the studio working on some new tracks including 'Three Blind Mice', 'One Fine Day' and 'Colwater High', the latter being a strong contender for a single in Ian's view. It was also confirmed that Mott would play an extensive European tour in October, UK concert dates in November and December and another US tour in spring 1975.

Griffin felt that Mott the Hoople "more-or-less broke up" in August after the "failure" of 'Foxy, Foxy'. The drummer said he tried to persuade Hunter to put out "a proper single" and though Ian was unenthusiastic, Dale said he convinced CBS that they had a great song and secured studio time even though the band had nothing. Griffin claimed he plotted with Fisher and Watts to get Mott to record a number he had written called 'Sunset Summer Nights' and a backing track was taped with Howie Casey playing saxophone. Ian admitted he was so horrified with what the band was offering, that he became sufficiently motivated to sit at the piano and run through a piece, titled 'The Saturday Kids'. Luther played a solo on an early version of Hunter's song, but Griffin would later say, "It was Grosvenor's last chance – and he blew it!"

> **IH:** "I think the band kind of thought I that I might leave, so Buff concocted this idea and they thought, 'We'll write this horrible song and get him in the studio, and then he'll hate it and he'll write another song for Mott.' So, they played me this horrible thing and that's how 'Saturday Gigs' started. I wrote it in a panic because this 'song' they wanted to record was NOT good!"

Despite the whirlwind energy, infectious personality and renewed spirit that Luther had injected into the group, they now considered that Grosvenor was no longer suitable. On 14th September *DISC* wrote 'Bender to Quit Mott' and a week later came news of Grosvenor's official departure from Mott the Hoople. 'ARIEL ON A SOLO BENDER' said *Sounds*, reporting that the guitarist had been writing material and had left Mott to begin recording a new album immediately and to plan an American tour. A formal statement from Mott the Hoople's management read that the band and Bender had compromised their playing to try and fit together and decided, although they were the best of friends, that the guitarist should form his own band. H&H added the split had absolutely nothing to do with "the feud" that Bender and Ian cooked up for fun. Whilst Fisher felt that Grosvenor didn't deliver the goods in a way that he could have done, he and Tippins held much admiration for Luther. Stan Tippins said: "Bender truly was one of the boys – a local Worcestershire lad – very much the same as the rest of the band. But Ian knew that Bender couldn't contribute anymore in the studio and as much as he really loved him, he had to go. It was tragic, because Luther was one of the greatest people to have on the road that I have ever been out with."

> **IH:** "The two styles – Luther's and ours – would not go together, no matter which way we tried it. It was upsetting him, and I got depressed about it. We just couldn't work it out, but I would have done anything for Bender to have suited us. When Ralphs left, Luther was there. He was a wonderful guy, but he wasn't a natural player for Mott, so it skidded a bit through *The Hoople* situation, and I finally decided we had to make a change. I look back fondly on some tremendous nights with Luther. He didn't write with Mott, but he has written some beautiful simple acoustic-type melodies on his own albums. I think, in retrospect, he kept Mott going through an extremely tiring time with his boundless energy and enthusiasm. Mad as a hatter and smart underneath, Ariel could be hard work in the studio, but so could I. I thought he played Mott's stuff great, but he was capable of the occasional gaffe and, of course, with Ariel nothing was done by halves. Luther was a great morale booster for the band, but he never was a Mott guitarist. You had to play a certain way and be a good guitar player to play with Mott the Hoople."

Pete Watts would only comment that Luther's departure was very upsetting for the band and that they were immature and didn't want to be around when it happened. Some fans had embarked on Ralphs versus Grosvenor comparisons which Luther felt was unjust. Grosvenor was also saddened by the handling of his Mott departure.

"In hindsight, the only answer I have for people who say that Luther Grosvenor's or Ariel Bender's guitar playing didn't suit Mott, is that you should listen back to the material that was recorded on *The Hoople* LP, which contained some very fine songs and guitar. The performance I gave was very good, I think. I was never knocked out with the subsequent live album and my own personal performance on that, although if you were there at a concert you could relate more to Mott and it was great. As for the Ralphs comparisons, I love

436

Mick and we go back a long way. We played in telephone boxes with electric guitars as youngsters and we were buddies and had the same dream. We both had a little bit of magic here and there and I think the comparisons weren't fair to me or Mick.

"I don't know the complete story of the end, but Stan Tippins came to see me at Bedford Gardens where I was living, almost in tears and he said, 'Look, the boys don't know how to say this, because they love you dearly, but they feel it's time for a change of guitarist.' I can't say I was very happy at the time. I was actually most sad that Stan had to tell me, and the guys couldn't, because they didn't have the heart. I can honestly say I gave them as much as they gave me. I gave them a shot in the arm – not literally! Mott the Hoople on Broadway was the commercial highlight of my career. Those days will never come back but we were there, and it was real. I used to work in a factory in Evesham, but my dream came true because I had it in my heart."

After his Mott tenure Luther planned The Ariel Bender Band, flirted with an embryonic version of Motörhead, was asked to join Sparks, but formed Widowmaker with former Love Affair vocalist Steve Ellis instead. Retaining the Ariel Bender alter ego, the band signed with Don Arden, issuing the albums *Widowmaker* and *Too Late to Cry*. Grosvenor also recorded a single with Verden Allen in 1978 but his interest in music had waned. "I was fed up with the industry," says Luther, "and the whole fucking music business – and I left it completely."

In the Nineties, however, Luther formed Blues 92, played on a Peter Green tribute album, *Rattlesnake Guitar* and recorded a second solo album, *Floodgates*. He later worked with a re-united Spooky Tooth, released a third solo record, *If You Dare* and formed The Ariel Bender Band.

> **IH:** "Luther's one of the best friends I've ever had in my life but after his year with us, Mott just wasn't going anywhere. He gave us 120 per cent but I didn't have that musical

partner anymore. With Mick Ralphs I'd had it and that was important because I can go too far sometimes. You need a guy there to say, 'Don't be so fuckin' stupid, that's over the top.' Luther would simply do what you wanted him to do, so the band slipped – not media-wise or crowd-wise, but the music started to slip really badly."

In August 1974, the pressure was really building on Mott the Hoople – and Hunter was feeling it most. H&H Management was planning relentless recording sessions, gigs and engagements through 1975, but the band's survival relied on finding another new lead guitarist – and crucially on Ian's writing.

Hunter's wood was beginning to warp, and Mott's sustain was seemingly fading – but a star replacement was waiting in the wings. The combination would create the strongest and most exciting musical partnership that Ian Hunter would ever experience.

CHAPTER THIRTEEN
Play Don't Worry

I just gravitated towards Mick Ronson. A lot of people did.

In September 1974 the British music press announced a third Mott the Hoople line-up change: 'BENDER QUITS MOTT... But Hoople Plan Giant Winter Tour', proclaimed *Melody Maker's* front page, the feature revealing plans for October live dates across Europe, followed by twenty-five British concerts billed as: 'A Rock 'n' Roll Evening with Mott the Hoople'. The group's next single release, 'Do You Remember the Saturday Gigs' was also announced as a prelude to the tour and the report claimed that Bender's replacement was to be Derek Griffiths, after Mott had been unable to secure the services of guitarist Mick Ronson. Griffiths had been associated with Epic artists Colin Blunstone and Argent, but despite *Melody Maker's* report, Derek *never* received any Mott the Hoople approach.

"There were loads of stories going around and I do have good recall of those days," says Derek Griffiths. "I was mentioned on the front of *Melody Maker* and was meant to be joining Mott the Hoople. I saw the feature and was also hearing about this rumour from people in the business, but it took place without me knowing anything official about it. No Mott guys ever rang me and asked

439

if I'd be up for the gig and no Mott management called me either, as I recall. They *were* convoluted and kaleidoscopic times!"

As well as the Griffiths speculation it was erroneously claimed again that former Man guitarist Deke Leonard might join Mott, but this had already been ruled out because Deke's propensity towards extended solos was not in Hoople vein. The Griffiths-Leonard and 'Is Ronson joining Mott?' rumours were finally expunged when Ian announced that Mick *was* a member of the band after all, and the follow-up headlines – 'MICK MAKES MOTT' and 'Mott moves for Ronson as new Hoople' – suppressed the speculation with further confirmation given at press conferences in London and New York.

> **IH:** "After Luther left Mott, I was thinking about looking for another guitar player and a couple of people were telling me I should speak to Mick Ronson. Following the Bowie retirement episode, Mick Rock told me that Ronson was sitting around doing nothing, so I went over to Mick's, we stayed up all night chatting and he called Tony Defries in America. Bang – in came Ronno, a totally different animal to Bender. Immediately, Ronson was all for Mott the Hoople and showing Bowie that he could do it somewhere else. Mick was great."

Although Ronson had his second album, *Play Don't Worry*, ready for release, he had agreed to suppress his solo career for Mott the Hoople, the "deal" being that he would feature some songs on stage with the band, share vocals with Hunter and remain under contract to MainMan and RCA. On paper, the union seemed earth-shattering as Mick had already become renowned for his playing, production and arrangement skills. Ronson's guitar style embraced harmony, tone and power, his stage presence and looks were iconic and he was a supreme sideman. To almost everyone who met him, Mick was also a modest, thoughtful and generous figure.

Michael Ronson was born on 26th May 1946 in Hull, the first son of George and Minnie Ronson. Mick took piano lessons from age five but wanted to learn the cello and attended violin lessons in preparation. Hull was a tough city and carrying a violin case made Mick a target of fun, but his musical grounding had taken root. Ronson described himself as a shy and nervous kid, but he would ultimately find expression in the guitar, claiming that the instrument made him another person.

Mick was influenced by The Everly Brothers and The Shadows, and he rated George Harrison's guitar solos highly. He also enjoyed The Yardbirds, adored the skills of Jeff Beck and later described NRBQ as his favourite band. Acquiring a Fender Telecaster when he was nineteen, Ronson started playing in bands. He left school and worked variously as a delivery man, car mechanic and municipal gardener but Mick became one of Yorkshire's best guitar talents although, like Ian Hunter, his musical desire caused friction with a disapproving father. One of Hull's finest vocalists was Benny Marshall who worked with Mick during his early career.

"Ronson played in various groups, mainly in Hull: The Insects (short-lived), The Buccaneers (very short-lived), The Mariners, The King Bees (short-lived), The Crestas, The Voice and Wanted (both in London), The Rats, Treacle, Ronno and the Hype (in London again). One night when The Crestas played, the hotel venue had DC electrics and while Mick was touching his guitar strings, he took hold of the microphone stand. He completed the circuit giving himself a massive electric shock causing the stand and guitar to stick to his body, throwing him off stage on to the front tables. His guitar had to be literally kicked away and Mick was badly burned and ended up in hospital."

In 1965, Mick moved to London and joined The Voice not knowing that the band was sponsored by a religious sect. Their guitarist was Miller Anderson, Ian Patterson's friend. Miller was quitting The Voice but recruited his replacement. "I selected Mick from loads of guys trying for the gig," says Anderson. "He sounded great and looked great – and he played great too. I stayed with The Voice until Ronson settled in and we became good mates. The Voice soon decided to go to Mexico, to some deserted beach, to continue being a bunch of cults. They dropped poor Mick off at the side of the M1 in the middle of the night, without any notice."

Ronson decided to play in a Tamla Motown covers band, worked in a paint factory, then joined one of Hull's most popular groups, The Rats. Ronson was now mastering Jeff Beck's string-bending style and used a banjo string for the top E, moving all the others to create a light-gauge set. He traded his Telecaster for a new 1968 Gibson Les Paul Custom 'Black Beauty' and created vibrato effects by pushing and pulling on the strings between the bridge and tailpiece. Mick became fascinated with a Django Reinhardt and Stéphane Grappelli album, but The Rats blasted out Hendrix, Zeppelin, Beatles, Cream and Jeff Beck covers. Free's *Tons of Sobs* LP also supplied some of their live material. Marshall, Ronson, drummer Mick Woodmansey and bass player Geoff Appleby utilised Fairview Studios at Willerby near Hull to make some recordings – retrospectively issued in 1995 as *The Rise and Fall of Bernie Gripplestone and the Rats from Hull*. In 1969, Ronson almost joined forces with another of East Yorkshire's up-coming stars – The Mandrakes' vocalist Alan Palmer – later Robert Palmer – but this collaboration didn't bear fruit as Alan and Mick were core members in their respective groups.

During Mick's stint as a municipal gardener with Hull City Council, local drummer John Cambridge pursued a reluctant Ronson asking him to give the London music scene another shot, with a singer he had joined named David Bowie. Cambridge found Ronson marking out lines on a rugby pitch, dressed in a navy donkey jacket with trousers tucked into wellington boots – the antithesis of "glam". Mick auditioned with Bowie on his first BBC radio session, played with David's band, The Hype and joined "The Court of Bowie" with Tony Visconti, living at Haddon Hall, the neo-Gothic Beckenham house where David would write *The Man Who Sold the World*, *Hunky Dory* and *Ziggy Stardust*.

Ronson also played on Michael Chapman's *Fully Qualified Survivor* and recorded a version of 'Madman Across the Water' with Elton John.

Mick was a striking figure with blonde hair, aqualine nose and good looks, but his onstage aura was further enhanced when the top face of his beloved 'Black Beauty' was stripped to reveal the instrument's underlying maple cap. Michael Chapman's roadie had prompted Ronson about the sonic improvements of stripped Gibsons and the black paint was removed from the face of Mick's Custom to reveal the natural wood beneath. The honeyed Les Paul look became uniquely identified with Ronson as he delivered his trademark sound through a Marshall Major 200-watt amp, nicknamed The Pig, a wah-wah pedal and a Tone Bender, Mick finding the pedal's "edge-of-feedback sweet-spot" to create a mid-range boosting tone control.

Ronson's was a tough musical apprenticeship and he brought real substance to Bowie's *The Man Who Sold the World*, the opening guitar feedback flashing from the grooves becoming a notable trademark on David's records. Mick's musical approach instantly influenced Bowie, as he transformed David's acoustic demos to electrifying, theatrical classics. Producer Tony Visconti was also intrigued by the guitarist's skill: "Mick Ronson was a blessing but didn't say much. We thought he was just a cool, silent type. Soon he became comfortable in his new surroundings, started to banter in semi-intelligible Hull-ese and his sense of humour surfaced. He referred to Bowie as 'Norman Wisdom' once and when he saw that it irked him, he didn't stop. Mick brought drummer Woody Woodmansey to David, then bassist Trevor Bolder from Hull stepped into my boots so, essentially, The Spiders from Mars was The Rats, with a new singer."

For his part, Bolder would praise Mick as a humble man who never had any rock star ego, and Ronson was also generous describing Bowie. "I loved David's music from the start," he said. "I just thought he was the most creative person ever. He knew what he wanted to do, and he got on and did it. He was quite a giving sort of person too and that's what really struck me about him. You knew he was going to be a star."

As Bowie temporarily lost interest in live performance, Mick formed another short-lived band, Ronno, with Benny Marshall, taking *The Man Who Sold the World* into heavier territory. Upon returning to work with Bowie, Ronson was encouraged to write his first string parts for the 1971 classic, *Hunky Dory*, but his bold, biting, wildcat guitar sound was also stamped on to Bowie's 'Queen Bitch', written in direct response to The Velvet Underground's *Loaded*. Mick was now the crucial linkman in the transformation of David's acoustic-based creations to a grander rock format.

Within three weeks of *Hunky Dory*'s release, Bowie and Ronson were back in Trident Studios to record *The Rise and Fall of Ziggy Stardust and the Spiders from Mars*. David had crafted a clever backdrop to his story of a doomed futuristic rock star, but a key element to success was Mick's muscular firebrand guitar and inventive playing. Bowie also liked Ronson's buoyant persona that kept band morale at a high point, and he saw Mick as a natural performer and a great foil for the Ziggy character. The Rats from Hull had become The Spiders from Mars and Ronson felt that they injected a new impetus into early Seventies music.

"*Ziggy Stardust* was a very quick album to do," Mick would say. "They were great songs and even just playing the chords had some sort of melody to it which I liked. The guitar sound on the records was played with a Les Paul, and a Cry Baby set to a middle 'honking' tone. You can't help but get a decent sound when you turn an amp full on, although a lot of it is in the fingers and your own personality. If you're going to play rock music, hit the chord – don't tickle about with it!"

Suzanne Fussey became Bowie's wardrobe mistress and hair stylist. She would marry Ronson in 1976 and knew that the quiet boy from Hull was uncomfortable with the Spiders' glam look and David's androgynous image. When Bowie draped his arm around the guitarist's neck during their infamous *Top of the Pops* 'Starman' performance, viewers and future pop stars like Boy George, Marco

Pirroni and Gary Kemp saw it as a life-changing moment. David's *Melody Maker* interview where he said he was bisexual also embarrassed Ronson, and his family faced flak, especially when Mick gave his parents a car and somebody threw paint over it.

"After joining David, Mick was unsurprisingly reluctant to adopt make-up," says Suzi Ronson. "He was from Hull and nervous of what people would think. He was not the type to put on make-up, but he got surprisingly used to it after a short time."

Two renowned British guitarists retained fond memories of Mick. Phil Manzanera of Roxy Music first met Ronson at a Croydon gig supporting Bowie. "I admired Mick for his fantastic melodic playing and tone," says Manzanera. "He was the perfect foil for David at that point and Ronson was a lovely man." A young Kirby Gregory who carved out success with Curved Air and Stretch was also impressed. "In the early Seventies, I played two gigs in Armada supporting David Bowie. The Spiders were wearing their jump-suits and looked like they had just arrived from another part of the galaxy. As an eighteen-year-old guitarist who listened to *Hunky Dory* every day of the week, I was in awe of Mick Ronson – his playing was melodic but tough – he had a fantastic tone – and he looked like a star! Mick treated us, 'the support band', with respect – a lesson I have tried to retain – and left me with the memory of a man who had a rare combination of stellar talent and humility."

Photographer Mick Rock described Ronson as Ziggy's anchor and considered it impossible to imagine Bowie's magical rise without him. "All the years I knew Mick, he remained very unspoiled and he never showed any interest in stardom," says Rock. "I don't think he understood the depth of his own talent; he was too busy being in awe of the talent of others." Mike Garson, a highly-talented American avant-garde jazz pianist joined the Spiders and Ronson "reached" him more than any guitarist he ever worked with. "Mick emanated a sparkle and was very warm-hearted. He was and still is my favourite guitarist. His arrangements and orchestrations were all stunning."

Ronson had made an emotional contribution to Mott the Hoople's *All the Young Dudes* album, arranging superlative strings and brass for Ian Hunter's 'Sea Diver', and his nasal guitar tones gave Lou Reed's *Transformer* an identifiable sound. Mick also assisted three more RCA acts, producing and playing on records by Dana Gillespie, Bob Sargeant and country-rockers Pure Prairie League. Craig Fuller of "PPL" recalls Ronson travelling to Toronto to work on their *Bustin' Out* album.

Craig Fuller: "Mick came over to do string parts on a couple of songs. He instantly became one of the guys, stayed until the end of the summer and revealed himself to be an all-round great guy. He'd played with David Bowie but was completely at ease with an up-and-coming country-rock band. His dream car was a Ford Torino – no Ferraris for Mick."

"Ronson was a great guy to be with and was brilliant in the studio," says Dana Gillespie. "We recorded at Trident and even though he was a guitarist first and foremost, he was superb as a producer. Ronson was mad for his work – that was his passion. All he ever wanted to do was work – it was his God. He was just a conscientious humble guy from Hull. He was also great 'eye candy' for the girls!"

Suzi Ronson says: "Mick would strive to make his productions sound like the person he was producing. He would colour and enhance what was there, rather than put his stamp on it. It always amazed me that he was born with such talent. I told him he was lucky as he really didn't have to worry about what he wanted to be, because he was born a musician."

During their 1972 US tour, Bowie and the Spiders recorded 'The Jean Genie', memorable for Mick's prominent Yardbirds guitar pattern that created a cool but stunningly simple single. Ronson's fourth LP with Bowie, *Aladdin Sane*, was co-arranged and mixed by Mick, and his stinging guitar riffs took 'Panic in Detroit' and 'Cracked Actor' to new levels. Ronson was directing everything in a musical sense and former Beatles engineer Ken Scott praised Mick's contributions.

Ken Scott remarked: "Was David Bowie talented? Absolutely! Was David Bowie worthy of the adulation often heaped upon him? Sometimes! Would everyone know his name if not for his pairing with Mick Ronson? Quite possibly not! Mick made my job as an engineer and producer so much easier and enjoyable. One of the great things about his arrangements was that he thought like a guitarist, and so they were never quite what one would expect. His string arrangements were amazing and his contribution unique. I would put Ronson up there among the best I've ever worked with. I think Ronno was better than any of The Beatles as a guitarist."

After Bowie retired his Ziggy character in July 1973, Dana Gillespie felt that Mick was very hurt by David's decision to move on, but Tony Defries now positioned Ronson for solo stardom. Having collaborated with Mott the Hoople and Lou Reed, Bowie and Ronson recorded with Lulu and 'The Man Who Sold the World' became a Top Ten hit. Lulu became a confirmed Ronson fan too.

"One of the most incredible things about Mick Ronson was that he was the first guitarist who ever accessed and combined a pop-rock and punk ethic in his guitar playing. His style was totally unique. I loved working with Mick in the studio – he was not a diva – he was a kind and gentle soul."

Ronson had contributed a vast amount to Bowie's breakthrough and success, the duo producing five classic albums, eight chart singles and playing over 200 concerts. Much of the credit for the overall strength of those recordings and stage shows was due to Ronson and Mick had a firm sense of what he brought to the projects after Bowie moved on to new musical pastures. "The newspapers wrote about disagreements but, in truth, David is very obliged to me," he said. "His albums are very much based on my character too and I often realised musically, things he just had in his mind."

MainMan moved to market Mick as a teen heart-throb in 1973, where a glamorous Jeff Beck may have been more appropriate, Ronson later admitting that he never believed in Defries' master plan. "Tony had this idea that I was to become the next David

Cassidy or something like that," he said, "a total money-making venture. David Bowie wasn't quite sure what he was going to do, so Tony said to me, 'Okay, we can make you a big star and get you a deal with RCA.' So, I said, 'Wonderful' and went off to make my own record."

At the Château d'Hérouville near Paris, Ronson cut his solo debut taking some inspiration from RCA artiste Annette Peacock's 1972 album *I'm the One.* "I was thrilled Mick covered several pieces from *I'm the One* on his first solo release," said Annette. Released by RCA in March 1974, *Slaughter on 10th Avenue* was an assured debut from Ronson and featured his first single, 'Love Me Tender', backed with 'Only After Dark', a song subsequently covered by The Human League, Def Leppard and Siouxsie and the Banshees. The album's climax was Mick's stunning guitar interpretation of Richard Rodgers' 'Slaughter on 10th Avenue', released as a second single. MainMan intensified their solo stardom campaign with a promotional film of the title track shot in a bar and street corner on New York's 10th Avenue, with Suzi Fussey playing the role of Mick's love interest. Tony Defries' marketing campaign included a six-storey billboard promoting *Slaughter on 10th Avenue* in New York City at a cost of 5,000 dollars a week plus a further ad on LA's Sunset Strip.

> **IH:** "Mick told me he was doing his album and David came in with the gang and sort of took over, which was alright with Mick, because he was fine that way. But then there was less and less time to do Ronson's album and the deal was that David was supposed to do lyrics for Mick. So, it got to the end and Ronson finally managed to say, 'David what about the rest of the lyrics?' Bowie said he didn't feel like writing and wandered off. Mick was left to complete the record in two days – but he did it. I remember that huge picture of Mick in Times Square. They put it up and then the bill posters went on strike – and it stayed up there for months."

Promoting Ronson at Bowie levels showed how MainMan was over-reaching. Mick was ill-prepared for solo stardom because whilst he possessed a full array of musical skills, he did not have the necessary ego. With *Slaughter* he had produced a record that was more idiosyncratic than David's work but still commercial enough to hit the charts, even out-performing John Lennon's *Mind Games*. But Mick was not given time to develop in Suzi Ronson's view. He was an imaginative guitarist and arranger but seemed unsuited to frontman status. Martin Turner of Wishbone Ash witnessed one of Mick's solo performances at London's Rainbow Theatre.

"I saw Ronno when he was promoting *Slaughter on 10th Avenue*. The Rainbow was packed that night and anticipation was high. Ronson had a large band on stage including Trevor Bolder and Mike Garson and he even had horns and girl singers. Mick really did look the part and was a stunning guitar player, producer and arranger, but it seemed that he was genuinely uncomfortable being band leader and vocalist. I liked his records very much, but I think it hit home at The Rainbow that Mick really wasn't cut out to be a solo figure."

A No.9 chart placing for *Slaughter on 10th Avenue* came as a shock to Ronson and he found solo success strenuous, admitting that he liked the company of other musicians and that he always wanted to hear what they had to say. That creative and collaborative attitude was an encouraging signpost for Ian Hunter and Mott the Hoople. Mick felt that he had been "bamboozled out of the last David Bowie concert" and approached with an offer that he could be "the next star". He complied, but, on the road, Ronson felt uncomfortable within himself. Nevertheless, by July 1974, as Mott was waning, Mick commenced work on a second LP, *Play Don't Worry*, which he arranged and produced at studios in London and Southern France. Playing several drum, bass and keyboard parts himself, the LP included covers of Velvet Underground, Claudio Baglioni and Pure Prairie League songs. Ironically, *Slaughter on 10th Avenue* was meant to express a loose concept, but Mick's follow-up seemed to flow more and was arguably stronger. *Play*

Don't Worry included a cover of Little Richard's 'The Girl Can't Help It' featuring 'Ian Hunter and The Microns' on backing vocals and 'This Is for You', a wonderful song written by actor-turned-musician Laurie Heath. Ronson had arranged a single for Heath who was a member of Milkwood, a New Seekers spin-off trio managed by Tony Defries.

"One day when we were recording Milkwood, Mick heard a song I had written called 'This Is for You'," said Laurie. "Mick's arrangement of the song and Mike Garson's piano was very sensitively interpreted. One morning, Mick and I shared a taxi on the way to a recording session. He'd been up most of the night writing string arrangements for a track he and David Bowie were laying down. I had no idea Mick could write string arrangements and told him how I wished I could write for strings. Mick pulled from his pocket a small blue book titled *Teach Yourself Orchestration* by King Palmer and placed it in my hand before telling me I could learn too. I still have the book, but I still cannot write string arrangements."

Play Don't Worry marked a solid progression for Ronson because he had begun to write lyrics. However, deep down, Mick hadn't really wanted to make the LP and was now unsure of his future. "I decided that solo vocal projects weren't quite right for me," said Ronson. "I felt uncomfortable as I didn't quite believe in what I was singing, so I decided to knock my solo recording career on the head."

> **IH:** "Tony Defries wanted to make Mick Ronson the next Bowie when David retired, so he started making Mick the frontman. The only thing was Mick wasn't a frontman. Ronson couldn't take the guitar through monitor systems – he hated that – he was a purist. He had to hear it straight from the amp and you can't have an amp behind you in the middle of the stage, on the front mike, because it's going to leak. So, Ronson was a side man – that everybody thought would be a great frontman."

450

'Billy Porter' was issued as Ronson's third RCA single, from his second album, in October 1974, but the release of *Play Don't Worry*, originally scheduled for November, was delayed when he joined Mott the Hoople. Mick was delighted at the prospect of offering his strengths as a musical partner again. Bowie wrote at the time that he was very intrigued about Ronson joining Mott. "It could be a really interesting partnership," he said. "It sounds great and nobody's more pleased about it than I am."

Hunter had witnessed Ronson's stage presence alongside Ziggy Stardust and felt drawn towards the guitarist as he found Bowie to be "remote". As a "rocker", Ian had gravitated towards Ronson.

> **IH:** "David looked like he'd arrived from another planet and Mick was God's gift to women – he looked amazing. Ronson's playing also seemed human. In the end, I think that financially the whole situation had to come to a head sooner or later with Bowie and MainMan, and, in turn, Ronson. How long can you hypnotise somebody? The odd thing is Mick told me that David rang him up a few years later to reform the Spiders. I asked Ronson, 'What did you say?' and Mick told me he'd said to David, 'Don't be so fuckin' daft. It's been done.' I can't remember when he told me that happened – 1978, I think. There were certainly two facts about Ronson – he was like me in that it wasn't about moves and fucking money – and he was also very modest – so I believed him."

During the summer of 1974, Ian had become increasingly concerned about how he might address Mott's next chapter following the departures of Verden Allen, Mick Ralphs and Luther Grosvenor. Now the band featured Mick Ronson: a bona-fide rock guitarist, a genius musician and arranger, and an iconic stage figure who could be committed, creative and open in the studio. Crucially, Ronson could work *with* Hunter, as Mick Ralphs had done.

All that Mott the Hoople had to do was capitalise on their star signing.

CHAPTER FOURTEEN

Marionette

Mott had run its course. The flame had died.

'**R**ONNO JOINS THE YOUNG DUDES' proclaimed *Record Mirror* on 28th September 1974 and so 'The Great Mott Mystery' was finally solved – Mott the Hoople had got their man. A comedic contingent at *NME* had started taunting Bryan Ferry and Mick Ronson, dubbing them Byron Ferrari and Ricky Monsoon – and their rib-tickling Mott splash carried the headline – 'Killer Monsoon Strikes'.

The amazing news of the guitarist's recruitment into Mott the Hoople had been announced by Ian and Mick at press receptions in London's Grosvenor House Hotel on 18th September, and the following day at the Hotel St Moritz in New York City. Arriving in front of the American press at a conference suite in the Sky Garden overlooking Central Park South, Hunter generously offered congratulations to former Mott-man Mick Ralphs, whose *Bad Company* album had just reached No.1 in America – but the main item on the agenda was Mick Ronson! Ironically, at the time of Luther Grosvenor's Mott arrival in 1973, Ian had claimed, "Bender will be here until the end. My entire future's bound up with Bender." A year later, Ian nodded towards Ronson and said, "Now my entire future's bound up with him."

Mick Ronson had been on Mott the Hoople's "Wanted" list shortly after David Bowie's "retirement" in July 1973. Ronson had also been interested in joining the band following Mick Ralphs' departure that summer but, when differences surfaced between MainMan and H&H Management, Luther Grosvenor was recruited instead. Now the deal was on and Ian was delighted saying that he felt Ronson's presence would give Mott a more electric sound and that the group had already recorded two tracks for single release. Angie Bowie sent a telegram saying that Mick joining Mott was, "the wedding of the year" and *Circus* magazine considered Ronson would lend Mott a new lease of life production-wise, with the band becoming harder-hitting. No Hoople contract was signed by Mick and he remained under MainMan Management; he would be a full band member whilst continuing solo work and the production of other artists.

> **IH:** "1974 was quite a year! I'd been panicking slightly because we were on the slide but Ronson and I met, and he rang Defries in the States. Mick had a second solo album coming out and I think Tony was figuring, 'Get him out on the road with Mott and I can plug the album.' They'd tried him as a solo artist, and it hadn't worked so it just seemed like a great move. It was the start of endless complications, but I didn't care and neither did Mick because we were getting on great. In the studio, he was brilliant as an arranger and a producer, so I thought, naturally, this is going to be wonderful because all the creativity will come back."

Dale Griffin's view was that Mott the Hoople had temporarily halted activities after Bender, when the name of Ronson came up and that whilst Hunter was enthusiastic, he and Watts were concerned about re-uniting with MainMan. Griffin described 'Ronno' as "elite" and "a feted and widely respected musician". Mick had the talent to add a new dynamic dimension to Mott and his arrival seemed too good to be true for the band's fans – but the excitement would be short-lived.

Mott the Hoople 'Mark IV' moved swiftly into AIR No.2 Studio to work on a single, Ronson taping guitar parts and Fisher adding synthesizer interludes on Ian's 'Saturday Gigs' composition, previously demoed as 'The Saturday Kids'. Mott also cut another new Hunter song – 'Lounge Lizard' – a medium-paced rock number and the only Hoople track ever originated with Ronson on guitar. Mick was pleased with the recordings and his mixing involvement, describing the 'Lounge Lizard' B-side as a jam. "Everybody is really happy about it and seems to think that it has been a good move," said Ronson. "It wasn't a planned move. It just happened. It was what I was looking for and I guess what they were looking for." Behind the façade, Dale Griffin became perturbed about 'Saturday Gigs' and Mick Ronson, but Ian Hunter was excited.

> IH: "Mick took time on 'Saturday Gigs' and it showed he really cared and how much he wanted to make the song and Mott the Hoople work. A good guitarist will always find a way to 'intro' a song, as Ralpher did on 'Dudes' and Ronno did on 'Saturday Gigs'. Mick tried to make the song better and had a lot to do with the track. It was typical Ronson and one of his best production jobs ever – spot on!"

Technically, 'Lounge Lizard' was not fully completed by Mott and the intended B-side was dropped, remaining shelved until it was issued on a 1993 Columbia collection. Dale Griffin was pleased with the drum sound captured by Bill Price at AIR but was annoyed that 'Lounge Lizard' was archived to accommodate a four-minute collage comprising live snippets of 'Jerkin' Crocus', 'Sucker' and 'Violence'. Griffin felt the two new studio tracks were a good package of previously unavailable cuts and said he was angered that Ian suddenly excluded 'Lounge Lizard', even though he later described it as "nothing more than a dirty, messy, rock song". An enraged Dale collated a "horrible-edited-together" live medley as the B-side of 'Saturday Gigs'. Why Griffin would glue the sonically sharp 'Sucker' from Broadway between two warmer-sounding fragments from Hammersmith is not clear, but it didn't work. He described the 'Medley' B-side as "crap" and termed it "a two-finger job at Ian who refused to explain why he was withholding 'Lounge Lizard'."

Produced by Mott the Hoople, the elegiac and valedictory 'Saturday Gigs' was released by CBS in Britain and Europe on 18th October 1974, just after the band had left to tour the continent. Griffin complained that 'Saturday Gigs', printed on record labels, was another CBS error, emphasising that the "full title" was '(Do You Remember) The Saturday Gigs?' Further fun followed when discs were issued internationally with 'Saturday Gig' and 'The Saturday Gigs' on different single pressings, the latter by MOTT THE HOPLE in Japan. In 1992 Columbia would re-release 'All the Young Dudes' as a single by MOTT THE HOPPLE. Island had seemingly been puzzled about the group members in 1972; Columbia remained confused about who they had signed twenty years later!

What mattered most in 1974, was that Hunter's inspired composition was a beautifully nostalgic song that celebrated Hoople history in epic terms; 'Saturday Gigs' was a clever précis of Mott's career, acknowledging The Roundhouse, Croydon, The Royal Albert Hall riot and their Broadway "first", with a short satirical stab at *Top of the Pops* thrown in for humorous effect.

> IH: "Croydon was referenced in 'Saturday Gigs' as there was a pub there, The Greyhound, opposite The Fairfield Hall. We must have played that venue half a dozen times but were always thinking, 'We'll play The Fairfield Hall one day' – and one day, we did. Mott crossed the road, the fans crossed with us and that was very special. We sold the place out that night at Fairfield Hall and when we arrived on stage the roar went on for ten minutes – the longest ovation I ever heard."

'Saturday Gigs' referenced Mott's lows, Ian singing, *"In '72 was born to lose, we slipped down snakes into yesterday's news"* – and their high points, but Hunter's repeated *"Goodbye"* on the song's coda hinted at another downturn. The band's original plan had been a farewell note to their fans, saying that Mott was "going to sleep for a while" and Ian voiced those lines on the demo. The single had been conceived as a temporary finale before the cavalry arrived in the form of Ronson but, ironically, the recharged recording would still prove to be Mott the Hoople's final studio piece.

Mott's new single received a mixed reception in the press. *Sounds* wrote 'Mott blow gig' but confusingly claimed: "With 'Saturday Gigs' Mott the Hoople are back on course and showing the kind of form that brought us the *Mott* LP, one of my top 10 LPs of last year." *NME* continued to whinge saying, 'Mott: The Obsessions Are Starting to Pall'; but 'Saturday Gigs' entered the UK singles chart at No.47, two weeks after release, and Mott recorded a promotional *Top of the Pops* appearance in anticipation of another high-flying hit. Filmed in an empty BBC studio for once, Dale Griffin fussed about having no microphone at his kit to sing backing vocals, and there was further grief behind the scenes, Watts admitting that Buff was angry as Ian and Mick had attracted most camera attention. Suddenly, another fracture appeared as it became clear that Mott was now a group with a rhythm section but two front-line stars – Hunter *and* Ronson. 'Saturday Gigs' only stayed in the charts for three weeks peaking at No.41, the band's lowest CBS single placing. The BBC film never aired.

As Mott was active long before the advent of MTV, Hoople history is sparsely represented in terms of professional film footage. Surviving clips comprise German 1970 *Beat Club* performances ('At the Crossroads' and 'You Really Got Me'), live 1971 French TV tracks ('The Moon Upstairs', 'Walkin' with a Mountain', 'Rock and Roll Queen' and 'Keep A-Knockin') and *Don Kirshner's Rock Concert* from 1973 ('Sweet Angeline', 'All the Young Dudes', 'All the Way from Memphis' and 'Drivin' Sister'). The *Top of the Pops* archive only holds appearances of 'Roll Away the Stone' and 'The Golden Age of Rock 'n' Roll', and European TV film remains of 'Honaloochie Boogie' and 'Drivin' Sister' from *Top Pop* and 'Roll Away the Stone' from *Disco*. Mott's promo videos of 'Downtown', 'All the Young Dudes', 'Honaloochie Boogie' and 'The Golden Age of Rock 'n' Roll' also survive. Wiped film includes seven *Top of the Pops* performances of 'Midnight Lady', 'All the Young Dudes', 'Honaloochie Boogie', 'All the Way from Memphis' and second takes of 'Roll Away the Stone' and 'The Golden Age of Rock 'n' Roll'. The German *Disco* performance of 'Foxy, Foxy', 1970 BBC *Disco 2* TV films plus the never-broadcast 'Saturday Gigs' are also lost.

Privately, Ian was upset with the fraught *Top of the Pops* 'Saturday Gigs' filming and devastated that Mott's single was poorly received by the record-buying public.

> **IH:** "On *Top of the Pops*, there was a run-in backstage because they felt that the cameras were showing more of Mick than the drummer. It was bullshit! Who cares! You're on *Top of the Pops* and your single might be a hit. That record *should* have been huge. I loved 'Saturday Gigs' and thought, 'If that's not a hit, sod it!' It didn't sell and, when it stopped at No.41, I think the writing must have been on the wall because that was a good single. The production's brilliant. We all did it, but it was mainly Mick. Morgan sang, *'Oh dear, oh God, oh my, oh my'* when we voiced the *'did you see the suits and the platform boots'* bit, and the *'Goodbye'* chant on the end was weird – it was like something was telling us time was up. Ralpher was long gone and it seemed we'd run our course. If 'Saturday Gigs' had been a hit I think Mott would have probably gone on longer, but how much longer, is anyone's guess. I wasn't that stable by that time, but it's amazing what a hit does for the constitution."

Dale Griffin thought that the 'Saturday Gigs' single was "too downbeat" with a "muted introduction that lacked presence" –

while Watts perceived Ian "started to panic about writing" and that two lower chart placings demotivated the group.

"Hunter had written 'Foxy, Foxy' which wasn't supposed to be a single and that wasn't a big hit," said Pete. "Then 'Saturday Gigs' was a great record, but it wasn't a hit and I think he probably got a few panic blocks about writing. I believe Ian went through the mill after Ralphs left, effectively leaving him responsible for all the writing. I do like 'The Gitterday Sags'. It's a lovely, nostalgic number. I thought that was a good record – one of the best we ever made – and that it would do well. It went straight to No.2 on the Capital Radio chart, but it failed to climb on the main chart and that was a crippler. Then the *Top of the Pops* session with Ronson was all wrong and horrible, and Buff threw a wobbler on it."

As Ronson prepared for his first live dates with Mott the Hoople, Steve Hyams, a friend of Watts and the band from their Island days, encountered Mott's latest recruit at one of his rehearsals. "I first met Mick Ronson in late 1974 at Manticore Sound Stage in Fulham, when he was rehearsing his new role as guitarist with Mott the Hoople," said Steve. "Ian Hunter introduced me as an old friend of the band and Mick introduced himself and was very polite and so charming. I immediately liked him."

Mott the Hoople's European tour was to be followed by twenty-five pre-Christmas concerts in Britain, recording sessions for an album during January and a US tour from April to June including the band's first appearance at New York's Madison Square Gardens. Opening at the 2,500-seater Olympen in Lund, Sweden on 10th October, Mott's continental schedule included nineteen gigs and their live set now incorporated 'Saturday Gigs', 'Lounge Lizard', 'Angel No.9' and 'The Girl Can't Help It'. Mick also added an interesting portion of Hendrix's 'Voodoo Child' to 'Born Late '58' and Mott amended their walk-on introduction to include Bryan Johnson's 'Looking High, High, High', a 1960 Top Twenty hit and Britain's Eurovision Song Contest entry from that year.

Concert reports carried upbeat headlines including 'Cancel the Wake' and 'Hot Mott on the Spot', one journalist saying that the group now possessed "added Mick Ronson fuel injection". Phil John recalled front-page coverage after Olympen while Griffin would remember mob scenes at Stockholm's Konserthuset. The local press reported on wild events, baton-wielding police and screaming fans, much to Watts' amazement. "We couldn't believe it when we went back to Sweden," said Pete. "We got out of the bloody plane and we were greeted like The Beatles. The last time we went there we played to two people in a village hall in the middle of nowhere, with Fairport Convulsion."

Behind the scenes in Europe however, Tippins worried that the Mott-Ronson live combination didn't seem right. "It was very weak," recalled Stan. "That's what surprised me out front in the audience. Mick didn't come through forcefully. Added to personality problems, another disappointment was that British tour tickets were not selling well and that was feeding back to the band."

Realising that unrest was now brewing between Watts, Griffin and Ronson, Ian was saddened. Hunter felt Mick had been the only guitar player that could save Mott and had tried to secure Ronson for the band and "play him in" in Europe, away from the British press. Watts also claimed that he felt the future for Mott the Hoople looked ominous at that point.

IH: "I wanted to make Mick feel comfortable in Mott, but the others didn't like him. The band sat apart at breakfast on tour and after three days it suddenly dawned on me what was going on. We were in our thirties, but I thought that was infantile."

"It seemed so great on paper, the idea of Ronson joining us," recalled Watts. "Mick and Mott were going to be the perfect match, but they weren't. I think it was probably Tony Defries that suggested we get rid of the thigh-length boots and get our hair cut short so that I ended up *without any image*. I just felt naff. I was in a blue boiler suit, Ian was in dark denim and the clothes were all dowdy, except Mick who was in a sparkling white jump suit which stood out brilliantly under the stage lights. It seemed like Ronson was being made to look real good and the rest of us to look real bad. We didn't really see much of Hirschman and Heller by this point. Stan managed us more than anybody."

Drum technician Phil John recalled Mott's European performances and described Ian "looking mean... in leather buckle fly strides, pointed boots and black shirt," while Pete resembled, "a Butlin rep, in jeans and an ill-fitting red short-sleeve shirt." Phil still perceived that by the time of the Zurich Volkhaus show on 18th October, the gigs were very good.

As Mott toured Europe, CBS finally released *Mott the Hoople Live*. There had been talk of a US-only release initially, and Ian had earlier remarked;

> **IH:** "Dale Griffin has finished the live album and it sounds great to me. I don't think it's being released in Britain. There's a big demand for it in America, but not so much demand for a live album here. Maybe it'll come out there and we'll see what happens with it later on."

Mott the Hoople Live was finally issued worldwide by CBS-Columbia on 1st November 1974. and featured eight tracks: Side One (Broadway): 'All the Way from Memphis', 'Sucker', 'Rest in Peace', 'All the Young Dudes' and 'Walkin' with a Mountain' and Side Two (Hammersmith): 'Sweet Angeline', 'Rose' and Mott's elongated 'Medley'. Presented in a single sleeve, initial UK copies contained a fold-out souvenir handbill and American pressings an inner bag, with black-and-white pictures and liner notes of the infamous Broadway and London concerts. The album was dedicated to the departed stable of "Guy, Phally and Ralpher, without whom..." and the record also marked Morgan's place as a fully fledged Hoople.

> **IH:** "Morgan Fisher was not a full member of Mott at first and was paid a salary. The band at that time was a four-

460

piece with two side men. We loved Morgan and eventually on *Mott the Hoople Live* he got his due."

The Broadway tapes had been re-mixed by Alan Harris and the Hammersmith recordings by Bill Price at AIR (London), while Dale Griffin was credited with production, editing tracks and sequencing. The band only taped their two London shows on the 1973 UK tour and two nights at The Uris Theatre, Griffin complaining that most live albums are made up from several different performances: "Not the Hoople!" There were notable aural differences on each side of the LP as the Uris sound was thin and sharp-sounding from a smaller hall, whilst the London tracks were warmer and highly charged. The second side possessed great energy, exemplified in 'Sweet Angeline' and the power of Mott's 'Medley' featuring 'Jerkin' Crocus', 'Rock and Roll Queen,' 'One of the Boys' and the sado-masochistic finale 'Violence'.

Ian's banter with the Hammersmith audience was a joy, especially the 'Medley' introduction – "Right, this is what you call get your arse up time… and we hope you're gonna get your arses up, 'cos it's been a bit nippy of late." The entrée to 'Angeline' was classic too… "Of course, we weren't always superstars – there was a time when we were just ordinary commoners just like you – and I remember doing some godawful gigs, in some great places, with some great people. The last bit of bad luck, or good luck, we ever had was an album called *Brain Capers*. We'd like to do a number called 'Angeline'." Pre-encore, Ian also thanks Mott's audience saying… "Three things made tonight so enjoyable – David Bowie, Mick Jagger and you. They've just gone – you're still here" – and concludes the night with… "On behalf of me and the firm, thanks for having us – God bless ya!" This was far removed from Bryan Ferry's typically laconic "Hello, we're Roxy Music" – and proof that Hunter was one of rock's natural communicators.

Mott the Hoople Live contained superb versions of 'Rest in Peace' and 'Rose', the former with Morgan's classical piano introduction illustrating once again that the band was capable of sensitivity and dynamics, as well as gut-tearing rock and roll. It was brave to place these mellow cuts on the group's only official live album, in preference to more dramatic numbers such as 'Crash Street Kidds' or 'Marionette'. In America, *Phonograph Record* described *Mott the Hoople Live* as "a scorcher", reviewer Ken Barnes writing: "I can't think of a live album that tops Mott's fifty-minute opus." *The Scene* said: "Ian Hunter dominates the group, his voice and songs being the backbone – Hunter can write some of the best and most simple rock lyrics ever heard." *Hit Parader* described Ian as: "One of the most recognisable rock stars of the decade"... while another reviewer acknowledged: "The medley closing side two is as close to the spirit of Little Richard as anyone could hope to be in 1974."

British press reviews were low-key, however. *NME*'s headline proclaimed 'Whole Lotta Nothin' Goin' On' – while Jethro Tull and Yes fan, Allan Jones, penned a *Melody Maker* feature, 'Uninspired Mott', describing Bender as "the wrong man in the wrong place... frequently blowing number after number... going completely AWOL on 'Walkin' with a Mountain'." Nevertheless, the album entered the UK charts on 23rd November, staying for two weeks reaching No.32. In the US, the LP climbed to No.23 but there was a signal of further fracturing when Columbia Records' press ads proclaimed: "Mott the Hoople Live Featuring Ian Hunter! Mott the Hoople's first live album catches all the electrifying excitement of Mott on stage and puts it together with all the superstar flash of Mott on record. Mott the Hoople Live! A transatlantic triumph! Their finest hour!"

The original *Mott the Hoople Live* LP sat uncomfortably with many fans of the group for a long time. Record company resistance and timing constraints meant that a heavily edited and dual-faceted single album did not work. The track listing was bizarre with only two hit singles, two B-sides and no material whatsoever from *The Hoople* and the album sleeve featured a great back cover shot of the band performing beneath life-sized puppets suspended over the Uris stage, but with no showcase 'Marionette' on the track listing. Roslav Szaybo recalls that Columbia New York designed

462

the *Live* LP cover and album insert, and he was unhappy when his original idea was not employed.

"I had a different concept for the cover of Mott's live album," said Roslav, "and it certainly was not an average stage-shot with a blue-and-white light beam placed across Ian's face! Columbia dropped my idea, changed the cover and came up with the Art Nouveau design for the insert. I didn't like that package particularly."

> **IH:** "Columbia in America did the original budgeting for the live album and for some reason they had the artwork of the props for 'Marionette' on the back of the sleeve, but no 'Marionette' track on the record. You could say it was our fault, but we were running around a lot in those days. By *Mott the Hoople Live*, Buffin and I had grown so far apart that he just did the whole thing. I was also sick of the songs having sung them so many times. I remember some stuff where they had to put on phoney applause because the ambient mikes hadn't kicked in, but the mix was fine as far as I can recall. I also remember in 1990 that a Texan gentleman came up to me in Halmstad, Sweden, and apologised. He said he was the guy who had added the 'canned' applause to *Mott Live*. His name was Joe B. Mauldin – Buddy Holly's original bass player. I told him, 'You don't have to apologise for *anything!*'"

Columbia had refused to countenance a double *Mott the Hoople Live* album and originally wanted a US-only release. A last-ditch attempt to include a ten-inch bonus disc was shelved and a special pressing accommodated nearly fifty-four minutes of material, but the track sequencing did not capture or reflect the shows well. The sacrificial lambs included 'The Golden Age of Rock 'n' Roll' and 'Hymn for the Dudes' and even Bender's guitar showcase was slashed from 'Walkin' with a Mountain'. Thankfully, a 30th Anniversary expanded 2CD set would be released by Sony, rectifying the original omissions and presentation.

As their live album was released, Mott the Hoople blazed across Europe with their new guitar hero and were scheduled to commence British concerts at the Glasgow Apollo on 10th November. Externally, all seemed well, and Mott was embarking on a new and exciting part of their career. Hidden from public view however, personality problems festered and took their toll with the continental live dates becoming the band's irrevocable undoing. The perception later fed to fans was that Mott had broken into two factions – Watts and Griffin plus Fisher, versus Hunter and Ronson – with the two parties often travelling and dining apart, but, by now, even worse, Ian and Dale could hardly bear to look at each other. As internal band gloom descended and deepened on the road, five German gigs were pulled, including the Brienner Theater in Munich where the stage was too small. Richie Anderson remained amused at the usual Hoople howlers, especially another Swiss "cock-up".

"I laughed at the 20th October gig where they gave us the wrong city on the tour schedule. That could have been interesting. How much time would it have taken driving around Switzerland only to find there was no Congress House in Biel – also known as Bienne in the French and German speaking canton of Bern – and then, somehow, finding out that the show was actually in Bern near the border with France."

Phil John remembered Stan Tippins delivering a bombshell in Frankfurt: the rest of Mott's European tour was cancelled, and the entourage was going home. No real reason was given but the future looked shaky. In the end Mott's Heidelberg, Hanover, Rendsburg and Hamburg concerts were scrapped but the group was compelled to play the Paris Olympia and a final gig at Amsterdam's Concertgebouw. Trudi Hunter recalled how the band met formally with Tony Defries in Paris. Fred Heller was unable to attend the meeting and Trudi felt that if Mott's manager had been there, the group could have been saved. Some of the band's perception was that Defries "despised" Mott the Hoople.

IH: "Paris Olympia was the pivotal night when I raved post-gig to Tony that the show had been great, to which Defries sarcastically replied, 'Yes Ian, but it's *always* great.'"

Trudi Hunter has always been resistant to talk about Mott the Hoople publicly, but she described the final dissolution of the band as "a Pandora's box" and stressed it is important to understand that the unravelling of Mott the Hoople was a process of evolution, not revolution.

"The Defries meeting in Paris happened because Fred failed to turn up," says Trudi. "Tony's reply – 'Yes Ian, but it's always great' – was not necessarily sarcastic. Defries didn't hate Mott – he hated the fact that there was no leader. David Bowie advised Ian in December 1972 to take the reins of the group, but the band would not have it. Things were moving too fast and Tony disliked the internal dynamics of the band. Without 'a leader' and one person to deal with, Defries felt Mott was handicapped. When Ian returned from Tony's meeting that night in Paris, he said that Ronson was fed up and he thought Mick was going to leave. At that point, Ian didn't see a future. He had been trying so hard to keep it all together – to keep both camps happy – but it was now doing him in mentally.

"Buffin complained on that tour that 'the Hunters' and 'Ronsons' were eating in hotel restaurants that they couldn't afford, but the band didn't realise we were sitting in, after 'the Ronsons' had finished their breakfast. We were having a cup of tea and perhaps eating left-over toast, not 'joining' Suzi and Mick for breakfast. Ian was also paying more than half his wages in alimony and child support, something they never considered. In my view, the seeds of the petty jealousies and resentments of the rest of the band towards Ian and Mick were sown in the arrangement Tony made with Mott's managers for Ronson's services. The band had wages of only £60 per week. Tony 'magnanimously' offered Mick 'for free'. Mott would only pay Ronson's expenses. Think about that – £60 per week versus all expenses paid – in a very expensive Europe."

It had become clear to Ian that within only six weeks, Mick had already had enough of Mott. Ronson had said that he favoured a collaborative band environment as it made artistic life easier, but he swiftly discovered that life was not easy in Mott the Hoople. Columbia Records grasped at straws and pressed a single, coupling live versions of 'All the Young Dudes' with 'Rose' for a January 1975 release – but the game was up. When Hunter returned to his Paris hotel room after the Olympia gig, he realised that Mott was shot. Moving on for their final European show, Ian tried to rescue the situation, but it was to be a last tango in Amsterdam.

> **IH:** "To try and sort things out, I said to Dale, 'Let's go for a drink,' but he replied, 'Don't tell me what to do' and stormed off. My heart sank into my boots. It was all too much to handle. I just needed support at that time, and I didn't get it. There I was, writing all this stuff, but running out because Ralpher's gone. We'd been running on empty with Luther but then here comes Ronno – lovely guy – lots of problems – but right at the top of his game. So, the music's going to be great again and then more problems come from the side that I never expected. Mick could have saved Mott but for one reason or another it was gone."

On 5th November, Mick Ronson appeared in a pre-recorded BBC TV interview on *The Old Grey Whistle Test*. Every inch the rock star with shorter hair and dressed in a zebra-striped shirt, black leather pants and sporting a huge gold buckle belt, Mick talked calmly to host Bob Harris about Bowie, solo records and Mott, explaining the future with his new band mates. Hidden behind the scenes, Mott the Hoople was finished, but Ronson appeared cool on the *Whistle Test* and seemed focused about recording the group's next album. The working title for the LP was *Showtime* and January sessions were booked at AIR Studios, even though Ian was short of new material.

IH: "I hadn't mapped out the follow-up album to *The Hoople* much, to the best of my recollection, apart from 'Lounge Lizard' there was nothing. A song called 'Henry and the H-Bomb' had been around for a while, but I could never get the lyrics."

Mick Ronson would later confess that his short Hoople tenure turned out to be an unhappy period, but he gallantly accepted some of the blame. "I enjoyed the idea of joining Mott," he said. "I thought it was all going to happen, but I was surprised after being with Mott the Hoople for a month. I was getting disgusted by the behaviour of the band. We played together on stage but off stage everyone was on his own. As soon as we started playing gigs, I knew what was going on and it was ridiculous. It was Ian that I did it for, but I got disillusioned real fast, which was partly my fault I suppose. It just didn't gel."

After their Amsterdam gig on 3rd November, Mott the Hoople's British tour was scheduled to commence a week later in Glasgow. 'Saturday Gigs' was peaking at No.41 in the charts and in the week before the UK gigs, Ian made a short visit to America. Suddenly, there were reports via Mott's publicist that Hunter had collapsed whilst staying at Fred Heller's home. Ian had been taken to nearby Morristown Memorial Hospital in Morris County where he was diagnosed as suffering from physical exhaustion and was kept under sedation and detained for five days complete rest. Then, suddenly, *NME*'s front-page read, 'MOTT SHOCK: Ian Hunter hospitalized in US; tour re-scheduled.'

Despite Hunter's olive branch in Amsterdam, Griffin was unhappy about Mott's European tour and Ian's American trip. Questions would be asked by the drummer as to why Hunter as group leader "never pulled the band together" and why he went to the USA when the start of a major UK tour was imminent. Dale later said he remained convinced that Ian had "harboured solo aspirations" for a long time.

With Ian hospitalised, the first four dates of Mott's tour were re-planned for late December. The opening show became Leeds on 15th November with the concerts in Scotland moved to the end of the schedule, but the British gigs were never played. One week after Ian's collapse, Bob Hirschman confirmed that the entire tour was cancelled because Hunter had not recovered as quickly as expected. It was hoped that the live dates would be re-scheduled while Mott's plans for recording a new studio album in January were unaffected. *Record & Popswop Mirror* wrote: 'IAN BOMBS MOTT DATES: Is he cracking up?' – sources saying that the band had sold over 50,000 tickets for their British tour and that they expected to lose a five-figure sum from its postponement. Speculation then grew, that Ian's illness may lead to Mott splitting with the next album recorded using a changed line-up. While Fred Heller was reportedly talking "cooperatively" with Tony Defries, Tippins was despatched to America to talk to Hunter.

"We'd had a call from Heller to Hirschman that Ian was in a collapsed state in New York having suffered a breakdown," recalls Stan. "So, Bob Hirschman sent me over to see if I could retrieve the situation, but when I got there, I couldn't do much about it. Ian was adamant that he had left the band. I tried to coax him back, but it was no good. In fact, I don't think there was much to be said. When I was going over, I thought I was going to say a lot more, but when I got there it was a complete waste of time saying anything. So that basically was the end of it. I think Heller had it in his mind that he would have Ian as a solo artist or as a duo with Mick. When we got Ronson in, Buffin and Pete seemed uneasy almost from day one. Buff always sensed 'happenings' and became a bit upset, but the band was already drifting apart. Ian got worried, then nervous, depressed and finally stressed, although there's a difference between a breakdown in a hospital and being at the end of your tether."

"I remember learning of Ian's breakdown in the US," says Bob Hirschman. "I was worried, and I was concerned, so Tippins was sent over to see Hunter. Stan was a great person. How he coped with the characters in Mott and facilitated those guys was amazing.

I take my hat off to him, but he could not convince Ian at the end. The response to Mick joining Mott by the other band members had been predictable, as someone else had come in and taken a second spotlight alongside Ian. Hunter welcomed having Ronson and knew how to handle it, but from Griffin's point of view, sitting behind that frontline, I can see why he became annoyed. You have these huge egos squeezed into a room for recording and then they're on stage every night performing. I think Pete Watts understood his role, strengths and weaknesses, and he handled it pretty well. Dale was fine in my dealings with him as a person, but the Ronson situation upset him. I guess I could see his point of view. I do have a recollection of the 'Buffin outburst' at *Top of the Pops* after the 'Saturday Gigs' filming. The writing was on the wall then I guess although the biggest disaster for Mott the Hoople, in my opinion, was Ralphs' departure. The band descended after that and, in some cases, I'm not sure that they made good choices. Ian was the heart and soul of the group, but Mick was a wonderful player – terrific in every way – and I say that as a schooled musician."

IH: "Ronson joining Mott the Hoople became the final nail in the coffin and it shouldn't have been that way. Mick joined only six weeks before the band's demise and it had a lot to do with our downfall. It was a real shame because Ronson could have revived Mott and bridged the gap, but he was never given a chance. Through 1974 I'd been doing all the interviews and writing all the songs, and I was getting a real snidey attitude in return. I think I finally realised that my days with Mott were over and the thought of that did me in. When Tippins flew over to see me I said to him, 'We're done Stan' and he agreed; that made me feel better because I really thought I was going mental. 'Saturday Gigs' had slipped from No.41 to No.46 after only two weeks on the chart, so we both knew it was over. In those days missing the Top Forty meant you were finished. Sabbaticals and breathers hadn't been invented in 1974 – bands simply broke up. The

Ronson episode was illogical and we blew the shot that we had. I felt really bad about dropping the other members in the shit, but I knew I couldn't play with them anymore. It was irrevocable, and it was horrible getting on the phone and saying, 'Look, I just can't do it anymore.' I got real sick with it and that was that. At times though, I felt that I didn't leave Mott the Hoople – I was forced out."

Ronson also flew to New York to visit Hunter while he was ill and on 23rd November one British headline read: 'Mott Split? Run its course with Hunter'. Based on London sources, the article stated that the band may quit after American dates, a final studio album and a farewell UK tour. Hunter then arrived back in Britain earlier than expected to record a solo LP, assisted by Ronson as co-producer. The duo hoped to complete Ian's tracks before starting work on a new Mott the Hoople album. Ian and Mick would use Mott's January recording time booked at AIR Studios, but this scenario simply increased the mounting speculation. Official sources repeatedly refuted any Mott break-up, but the truth was, Ian had already quit the band.

Finally, Mott's fans received the confirmation that they were dreading with the headline: 'HUNTER RONSON SPLIT HOOPLE'. Ian and Mick had broken away from the group, Hunter would pursue a solo career for recording and live work with Ronson as his second-in-command and the pair planned to form a new band. All forty dates booked for Mott the Hoople's 1975 US tour, including Madison Square Garden were cancelled and Ian intended to move to America for a year. There were press suggestions that Hunter was offered a reported 750,000 dollars solo deal from CBS, but the claim was hotly refuted.

IH: "I could have sued over that. Put simply, Mott was just getting negative and I didn't want to go on unless it was positive. After five years I'd just had enough. Mott had gone as far as it could."

470

"At the time of the Mott break-up I was finishing putting tour dates together in twenty thousand seat venues, including Madison Square Garden." says Fred Heller. "Hunter had his nervous breakdown, which I think he could have dealt with. There were legal implications and I well remember having a conversation with Ian that Mott's US tour was not going to start for weeks, and that it would set him and his band mates up financially for a long time. The rest of Mott never accepted or liked Ronson, no matter what they said. I also think Hunter was a bit insecure and self-conscious about how he was perceived as a performer with Mott the Hoople. As a songwriter I believe Ian was passionate and honest. I also believe *Mott* and *The Hoople* were two under-rated albums of truly great songs."

Bill Henderson wrote an excellent Mott the Hoople valediction in *Sounds* expressing the view that even before Mick Ralphs had left, Ian was Mott the Hoople. "Mott without Hunter – is the Stones without Jagger – The Who without Townshend," said Henderson. "For Hunter, it was obviously the end of the line within the group." Reported rows between Hunter and Griffin over production of *The Hoople* and *Mott the Hoople Live*, and suggestions that Dale disliked Ian's writing on 'Marionette' and 'Trudi's Song' were refuted. Tensions *had* increased between the pair however, and Ian gave little input to the production of the live album. On tour, Ronson and Mott's rhythm section hardly spoke, and it was claimed that Hunter had become so stressed with the atmosphere on one European gig that he threatened to fire the band's trusty roadies.

Mott the Hoople had long suffered from internal trauma and Hunter and Griffin had often not seen eye to eye. The animosity between them had grown stronger over the years and, tired of the tension, at one point, following a few drinks one evening, Ian had approached Roxy Music drummer, "The Great Paul Thompson", in London's Marquee to ask if he would be interested in joining Mott. Paul was a powerful player with a precise but liquid feel, so good that in 1983 he would audition with AC/DC in New York and almost joined the band. Hunter recalls that Thompson was very discreet regarding his Hoople enquiry, saying that he was happy in Roxy and that Bryan Ferry had told him he would always look after him.

As Mott's split was confirmed, their management told the US press that "the whole show" had been on Ian's shoulders in Mott the Hoople and that touring Europe using unprofessional promoters was "the pits". Fred Heller also observed that the band's reputation had trapped Hunter into writing 'Sucker' and 'Jerkin' Crocus' whereas he preferred sensitive numbers like 'Rose' and 'Rest in Peace' which were often overlooked. 'One of the Boys', 'Violence' and 'Crash Street Kids' had strengthened Mott's feral aura but Fred felt the aggression had started to destroy the band's creative force. A frenetic Hoople had become Ian's monster and it had taken him eighteen months longer than Mick Ralphs to reach the same sense of disillusionment. Luther Grosvenor was unsurprised when he heard of the group's demise so soon after his departure, saying that he believed when Ronson joined, "Mott was already split in half."

Dan Loggins reflected that Mott the Hoople had started to wane and considered that while 'Foxy, Foxy' and 'Saturday Gigs' (which were not issued as US singles by Columbia) remained melodic and "hooky", they were anti-climactic after *Mott*. 'All the Way from Memphis' and 'Roll Away the Stone' had been Hunter's templates to success in Britain and America but some of the press were no longer convinced. "I think Robert Christgau, rock critic and an early champion of Mott in the States felt that with 'Saturday Gigs', Ian was re-writing the band's history again," says Loggins. "To Robert, the last chapter had already been written."

> **IH:** "Robert Christgau was America's foremost music critic and almost defined the genre. Christgau had some interesting angles on Mott the Hoople, placing us in what he called 'art rock'. He could be a harsh critic and we weren't spared at times, but his observations regarding art rock were right on the money and you can tell that he 'got' us – despite apparently falling asleep during one of our gigs!"

Hunter knew that something crucial had been lost with Ralphs' departure and he had seemed intent on parking Mott the Hoople beneath the nostalgic tone and reflections expressed in 'Saturday Gigs'. Then, suddenly, Ronson brought a wave of renewed hope – but the five-year "snakes and ladders" slog had drained Ian and with more internal back-biting Hunter *was* "done". Fred Heller claimed that the split from Mott became inevitable. Now the uncertainty was gone and even the pleadings of Guy Stevens at the Hunters' home could not change the singer's mind. Ian had carried the weight of the group, its direction and creative blood for too long and, after two "less successful" Mott singles, Hunter felt he had exhausted any musical possibilities that remained.

> **IH:** "Guy sat in my Wembley flat and pleaded with me to take the name Mott the Hoople, but I couldn't do that, as I felt it would put the other guys out of business. Guy also told me to fire Buff, but I couldn't do that either as I felt we were on equal standing. I still think I could have pulled it off with Dale's cooperation. It was the negativity that finished me off and put me over the edge. I knew that Ronson could contribute and, to me, that was all that mattered. There had to be that guitarist there to fight me. That's how it worked with Ralpher, and Ronson was the only one out there that I knew could do it."

Just like their Island swansong, Mott was burned out from relentless live work and more internal tensions had foamed and fermented in Europe. As Free's vocalist, Paul Rodgers once noted, songwriting is the lifeblood of any band and Mott's creative flow had become Ian's responsibility and pressure. The rhythm section had been reluctant to bend and soon bristled at any musical or tactical suggestions from Ronson. The cocktail was further complicated by Tony Defries and MainMan who looked after Mick, while Heller represented a band where he really rated the frontman more than the other players.

IH: "After *Mott* I had to write the whole *Hoople* album. I did all the press and we seemed to play six gigs a week. A democratic business is fine, if you've got five genuine democrats, but if you've got two closet fascists in there, which most bands have, it's tough. Ronson joined and with all the distress on top of my stress, I ended up with nervous exhaustion. You get different stories from Mott members about the Mott split, but when Ronson joined it was difficult. He had a different manager. He had a different label. But Ronno came into Mott with a great attitude. He wanted to show Bowie that he could do it somewhere else, so bad. The rest of the band just looked at him as if he was taking over but if they'd gone for it, it would have been huge, because I saw Mick on fire. The band just didn't take to him and I could not understand that. To me it was music and Mick was great. I think from the outset he said, 'Let's rehearse – *now!*' So, I rang the group and they were too busy. That's not a good thing to lay on a guy who's just at the beginning with a new band. That's my version of what happened. Talk to somebody else and you'll probably get a different view. It was very difficult after Ralphs joined Bad Company as it was hard to tour constantly – and write songs, and singles, and albums of real quality every year. I think the whole band was half-dead and tired from touring, so when Ronno joined tempers were maybe a bit frayed and petty inter-sniping ruined it. I don't think it was anyone's fault. It was just five years of continual hard work and it didn't work out, but I found the Ronson rejection so stupid."

The Sea Divers' last gesture was to sell off a newly arrrived stock of freshly printed programmes for Mott's cancelled British tour to fan club members, the artefacts becoming a coveted rarity. Bob Hirschman was credited erroneously with the startling colourful shot that graced the front of Mott's collectable programme, but he does not remember *anything* about the photograph.

The break-up date for Mott the Hoople was claimed to be 16th December 1974, but Dale Griffin recalled that Hunter telephoned him on 12th December to tell him that he had left the group. For years the "Hunter split" and "Ronson dilemma" would be aired by Griffin. He stated that the intent had been to make Mott an equal-shares five-man outfit again, but the band learned Ronson was not receiving his "Hoople wage". The group discussed this at Mick's MainMan apartment near The Royal Albert Hall and Griffin claimed that Ronson seemed startled at the suggestion he should be paid Mott money. It was left that Mick would sort things out with Stan Tippins, but Ronson never took any wages.

"When I went to Ronno's flat the atmosphere was horrible," said Pete Watts. "It was full of obvious Bowie hangers-on just helping themselves to everything. I felt very uncomfortable and didn't like it at all. I remember Mick wandering into the kitchen and he was very friendly saying, 'Help yourself Pete. There's champagne there, vodka, whatever you want. I'll make you a special milk shake if you like.' I'd have preferred a nice cup of slop."

"After the difficulties with Bender, we desperately wanted a guitarist who could be part of the group and contribute musically," Griffin would say. "Ronson seemed perfect. The reality was a nightmare. Everyone who knew him or worked with him says what a good, kind guy Ronson was. Inexplicably, this was not our experience. We wanted Mott to survive for as long as possible. In retrospect, the strange thing is that our management and record label showed no real wish to continue Mott the Hoople. All of them, including Stan, seemed to enter a period of slumber."

Watts believed Hunter had simply had enough of Mott the Hoople although he described Ian as "coherent" when he phoned him from America.

"Ian was getting on with Mick, but it wasn't happening as a group. The last few tracks we'd done hadn't been very big hits and I think Hunter felt that he might be losing it writing-wise. The management was all to cock and we never really felt convinced about Heller or Hirschman. America was another thing that caused the split really; Ian wanted to go, Dale would probably have gone, and I just never liked the idea of it. Also, we never had any real money in Mott the Hoople. When I got my Bentley, I nearly had to strangle Bob Hirschman to get the money to buy it. We were an image band, but clothes came out of our wages. I was buying leather suits at seventy-five pounds each and yet our top wage was seventy-five pounds a week at the height of our fame. I used to bring back the guitars I bought in the States and sell them to supplement my income. This was in a group, who'd had hit records, was nationally known, had adverts on the sides of buses driving round London, *Top of the Pops* – the lot. I once saw a documentary on Sweet and they had Rolls-Royces and were saying they had so much money they didn't know what to do. We had so *little* money we didn't know what to do.

"When Mott split, I was in a twenty-pounds-a-week flat in Ealing and when the roadies came around with my gear I didn't know where to put it. Phil and Richie turned up with a big van and said, 'Well, there's your stage clothes – there's your amps.' They had a wardrobe trunk full of silver hair spray and crab cream and that's when it really came home to me it was the end. I had to take all my stuff up a flight of stairs to this little flat and it was a horrible feeling – one of the worst days of my life. I always felt I was a mug in Mott the Hoople. You signed anything that was put in front of you. You then discovered that record deals were terrible – and then we found out years later that Mott was actually signed to Guy Stevens! We seemed to be a non-profit-making concern. I was glad I was in Mott the Hoople and did it – but I'm bloody glad I got out of it too. We were never afraid to try things and go in different directions, and I always felt that we only scraped the surface. We were dynamite live, and I don't know how we got to be in that position. It was very difficult after *The Hoople* but some of our work I thought was great – like 'The Saturday Gigs' and 'Waterlow' – and it was fantastic when people said *Brain Capers* was so influential."

After the split, Ian admitted that during Mott's final weeks he thought Ronson was seeking an exit route almost as soon as he joined when, in fact, Mick just wanted to record any album with Ian. On his visit to the US, Ian realised that he loathed aspects of the group so much. He had dropped "hints" to Pete and Dale that the band could not go on for ever, but they didn't register.

> **IH:** "I would have been there for Watts at any time, but Buff often got nervous and was upsetting me to the point that I got into a worse state than him. Frankly, it reached the stage, personality-wise, where I just couldn't take anymore in Mott the Hoople. I was supposed to write the songs and keep these people together, but it was fucking impossible. The whole Mott-Ronson thing was illogical and annoyed me. There was all manner of personal bullshit between band members and I can see both sides of it now, but at the time you're in this little goldfish bowl and everything is exaggerated. You feel so important. Everything's a mountain instead of a molehill and none of us were university educated so we didn't stand back. Mott the Hoople was this dark cloud that would not go away."

"I think when Bender left a lot of the spirit went out of the band because he was an incredible catalyst," says Morgan Fisher. "When Mick Ronson joined, Mott was set to become even more amazing and it was incredible for me, as I was a huge fan. Ronno was really good on stage and we were quite willing to go his way, changing our wardrobe and hairstyles as soon as he joined. The problem was we didn't have enough time to play together as it all happened so suddenly. I got on well with Mick, and certainly better than Pete and Buff because I was interested in new musical experiences and Ronson could provide that. It was mostly me that had the task of teaching him the Mott repertoire and I visited his flat a few times. Ian and Mick were close, and with Pete and Buff on 'the other side', I could see a distinct rift developing as we toured. Unfortunately, we only did one single and then it was all over. It was a stunning shock when it all came crashing down. There was no discussion before or after the split. It was a *fait accompli* and the timing couldn't have been worse. If it had happened six months later, we would all have been in a much better position, including Ian, so that's how strongly he felt about it."

Dale Griffin once opined that other events and external influences had impacted on Mott the Hoople including, "wives, girlfriends, families, friends, managers and record company people". He described the 1974 European tour as "divisive" and "hateful", perceiving that he and Watts had almost become a backing band whereas Mott had been a team of five people. Ian was acutely disappointed that the Mott-Ronson collaboration had failed amidst such petty perceptions.

> **IH:** "Mick was 110 per cent for Mott but his presence had a real effect on Pete and Buff and that pissed me off because I thought Ronson was the only guy that could save us. I knew we had to make concessions with RCA and Defries but, I think they thought I was on Mick's side, whereas I began to feel like the failed bridge. Mick had good ideas but some of the band just looked at him with suspicion. Ronson had only been in Mott a few weeks and came to me and said, 'What do I need this for?' I was doing all the press, all the writing, had a handle on what Mott was and I understood the press, but by the end of the European tour I was gone. I remember sitting with Charles Shaar Murray and I looked down and my hands were really shaking. It was horrible, but I never blamed anybody. The band was over. We'd hit the brick wall, creatively. There was too much aggravation and my nerves were shot. With Mott the Hoople I wound up a wreck, and rock 'n' roll's not much good to you when you're lying on your back in hospital!"

After Mott the Hoople's break-up, Watts and Weaver set out to write some songs, but Blue accepted an offer to play with The Bee Gees in America. Morgan, meanwhile, scored music for an exhibition at

London's ICA, then Fisher, Watts and Griffin worked together. "We used to go around to Pete's rambling house which was a great place to visit because it was full of pinball machines and juke boxes," recalled Morgan. "It became our pre-rehearsal, rehearsal room. Pete had this horrendously out of tune piano and Buffin would use cardboard boxes as drums, which sounded really good."

At Gooseberry Sound in London's Gerrard Street, the trio demoed songs and when CBS retained commitment to a new band, they decided to stay together in a reshaped line-up and search for a vocalist and guitarist. Nils Lofgren, Zal Cleminson and John Miles were considered while CBS proposed Russ Ballard of Argent. Ballard possessed formidable songwriting talent, but Griffin pointed out their eagerness to remain distant from "dark sunglasses" and "any Ian Hunter comparisons." Russ admitted in 2012 that he never knew CBS might be interested in him joining Mott and, in the end, Watts picked former Hackensack guitarist Ray Smith. Fisher termed Smith "a cool dude" and a great band member who was a joy to work with. Ray changed his surname to Major after Watts' suggestions for a new identity – Jesus Smythe Briggs, The Pink Punk or Damage Massacre – were not accepted!

The options for a lead vocalist were simple; recruit a singer that was a facsimile of Ian Hunter or take a 180-degree turn. Watts ambitiously wanted Stevie Wright from The Easybeats, there were flirtations with John Otway and John Butler, and CBS favoured Terry Wilson-Slesser who joined former Free guitarist Paul Kossoff in Back Street Crawler instead. Mick Ralphs proposed Nigel Benjamin who had sung with Grot, Fancy, The Billion Dollar Band and Royce, and Watts described Nigel's voice as incredible. Benjamin was no counterfeit Hunter, so he was "in". The new band would be radically different, Pete Watts devising various names including The Hooples, Shane Cleaven and the Clean Shaven, Twentieth Fontury Sex, Broadside Outcasts, Dignose & Dognose and Cunning Stunts. Finally deciding to keep some vestige of their past, they became 'Mott' and Fred Heller adopted a dual role as manager for Ian Hunter as well as the new group.

479

"Mott without Ian became more rewarding for us, because we all had a chance to pitch in," says Fisher. "Ian was a man with a message, and we liked the way he wrote musically, but he would never discuss or explain his lyrics and we never really asked him. It happens with a lot of bands. Ian used to play us a new song, even with scat singing if he hadn't finished the lyrics and it was inspiring to see him do that. When we wrote in the new Mott it was more like a musician's approach, looking for riffs and chords before melody and lyrics. Mott was more music-based and less vocal-orientated, but Hunter was a better songwriter all round."

Mott's first album, *Drive On*, named after a band catchphrase, was released in September 1975 and featured eleven tracks. Against Mott's wishes, CBS lifted three singles from the LP, but some press reviews opined that a once-great group had been reduced to a standard hard-rock outfit. Mott was criticised for "crudity" and "sappiness", exhibited in the lyrical banality of 'She Does It' and 'Love Now'. 'By Tonight' and 'Stiff Upper Lip' were real highlights but, even after several re-issues, critics were never sold on the post-Hoople band or their output. Classic Rock wrote of *Drive On* in 2018: "Mott the Hoople without Ian Hunter (or Ronson, or Ralphs, or even Bender). Houston, we have a problem. Perky Watts songs, but it still sounds like a shrill Heavy Metal Kids demo."

'I Can Show You How It Is' and 'Shout It All Out' by the re-vamped Mott were "pointed lyrically" at Hunter by Watts and Griffin, but Pete expressed unhappiness about songwriting describing his inspiration as desperation: "Somebody had to write, and I was landed with it after Ian left. I was composing half-songs that were half-good, because I didn't know about choruses and wasn't writing about incidents directly; they were more general and imaginary. It was horrible writing, but it was good fun recording *Drive On*, shaking off the burden of Mott the Hoople and all the saxes, and girl singers and orchestras."

Following the release of *Drive On*, Mott toured Britain to a good reception, played forty American gigs and sales of their LP exceeded 120,000 copies in the US. Ray Major got to know his new

Mott colleagues and liked them as personalities. "Pete wasn't that serious about the business. He told me once he'd only ever been in music for birds and money. I'd never been in America and was out of sorts with the time change but all Pete could think about was hitting the town and 'raging'. Dale on the other hand was serious. He wanted to get it right and sometimes it wasn't right, and we fell out a few times. I saw Ian Hunter again and met Mick Ronson for the first time in New York on the *Drive On* tour. They were gentlemen. I went to pick up this message at the hotel desk and Ronson was there and said, 'Hello, how are you doing? Are you playing with Mott and is this your first time in the States? You'll love it. It's great. They're alright. They're good guys.' And yet there was all that crap about Mick, and Pete and Buff, calling his album *Worry, Don't Play*. I told them I wasn't into that and they should have got it all out in the open and sorted things out with Ronson."

Richie Anderson and Phil John stayed with Mott initially but switched to working with Ian Hunter. The crew saw that Ray was a fine guitarist but felt Nigel's vocals were too far removed from the Hunter heritage. A further American tour was planned so by February 1976, Mott was camped at Manor Studios in Oxfordshire to commence work on their second LP, *Shouting and Pointing*. The title was inspired by an Oliver Reed interview where he claimed he disciplined his sons with "a lot of shouting and pointing" – Watts' working title had been *The Side of a Wedding in Germany! Shouting and Pointing* was released in June and the tracks 'Collision Course', 'Storm', 'See You Again' and 'Broadside Outcasts' were sublime. No singles were lifted to promote the LP and Griffin suspected that CBS had already lost interest in the band. The label did spend money though, for Roslav Szaybo to direct a brilliant cover featuring a "rock 'n' roll battlefield" with Mott marauding over scattered music bric-a-brac including amps, instruments, tapes and records. The sleeve was shot by Gered Mankowitz who had photographed Hendrix and the Stones.

"Roslav had the original idea that we would create a stylised First World War landscape for *Shouting and Pointing* using rock 'n' roll memorabilia, and my role was to bring that to life," says Gered. "CBS procured hundreds of reels of old tape and musical debris, and even hired and borrowed broken instruments, including some of Mott's. We shot photos in my Great Windmill Street studio, on the third floor. It was a pain to lug all the gear upstairs, but Mott's roadies were great. The room full of all this stuff dominated the studio for three days. For the setting I created smoke and a reddish sky with paper and lights, then Mott came up in their stage gear and Morgan Fisher's Kitchener-style uniform made him particularly appropriate to the theme. The band was great at screaming – and shouting and pointing."

Mott only played three British gigs to promote *Shouting and Pointing* and toured America for a further three months. Despite enmity conveyed in the press, the band included 'Violence' and Hunter's 'All the Way from Memphis' in their live set, plus an excellent version of The Doors' 'Love Me Two Times'. *Drive On* had hit No.45 in Britain and made the US charts, but none of Mott's other records charted. In 1975, had Watts, Griffin and Fisher opted for an entirely new "brand", the outcome may have been different. Attempted continuity by name, inevitably led to Hoople-Hunter comparisons and it was unfortunate because Nigel was not Ian, nor did he try to be. Mott was Not the Hoople and whilst it should never have been judged as such, it was.

Following two commercially unsuccessful albums and three stiffed singles, CBS was edgy, and the band now considered that Benjamin's vocals and direction were not suited to Mott. They taped a new single at Pye Studios, but the cut was canned. "On 8th September 1976 we recorded 'Get Rich Quick'," recalled Griffin, "and Nicky Graham, A&R Executive of Columbia, enthusiastically said, 'It's Top Ten!' On 9th September we were dropped!"

Mott was committed to play a twenty-six date UK tour and taped a BBC Radio 1 *In Concert* session, but amid more wrangling, a secret rehearsal was held aimed at introducing former Hoople fan, Kelvin Blacklock, as lead singer. Griffin was later disparaging about Blacklock while Benjamin subsequently said that he couldn't wait to tell CBS he had left Mott. Nigel bristled over the contention that track selections for the two albums were based on who wrote material, rather than great songs. Benjamin likened himself to a low-paid, hired hand and Major admitted there was "friction and sarcasm" within the group. "Part of the problem with Mott not taking off, was that the name was more charismatic than the band, apart from when Ian Hunter was in the group," says Ray. "A Mott without Ian Hunter never had much chance."

"Mott didn't really work out," says Morgan Fisher. "None of us were great songwriters and Nigel never felt comfortable and we never really gave him a chance to do what he wanted. Well, we gave him chances, then flattened him when he came up with something, because we couldn't get into what he was doing. After a lot of touring, Mott was encouraged by Columbia to record a second album. We complained that we needed more time to write but were forced to do *Shouting and Pointing* in a rush. It didn't sell enough so CBS said, 'We don't need any more albums. Goodbye.'"

Dropped in March 1977 Mott collaborated with Steve Hyams, who had befriended Mott the Hoople in their early years. Hyams came from a well-to-do family with a boarding school background and had been a close friend of Watts' when he moved to London. Hyams, who had cut an unreleased album, *Mistaken Identities*, was an interesting writer and singer and he agreed to help the fractured Mott.

"After Nigel Benjamin left Mott, Pete said, 'Look Steve, we're getting all these tapes from different people and none are better than yours. Do you want to come and have a go with us?' So, I went to Pete's house and Mott were demoralised by this time. Mick Ralphs had gone, Ian had gone, the deal with CBS was up and the punk thing was happening. Nobody had any money, so I asked a contact if he could get me some studio time through Arista Records."

Mott and Hyams recorded five tracks at The Argonaut, Richard Branson's floating barge studio on Regents Park canal near Maida Vale. The demos were crying out for good production and Watts,

ROCK 'N' ROLL SWEEPSTAKES

Griffin and Fisher played tapes over tea at The Dorchester Hotel to an impassive and "matter-of-fact" Frank Zappa, but the legendary American was more eager to return home than produce Mott, according to Dale. The "new" Mott held "a press showcase" at The Rainbow as Mott the Hoople but failed to impress journalists and Arista was not interested in the demos. Griffin blamed Hyams for The Rainbow "debacle" and said he would never work with him again. In 1993, a six-track CD, *Mott the Hoople featuring Steve Hyams* was released, against Watts' wishes and much to Griffin's rage. He described the CD as a "rag bag collection of hurried demos" and "the darkest, most shameful episode in Mott's history". Steve Hyams went on to issue a fine solo album, 1997's *Feather and a Tomahawk*.

Mott decided to re-group again and having collaborated with Medicine Head, Fisher proposed the band's affable writer, guitarist and vocalist John Fiddler as their next frontman. Fiddler had penned several great songs including 'Pictures in the Sky' and 'Rising Sun' and he knew Watts and Griffin from earlier support slots with Mott the Hoople.

"I helped recruit John Fiddler as we were a band with no singer and he was a singer with no band," says Morgan. "I'd known John for years and adored him and Medicine Head. He invited me to play their farewell tour and when the time came to replace Nigel, John was the glaringly obvious choice. The guys in Mott respected Fiddler but John demanded a new identity. He didn't want to be just another frontman for just another incarnation of Mott. We would be playing some of his songs and it needed to be a new band. We agreed."

"One night I invited Morgan round to dinner," says Fiddler, "and the phone kept ringing for him, and it was Pete Watts saying, 'Have you asked him yet? Have you asked him?' So, Morgan asked what I thought about going down to their rehearsals which I did, and it was good. I hadn't been thinking about what I was going to do at all. Suddenly, there was this great rock 'n' roll band around me, with guitars and basses and lots of noise."

Watts devised another plethora of "new" names for the "new" group including The Huge Terappins, Bex Bissell, Gretna Brown, Elegant Mess, Safety Last, Public Enemy No.1, British Lay Land and Brain Haulage (the latter a throwback to Mott the Hoople days). He even suggested Mott the Lion to try and connect with the former group and reinforce their pedigree. Shelving the briefly-adopted Big Ben, the band was launched as British Lions. John Fiddler loved rugby but hated British Lions and preferred Watts' bastardisation, Burtish Loins, however it was perceived that the "Brit" moniker might attract American audiences. Fiddler thought that the band was exciting although their timing was wrong, but he embraced the new spirit at the time, shaving off his moustache and sporting much shorter hair.

Represented by Status Quo manager Colin Johnson, British Lions signed to Vertigo Records in the UK and RSO for America, releasing their eponymous debut in February 1978. Recorded at The Manor in only two weeks, the nine-track LP featured two singles, 'One More Chance to Run' and 'International Heroes'. The album hit the US Top 50 as the Lions toured the USA and John Peel championed the group with a three-song BBC radio session, but Griffin thought Peel didn't like British Lions and only felt loyalty towards Fiddler from his Medicine Head days. Fisher tried to get Mott to think more "new wave", as he admired the punk music scene that had ignited in Britain.

"I thought it was good to start afresh and British Lions expressed our Englishness and was cool. Unfortunately, we chose a name that John didn't like at all, mainly to try and catch the US market. Fiddler had good songs and the first album was easy to make but punk was happening, so we were considered 'old farts' in Britain by this time. We aimed for America but touring and promotion didn't happen, perhaps because Quo never made it in the States with Colin. I was totally fascinated and thrilled by the amateur nature of the punk phenomenon though. I often went to The Roxy club in London, still sporting my handlebar moustache, trilby hat and raincoat, while mayhem and 'gobbing' went on all around me."

A second "difficult-to-do" Lions album was recorded in late 1978 at Mickie Most's RAK Studios, Watts describing the process as absolute hell. "We had no money and we hadn't got a lot of material," said Pete. "Three of us were having personal problems with our ladies, which is why it's called *Trouble with Women*. Ray had hepatitis and Morgan was playing on other people's albums. Some days at RAK, there was just one of us turning up and working on the tracks. It was no kind of atmosphere to be productive."

Having cut *Trouble with Women*, RSO Records asked for some songs to be changed for the US market, but eventually passed on their option to release the LP. The rejection was mirrored by Phonogram in the UK. Two major British treks supporting Status Quo and AC/DC had not helped the Lions' cause and, amidst arguments over group policy, they disbanded. Fisher recalls the demise as one of the most depressing times in his career while Griffin was critical of Colin Johnson and the group's management. Tippins went on to "tour-manage" The Pretenders, Lou Reed, Simple Minds, Adam and the Ants, Sade, Transvision Vamp, King Crimson and Paul Young, but he loved Mott the Hoople and recalled the end of Mott and British Lions with sadness.

"I remember being in the office, which we ran from Pete's house in Acton, and after all those years of Mott the Hoople, Mott and The Lions, the phone stopped ringing – no record companies – no agents – no label – nothing. I just sat in this office thinking, 'This is the end. I'm the last one left!'"

> **IH:** "Stan was 'the bee's knees' of tour management. There was nobody better. He was an amazing guy who liked to mess things up. If it was all running smoothly, he'd go out of his way to create havoc and that was a great attribute to have as the road does get boring. Stan would find things to do that you couldn't imagine because he thinks differently. He's a legend but, sadly, he stopped tour-managing, preferring life in the country and all that it entails. I've always been a Stan Tippins fan."

The Lions' tapes lay in Phonogram's archive until Cherry Red Records, led by Iain McNay, released *Trouble with Women* in 1980. The songs 'High Noon,' 'Lady Don't Fall Backwards' and 'Any Port in a Storm' were particularly strong and the earlier rejection by RSO and Vertigo was puzzling.

"British Lions was potentially great," said Watts, "and Fiddler was good, but it was a bad time to start during punk. Our management wasn't right, and the band members wanted to go in different directions. We did all these horrible clubs to get tight and it was fun. After that we had a meeting with Colin Johnson to decide what we were going to do. The first thing he said was that Phonogram liked the second album but there were four tracks they wanted us to leave off, so, I got up and said, 'Well fuck 'em. We're not doing any more.' Then Colin said, 'I've got a gig list prepared. We're going to go back to P.J.'s Club, in Harrogate to do that again… you went down very well there… then we're going to go back to that little club in Plymouth.' And me and Buffin said, 'Oh no… no we're not… we are *NOT!*' I came out of that meeting knowing things were not looking good and then we met our accountant who revealed my tax liability. I had nothing. As we left the building, Colin Johnson was falling about laughing, saying, 'I can't believe it. How the hell did you get yourselves in that position?' I recall walking down the street thinking, I've done this for fifteen years and I owe the taxman fifteen thousand quid. I'd been a mug to the music industry long enough. I felt out of control because I didn't really know what was going on with the business side of things or money, so, I packed it in."

Hunter recalls that Tippins and Griffin contacted him after the demise of British Lions. Roxy Music, who Ian admired, had re-formed in 1979 to record and promote a great new album, *Manifesto*, but he knew for sure that he would not go back to working with Mott anymore. "I like all of the boys very much, but I'd rather keep Mott the Hoople as a souvenir," said Hunter at the time. "A re-union would mean nothing. Roxy was a good example of that, in my opinion."

Post-Lions, Fisher pursued a fascinating solo career; he recorded diverse albums, including *Hybrid Kids* and *Miniatures*, joined Queen for their 1982 tour and moved permanently to Japan in 1985. Mott always remained closer to his heart than Queen or the Love Affair. The band had been complicated and intense for Fisher, who worked hard to the extent he almost collapsed – just like Ian had done in 1974. Fisher's later creative work included fine art photography, albums, a book titled *Far East Tour Diary*, about his time with Japanese band The Boom, and a Mott the Hoople tribute CD, *Moth Poet Hotel*. He was pleased that his contributions to *The Hoople* broadened the band's horizons but could see why many fans preferred Mott's rawer, earlier output and described *Brain Capers* as stunning.

Fiddler and Major moved on to work together in Box of Frogs with founding members of The Yardbirds. Fiddler released solo albums including *State of the Heart* and *Return of the Buffalo*, while Major played with Steve Hyams, The Yardbirds and issued a solo record, *First Poison*. Major also overcame Stage 3 throat cancer showing great courage and released *7% Solution* in 2014 to celebrate survival against incredible odds.

After the demise of British Lions, Watts and Griffin formed Grimtone Productions and worked with Slaughter and the Dogs, Department S and Hanoi Rocks. Dale became a renowned producer of Radio One sessions at the BBC and recording engineer Martin Colley remembers him being angry at some sessions, exhibiting impatience with bands he deemed unprofessional. The Beeb engineers' "view" was that Griffin genuinely struggled to understand why so many groups didn't seem to take the sessions seriously and "exchanges" occurred with a few bands. Colley recalls Griffin describing Ian Hunter as "difficult" and confessing that he "didn't like" Mick Ronson. After a week of grumbles about Ronson, Martin sneaked off to the BBC reception one day for fun and asked a telephonist to phone down to Mr Griffin saying that Mr Ronson was in reception to see him. Dale was not amused and stomped out of the studio, white-faced.

The Smiths' frontman, Morrissey, once reflected on his love of Mott the Hoople and his brushes with Buffin as a Manchester concert-goer and musician: "In 1973 Ian Hunter asks me, 'What's your favourite Mott album?' *'Brain Capers,'* I say. 'Uhh, that's our LEAST favourite,' says Buffin. Crushed. Ten years later, as singer in the Smiths, we do a BBC radio session with Buffin at the control desk. We are oddly warned beforehand that he will not talk about Mott the Hoople. In fact, he says neither hello nor goodbye. Crushed."

The accuracy of Griffin's Mott claims was sometimes thrown into doubt, not least when Dale said that he remembered Morgan playing the band an early 1900s French recording with a melody identical to 'All the Young Dudes', hinting at plagiarism. In fact, Fisher had cut a spoof recording. "I created the 'Dudes' track for a laugh and played it to the lads," admitted Morgan. "I had them going for a couple of delicious minutes. I used my trusty old British VCS3 synth, as played on *The Hoople*, 'Roll Away the Stone' and 'Saturday Gigs', to create a sort of Palm Court Orchestra arrangement, with scratches recorded off a real 78 rpm record. I later released it on my 1979 album, *Hybrid Kids*."

Dale Griffin assembled a colossal Mott the Hoople compilation LP for Island, *Two Miles from Heaven (Rare Tracks 1969-1972)*. Released in 1980 and containing fourteen hard-to-find and previously un-issued cuts, Griffin engaged Fisher, Major and Watts to overdub on several original tapes, the collection being notable for the demo tracks 'Ride on the Sun', 'One of the Boys' and 'Black Scorpio'. The two sides of vinyl were branded 'Dark Cargo' (one of Watts' favourite Barrow Poets' poems concerning defecation) and 'Bald at the Station' (a reference to a rejected, hairless, bass-playing Bad Company candidate noted down by Ralphs in 1973). Dale Griffin also oversaw *Walkin' with a Mountain*, a 1990 Island retrospective that featured an edit combining 'You Really Got Me' and 'Wrath 'n' Wroll' as 'Crossfads'. A pointless shortened live version of 'Keep A-Knockin' was included too and yet 'Downtown' and 'The Debt' remained elusive on compact disc.

489

In 1997, Griffin reflected on his involvement in the industry and the fact that he could never resist the attraction of music. "There has to be something in you of the crazy man to be in a rock group, because before I became a professional musician, everything warned against doing anything like that. Music hypnotises you and perhaps against your will you must do it. I remember when Watts became a pro musician, and I was still at school gnashing my teeth and thinking, 'The bastard, that's what I want to do.' Of all the groups that Watts and I had at school, only he and I turned professional. The singer in one of the bands went into accountancy and became incredibly successful, but he was bitter that he never became a professional musician. He managed to subdue the crazy man, and stop himself doing it, but we couldn't. It is a drug."

Watts produced Hanoi Rocks but removed himself from music running a London antique shop and enjoying carp fishing. In 1990, he contributed to Rockfield sessions with members of The Silence. The subsequent CD, *Shotgun Eyes*, contained thirteen covers that the band used to perform in the Sixties and was released in 1998 coupled with the original *Doc Thomas Group* album, as *The Italian Job*. Eventually Watts returned to Ross and opened The Dinosaw Market in Hereford, a vintage shop that sold clothing, records and antiquities. He later revelled in walking trips around the British countryside covering 650 miles along the South West Coast Path in boots acquired at a car boot sale! Watts eventually wrote a book about his experiences titled *The Man Who Hated Walking*, published in 2013.

Mott's road crew had been invited by Roger Taylor to leave Mott the Hoople when the drummer declared Queen was going to be the biggest band in the world. Anderson and John were unconvinced by the offer and Taylor's claim but, following Mott's demise, Phil John became Taylor's drum roadie for twelve months and Richie Anderson was Brian May's guitar tech for seven years. The pair saw that Queen were totally dedicated to success and far more organised and disciplined compared to Mott's easy-going atmosphere. Anderson reflected that Mott had been "a ramshackle mob" whilst Queen, Bowie, the Spiders and MainMan exhibited "lessons in professionalism". The duo's best memories with Mott included playing alongside Joe Walsh and simply being in the USA, which was always a high point.

"Sadly, on the verge of greatness, Mott the Hoople imploded," says Phil John. "A prestigious headlining gig at Madison Square Gardens was in the pipeline, but it was not to be. Luther had been undisciplined but sensational – he was just what US audiences loved and America was where the money was. Ronson did not work out, so with a click of the fingers Mott the bloody Hoople was no more. No more verses to be added to the Ballad of Mott. No more Saturday gigs for the Saturday kids. After five years with Mott, I was left with a wealth of great memories that no one, including the HMRC, could ever take from me, plus a handful of photographs and a tatty notebook – my diary of that fateful, final 1974 European tour."

Mott the Hoople had their greatest commercial success during their CBS era between July 1972 and December 1974 scoring seven chart singles and four hit albums. They left behind a legendary live legacy that included a Royal Albert Hall "ban", a Hammersmith Odeon "riot" and an unprecedented week of sell-out concerts on Broadway. For decades Mott the Hoople would be cited as an important influence by some of popular music's biggest names including The Clash, Def Leppard and Mötley Crüe, but Watts expressed amazement when other artists acknowledged Mott as an inspiration. Prone to eccentricity and exaggeration, Pete would claim he loved the freedom he found when he finished being in bands, saying it was awful to see Mott live dates booked up for "three years in advance." Watts also opined in 1997 that Mott the Hoople was much ado about nothing.

"Sometimes I can't see what all the fuss is about to be honest although, I think in the early days, Ian's lyrics were very pointed and that was a big part of it. Before Mott started, Ian had lived quite a full life whereas most kids in a band, when they start, haven't really got anything to write about at all. I think Hunter had had a difficult time and was able to express things well lyrically, like 'The Moon Upstairs' – you can see the anger in it. He was older than the rest of us. He'd been through horrible, hard times. He'd lived it, but he also had unmatched ability to express it, in a cutting kind of way. If people say they love Mott, I just can't see it. I don't know why. I *do* think our strong point was our live show, but none of that remains as there's very little film. If we were good live, there's no real evidence – all you can really go by is the testimony of people like *ZigZag* editor Pete Frame, who seemed to be quite impressed by us. It felt good on stage at the time, but was there really something there or not?"

> **IH:** "There was something there! The band was great with Ralphs because he was a very tasty guitar player at a time when there weren't too many tasty guitar players around. Mick loved all those West Coast bands, but I was Jerry Lee Lewis and Little Richard forever – I was blood and thunder. That's what I grew up on, that's what I always loved and that's what Mott was – a combination of assets, slamming into each other. I don't think as a band Mott was that great musically. It just seemed to have a lot of things going for it. I was always a personal fan of Mick Ralphs. He had been great from the start – he wrote some great songs with good song sensibility, was very creative and would always turn an idea into something. Ralphs was hilarious too.
>
> "Verden and Mick were by far the best musicians in Mott. Verden was an excellent organ player and whilst he could be his own worst enemy, he was funny and loyal. Pete could be a bastard and he was a lazy sod, and a selfish sod too, but I think he was probably the backbone of Mott the Hoople. Watts *was* eccentric and often hilarious. I remember staying at Pete's parents' house near Hereford once and it was known to be haunted, but they forgot to tell me! His Dad, a college professor, had a couple of run-ins with the lady ghost and she checked me

492

out. Dale was Mott's facts and figures man. When it came to the live album and mixing and all the incidental stuff, we got Buff because he seemed to have a clearer mind than the rest of us. Morgan Fisher was a very intelligent, warm character and a great player. Bender was one of the best friends you could ever have in your life and although I don't think he suited Mott musically, as most guitar players wouldn't, he was a great guy. Ronson, I thought, could and would have suited Mott the Hoople had he been given the chance. Mick could have revived Mott. If he'd come in off the street with no management, walked in and taken the guitar job, I think it could have been sensational, so the end was sad. There tends to be a certain amount of acrimony when bands split, so you try to forget it, but the drama went on for years."

After the rock cognoscenti branded Mott "glam", some considered that the band's original DNA had been destroyed: that 'All the Young Dudes' had turned Mott the Hoople into corporate product and ultimately ripped out its heart. The loss of Allen and Ralphs were damaging wounds and Ian knew that Mott was limping after their departure but, despite this, he remained "loyal to the cause". Only a few months before he left, during the Broadway tour, Ian had said of Mott the Hoople: "I'm an ace frontman because I've got an ace band behind me. I'll never leave. I'd be a mug on my own."

As 1974 advanced however, deep down, Ian knew that Mott the Hoople had played *"the suits and platform boots"* line to the limit. Glam would crash and burn by late 1974 – Bowie moved towards "plastic soul" and Roxy Music's *Country Life* audaciously displayed Teutonic oom-pah and harpsichord instrumentation – only Marc Bolan stayed rooted to the genre with a *Zinc Alloy* album title that echoed *Ziggy Stardust*. Mott had wallowed in glam rock for a while and had sportingly ridiculed it too, but Hunter was astute enough to know that Mott the Hoople faced an endless continuum rather

493

than a progressive trajectory. The sparkle had faded – and Ian felt that Mott had run its course.

IH: "I remember in 1972 that Tony Defries gave us all £200 each and told us to go out and buy some clothes. Pete and Dale really enjoyed dressing up and I enjoyed going along with it – for a while. Watts had his own way and decorated his head and chest hair with silver car paint! He was always aware of looks and liked all that. Ralphs wasn't that keen on the glamour, but Luther loved it, as did Morgan. Dropping in on 'glam' to make it, hurt us in a way, because we did have good material. We were a deep band but during the glam fad some people got the wrong idea about Mott. It took them a while to understand that the group was valid. The tarting-up was all for some showbiz. 'There's nothing wrong with a bit of ballet,' as Freddie Mercury always said.

"After the Bowie association we were semi-glam I suppose, but Mott was called punk too, so we were many things. I was uncomfortable with the Defries aspect though, because I was an ordinary working-class bloke and the MainMan set-up was a little effete for me. Anyway, glam rock was there, and we were for it because that's what it was going to take to make it. I remember I went up to Wembley and watched the ice shows once and went backstage and asked them where they got their costume material from. By the time we played Broadway I think we were looking pretty classy but when we came down off the platform boots it was hilarious. I felt like I'd fallen down a hole with a huge stomach at the front and flat-feet at the back. Roger Taylor of Queen said later on that we were hod-carriers in gilt and that type of tag is the cross that Mott the Hoople has had to bear. People who listened understood that we were much more than clothes, but the ass-end of the media never really noticed. Glam camouflaged what we were, and it was all a bit silly. We stopped the glamour on the European tour in 1974. The heels and hair went, and we were a respectably clad rock band again. The clothes and boots were props but of course you just get lumped in with the fuckin' glam thing for the rest of your life, which detracted from the music we made. I was a fan of Jerry Lee and Little Richard, so I knew what you had to look like, but Phally and Ralpher weren't happy. Mott the Hoople was really 'flash rock' like the Stones, but with Bowie and 'Dudes' we were branded glam. It was all a backlash to blues and psychedelia anyway, and the backlash to us was punk. Dressing up was stupid, but if you can't be stupid in your younger years, when can you be?

"Mott the Hoople was a lot of aggravation, a lot of trouble and total madness. There was a lot of craziness in that band and I don't think I had much to do with that craziness. After we split up the first time, in Switzerland, we were great mates again, when all the trouble and the pressure of trying to get there wasn't in the way. You join a rock 'n' roll band for freedom. Then you reach successful heights and there is no freedom. Mott the Hoople was also a very stressful group, which added to the strains. We never relaxed and the band was always high drama. Mott was also a 5-Nil democracy; if we voted 3-2, then two of them would sulk; then there would be weeks of debate, going back and forth and so nothing would get done. It really became impossible.

"I think my happiest days were in Hamburg, with Freddie Fingers Lee before Mott, because there was no pressure. Mick Ralphs would probably mention intensity in Mott and there was a lot of that and maybe that was my fault. It was a very intense band, driven on by desperation. I don't think Mott was brilliant musically. Mott were rambunctious... and there's something nice about that. If you can't play that well but you play with desperation, then they say you're a punk band. So, we were a punk band, years before punk came in. We could be sensational live and when Mott 'hit it' on stage, it was better than anything else in the world, including the sexual act. I saw The Who 'hit it' one night at The Roundhouse and it was breathtaking. Mott was strange too and dealt with a lot of areas. There were songs like 'Crash Street Kidds' which predicted what was going to happen a few years before it happened, with the Pistols and The Clash. There was desperation because there were so many bands and we had to do something different. Yes, we hitched our wagon to the period, but we ran parallel with Bowie and we ran parallel with Dylan. Mott was commercial latterly, but some people thought we were profound and deep. Frankly, we just wrote songs and recorded them – and we were lucky."

Mott the Hoople's essence was plain to see during their Island years; they offered light and shade in their music, sometimes went to extremes and their overwhelming power often disguised a charming innocence. Hunter was a charismatic, intelligent figure and a truthful, soul-bearing writer. Guy Stevens, the impossibly driven music fanatic, stoked Ian's ideas and drew unpredictable music from his charges, much of the mania and mayhem creating deeply moving and schizophrenic songs.

Mott's recorded output was esoteric, eccentric and electric; chaotic, sensitive and autobiographical at varying times, across several stunning albums. They became a feral, peerless live act that struggled in the studio, but following David Bowie's intervention with one of rock music's greatest-ever songs, the band charted a new course, with Ian freshly inspired to write more hit singles and sensational album tracks. Silence from Herefordshire had provided a rhythmic rock 'n' roll sound, but the struggling London bassist and songwriter that they found via Guy Stevens, in a Denmark Street basement, blossomed into a unique composer and performer. In 1969, Mott the Hoople first caught attention with an album that was the charming equal of Bob Dylan's *Highway 61 Revisited*... in 1971 the group captured amazing power with the "pre-punk" *Brain Capers*... then they produced the polished and near-perfect *Mott*.

By the end of 1974, the band had run aground – but Ian Hunter was just setting sail.

Mott the Hoople chronicled the early Seventies as much as David Bowie, Roxy Music or Lou Reed. They helped Ian Hunter pursue his fascination with America and he became the creative centre and authority of the group. In 1974 they were reaching a commercial zenith but true to form, the tempestuous Mott fractured again, leaving behind a treasure trove of classic songs.

To many followers and observers, Mott the Hoople had been the ultimate experience; they "really rocked" in a live setting, their records sparkled with Hunter's exceptional writing and Mott's music had offered intelligence, craziness and fun! They had also provided many fans with an emblematic soundtrack to their lives.

Never given their real due and imploding before they reached their full potential, Mott the Hoople still merits a place in America's Rock and Roll Hall of Fame, as artists like Cheap Trick's Robin Zander will testify today. Mott had fought, struggled and proved their worth to many upcoming bands and rock stars. Referenced as an inspiration by artists like Queen, The Clash and Mötley Crüe, Britpop's Blur bore much resemblance to Mott the Hoople. In 1992, Bobby Gillespie, lead singer with Primal Scream, would pick his favourite tracks for *Select* magazine and include 'Trudi's Song' from *The Hoople*, admiring the song's calmness and lyrics. Name-checks would abound over the years from the likes of John Taylor (Duran Duran), Billy Duffy (The Cult), Jim Kerr (Simple Minds) and actor Johnny Depp who all adored *Diary of a Rock 'n' Roll Star*.

Ian had signposted personal and musical change in 1974. He had also indicated that 'Marionette' was the most important song on *The Hoople*, and ironic lines had oozed from his pen. The frenzy that was Mott the Hoople really had become Hunter's overpowering ogre, and he had *"lost the will to fight."* Mott had flailed and thrashed but succeeded. Ian had expressed toughness and tenderness through many exceptional songs while the band made fun of their own pretensions. Hunter had also revealed soulful songs that were transparent and true, demonstrating his great compositional flair. As Ian later admitted, "ends are never easy" and Mott the Hoople's demise was sad, but the final chords of their "blistered psalms" would carry great sustain and echo, not only in terms of their original recordings, but "cover versions" by other artists.

There would be continued enmity after Hunter and Ronson split from Mott and several tiresome reformation rumours... there would also be untold re-issue discs and several cherished collections including *Two Miles from Heaven*, *Original Mixed-Up Kids: The BBC Recordings*, *The Journey* and *All the Young Dudes: The Anthology*... and, given time, there would also be eventual re-engagement and hatchet-burying.

Meanwhile, as the sun rose on 1975, alongside Mick Ronson, Hunter could collaborate with another creative partner. Ian would unleash the full potential that had been untapped by Mott the Hoople, via a new solo project and it would feature some of his best work. The album title would be simple – *Ian Hunter* – but the record would be a sparkling statement of intent, illustrating the Mott that might have been.

Mott the Hoople had taken wrong turns and experienced highs and lows. Hunter had written creatively about their travails with great knowing and skill. Ian also discovered that the strains and struggles are the fuel and the essence of rock and roll.

He had gained so much on the journey... but the Ballad of Ian Hunter had just begun.

Ballad of Mott the Hoople (26th March 1972, Zurich)

I changed my name in search of fame, to find the Midas touch
Oh, I wish I'd never wanted then what I want now twice as much
We crossed the mighty oceans, and we had a few divides
But we never crossed emotion, for we felt too much inside

You know all the tales we tell, you know the band so well
And still, I feel, somehow we let you down
We went off somewhere on the way, and now I see we have to pay
The Rock 'n' Roll Circus is in town

Buffin lost his child-like dreams, and Mick lost his guitar
And Verden grew a line or two, and Overend's just a rock 'n' roll star
Behind these shades the visions fade, as I learned a thing or two
But if I had my time again, you all know just what I'd do

Rock 'n' roll's a loser's game, it mesmerises, and I can't explain
The reasons, for the sights, and for the sounds
The grease paint still sticks to my face, so what the hell I can't erase
The rock 'n' roll feeling, from my mind

(Ian Hunter 1972)

Afterword

A ROCK 'N' ROLL GODSEND

To young Americans in the Seventies, Ian Hunter was a rock 'n' roll Godsend; an explosion of corkscrew hair and jubilant confrontation who sparkled in wit and satin from behind black-windshield shades, like a perfect union of English Bob Dylan and earthbound David Bowie.

Hunter came to our towns like clockwork too, first at the head of the brawling-glam juggernaut Mott the Hoople; then, into the New Wave Eighties with guitarist and glitter brother Mick Ronson – and always packing masterful songs about the war on jive and the constant, precious salvation in music.

It is a life I can chart through my own, transforming encounters – the crash-landing force of late '69's *Mott the Hoople* – the lethal impatience of 'The Moon Upstairs' on 1971's *Brain Capers* – *"We ain't bleedin' you, We're feedin' you, But you're too fuckin' slow"* – the hypnotising fury of my first Mott show in Philadelphia in 1974; then many Hunter-Ronson gigs over three more decades, the singer on his long, solo trail.

At a 2015 New York show, Hunter was reaffirming his chorus in 'All the Way from Memphis' – *"It's a mighty long way down rock 'n' roll"* – with vintage fervor and new-song ammo.

More than anything, Ian Hunter has argued and proved in each classic recording, at every crossroads, that rock and roll is a lifer's work – and that the road never ends, if you always face forward.

David Fricke
Rolling Stone

Mott the Hoople Discography

Albums

Mott the Hoople

You Really Got Me (Davies) 2.55
At the Crossroads (Sahm) 5.33
Laugh at Me (Bono) 6.32
Backsliding Fearlessly (Hunter) 3.47
Rock and Roll Queen (Ralphs) 5.10
Rabbit Foot and Toby Time (Ralphs) 2.04
Half Moon Bay (Hunter/Ralphs) 10.38
Wrath and Wroll (Stevens) 1.49

Recorded: Morgan Studios (No.2), London – July 1969
Released: Island Records ILPS 9108 – November 1969
Personnel: Ian Hunter (Vocals and Piano); Mick Ralphs (Lead Guitar and Vocals); Verden Allen (Organ); Overend Watts (Bass and Backing Vocals); Buffin (Drums)
Producer: Guy Stevens, Engineer: Andy Johns

Moulded by Guy Stevens with M.C. Escher's 'Reptiles' artwork providing a wonderful sleeve. This eponymous LP is a gem containing fine covers of Kinks, Sonny Bono and Doug Sahm numbers plus Ralphs' brilliant 'Rock and Roll Queen'. It also features the epic eleven-minute 'Half Moon Bay', Ian's first major Mott composition and Hunter's lyrical skill was further revealed in the colourful and descriptive 'Backsliding Fearlessly'. *Mott the Hoople* was recorded before the band played their first live gig. Guy wanted to call the LP *Talking Bear Mountain Picnic Massacre Disaster Dylan Blues* and another contender was *The Twilight of Pain through Doubt*, but sanity prevailed... or did it?

Mad Shadows

Thunderbuck Ram (Ralphs) 4.50
No Wheels to Ride (Hunter) 5.50
You Are One of Us (Hunter) 2.26
Walkin' with a Mountain (Hunter) 3.49
I Can Feel (Hunter) 7.13
Threads of Iron (Ralphs) 5.12
When My Mind's Gone (Hunter) 6.31

Recorded: Olympic Studios (No.1), London – February to April 1970
Released: Island Records ILPS 9119 – September 1970
Personnel: Ian Hunter (Vocals and Piano); Mick Ralphs (Guitar, Recorder and Vocals); Verden Allen (Organ); Overend Watts (Bass); Buffin (Drums) Guy Stevens (Spiritual Percussion, Psychic Piano)
Producer: Guy Stevens, Engineer: Andy Johns

Originally titled *Sticky Fingers* but Guy Stevens told The Rolling Stones and the rest is history. Jagger was present during the session for 'Walkin' with a Mountain'. 'No Wheels to Ride' and 'I Can Feel' are two dynamic Hunter ballads while 'Thunderbuck Ram' was Mott in semi-metal vein. Guy Stevens had become "a sixth band member" and decided to capture his creation live in the studio.

The outcome was Mott's dark album – poorly recorded and all rather serious. 'When My Mind's Gone' was allegedly taped while Ian was hypnotised under Guy's influence. The exaggerated claim made for good press; the monochrome split-image of "flames from somewhere" made a great demonic cover.

Wildlife

Whisky Women (Ralphs) 3.42
Angel of Eighth Avenue (Hunter) 4.33
Wrong Side of the River (Ralphs) 5.19
Waterlow (Hunter) 3.03
Lay Down (Safka) 4.13
It Must Be Love (Ralphs) 2.24
Original Mixed-Up Kid (Hunter) 3.40
Home Is Where I Want to Be (Ralphs) 4.11
Keep A-Knockin' (Live) (Penniman) 10.10

Recorded: Island Studios (1 and 2), London – November and December 1970
Released: Island Records ILPS 9144 – March 1971
Personnel: Ian Hunter (Vocals and Piano); Mick Ralphs (Lead Guitar and Vocals); Verden Allen (Organ); Overend Watts (Bass); Buffin (Drums)
Producer: Mott the Hoople
Engineer: Brian Humphries assisted by Richard Digby-Smith and Howard Kilgour
Strings on 'Waterlow' arranged and conducted: Michael Gray
Solo Violin on 'Angel of Eighth Avenue': James Archer
Pedal Steel Guitar on 'It Must Be Love' and 'Original Mixed-Up Kid': Gerry Hogan
Backing Vocals on 'Lay Down': Jess Roden and Stan Tippins
'Wrong Side of the River' recorded at Olympic Studios 10th February 1970
Engineer: Andrew Johns. Producer: Guy Stevens

'Lay Down' recorded at Island Studios 10th September 1970
Engineer: Philip Brown. Producer: Guy Stevens and Mott the Hoople
'Keep A-Knockin' recorded at Fairfield Halls, Croydon, London, 13th September 1970
Engineer: Andrew Johns

After the darkness of *Mad Shadows*, Mick Ralphs hustled for a "nicer" album. He laid bare his West Coast American influences on *Wildlife* while Ian contributed three astonishing songs – 'Original Mixed-Up Kid', 'Angel of Eighth Avenue' and 'Waterlow' – the latter a tear-jerking reflection on the breakdown of his first marriage. The band dubbed the LP *Mildlife*, but the engaging ether was shattered by a crunching ten-minute version of 'Keep A-Knockin', "salvaged" from the tapes of a typically riotous concert at Croydon Fairfield Hall. Ian has more of a fondness for *Wildlife* than practically all other early Mott records, but he claims it was the worst-selling album the band ever released. The fact that the peace is pole-axed by a feral live track is trademark Hoople schizophrenia.

Brain Capers

Death May Be Your Santa Claus (Hunter/Allen) 4.55
Your Own Backyard (Dimucci) 4.13
Darkness, Darkness (Young) 4.33
The Journey (Hunter) 9.15
Sweet Angeline (Hunter) 4.53
Second Love (Allen) 3.46
The Moon Upstairs (Hunter/Ralphs) 5.07
The Wheel of the Quivering Meat Conception (Hunter/Stevens) 1.21
Recorded: Island Studios (No.1), Basing Street, London – September 1971
Released: Island Records ILPS 9178 – November 1971

Personnel: Ian Hunter (Vocals and Piano); Mick Ralphs (Lead Guitar and Vocals); Verden Allen (Organ); Overend Watts (Bass and Backing Vocals); Buffin (Drums)
Trumpet on 'Second Love': Jim Price
Producer: Guy Stevens, Engineer: Andy Johns

Having ditched a covers album concept (pre-*Pin Ups*, pre-*These Foolish Things*) Mott started to produce their fourth studio LP, originally titled *AC/DC*, but stopped after one week and summoned their mentor. Guy arrived resplendent in a black cape and Zorro mask and the ensemble trashed and set fire to Island Studios under Stevens' direction. In five days, Mott cut an incendiary record that is often referenced as a precursor to punk rock. 'The Journey' proved that Ian had become a majestic writer and 'The Moon Upstairs' exemplified bitter frustration at Mott's lack of commercial success. Guy was still a magpie with strange titles and christened two tracks 'Death May Be Your Santa Claus' and 'The Wheel of the Quivering Meat Conception', lifted shamelessly from a disturbing art house film and a Kerouac poem. For some die-hard fans, this remains Mott the Hoople's greatest album.

All the Young Dudes

Sweet Jane (Reed) 4.21
Momma's Little Jewel (Hunter/Watts) 4.26
All the Young Dudes (Bowie) 3.33
Sucker (Hunter/Ralphs/Watts) 5.03
Jerkin' Crocus (Hunter) 4.00
One of the Boys (Hunter/Ralphs) 6.46
Soft Ground (Allen) 3.17
Ready for Love/After Lights (Ralphs) 6.47
Sea Diver (Hunter) 2.55

Recorded: Trident Studios, Soho, London, June and July 1972

'All the Young Dudes' & 'Sucker' recorded at Olympic No.2 Studio, Barnes, May 1972
Released: CBS Records CBS 65184 – September 1972
Personnel: Ian Hunter (Vocals and Piano); Mick Ralphs (Guitar and Vocals); Verden Allen (Organ); Overend Watts (Bass and Backing Vocals); Buffin (Drums)
Saxes and Acoustic guitar: David Bowie
Strings and brass on 'Sea Diver' arranged and conducted: Mick Ronson
Producer: David Bowie, Arrangers: Mott the Hoople and David Bowie
Engineers: Ted Sharp, Dave Hentschel, Keith Harwood

Although Bowie-driven, with relatively thin-sounding production, this album retained some of Ian's influence via 'One of the Boys' and the Stones-styled 'Jerkin' Crocus.' 'Ready for Love' is one of Mick Ralphs' finest songs and Hunter's 'Sea Diver' features a moving Mick Ronson orchestral score. The title track, a UK No.3 hit single, is often classified as *the* definitive Seventies glam anthem but it was really linked to Bowie's sci-fi parable, *Ziggy Stardust*. The bulletin of imminent Armageddon revealed by the "news guy" in David's 'Five Years' was the same "news" carried by the Dudes. Mott's single was praised as a hymn to youth, but it was an apocalyptic tale. Hunter's vocal embellishments made 'Dudes' an infectious classic and the band's indelible stamp made it Mott's song – forever! Clever 1920s concept cover and artwork under the great Mick Rock's direction.

Mott

All the Way from Memphis (Hunter) 5.02
Whizz Kid (Hunter) 3.25
Hymn for the Dudes (Hunter/Allen) 5.24
Honaloochie Boogie (Hunter) 2.43
Violence (Hunter/Ralphs) 4.48

Drivin' Sister (Hunter/Ralphs) 3.53
Ballad of Mott the Hoople (March 26, 1972, Zurich) (Hunter/Ralphs/Allen/Watts/Griffin) 5.25
I'm a Cadillac/El Camino Dolo Roso (Ralphs) 7.50
I Wish I Was Your Mother (Hunter) 4.53

Recorded: AIR No.2 Studio and Abbey Road No.2 Studio, London – February to April 1973
Released: CBS Records CBS 69038 – July 1973
Personnel: Ian Hunter (Vocals, Piano and Guitar); Mick Ralphs (Guitar, Organ and Vocals); Overend Watts (Bass); Buffin (Drums and Backing Vocals)
Producer: Mott the Hoople, Arranger: Ian Hunter
Engineers: Bill Price, Alan Harris (AIR), John Leckie (EMI)
Saxophones on 'All the Way from Memphis' and 'Honaloochie Boogie': Andy Mackay
Electric Cello on 'Honaloochie Boogie': Paul Buckmaster
Violin on 'Violence': Graham Preskett
Backing Vocals: Thunderthighs

Mott remains a Seventies classic chronicling the trials and tribulations of rock 'n' roll. The band considered John Lennon, Mike Leander or Roy Wood as producer for their sessions but, encouraged by Roxy Music who was recording *For Your Pleasure* in an adjoining studio at AIR, they took the reins themselves and delivered their finest album. 'Ballad of Mott the Hoople' immortalised their Swiss split, 'Hymn for the Dudes' exposed the absurdity of music-related fame and 'I Wish I Was Your Mother' remains one of Hunter's finest songs. The proto-punk 'Violence' retained Mott's earlier anger and Ian penned two cracking hit singles – 'Honaloochie Boogie' (UK No.12) and 'All the Way from Memphis' (UK No.10). *Mott* = Mott's masterpiece!

508

The Hoople

The Golden Age of Rock 'n' Roll (Hunter) 3.25
Marionette (Hunter) 5.08
Alice (Hunter) 5.20
Crash Street Kidds (Hunter) 4.31
Born Late '58 (Watts) 4.00
Trudi's Song (Hunter) 4.26
Pearl 'n' Roy (England) (Hunter) 4.31
Through the Looking Glass (Hunter) 4.37
Roll Away the Stone (Hunter) 3.10

Recorded: Advision Studios, London – January 1974
Re-mixed and dubbed: AIR London Studios 2 and 3 – February 1974
Released: CBS Records CBS 69062 – March 1974
Personnel: Ian Hunter (Vocals and Rhythm Guitar);
Overend Watts (Bass and Backing Vocals); Dale Griffin (Drums);
Ariel Bender (Lead Guitar); Morgan Fisher (Keyboards)
Producers: Ian Hunter, Overend Watts and Dale Griffin
Arranger: Ian Hunter – except 'Born Late '58' arranged by Overend Watts
Engineers: Alan Harris, Mike Dunne and Paul Hardiman
Engineers: Bill Price with Sean Milligan, Gary Edwards, Peter Swettenham
Production Supervisor: Dan Loggins
Saxophones: Howie Casey and Rockin' Jock McPherson (Andy Mackay)
Violin on 'Marionette': Graham Preskett
Cello on 'The Golden Age of Rock 'n' Roll': Mike Hurwitz
Orchestral arrangement and conductor on 'Through the Looking Glass': Graham Preskett
Guest appearances: Mick Ralphs, Blue Weaver, Lynsey de Paul
Backing Vocals: Barry St John, Sue and Sunny

Book-ended by two more hit singles – 'Roll Away the Stone' (UK No.8) and 'The Golden Age of Rock 'n' Roll' (UK No.16) – Ian composed some tough and percipient songs for Mott's final studio album. 'Crash Street Kidds' and 'Marionette' were of considerable note, the latter a mini-opera addressing the constrictive, corporate side of the rock business and its effect on the writer. Crazed violin, staccato cellos, Quasimodo choruses and manic laughter surround Hunter's nightmare of a rock star driven to submission. Ian described it as a nervous breakdown on record! Queen followed with their operatic 'Bohemian Rhapsody' and "marionette" was used to describe David Essex in his portrayal of a fading pop idol in the movie *Stardust*. In under six months Hunter was confined to a hospital bed and Mott was done. Hoople's blood and thunder!

Mott the Hoople Live

Broadway
All the Way from Memphis (Hunter) 5.05
Sucker (Hunter/Ralphs/Watts) 6.06
Rest in Peace (Hunter) 5.57
All the Young Dudes (Bowie) 3.49
Walkin' with a Mountain (Hunter) 5.02
Hammersmith
Sweet Angeline (Hunter) 7.03
Rose (Hunter) 4.46
Medley – Jerkin' Crocus/One of the Boys/Rock and Roll Queen/ Get Back/Whole Lotta Shakin'/Violence (Hunter/Ralphs) 16.00

Recorded: Hammersmith Odeon, London – 14th December 1973 and The Uris Theatre, Broadway, New York – 9th May 1974
Released: CBS Records CBS 69093 – November 1974
Personnel: Ian Hunter (Vocals and Rhythm Guitar);
Overend Watts (Bass and Backing Vocals); Dale Griffin (Drums);
Ariel Bender (Lead Guitar); Morgan Fisher (Piano); Mick Bolton (Organ); Blue Weaver (Organ)
Producer: Dale Griffin, Engineers: Bill Price, Gary Edwards Mastering: Howard Thompson

Executive Producer: Fred Heller, Associate Producer: Robert Hirschman
Mastered at: The Record Plant, Los Angeles

Capturing the "real Mott" on tape was always a conundrum and although they had wholesome material from London's Hammersmith Odeon and Broadway's Uris Theatre to work from, the resultant single LP was a few notches down on what it could and should have been. *Mott the Hoople Live* fell short of the mark in 1974 but Sony's 30th Anniversary Edition in 2004 hit the bullseye. The 1973 Hammersmith Odeon set is worth the price of admission alone. Very flash! Very rude! Very much '74 rock 'n' roll!

UK Singles

Rock and Roll Queen/Road to Birmingham
Island WIP 6072 – October 1969

Midnight Lady/The Debt
Island WIP 6105 – July 1971

Downtown/Home
Island WIP 6112 – September 1971

All the Young Dudes/One of the Boys
CBS 8271 – July 1972

Honaloochie Boogie/Rose
CBS 1530 – May 1973

All the Way from Memphis/Ballad of Mott the Hoople
CBS 1734 – August 1973

Roll Away the Stone/Where Do You All Come From
CBS 1895 – November 1973

The Golden Age of Rock 'n' Roll/Rest in Peace
CBS 2177 – March 1974

Foxy, Foxy/Trudi's Song
CBS 2439 – June 1974

Saturday Gigs/Live Medley (Jerkin' Crocus/Sucker/Violence)
CBS 2754 – October 1974

US Singles

Rock and Roll Queen/Backsliding Fearlessly
Atlantic 45-2749 – July 1970

All the Young Dudes/One of the Boys
Columbia 4-45673 – August 1972

One of the Boys/Sucker
Columbia 4-45754 – September 1972

Sweet Jane /Jerkin' Crocus
Columbia 4-45784 – January 1973

Honaloochie Boogie/Rose
Columbia 4-45882 – June 1973

All the Way from Memphis/Ballad of Mott the Hoople
Columbia 4-45920 – September 1973

The Golden Age of Rock 'n' Roll/Rest in Peace
Columbia 4-46035 – April 1974

Roll Away the Stone/Through the Looking Glass
Columbia 4-46076 – June 1974

All the Young Dudes (Live)/Rose (Live)
Columbia 3-10091 – January 1975

Rare Tracks

There have been over fifty Mott the Hoople compilations and collections, largely based on their eight original albums... but there have also been several releases encompassing rare songs, previously unheard material and bonus tracks... including:

Two Miles from Heaven (Rare Tracks 1969-1972) – (Island 1980)

You Really Got Me (Vocal Version) (June 27, 1969) (Davies)
Road to Birmingham (July 7, 1969) (Ralphs)
Thunderbuck Ram (Alternate Mix) (November 15, 1969) (Ralphs)
Going Home (January 16, 1970) (Ralphs)
Little Christine (June 24, 1969) (Ralphs)
Keep A-Knockin' (Studio Version) (February 18, 1970) (Penniman)
Black Hills (October 17, 1970) (Ralphs)
Growin' Man Blues (November 16, 1970) (Hunter)
Til I'm Gone (April 11, 1971) (Ralphs)
One of the Boys (Hunter/Ralphs)
Ride on the Sun (Hunter)
Surfin' UK (December 14, 1970) (Ralphs)
Black Scorpio (Hunter/Watts)
Ill Wind Blowing (April 14, 1971) (Hunter)

Walkin' With A Mountain (1969-72) – (Island 1990)

Crossfads (You Really Got Me/Wrath and Wroll) (Edit)
Keep A-Knockin (Live Edit)

The Ballad of Mott: A Retrospective – (Columbia 1993)

Henry and the H-Bomb (Demo) (Hunter)
Through the Looking Glass (Hunter) (Profanity Take)
Lounge Lizard (Aborted Single B-side) (Hunter)

Original Mixed-Up Kids: The BBC Recordings – (Windsong 1996)

Studio Sessions: Whisky Women, Darkness, Darkness, The Moon Upstairs, Original Mixed-Up Kid, Thunderbuck Ram
In Concert: Your Own Backyard, Death May Be Your Santa Claus, Darkness, Darkness, The Moon Upstairs, Whisky Women, The Journey

All the Way from Stockholm to Philadelphia 1971-72 – (Angel Air 1998)

CD1: Konserthuset, Stockholm 1971 – Long Red, Original Mixed-Up Kid, Walkin' with a Mountain, Laugh at Me, Thunderbuck Ram, Keep A-Knockin'
CD2: The Tower Theatre, Philadelphia 1972 – Jerkin' Crocus, Sucker, Hymn for the Dudes, Ready for Love, Sweet Jane, Sea Diver, Sweet Angeline, One of the Boys, Midnight Lady, All the Young Dudes, Honky Tonk Women

All the Young Dudes: The Anthology – (Sony Music 1998)

CD1: *The Twilight of Pain through Doubt – Three Years on Treasure Island (1969-1972)*

CD2: *Temptations of the Flash – Columbia Hitts & Hottrax (1972-1974)*
CD3: *Blistered Psalms – Demos & Rarities (1964-1978)*
Like a Rolling Stone (Impromptu Jam)
Rock and Roll Queen (45 rpm version)
Find Your Way (Backtrack demo)
Wrath and Wroll (God Save the Queen coda)
Moonbus (Baby's Got a Down) (1998 Mix)
It Would Be a Pleasure (Demo)
Ohio (Live)
The Debt (Hunter)
Downtown (1998 Mix)
Long Red
It'll Be Me
The Journey (Alternate Version)
Mental Train (Demo/1998 Mix)
How Long? (Death May Be Your Santa Claus)
Movin' On (1998 Mix)
The Hunchback Fish (Backtrack)
All the Young Dudes (Bowie/Hunter Vocals)
Shakin' All Over (Demo Version)
Please Don't Touch (Demo Version)
So Sad (To Watch Good Love Go Bad) (Demo Version)
Honaloochie Boogie (Demo)
Hymn for the Dudes (Demo)
Nightmare (Demo)
The Saturday Kids

Rock and Roll Circus, Live 1972 – (Angel Air 2000)

One of the Boys, Ballad of Mott the Hoople, Mr Bugle Player

Mojo presents... an introduction to Mott the Hoople – (Sony Music 2003)

Live Medley ('Saturday Gigs' B-side)

515

Mott the Hoople Live: 30th Anniversary Edition – (Columbia 2004)

CD1: Uris Theatre, Broadway, New York, May 1974 – Jupiter, American Pie, The Golden Age of Rock 'n' Roll, Sucker, Roll Away the Stone/Sweet Jane, Rest in Peace, All the Way from Memphis, Born Late '58, One of the Boys, Hymn for the Dudes, Marionette, Drivin' Sister/Crash Street Kidds/Violence, All the Young Dudes, Walkin' with a Mountain
CD2: Hammersmith Odeon, London, December 1973 – Jupiter, Drivin' Sister, Sucker, Sweet Jane, Angeline, Rose, Roll Away the Stone, All the Young Dudes, Medley – Jerkin' Crocus/One of the Boys/Rock and Roll Queen/Get Back/Whole Lotta Shakin'/Violence, Walkin' with a Mountain

Concert Anthology – (Cleopatra 2005)

Death May Be Your Santa Claus (Wild 'n' Rude Mix), The Ballad of Billy Joe (Demo), If Your Heart Lay with the Rebel (Demo), It Would Be a Pleasure (Demo)

The Hoople – (Sony Music 2006)

The Saturday Kids (Work in Progress)

Live Fillmore West, San Francisco 1970 – (Angel Air 2006)

The Wreck of the Liberty Belle (Instrumental outtake)

Fairfield Halls, Live 1970 – (Angel Air 2007)

Ohio, No Wheels to Ride, Rock and Roll Queen, Thunderbuck Ram, When My Mind's Gone, Keep A-Knockin', You Really Got Me

Family Anthology – (Angel Air 2012)

Can You Sing the Song That I Sing? (Edit), The Chosen Road (Demo)

Mental Train: The Island Years 1969-1971 – (Universal 2018)

You Really Got Me (Full take), Rock and Roll Queen (Instrumental backtrack), The Hunchback Fish (Vocal rehearsal), No Wheels to Ride (Demo), Brain Haulage, Blue Broken Tears, Midnight Lady (Backtrack), Where Do You All Come From (Instrumental backtrack), Can You Sing the Song That I Sing? (Full version), I'm a River

Compilations

Rock and Roll Queen (LP/CD) – Island 1972
Pop Chronik (2LP) – Island (Germany) 1974
The Golden Age of Mott the Hoople (LP) – CBS (Germany) 1975
Greatest Hits (LP/CD) – CBS 1976
Shades of Ian Hunter and Mott the Hoople (2LP/CD) – CBS 1980
All the Way from Memphis (LP) – Hallmark 1981
Rock Giants (LP) – CBS (Germany) 1982
The History of Rock Volume 27 (2LP) – Orbis 1984
The Golden Age of Mott the Hoople (Cassette) – CBS 1985
The Collection (CD/2LP) – Castle 1987
Walkin' with a Mountain (CD) – Island 1990
Mott the Hoople II Rock (LP) – De Agostini/CBS (Italy) 1990
London to Memphis (CD) – Columbia 1992
Backsliding Fearlessly (CD) – Rhino 1994
Six Pack: London to Memphis (CD) – Sony 1996
Super Hits (CD) – Columbia 1997
The Best of the Island Years 1969-72 (CD) – Spectrum 1998
Friends and Relatives (2CD) – Eagle 1999
Live Dudes (CD) – Demon 2000

A Tale of Two Cities (2CD) – Snapper 2000
Greatest Hits Live (CD) – Purple Pyramid 2000
Two Miles from Live Heaven (2CD) – Angel Air 2001
Hoopling: Best of Live (CD) – Angel Air 2002
Walking with the Hoople (2CD) – Snapper 2004
Concert Anthology (2CD) – Purple Pyramid 2005
Essential Young Dudes: Live and More (2CD) – Music Club 2006
The Journey: A Retrospective of Ian Hunter and Mott the Hoople (3CD) – Columbia 2006
An Introduction to Mott the Hoople (CD) – Fuel 2000 2006
All the Young Dudes: Their Best (CD) – Music Session 2007
All the Young Dudes: Demos and Live '71 to '74 (LP) – Cleopatra 2007
All the Young Dudes (2CD) – Black Box 2007
Roll Away the Stone (2CD) – Music Club Deluxe 2008
In Performance 1970-1974 (4CD) – Angel Air (2008)
Old Records Never Die (2CD) – Shout 2008
The Definitive Mott the Hoople Live (2CD) – Store for Music 2008
The Golden Age 1969-97 (2CD) – Raven 2009
Original Album Classics (5CD) – Sony 2009
All the Live Dudes (CD) – Airline 2009
The Very Best of Mott the Hoople (CD) – Sony 2009
Live at HMV Hammersmith Apollo 2009 (2CD+CD Rom) – Concert Live 2009
The Collection (CD) – Camden Sony 2010
Live in Sweden 1971 (LP) – Sireena 2010
The Ballad of Mott the Hoople (CD) – Sony (Japan) 2012
Mott the Hoople Live 2013 (at Manchester Apollo) (2CD+DVD, 2LP) – Concert Live 2013
The Essential Mott the Hoople (2CD) – Columbia Legacy 2013
Complete Atlantic Studio Albums (4LP numbered box) – Rhino Custom Products 2014
Mott the Hoople Live at Hammersmith 1973 (2LP) – Madfish Records 2019

Permissions

'Violence'
Words & Music by Ian Hunter and Mick Ralphs
© Copyright 1973 Island Music Limited.
Universal/Island Music Limited.
All Rights Reserved. International Copyright Secured.
Used by permission of Hal Leonard Europe Limited.

'Ballad of Mott the Hoople'
Words & Music by Verden Allen, Peter Overend Watts, Mick Ralphs,
Terence Dale Griffin, Ian Hunter
© Copyright 1973 Island Music Limited.
Universal/Island Music Limited.
All Rights Reserved. International Copyright Secured.
Used by permission of Hal Leonard Europe Limited.

'The Moon Upstairs'
Words & Music by Ian Hunter and Michael Ralphs
© Copyright 1971 Jesse John Music.
BMG Rights Management (US) LLC and Cee Dee Music.
All Rights Reserved. International Copyright Secured.
Used by permission of Hal Leonard Europe Limited and Angel Air
Records.

'Shades Off'
Words by Ian Hunter
© Copyright 1975 Jesse John Music.
All Rights Reserved. International Copyright Secured.
Used by permission of Jesse John Music.

MOTT THE HOOPLE
TWO MILES FROM HEAVEN

FEATURING
IAN HUNTER MICK RALPHS OVEREND WATTS BUFFIN VERDEN ALLEN
NEW AND RARE TRACKS 1969-1972

THE BEST OF

MO**TT** THE

H**OO**PLE

1969-1972

THE BEST OF

MOTT
THE
HOOPLE
THE ISLAND YEARS 1969–197

MOTT THE
HOOPLE

Backsliding
Fearlessly:

The Early Years

Mott
the Hoople

Original Mixed Up Kids